WRITING FOR LIFE

Also by John D. Bessler

Death in the Dark:
Midnight Executions in America

Kiss of Death:
America's Love Affair with the Death Penalty

Legacy of Violence:
Lynch Mobs and Executions in Minnesota

WRITING FOR LIFE:

The Craft of Writing for Everyday Living

by John D. Bessler

Bottlecap Books
MINNEAPOLIS

Bottlecap Books

Requests for permission to make copies of any part of the work should be mailed to the following address: Bottlecap Books, 514 N. Third Street, Suite 105, Minneapolis, MN 55401.

Library of Congress Cataloging-in-Publication Data
    Bessler, John D.
      Writing for life: the craft of writing for everyday living / John D. Bessler
      ISBN 978-0-9792718-0-9
      Preassigned Control Number: 2007920801

Designed by Andrew Bessler and Victoria Hakala
Printed in the United States of America by Sentinel Printing on Wausau 50# Exact Vellum Opaque acid-free stock and bound by Midwest Editions.

To Amy and Abigail

Writing is an exploration.
You start from nothing and learn as you go.

–E. L. Doctorow

That it will never come again
Is what makes life so sweet.

–Emily Dickinson

CONTENTS

The greatest part of a writer's time is spent in reading, in order to write; a man will turn over half a library to make one book. –Samuel Johnson • Putting an idea into written words is like defrosting the windshield: The idea, so vague out there in the murk, slowly begins to gather itself into a sensible shape. –William Zinsser • Writing is like training for an athlete or practice for a musician. If you stop entirely, it takes a long time to get your pace back. –Haruki Murakami • Let's face it, writing is hell. –William Styron • I simply write and in the act of writing discover what it is I knew. –Sandra Cisneros • Whatever is worth doing at all is worth doing well and nothing can be well done without attention. –Earl of Chesterfield • Writing is a compulsive, and delectable thing. Writing is its own reward. –Henry Miller • In the richness of language, its grace, breadth, dexterity, lies its power. –James Salter • Life is nothing without friendship. –Cicero • Influenced by my dad, I felt that the finest thing in the world was to be a writer. –Carolyn See • A faithful friend is the medicine of life. –The Bible • Writing is neither holy nor mysterious, except insofar as everything we do with our gathered powers is holy and mysterious. –Scott Russell Sanders • Everyone thinks writers must know more about the inside of the human head, but that is wrong. They know less, that's why they write. Trying to find out what everyone else takes for granted. –Margaret Atwood • The words of the world want to make sentences. –Gaston Bachelard • The minute you start putting words on paper you're eliminating possibilities. –Joan Didion • In general I think you usually do write for someone. –Gabriel García Márquez • Failure is inevitable for the writer. –Irwin Shaw • I wish I were more at home with writing. –Edmund White • To write is to make oneself the echo of what cannot cease speaking. –Maurice Blanchot • At some stage in the process of creation the creative product—whether painting, poem, or scientific theory—takes on a life of its own and transmits its own needs to its creator. It stands apart from him and summons material from his subconscious. –George Kneller • We are cups, constantly and quietly being filled. The trick is, knowing how to tip ourselves over and let the beautiful stuff out. –Ray Bradbury • I write about violence as naturally as Jane Austen wrote about manners. Violence shapes and obsesses our society, and if we do not stop being violent we have no future. –Edward Bond • I want to go on living even after my death! And therefore I am grateful to God for giving me this gift, this possibility of developing myself and of writing, of expressing all that is in me. –Anne Frank • All my life I've looked at words as though I were seeing them for the first time. –Ernest Hemingway

ACKNOWLEDGMENTS

We must use time as a tool, not as a couch. –John F. Kennedy • Make your friends your teachers and mingle the pleasures of conversation with the advantages of instruction. –Baltasar Gracián • I'm glad I understand that while language is a gift, listening is a responsibility. –Nikki Giovanni • A stander-by may sometimes, perhaps, see more of the game than he that plays it. –Jonathan Swift • Find a subject you care about and which you in your heart feel others should care about. It is this genuine caring, and not your games with language, which will be the most compelling and seductive element in your style. –Kurt Vonnegut • The writer should be very detached from his work. I've always used the comparison that a writer should be as detached as a heart surgeon is from his work. To write well, you can't be crying as you're cutting someone's heart out. –Ernest Gaines • To me the greatest pleasure of writing is not what it's about, but the music the words make. –Truman Capote • Talent is cheaper than table salt. What separates the talented individual from the successful one is a lot of hard work. –Stephen King • Like stones, words are laborious and unforgiving, and the fitting of them together, like the fitting of stones, demands great patience and strength of purpose and particular skill. –Edmund Morrison • Rewriting is like scrubbing the basement floor with a toothbrush. –Pete Murphy • To be a writer is to throw away a great deal, not to be satisfied, to type again, and then again and once more, and over and over. –John Hersey • My most important piece of advice to all you would-be writers: when you write, try to leave out all the parts readers skip. –Elmore Leonard • The creative impulse suddenly springs to life, like a flame, passes through the hand onto the canvas, where it spreads farther until, like the spark that closes an electric circuit, it returns to the source: the eye and the mind. –Paul Klee • Tolstoy went through and rewrote War and Peace eight times and was still making corrections in the galleys. Things like this should hearten every writer whose first drafts are dreadful, like mine are. –Raymond Carver • Fall seven times, stand up eight. –Japanese proverb • I have rewritten—often several times—every word I have ever written. My pencils outlast their erasers. –Vladimir Nabokov • If anything can go wrong it will. –Murphy's Law • Beware thoughts that come in the night. They aren't turned properly; they come in askew, free of sense and restriction, deriving from the most remote of sources. –William Least Heat-Moon • As we express gratitude, we must never forget that the highest appreciation is not to utter words, but to live by them. –John F. Kennedy • Words can have no single fixed meaning. Like wayward electrons, they can spin away from their initial orbit and enter a wider magnetic field. No one owns them or has a proprietary right to dictate how they will be used. –David Lehman • I was brought up to believe that the only thing worth doing was to add to the sum of accurate information in the world. –Margaret Mead • Writing a first draft is like groping one's way into a dark room, or overhearing a faint conversation, or telling a joke whose punch line you've forgotten. As someone said, one writes mainly to rewrite, for rewriting and revising are how one's mind comes to inhabit the material fully. –Ted Solotaroff • To write or even speak English is not a science but an art. –George Orwell

This book began, as I suspect many books do,
in a conversation; or a series of conversations.

−Page Smith, *As a City upon a Hill*

A friend may well be reckoned the masterpiece of nature.

−Ralph Waldo Emerson, essayist

It's what you learn after you know it all that counts.

−Harry S. Truman, U.S. President

If I have seen further it is by standing on the shoulders of Giants.

−Sir Isaac Newton, English mathematician

ACKNOWLEDGMENTS

Thank-yous

Every creative endeavor has a genesis, often no more than an abrupt vision. When filmmakers Joel and Ethan Coen set to work on their movie, *Miller's Crossing*, they were captivated by the image of a hat blowing in the wind. When Michelangelo, who carefully chose a block of stone for a sculpture, was asked about the resulting masterpiece, he replied, "I saw the angel in the marble, and I chiseled until I set it free." For me, that moment of revelation came several years after I read Betty Edwards's ground-breaking book about the drawing process, titled *Drawing on the Right Side of the Brain*. That book explained the artistic process to me in such clear language that, in just a few weeks, I went from drawing nothing more than doodles and stick figures to sketching realistic-looking human faces. I don't remember exactly when the idea hit me, but one day it occurred to me that a similar type of book about the writing process would be extremely helpful to a lot of people. *Writing for Life*, which took approximately six years to research, write and revise, is the result of that vision, however abstractly conceived when it first came to me.

I actually wrote this book as the final project for my Master of Fine Arts degree from Hamline University in St. Paul, Minnesota. When I entered the M.F.A. program in 1997, I did not know quite what to expect. I thought then that I already knew a lot about writing, but I had the nagging sense that I should know more. This led me to enroll in the program and take night classes off and on in what became a nearly decade-long venture, culminating with my graduation in 2005. What I found in the courses were wonderful, hard-working teachers and an array of talented writers, and what I discovered is that every writer can always improve his or her writing abilities. As it turned out, I did have a lot to learn, and that learning process—I certainly know now—will never stop. Writing is a craft that is learned over time, and though this book sets forth what I've discovered about the writing process thus far, I can't profess to know everything there is to know about writing. As Michelangelo was fond of saying, "I am still learning."

All of my Hamline instructors—Mary François Rockcastle, Deborah Keenan, Jim Moore, Julie Landsman, Margot Fortunato Galt, Sheila O'Connor, Patricia Kirkpatrick, and Anne Czarniecki —were, without exception, devoted to the writing process and passionate about the English language and its possibilities. The marvelous students I encountered in every class are too numerous to mention, but suffice it to say that they, too, had great insights on the craft of writing and that I immensely enjoyed getting to know them. For someone like me, who is always interested in bettering my writing skills, Hamline's M.F.A. program was a godsend. I got exposed to literature and nonfiction books I never would have found on my own, and it was thrilling to see my fellow students, through their writing and revision, turn thoughts and blank pieces of paper into creative works of art. Special thanks must be extended to Anna Sochocky, now a graduate of Hamline's Graduate Liberal Studies program, who let me know about the program while she was enrolled in it.

I also need to thank those who have helped me along the way. I'm a lawyer by training, and over the years I've had the opportunity to work with a host of good writers, including U.S. Magistrate Judge Jack Mason, Professor Gene Shreve, and many lawyers at the law firms of Kelly & Berens, Faegre & Benson, and Leonard, Street & Deinard. I would like to pay special homage to Judge Mason, as well as my late friend and former law partner, George Ludcke, larger-than-life figures who taught me a great deal about writing before dying at young ages, one while bicycling and one after playing hockey with friends. I also need to thank Katie Haagenson, who helped me track down a much-needed source (in minutes no less), as well as Mary François Rockcastle, Patricia Kirkpatrick, Stacey Foster, Kellie Hultgren and Stephanie Lake, who gave me useful comments on the manuscript.

I'd also like to express my gratitude to all of the high school teachers and college and law school professors that I've learned from, not only about English and writing, but about topics as diverse as politics, religion, rhetoric, chemistry, law and history. I still count the set of extraordinary teachers I had at Loyola High School—among them, Pam Cady, Carol Goodrich, Chris Thiem, Peter Myhrwold, and the Rev. Robert Schneider—as some of the greatest influences on my life. My instructors and professors in college and law school also taught me how to think critically, which is as important as anything to the craft of effective writing. The dedication of teachers, who perform a priceless public service but who are all too often underpaid and undervalued, is something that I, for one, will always appreciate and will never forget.

I want to especially thank my parents, Marilyn and Bill Bessler, who helped proofread the manuscript, as well as my wife and daughter, Amy and Abigail, who gave me continual encouragement on this project and who are both talented writers themselves. Amy had her senior essay at Yale published as a book when she was only twenty-two-years-old, and she still writes a great deal in her own life and work as a public servant. Abigail, as a sixth grader in the public schools, is already a voracious reader and loves writing her own poetry and stories. She's already taken summer writing classes through Minneapolis's Loft Literary Center, and she even started a student-run school newspaper, *The Pratt Post*, which taught her a lot about the editorial process. I am extremely proud of both of them, and I am blessed to live with two such lively, fun-loving people who hold words in as high esteem as I do.

John D. Bessler

In the beginning was the Word. –St. John, Gospel 1:1 • Beginnings are always troublesome. –George Eliot • My way is to begin with the beginning. –Lord Byron • What one has to do usually can be done. –Eleanor Roosevelt • Creative writing is simply writing produced by a creative mind regardless of the form or genre the writer uses for his expression. –Mary M. Colum • Nobody is ever met at the airport when beginning a new adventure. –Elizabeth Fernea • A writer is somebody for whom writing is more difficult than it is for other people. –Thomas Mann • Life is a voyage. –Victor Hugo • A writer not writing is practically a maniac within himself. –F. Scott Fitzgerald • I'm only really alive when I'm writing. –Tennessee Williams • One of the things a writer is for is to say the unsayable, speak the unspeakable and ask difficult questions. –Salman Rushdie • It is very difficult to write. –Marianne Moore • You've got to want very much to write. Writing must become the most important thing in the world to you. –Sigurd Olson • I hope that what you'll read here will have some meaning. I want it to, as much as I've ever wanted anything. –Earvin "Magic" Johnson • Why do I write? Perhaps in order not to go mad. –Elie Wiesel • Wordstruck is exactly what I was—and still am: crazy about the sound of words, the look of words, the taste of words, the feeling for words on the tongue and in the mind. –Robert MacNeil • I've had great joy writing screenplays. Every single one has been a matter of joy. –Harold Pinter • I write because I like to write. –Paddy Chafevsky • I love being a writer. What I can't stand is the paperwork. –Peter De Vries • If you want to find out what is happening in an age or in a nation, find out what is happening to the writers, the town criers. –Ben Okri • I wish there were some words in the world that were not the words I always hear. –Donald Barthelme • I have loved writing, especially in the winter, early in the morning, sitting with my back to the fireplace at a card table. –Joan Baez • First sentences are doors to worlds. –Ursula K. Le Guin • Genuine beginnings begin within us, even when they are brought to our attention by external opportunities. –William Bridges • Only those who dare to fail greatly can ever achieve greatly. –Robert F. Kennedy • I believed for the first time that I could actually be a writer. –Joan Rivers • The next thing most like living one's life over again seems to be a recollection of that life, and to make that recollection as durable as possible by putting it down in writing. –Benjamin Franklin • The greatest pleasure in life is doing what people say you cannot do. –Walter Bagehot • Start to write, and let one thing lead to another. –Ring Lardner • It is better to begin in the evening than not at all. –English proverb

BEGINNINGS

The way of progress is neither swift nor easy. –Marie Curie • Failure is only an opportunity to begin again more intelligently. –Henry Ford • With ordinary talents and extraordinary perseverance all things are attainable. –Thomas Buxton • Something awful happens to a person who grows up as a creative kid and suddenly finds no creative outlet as an adult. –Judy Blume • Language, like love, starts local. –Allan Gurganus • The very impulse to write, I think, springs from an inner chaos crying for order, for meaning, and that meaning must be discovered in the process of writing or the work lies dead as it is finished. –Arthur Miller • I love to write to the moment. –Samuel Richardson • "Where shall I begin, please your Majesty?" he asked. "Begin at the beginning," the King said, gravely, "and go on till you come to the end: then stop." –Lewis Carroll • The wish-to-write is very common. It is often vague, intermittent, a mere emotional itch, a weak yen, a daydream. –Gorham Munson • Skilled or unskilled, we all scribble poems. –Horace • If you tell yourself you are going to be at your desk tomorrow, you are by that declaration asking your unconscious to prepare the material. –Norman Mailer • We will not know unless we begin. –Howard Zinn • Why do so many people want to be writers anyway? –Sherwood Anderson • The hardest thing about writing, in a sense, is not writing. I mean, the sentence is not intended to show you off, you know. It is not supposed to be "Look at me!" "Look, no hands!" It's supposed to be a pipeline between the reader and you. One condition of the sentence is to write so well that no one notices that you're writing. –James Baldwin • Writing is a way of coming to terms with the world and with oneself. –R. V. Cassill • Writing is an act of concentration and reflection. It is an act of diving into the well of our inner lives. It is a process of healing and regeneration. –Susan Zimmermann • I have forced myself to begin writing when I've been utterly exhausted…and somehow the activity of writing changes everything. –Joyce Carol Oates • There were years in which I could have devoted myself to writing if I had wanted to. It is commonly known that everyone looks back and regrets not following through on more things that mattered to them. –Ann Beattie • A writer is someone who makes the tracks of her mind's thinking visible for anyone who wants to follow her. –Kelly Cherry • I find the great charm of writing consists in its surprises. –Oliver Wendell Holmes • For me, writing something down is the only road out. –Anne Tyler • We cannot do everything at once, but we can do something at once. –Calvin Coolidge • We should not let our fears hold us back from pursuing our hopes. –John F. Kennedy • If you want to write, you can. –Richard Rhodes • Advice to aspiring writers: Fasten your seat belts—it's going to be a bumpy ride. –Christopher Buckley • Real courage is when you know you're licked before you begin, but you begin anyway and see it through no matter what. –Harper Lee • Whoever wants to reach a distant goal must take many small steps. –Helmut Schmidt • To get started, I will accept anything that occurs to me. Something always occurs, of course, to any of us. We can't keep from thinking. –William Stafford • Beginnings are important. –John Irving • One thing is clear: We don't have the option of turning away from the future. –Bill Gates

Inspiration is wonderful when it happens, but the writer must develop an approach for the rest of the time. The approach must involve getting something down on the page: something good, mediocre or even bad. It is essential to the writing process that we unlearn all those seductive high school maxims about waiting for inspiration. The wait is simply too long.

–Leonard Bernstein, conductor and composer

Every writer I know has trouble writing.

–Joseph Heller, author of CATCH-22

I am beginning to learn that it is the sweet, simple things of life which are the real ones after all.

–Laura Ingalls Wilder, American writer

Until one is committed, there is hesitancy, the chance to draw back, always ineffectiveness. Concerning all acts of initiative (and creation) there is one elemental truth, the ignorance of which kills countless ideas and splendid plans: that the moment one definitely commits oneself, then providence moves too. All sorts of things occur to help one that would never otherwise have occurred. A whole stream of events issues from the decision, raising in one's favor all manner of unforeseen incidents and meetings and material assistance, which no man could have dreamed would have come his way. I have learned a deep respect for one of Goethe's couplets: "Whatever you can do, or dream you can, begin it. Boldness has genius, power, and magic in it."

–W. H. Murray, THE SCOTTISH HIMALAYAN EXPEDITION

CHAPTER ONE

Start Where You Are

Writing is hard work. It requires concentration to put words on paper, and it requires perseverance to revise one's writing and get the words right. I've practiced law for fifteen years now—writing almost every day as part of my job—but I still struggle with words. As an attorney at a Minneapolis law firm doing commercial litigation, I need to use words effectively to be a good advocate. I write demand letters. I write answers and complaints for filing in court. I write e-mails and memos to clients. And I read cases and statutes and write motion papers and appellate court briefs. In my work, it is critical that I choose my words carefully so that I present facts and arguments persuasively. Words convey meaning, so word choices matter a great deal to both my clients and me. Before meeting with opposing counsel or appearing before a judge, for example, I make notes about what I plan to say. If I didn't, I wouldn't be prepared.

At the law firm where I work, things move at a fast pace. Judges set filing deadlines that must be met, and corporate clients expect answers to questions—often the same day they ask them. Statute books and online legal research enable me to find those answers, but it is writing that allows me to quickly assemble and communicate what I've found and to understand complex cases and legal issues. Writing helps me unleash creative thoughts and ideas and harness information and then relay it. And whether I'm representing an individual, a small business, or a large corporation, or working on a pro bono file or a multi-million dollar dispute over insurance or the broadcast rights to a Major League Baseball team, I always strive to communicate effectively. Writing is not only an essential part of my job, it actually helps me think and prepares me for oral communications, no matter what the setting.

I've written a lot since I was a teenager, but writing has never been easy for me. When I'm writing, I often feel like I'm wrestling with words, trying to capture and then articulate concepts or ideas, some more elusive than others, as if I were trying to put a stronger, more limber adversary into a half nelson. My goal is always to pin down what I want to say in the clearest possible language, keeping in mind, of course, whatever filing deadlines or client-driven time constraints may exist. Usually I feel good about what I write, but other times I look back at what I wrote and think to myself that I could have expressed myself more clearly or succinctly, like the times I've had to pull all-nighters to meet a filing deadline or reply to a motion seeking a temporary restraining order. Writing has certainly gotten easier for me over time, as I've learned to work with words, but writing never has been, and never will be, effortless. It's just the nature of writing: it's hard work. One has to struggle to communicate with clarity and style, just as a wrestler has to struggle to hold an opponent against a mat long enough to claim a victory.

But writing offers valuable rewards that make the effort

worthwhile. Writing allows us to express ourselves, to communicate with others. Winston Churchill—a gifted communicator—thought writing so important that, as Great Britain's prime minister, he issued a national security directive stating that "all directions emanating from me are made in writing, or should be immediately confirmed in writing." Writing not only allows us to record events and memories, but it permits us to grapple with thoughts and ideas more effectively. It allows us to analyze and solve complex problems more efficiently than we could otherwise; it enables us to learn from our ancestors and the past; and it allows us to instantaneously transmit information across the globe via letters, faxes, blogs and e-mails. Without writing, communications and human and social progress would move at a tortoise's pace. It's no wonder that Abraham Lincoln, one of America's greatest presidents, called writing "the great invention of the world."[1]

For me personally, writing has offered tremendous opportunities. I grew up in a 12' x 60' mobile home, and later a modest house, in Mankato, Minnesota, with my parents and five brothers. My mom and dad, who are both teachers, didn't have much money, but they worked hard, valued education, and always encouraged me to read and write. They gave me free reign of their bookcases at home, and they let me use their Smith Corona typewriter at almost any hour of the day or night. Because I developed strong writing skills, I had the opportunity to go to college, to become a lawyer and earn a living helping others, and to buy a house for my own family. Through my prior books and published articles, I've also gotten the chance to reach a larger audience for my views on important social and political issues, such as America's death penalty. Because of my writings, I've even had the opportunity to study international human rights law at the University of Oxford. Through my words, I am able to express myself on topics as weighty as genocide, child labor, summary executions, the plight of refugees, and war and peace. Writing actually allows me to reach people I may never meet in my lifetime.

Many people write, but few do it well. Since 1969, the U.S. government has administered tests and reported the results through the National Assessment of Educational Progress, better known as "the nation's report card." That testing has assessed the writing skills of fourth and eighth graders, as well as high school students, from 1984 to 2002, with test scores not fluctuating much over that time. Disturbingly, in 2002, 26 percent of high school seniors rated as "Below Basic" in writing ability; only 51 percent were at the "Basic" skill level, denoting merely acceptable performance at grade level; and only 22 percent were considered "Proficient," denoting "solid academic performance" demonstrating "competency over challenging subject matter." Writing scores on the 1998 and 2002 tests showed that only *one to two percent* of twelfth graders had "Advanced" writing skills. The vast majority of students are thus not realizing their full potential and will be unprepared for college or the workforce. Because the SAT® added a writing assessment in 2005, many teenagers may fail to get into the colleges of their choice or fail to get in altogether.[2]

Writing skills are often lacking in workplaces, too. A 2004 report of the National Commission on Writing, which surveyed 120 major American corporations employing nearly eight million people, found that writing is a "threshold skill" for hiring and promotion and that two-thirds of salaried employees have writing responsibilities, with nearly universal e-mail usage. Even among hourly employees, between one-fifth and one-third of employees have some writing responsibilities. Yet, the commission's report—the result of a survey of human resource directors in corporations associated with the Business Roundtable—found that up to one-third of employees in blue-chip companies have deficient writing skills. "People who cannot write and communicate clearly will not be hired and are unlikely to last long enough to be considered for promotion," the report concluded, noting that more than 40 percent of responding firms offer or require training for salaried employees with writing deficiencies. This costs American businesses as much as $3.1 billion annually, a sum roughly equivalent to how much companies waste in electricity for office machines that are left on when not in use.[3]

Actually, everyone I know encounters difficulty writing from time to time—usually most of the time. To struggle with writing is not only common, it's completely normal and to be expected. *Writing for Life* aims to better one's writing skills, though I can't promise that writing will ever be as easy as, say, coasting downhill on a bicycle. If writing was that easy, books such as this one would be unnecessary. Indeed, it's because writing is hard—and takes so much patience—that many people give up on writing or grow so frustrated with it that they write only when necessary (and then, often, badly). Many people never learn that becoming a good writer takes time and continuous practice and that effective writing is really just about following some simple steps and meticulously *revising* what one first writes.

But there are tough questions to answer. Given that writing is hard, is it really worth the effort? And if so, how does one efficiently reap all of the rewards that writing has to offer?

The answer to the first question is simple: yes, it's worth it. In the world in which we live, every phase of life, from student to retiree, and nearly every job, from assembly line worker to accountant and from retail clerk to nurse, requires writing skills of some kind or another. A 2004 report of the National Commission on Writing found that more than 80 percent of companies in the service and finance, insurance, and real estate sectors assess writing during hiring, with half of all companies taking writing skills into account when making promotion decisions. In fact, more than half of all responding companies "frequently" or "almost always" produce reports, correspondence and memos, and for jobs requiring writing, 54 percent of companies require writing samples, with 71 percent of companies forming impressions of applicants' writing abilities based on cover letters. Eighty-six percent of human resource directors said they would hold poorly written applications against a job candidate either "frequently" or "almost always." "In most cases, writing ability could be your ticket in…or it could be your ticket out," said one survey respondent, noting how writing skills might mean the difference between getting hired or rejected or between a promotion and a lost job.[4]

With the rise of the Internet and e-mail communications, writing has become more common and is even more important than ever. E-mail messages, often drafted quickly, may invite sloppy writing, but if you want to excel in school or at a job, you need to learn how to write well, including in e-mails. More than 90 percent of mid-career professionals say that the "need to write effectively" is "of great importance" to their work lives, and accuracy in writing is listed as "Extremely important" by 95 percent of the human resource directors of blue-chip companies. In addition, more than 90 percent of human resource managers say clarity and conciseness in writing, as well as grammar, punctuation, and spelling, are either "Extremely important" or "Important" to them. Even if you only have to write occasionally, becoming a better writer is in your own best interest: it will help you do what you have to do, what you want to do, and give you more confidence and pride in your work and in yourself. Learning to write well may be challenging, but everybody should *want* to write effectively *for themselves*, not just because a grade might depend upon it or because a parent, teacher or workplace supervisor might say it's important to do.[5]

The real difficulty lies with the second question: how does one become an effective, or more effective, writer? Learning and making use of proven writing techniques certainly makes writing easier, but learning how to write well doesn't happen overnight, or even in weeks or months. *Writing for Life* will give you the insight and tools you need to write more effectively, but I would be doing you a disservice if I didn't disclose now that trial and error is the best way to learn to write effectively. Just as kids fall and skin their knees when they first try to ride bicycles, nobody can escape unscathed when they learn to write. Given that reality, how does one even begin to think about doing all the work it takes to become a more effective writer and communicator? Because I've struggled with the same question myself, let me suggest an approach at the outset by way of a story.

In the mid-1990s I worked as a law clerk for Jack Mason, a federal magistrate judge who had a zest for life and for languages in particular. He rode his bicycle to work from Minneapolis to downtown St. Paul during the summer, drove a foreign convertible, played piano and accordion, and loved watching *The Simpsons* and reading *Dilbert*. He spoke fluent German, and he studied Italian, French, Spanish, Korean and Arabic. A graduate of Harvard Law School and Minnesota's Macalester College, where he befriended fellow student and future United Nations Secretary-General Kofi Annan, Judge Mason was well-read, never without opinions on important civic issues, and a gifted writer who wrote and edited his own decisions. Judge Mason recognized the value of concise, clearly worded prose, and he expected his law clerks to do multiple rounds of edits to achieve that objective in their own work. As one of his clerks, I saw first-hand the benefits of revision as I watched sloppily worded drafts become polished orders.[6]

Tragically, in June 2002, Jack Mason died suddenly while biking around the upper Midwest's scenic Lake Pepin on an annual 70-mile trek. My father-in-law, former Twin Cities' newspaper columnist Jim Klobuchar, bicycled often with Jack. After Jim's close friend died, he e-mailed friends, recalling a conversation he'd had with Jack one evening at Gooseberry Falls State Park along Minnesota's North Shore. "The surf was faintly audible and the resident gulls floated in the current above the shoreline pines. The low sun was beginning to streak the woods and the sky with color and to darken the water," my father-in-law wrote of the sunset they took in together that day near Lake Superior. "You know, I've seen this a hundred times, but it's always better when you see it at the end of a day's bike ride," Jack said at the time. "You've had to work to get here, and all of those impressions you toss around in your mind while you're riding, with the sounds and the shifting scenes, it makes a good day great." Jim and Jack shared a love of adventure—my father-in-law as a mountain climber and adventure club leader and Jack as a frequent fellow traveler—but also a mutual respect for hard work and the power of words, whether in newsprint or in a court order.[7]

When Judge Mason swore in immigrants as new U.S. citizens or when he performed a wedding—I saw him do two, one of my brother Andrew and his wife Hongji and one in his courtroom in which he conscripted me to act as the impromptu photographer with the groom's camera—he was fond of quoting from a book called *Start Where You Are*. Written by Arnold Lowe, a Presbyterian minister, the book has a clear message: "We cannot live without dreams and we dare not be without hope, but the fulfillment of dreams and hopes belongs to tomorrow. That is where someday we hope to be; but to be what our dreams so alluringly promise, we must begin with ourselves today." "No one can escape the hard and often bitter lesson," Lowe wrote in his book, "that to arrive at the end of the road we must begin where we are." If you want to bicycle somewhere, you must peddle and expend the energy it takes to get there; to learn a new language, you must study and use it before you can become fluent. Lowe's directive: "start where you are." Though the prize, one's personal aspiration, may be a long way off, it is well worth seeking—and has all kinds of social utility. "To do something great for others, we must first do something within ourselves," Lowe wrote, explaining: "We cannot begin with perfection, nor can we begin with ultimate achievement. Achievement is a process. We must begin wherever we happen to be."[8]

Writing for Life offers similar advice. It urges you, the reader, to start where you are when it comes to the writing process. If you know almost nothing about the craft of writing, that's fine; if you already fancy yourself a proficient writer, that's okay, too. Self-improvement is always possible with writing, no matter what your current skill level. Either way, it's my hope that you presently find yourself reading the right book—a book intended to offer useful advice about the writing process regardless of whether you're a beginning writer or a fairly skilled practitioner. Writing is, fundamentally, about exploration and discovery, and in its own way—no matter how you use it—it can be as exhilarating as running or mountain climbing. There is an innate human desire to travel and explore, and writing helps satisfy that longing. Just as climbers converge in Nepal and trek up Mount Everest, writers engage in inner exploration when they write. And fully understood, the writing process is adventurous and fun, with any fear of writing—or incidences of writer's block—easily overcome. Indeed, the journey itself can be reward enough, even if one fails to reach one's chosen destination.

If you believe you can't ever be a skilled writer, I ask that you set that notion aside. Skills are developed through practice, and writing should never be a source of loathing or dread. Though misconceptions about the writing process abound, knowing more about it, combined with consistent practice, will make any fear of writing subside and become manageable. Even if you presently hate writing or you've given up on it and consider yourself a discouraged writer—the functional equivalent of a "discouraged worker" (that is, one who has stopped looking for work out of a belief that no job can be found)—don't give up hope. When it comes to learning the craft of writing, anything is possible because it's all *within your control*. If you set your mind to it, you'll be able to do it. It may take time, but what doesn't? As India's political and spiritual leader, Mahatma Gandhi, put it: "If I have the belief that I can do it, I shall surely acquire the capacity to do it even if I may not have it at the beginning."[9]

It's perfectly understandable why some people hate writing: they've only done *compulsory* writing. They've only written when told to do so, usually by a parent, teacher or employer, and often only on subjects they've been told to write about by others. Schoolwork and writing assignments, of course, are a necessary part of learning and life. Teachers must turn in grades, and assigning term papers allows them to assess student performance. Likewise, employees must often write letters, reports and presentations as part of their jobs. Although writing assignments force everyone to write, it's not exactly the most welcoming way of learning the craft. People resent doing what they're told to do, and such resentments can jade their views of the writing process. I've learned to like writing over time, but I didn't always like it and even now I look forward to some writing projects more than others. If all you're doing is homework or mandatory writing projects, writing can seem like a chore, particularly if what you're writing about doesn't especially interest you.

Ideally, one's first exposure to writing would be through voluntary wordplay, much like kids first discover the alphabet through toy blocks or the joys of baseball, basketball or football through sandlot or playground pick-up games. Unfortunately, we don't live in an ideal world. Though e-mails nowadays facilitate playful, written exchanges and kids at young ages have e-mail accounts, most people pick up writing skills primarily through homework, bland textbooks or handbooks, and projects at work. This, however, is not the best way to excite students, employees and others about the writing process. Time pressure and the pace of business can make academic and work-related writing stressful (believe me, I know!), and such stress can complicate one's views about the craft of writing. In fact, workplaces often lack sufficient mentors or resources to teach writing, and schools themselves often spend far too little time convincing students *why* they should write, let alone teaching kids *how* to write.

The statistics pertaining to schoolchildren are telling. According to data from the National Assessment of Educational Progress, 97 percent of elementary school students spent three hours a week or less on writing assignments. While some kids, like my daughter, do writing projects outside of schoolwork, many children never do, thus never gaining proficiency or confidence with the use of written words. The upper grades are often no better. Forty-nine percent of twelfth graders report that they are assigned a paper of three or more pages perhaps once or twice a month in English class, and 39 percent report that such assignments are given "hardly ever" or "never." And that's in English class! A 2003 report of the National Commission on Writing found that adding just fifteen minutes of writing four nights a week would add 33 percent to the amount of time the average elementary school student spends writing. In other words, students are writing far too infrequently, leading to profound deficiencies in writing ability.[10]

If you ask me, everyone should feel as comfortable writing as they do having a light-hearted conversation over dinner with a close friend. It's too bad that's not the case. Ironically, though people effortlessly learn to speak and, for the most part, confidently use that skill throughout their lives, many people never feel at ease writing. Often, they simply don't understand the writing process. Whereas speaking comes naturally because we've been doing it all our lives, writing skills are not innate and are acquired only through instruction and trial and error, making writing especially difficult for those who write infrequently. Many people, in fact, try to avoid writing or put off writing projects until the last minute, leaving insufficient time for revision—a key to effective writing, as I'll discuss more later. This leads to poor quality writing and exacerbates the writer's insecurities about his or her writing ability. Only after the writing process is demystified and people realize that they *can* write more effectively, including by revising what they write, do people blossom as writers.

This book seeks to convince everyone that learning to write well should be a lifelong objective because it will yield lifelong rewards, both personally and professionally. In that respect, *Writing for Life* is intended to be much more than a how-to book; it is also intended to be a *why* book. The why questions are, in my view, just as important as the how-to questions. Why do people write? And why should people write? If these questions aren't satisfactorily answered, why would anyone want to write or take the time to improve his or her writing skills in the first place? No matter what your perspective, if I can convince you that writing is enjoyable and beneficial and can show you some techniques for making writing easier, I will have accomplished my objectives in writing this book. *Writing for Life* is intended as a roadmap to effective writing, though you'll have to do the driving and navigating yourself to get there. I want to share what I know about the writing process so that you view it positively and so you can write more effectively. Writing offers tremendous rewards, and I want you to be able to write as well as possible and to be able to see through all the misconceptions about writing that I myself once harbored.

What you need to remember at all times is that writing—regardless of any pre-conceived notions you have about it or how you were first introduced to it—is really just a powerful way to help you organize and communicate your thoughts. All of us already record thoughts and images in our heads and then selectively filter and use them. We remember specific events and what people tell us, and we sometimes even meticulously plan what we're going to say to someone in advance of saying it. You might have crafted, tweaked, and then rehearsed what you were going to say to your first date before asking out that person, or you might have gone over and over what you ended up saying to a prospective employer in an interview. If you've ever had anything important to say, and I'm sure you have, you've undoubtedly asked yourself before: What's the best way of saying something? Would something sound better if a word or phrase was changed, expanded upon, or deleted altogether? That's only natural. Our minds work that way so that we can make a favorable impression on the people we meet.

Whenever you think to yourself like that, you are essentially writing and then rewriting *in your head*. This is cumbersome because your mind can only keep track of so many facts and ideas at once. Writing something down on paper often turns out to be a much better way to find the right words for a particular occasion or to capture the essence of what you're thinking. Without help, the mind can play tricks on us. We sometimes forget what we promise ourselves we'll never forget, or we may get flustered and forget to say something that needed to be said. That is why office workers keep to-do lists, why grocery shoppers carry lists, why politicians write speeches, and why salespeople create written presentations. Writing is no substitute for oral speech (nor would I want it to be), but writing does many valuable things, including making your thought process more transparent, permanent and capable of being analyzed. Writing even helps you discover what you want to say when, at first, you don't have a clue about what that might be.

If you like to create or think, writing is definitely for you. That's because the writing process assists—indeed, catalyzes—the creative and thinking processes. The mind can only focus on so much information at once, which is why writing—the transcription of thought—takes on such critical importance. What writing does is allow multiple thoughts, of whatever complexity, to be put in front of the writer at one time and in one place. When I start working on a commercial litigation matter, for example, I often feel daunted by the complexity of the legal issues and all the material facts, which may implicate dozens of witnesses or be scattered among numerous banker's boxes of documents, perhaps covering a span of many years—or even decades! Only after I start sorting through the materials, organizing them, and writing things down does my anxiety level decline and my confidence rise.

Think about it this way: writing performs the same function as a hockey star's relatively unknown teammate, the unsung player who provides key assists by putting the puck where it needs to be. Leading scorers only score lots of goals by maneuvering to the right position and then getting passes at opportune times. A talented writer understands that complex subjects are not manageable if exclusively kept in one's head; only by writing things down does a writer get positioned for being able to understand and take shots on goal at a given subject matter. In hockey, many shots get blocked by goalies—the equivalent of obstacles to clear thinking. But good writers, like good offensive players, know that by taking multiple slap shots at the net, goals can and will be scored. In writing, those multiple shots are taken not with hockey sticks and pucks, but through writing and revision.

Writing requires thinking, but if you think hard enough, you'll eventually find the right words to express your thoughts, however inexpressible you may have first thought them to be. As Linda Trichter Metcalf and Tobin Simon write in their book, *Writing the Mind Alive:* "You may not think in words but you can always turn thoughts into words," thus giving voice to your ideas, feelings, and beliefs. "The truth," they note, "is that, without writing, it is difficult for most people to go into their thought." "By writing you *slow thought down*," they explain, adding that writing "lets you project your thoughts onto a surface and interact with them." The writing process thus enables you to logically deal with, and contextualize, information, even material involving emotional content. The novelist E. M. Forster asked a question that all of us should consider in our daily lives: "How can I tell what I think till I see what I say?" If the writing process is seen as *a thinking process* (which is what it is), the benefits of writing are obvious: clearer thinking and better decision-making.[11]

I guarantee you: if you start to write, or try to learn to write more effectively, you will learn and discover things—things that may change the course of your life even if you never become (or don't aspire to be) a full-time writer. When you write, you grapple with thought. You may be seeking understanding, a workable solution to a problem, or simply exploring what you want to do with your life. By writing things down, you impose order on your mind, much like the Library of Congress or Dewey decimal classification systems organize the shelving of library books. You also may find greater clarity of purpose in your life. I've been writing for a long time now, and I can attest that the writing process has helped me on countless occasions. It's improved my communication skills; it's helped me navigate difficult projects at work; and it's given me focus, direction and a heightened sense of self. "I think, therefore I am," the French mathematician and philosopher René Descartes wrote in *Le Discours de la Méthode*. The father of analytic geometry easily might have added: "I write, therefore I am more effective."[12]

This book's premise is that *anyone* can learn to write well and that *everyone*, regardless of current proficiency, can improve his or her writing ability and should take concrete steps to do so. Writing well is not only an essential skill for living, but the writing process—though grueling at times—is a key to a life well-lived. It may take concerted effort to write well, but that goal—I can assure even the most skeptical readers—is achievable and well worth pursuing. Becoming an effective writer can lead to better grades, better reasoning, or a better-paying job. But far more important than any academic, monetary or work-related rewards, learning to write well offers the promise of greater personal satisfaction throughout one's life. Because the act of writing hones one's thinking skills, writing itself will be extremely beneficial to you no matter what you do with your life. As best-selling author Anne Lamott puts it: "Writing has so much to give, so much to teach, so many surprises. That thing you had to force yourself to do—the actual act of writing—turns out to be the best part."[13]

If you're reading this book, it's a fair assumption that you either *want* to write more effectively or that someone else—a teacher, mentor, or parent, maybe—thinks you *need* to improve your writing skills. *Writing for Life*, I'll confess up front and without apology, is not a textbook. If you want to read a treatise on writing, there are plenty available, replete with model writing samples, long chapters on punctuation and grammar, and exercises on writing everything from academic papers to personal essays to professional-looking business letters. In this book, I won't show you how to diagram sentences or lecture you on the finer points of syntax; you can look elsewhere to learn about subordinate clauses, subjects and direct objects, definite and indefinite articles, gerunds and intransitive verbs, and misplaced modifiers and dangling participles. *This* book seeks to show you what the writing process is all about and what that process can do for you. It aims to convince you that writing can enrich your life and that using simple, concrete techniques will make you a better writer, a more effective communicator, and a more thoughtful and productive member of society.[14]

Writing allows you to make connections with other people, and the rigorous use of one's mind can be pleasurable, just as bicycling or jogging can make one's body feel alive. Writing is not only a physical act, requiring the use of one's hands, but it is a mental activity requiring active engagement with one's surroundings and oneself. What could be more satisfying than to use words effectively to be a full participant in life's activities—to think and reason, to express oneself, to be passionate about one's endeavors, and to make a positive contribution to society? What writing well does is make you a much more effective player in the world. You may never be as good a writer as you'd like to be, but that's okay; none of us ever achieves perfection, and that's, in fact, what makes us human. But if you start to improve your writing skills now, just think what you'll be able to accomplish later. As Arnold Lowe wrote: "You have noble dreams? You want a better world? Then why don't you begin in the little world in which you live? How far that will carry you in the end."[15]

If you're disheartened by the prospect of all the work ahead of you, don't be. Hard work—as Judge Mason noted after his long bike ride with my father-in-law—makes getting somewhere all the more worthwhile. And all of us, whether we realize it or not, already know quite a bit about writing. We've read books and newspapers and magazine articles; we've had spelling and grammar lessons in school; and we've all written something, if only short papers or the occasional letter, e-mail or post card. Indeed, the average high school graduate possesses a vocabulary of approximately 40,000 words or more. This prior training and knowledge gives anyone—with the exception of newborns, toddlers and those with the most profound disabilities, making writing difficult or impossible—the tools and therefore the power to write well if the work ethic is there. Plainly, anyone reading this book starts with at least some skills and opinions—good or bad—about the English language and the writing process and has the *capacity* to write effectively. As you work toward becoming a better writer, you'll simply be building on the skills you already possess and—in some cases—abandoning bad habits.[16]

If you've had only positive writing experiences thus far, consider yourself lucky, perhaps akin to a lottery winner. Negative reactions to writing are common, so common, in fact, that many people associate writing with failure. All of us, I suspect, can remember our grade-school teachers asking us to write about what we did over our summer breaks. We wrote down our experiences on wide-ruled paper, whether dutifully or joyfully, and those assignments—about our own lives—were then turned in and graded. You may have thought you expressed yourself brilliantly on the page, but the red ink may have led you to believe the teacher thought otherwise. You may have experienced the same thing in middle school or high school. English teachers, after all, love to circle grammatical and spelling errors and often scribble "run-on sentence" or "awkward" in the margins of students' papers. Such comments, unfortunately, are often mistaken by a student as an indication that the teacher believes the student lacks writing talent or that the pupil's *thoughts*—the substance of what was said—were flawed or not worthwhile. It's a shame when that happens. Raw, rough-around-the-edges writing should never be confused or equated with a lack of ability.

Teachers, of course, just want us to learn from our mistakes. Too often, however, people mistake constructive criticism for a judgment that they lack aptitude or originality. As one writing teacher puts it, if you got a C-minus on a paper, you may have taken away this lesson: "You had a C-minus summer. You thought it was an A-plus summer, but it wasn't. It was only C-minus." What you need to remember is that people who read your writing are usually only trying to help. The joy of writing is diminished if well-intentioned comments, intended only to improve one's writing skills, are taken the wrong way. So just be cognizant of that as your writing is critiqued by others. It is, ironically, in schools—our places of learning—that fears of writing typically develop, and for many people, unfortunately, those fears never go away. "The blank piece of paper or the blank computer screen, waiting to be filled with our wonderful words," notes writing expert William Zinsser, "can freeze us into not writing any words at all."[17]

What people fail to recognize is that writing is really just a combination of speaking and listening skills. If you can speak and listen and have the patience to revise what you first write, you can become a skilled writer. First drafts demand speaking onto the page as you would while talking to someone, and long compositions are just like extended monologues. Revision, on the other hand, requires listening to how those words sound and are put together, then being patient as you strive to improve your words and their organization and content so that you say precisely what you want to say in the most effective manner possible. Your speaking voice—the way you say things—is something you already possess and is what gives your writing distinctive personality. But here's the rub: it is only through deliberate and dedicated revision—a kind of listening process that requires you to identify (and then rectify) the flaws in your initial thoughts and drafts—that your writing truly comes alive.

Remember, good writers are made, not born. Even the best writers—people such as Ernest Hemingway and Emily Dickinson—had to learn the craft of writing along with everyone else. Some people, no doubt, acquire a knack for writing (and even publishing what they write) when they're young, but many people don't develop their writing skills until much later in life. Two sisters and civil rights pioneers—Sarah "Sadie" Delany and Annie Elizabeth "Bessie" Delany—did not write their first book, *Having Our Say*, until they were both older than 100! Thus, it's never too late to start where you are and to learn how to write more effectively. "A journey of a thousand miles must begin with a single step," the philosopher Lao-Tzu once said, a reminder of the fact that any trip worth taking will take considerable time and endurance. What you will be able to accomplish is up to you, but I guarantee that if you make a conscious effort to improve your writing, it will improve over time. As former president Theodore Roosevelt—one of Hemingway's idols, and a famous writer in his own right—aptly advised, "Do what you can, with what you have, where you are." It's much like the advice that Jack Mason and Arnold Lowe were fond of giving, and I think it's very sound advice.[18]

I concede that learning to write well is a challenging endeavor. It was for me, and it is for everyone. I cannot emphasize enough, however, that the journey is well worth the bumpy ride, even if you never intend to publish a book or travel as far or climb as high as famous literary figures such as Kurt Vonnegut or Richard Ford or Ann Beattie or Louisa May Alcott. Not only does writing become easier with practice, but the writing process itself provides its own tangible benefits: it can help you better understand yourself, those around you, and the world we inhabit. Writing well, more than anything else, can help you make a meaningful contribution to society, giving your life meaning and greater significance. Plus, the writing process can be just plain fun once you get the hang of it. As writer James Salter explains: "The act of writing, though often tedious, can still provide extraordinary pleasure." The lines written "at the tip of a pen," he notes, "can be the most valuable thing I will ever own." What more could you want?[19]

Let's begin, shall we?

Seeing comes before words. –John Berger • I know a good many fiction writers who paint, not because they're any good at painting, but because it helps their writing. It forces them to look at things. –Flannery O'Connor • Great writers leave us not just their work, but a way of looking at things. –Elizabeth Janeway • Accuracy of observation is the equivalent of accuracy of thinking. –Wallace Stevens • Part of us is always the observer, and no matter what, it observes. It watches us. It does not care if we are happy or unhappy, if we are sick or well, if we live or die. Its only job is to sit there on our shoulder and pass judgment on whether we are worthwhile human beings. –Richard Bach • The only life we know well, the one on which we are the ultimate authority, is our own. The only experience to which we can bear witness is that which we have personally endured or observed. –Wallace Stegner • Painting is silent poetry, poetry is eloquent painting. –Simonides • I suspect that the reason that the ability to write good prose and good dialogue go hand-in-hand is simply that a good writer knows how to listen. –John Braine • Art is a technique of communication. The image is the most complete technique of all communication. –Claes Oldenburg • My task which I am trying to achieve is, by the power of the written word, to make you hear, to make you feel—it is, before all, to make you *see*! –Joseph Conrad • The purpose of art is not a rarified, intellectual distillate—it is life, intensified, brilliant life. –Alain Arias-Misson • Nobody sees a flower—really—it is so small it takes time—we haven't time—and to see takes time, like to have a friend takes time. –Georgia O'Keeffe • Look and you will find it—what is unsought will go undetected. –Sophocles • Yes, writing can be complicated, exhausting, isolating, abstracting, boring, dulling, briefly exhilarating; it can be made to be grueling and demoralizing. And occasionally it can produce rewards. But it's never as hard as, say, piloting an L-1011 into O'Hare on a snowy night in January, or doing brain surgery when you have to stand up for ten hours straight, and once you start you can't just stop. If you're a writer, you can stop anywhere, any time, and no one will care or ever know. –Richard Ford • Writing is one-third imagination, one-third experience, and one-third observation. –William Faulkner • Every child is an artist. The problem is how to remain an artist once he grows up. –Pablo Picasso • Through my own experience—and that of countless others that I have shared—I have come to believe that creativity is our true nature, that blocks are an unnatural thwarting of a process at once as normal and as miraculous as the blossoming of a flower at the end of a slender green stem. –Julia Cameron

OBSERVATION

I learned to read what lay behind the look that veiled people's faces, I learned how to sketch in human beings with a few rapid words, I learned to see; to observe, to remember; learned, in short, the first rules of writing. –Edna Ferber • There must above all be joy and excitement in learning, and I became convinced that field trips and observations were as important as books and laboratories. –Sigurd Olson • Only love (that is, jealousy) can train the writer's mind, since constant suspicious questioning of every motive, every movement, and the conversion of each innocent story into a guilty alibi—only this restless and piercing scrutiny can teach the writer to observe. –Marcel Proust • Often while reading a book one feels that the author would have preferred to paint rather than write; one can sense the pleasure he derives from describing a landscape or a person, as if he were painting what he is saying, because deep in his heart he would have preferred to use brushes and colors. –Pablo Picasso • Black and white is my canvas, words my pigments, interpretation of the wild my theme. –Sigurd Olson • I have always liked to let things simmer in my mind for a long time before setting them down on paper. –William Somerset Maugham • To evoke in oneself a feeling one has once experienced and having evoked it in oneself by means of movements, lines, colors, sounds, or forms expressed in words, so to transmit that feeling—that is the activity of art. –Leo Tolstoy • The greatest advantage of being a writer is that you can *spy* on people. You're there listening to every word, but part of you is observing. Everything is useful to a writer, you see—every scrap, even the longest and most boring of luncheon parties. –Graham Greene • The business of a poet is fundamentally to *see*, not to analyze. –Henrik Ibsen • Art is a human product, a human secretion; it is our body that sweats the beauty of our works. –Émile Zola • It is with the reading of books the same as with looking at pictures; one must, without doubt, without hesitations, with assurance, admire what is beautiful. –Vincent van Gogh • The poet produces something beautiful by fixing his attention on something real. –Simone Weil • By artist I mean of course everyone who has tried to create something which was not here before him, with no other tools and material than the uncommerciable ones of the human spirit; who has tried to carve, no matter how crudely, on the wall of that final oblivion, in the tongue of the human spirit, "Kilroy was here." –William Faulkner • The fiction writer is an incorrigible lover of concrete things. –Wallace Stegner • I date all my work because I think poetry, or any writing, is but a reflection of the moment. –Nikki Giovanni • I'm just going to sit down and tell the truth. –Jack Kerouac • The moment one gives close attention to anything, even a blade of grass, it becomes a mysterious, awesome, indescribably magnificent world in itself. –Henry Miller • When you walk into a room and you get a certain feeling or emotion, remember back until you see exactly what it was that gave you the emotion. Remember what the noises and smells were and what was said. Then write it down, making it clear so the reader will see it too, and have the same feeling you had. –Ernest Hemingway • He who asks questions cannot avoid the answers. –Cameroonian proverb • People only see what they are prepared to see. –Ralph Waldo Emerson

The life which is unexamined is not worth living.

−Plato, Greek philosopher

In the fields of observation chance favors
only those minds which are prepared.

−Louis Pasteur, French chemist

People are turning to their gardens not to consume
but to actively create, not to escape from reality but to
observe it closely. In doing this they experience the
connectedness of creation and the profoundest sources
of being. That the world we live in and the activity of
making it are one seamless whole is something that we
may occasionally glimpse. In the garden, we know.

−Carol Williams, BRINGING A GARDEN TO LIFE

Stare. It is the way to educate your eye, and more.

−Walker Evans, photographer

CHAPTER TWO

Learning to See

To be an effective writer, you must learn to observe things through a writer's eyes. Observation skills are of such crucial importance to writers because writers must vividly describe what they see. Fortunately, all of us possess those skills. Our eyes allow us to see what's happening around us, and our minds allow us to process that information, not only to make sense of visual stimulus, but to form opinions and beliefs about what we see. We all certainly possess the ability to describe in words what we see or experience, though our descriptive skills are dependent on how well our eyes and senses are trained and on how well we've learned to think and write. Actually, one does not even need aural or visual information to be able to write effectively. Even the deaf and the blind make accurate and insightful judgments and observations all the time about their surroundings, the people they meet, and the experiences they have. Through written description, anything or anyone can be brought to life—*by* anyone and *for* anyone.

In her book, *Art Objects*, English author Jeanette Winterson issues a thought-provoking challenge to anyone interested in the mind's ability to process and interpret information: make a pact with a painting and agree to sit down and look at it, all alone, with no distractions, for one hour. "To spend an hour looking at a painting is difficult," she explains, noting that those who take up the challenge encounter discomfort and irritation because they may be more accustomed to channel surfing and constantly flickering TV screens than looking at something for that long. Those who stick with the exercise, however, also experience what Winterson calls "increasing invention." Even couch potatoes, if situated in front of a work of art long enough, she says, will start "engaging with the picture" and begin asking themselves meaningful questions about it: "What is it about? Is it a landscape? Is it figurative?" Inevitably, such questions will lead to a more meaningful exploration of what a piece of art—what one is looking at—is all about.[1]

You may be asking yourself: what does this hour-long exercise involving a painting have to do with the craft of writing? That's a good question, and the answer—everything—is certainly not restricted to the realm of art appreciation or the ability to articulate what you like or don't like about a particular piece of art. The ability to observe and describe (and form opinions about) what you're looking at—and to make sense of it for yourself and others—is what good writing is all about. In fact, you don't have to look at a piece of art to learn the lesson; you could just as easily look at an oak tree or a lit candle for an hour and get the point, which is that writers need to pay close attention to what they see, experience and feel, and then be able to articulate in clear, understandable language what's seen, experienced and felt. Winterson's challenge—to spend an hour intently studying a painting—is a good one for any writer to take up because sitting still and staying focused forces the writer to develop his or her observation skills, as well as his or her descriptive skills. Just try it for yourself, and I bet you'll see what I mean.

Over a dozen years ago, I issued a somewhat similar challenge to myself that further illustrates the point I'm trying to make. After finishing law school—a three-year journey aimed at learning to "think like a lawyer"—I decided to take a six-week trip, all by myself, across Canada and the eastern United States. My first job as an attorney didn't start for a couple of months, and I wanted to take some time off and see if I could unleash a creative power a bit more exciting than learning how to interpret often ambiguously worded court decisions or statutes. My sophomore-year college roommate, now an electrical engineer, had once recommended a book authored by Betty Edwards called *Drawing on the Right Side of the Brain*—a book he'd sworn had taught him how to draw. Skeptical, yet still intrigued after the passage of many years, I finally went out and bought the book, a pad of sketching paper, some drawing pencils and a big eraser. My childhood drawings had consisted of little more than stick figures and one-dimensional houses with curlicues coming out of their chimneys to represent smoke, so my challenge to myself seemed far-fetched: learn to draw in six weeks.[2]

My road trip started in Minneapolis in the summer of 1991. When I set off, I had only a vague idea of where I wanted to go and what I wanted to see. I knew that I was packing a tent in the trunk and was headed first to the Windy City, Chicago, and then on to Detroit, at which point I would cross into Canada. I also knew I wanted to visit my brother Bill in West Virginia at some point on my trip, and that I wanted to see some art museums and national and state parks. But I purposely decided to leave my itinerary fairly open-ended. I left the Twin Cities with a tank full of gas and little more than my camping gear and what might be described as low expectations as to how my little experiment in learning to draw might turn out. At the very least, I knew that I would enjoy the drive and all the scenery, artwork and historic sites that I would see along the way. Little did I know then what any of this would have to do with the art of writing.

The subtitle of *Drawing on the Right Side of the Brain* is "A Course in Enhancing Creativity and Artistic Confidence." A boost in artistic confidence is certainly what I needed because, at least with respect to drawing, I knew exactly what I had: none. I had a close friend in high school, John Ostgarden, who could effortlessly draw pencil sketches of flowers and beautiful models out of magazines and still have the roses and tulips and women actually look beautiful when he was done. His artistic ability always astounded and fascinated me and, truth be told, made me a bit envious. If I had tried to do that, I wouldn't have known where to begin. I never excelled at art, and every time I tried drawing something it looked like I was stuck in a remedial kindergarten class. Everything I'd ever drawn, if you could even tell what the resulting object was, looked like a caricature of itself—the sun, with little lines coming out of it, to represent heat; a cloud, with little lines coming out of it, to represent rain; and so on and so forth.[3]

Those who write, it turns out, can learn a lot from artists and by studying art. In *Art Objects*, Jeanette Winterson recalls a life-changing snowy Christmas in Amsterdam when she wandered past a small gallery and saw a painting of a woman in blue robes that deeply moved her. As she described it, her heart "flooded away" at the "Renaissance beauty" of "the brush strokes in thin oils." It was a matchless moment, the kind of moment that true art inspires and that we experience when we see something that we love. "Here was a figure without a context, in its own context," Winterson wrote. Until that day, Winterson confesses to having little interest in the visual arts, though she realized later that her lack of interest was due to a kind of ignorance. To paraphrase Winterson's line in *Art Objects*, "I don't like this picture" is a common statement, but not one that tells us anything about a painting; it is a statement that tells us about the speaker. By going beyond first impressions—by asking the *what, why* and *how* questions—we learn and make discoveries.[4]

Winterson's experience is telling. Instead of leaving Amsterdam the next day as planned, Winterson stayed on and stood in line to get into the Rijksmuseum and the Van Gogh Museum, spending her afternoons at private galleries and her evenings reading about art and immersing herself in it. Her usual response, "This painting has nothing to say to me," had become "I have nothing to say to this painting." By becoming more conversant in the language of art through reading John Ruskin's *Modern Painters*, Walter Pater's *Studies of the History of the Renaissance*, and art writer Roger Fry, Winterson changed her own "way of seeing" and looking at pictures. Winterson's newfound knowledge led her to this insight: "There are no Commandments in art and no easy axioms for art appreciation. 'Do I like this?' is the question anyone should ask themselves at the moment of confrontation with the picture. But if 'yes', why 'yes'? and if 'no', why 'no'?"[5]

The sheer power of books and the written word—akin to the inexplicable force of the oil painting Winterson found hanging in the Amsterdam gallery—has never been more evident to me than it was that summer of '91. That summer, Betty Edwards's book not only taught me how to draw, but changed forever the way I look at people, at things, and at art. I learned about light and shadows and cross-hatching and about how to *see* things for the first time— things I'd experienced thousands of times before, like sunrises and people's faces, yet had never really *observed* before, at least not in the way Edwards's book taught me to do. "Ability to draw depends on ability to see the way an artist sees," Edwards explains in her book, noting that "this kind of seeing can marvelously enrich your life." Because of the long stretches of time that I had that summer, with little to do but observe the world and create, not only did I learn how to do pencil sketches on my trip, but I came to know myself better and what it means—and what tedious, hard work it takes—to be an artist. What I learned about drawing from Betty Edwards's book informs my own exploration of the writing process, which also requires meticulous attention to detail to produce quality work. If you want to write well, you must learn to see and think *like a writer sees and thinks.*[6]

Drawing on the Right Side of the Brain shows how artists think by discussing how the mind works. The book begins with Edwards's recitation of the discovery by Nobel Prize-winning psychobiologist Roger Sperry of the dual nature of human thinking—with verbal, analytic functions located mainly in the brain's left hemisphere and visual, perceptual functions located primarily in the right hemisphere. The left hemisphere, scientists have discovered, controls language function in 97 percent of right-handers and 68 percent of left-handers; the right hemisphere controls language in just 19 percent of left-handers, with language function centered in both hemispheres for some left-handers. Whereas the left hemisphere is typically more active while someone reads or writes, the right hemisphere is generally more active with drawing, painting and music. Brain scans reveal greater concentrations of activity in one hemisphere or the other depending on what one is doing, though both regions of the brain often work together during creative activities. One set of experiments found more right hemisphere activity, as measured by electroencephalograms, or EEGs, when subjects wrote fantasy stories. The *corpus callosum,* a large cable of nerve fibers, connects the brain's two hemispheres and allows communication between them. Good writers make use of both hemispheres when they write because effective writing requires keen observation as well as the logical use of words.[7]

Edwards explains that the left side of the brain—which scientists know from studying head injuries is where language function typically predominates—is where most people operate in their daily lives. "Left brain" or "L-mode" activities include speaking, reading, writing, and arithmetic, and account for analytic, sequential or linear thought. Everyone is endowed with perceptual skills—Edwards's book boasts that anyone with average eyesight and eye-hand coordination can learn to draw—but Edwards notes that the "visual, perceptual" function of the brain's right hemisphere, its "R-mode," is mystifying to most people. Even though the brain's right hemisphere is designed (and regularly used) to rapidly process global, constantly changing visual information—driving a car or playing a video game requires "R-mode" functioning—artists are regarded by non-artists as people with "rare God-given talent" because the drawing process seems mysterious and incomprehensible. Edwards's insights, I've come to see, are equally useful for thinking about the writing process, which many people struggle with, too, and often don't understand.[8]

The whole premise of Edwards's book is that the artist within each of us is not properly developed in schools and that, without justification, artistic skills go largely untaught. "The majority of adults," Edwards writes, "do not progress in art skills much beyond the level of development they reached at age nine or ten." Children's drawings of human figures, Edwards notes, often resemble one another, though each child adds special details (such as round or square buttons) to his or her own drawings as time goes on. "These favorite ways to draw various parts of the image eventually become embedded in the memory and are remarkably stable over time," Edwards explains, describing the process by which childhood memories become so deeply engrained that internalized *symbols* for objects or human features can prevent many adults from seeing those objects or features *as they really are.* The human head exemplifies the kind of subject for which most people have a strong, persistent symbol system. For that reason, adults' drawings of human faces often differ little from children's drawings of them. Because the artistic process is never fully understood, children may stop thinking of themselves as artists, and artistic skills and techniques may never be learned, as they might have been, thus necessitating Edwards's book to remedy the resulting artistic deficiencies.[9]

Just as people's artistic skills are often undeveloped, so, too, are writing skills often lacking. As an adjunct law professor, I have personally seen a major deficiency in our education system: the inability of some people to write effectively. I teach at the University of Minnesota Law School, a top-ranked institution, but I still regularly encounter law students who turn in papers that are disorganized, rambling, or that contain multiple spelling and grammar errors. Most of the students are proficient writers, but many of them are still writing at levels far below their potential effectiveness, in part due to deficiencies in prior schooling. I teach a seminar on the death penalty, but I always try to work in a little writing instruction, too. To emphasize the importance of revision, which is a crucial part of any writing project, I ask my students to turn in rough drafts of their papers midway through the course and I always give comments on those drafts. The vast majority of students are open to suggestions, but others, I've found, resist extensively revising what they first wrote—a stubbornness caused by a misapprehension of the writing process. No student, of course, can learn to write effectively in one class, though I'm convinced that better writing and revision skills can be learned.

Humans have a built-in *instinct* to write, with children beginning to scribble with pencils or crayons at about age one and a half. All of us, however, need to *acquire* writing skills through schooling or other means. Though we all possess "L-mode" skills, such as linear, sequential thinking, somewhere along the line a large number of people begin to shun writing or come to believe they lack the talent for it. This begins in schools, but does not end there. The 2002 Survey of Public Participation in the Arts, conducted as a supplement to a U.S. Census Bureau study, found that only seven percent of adults did creative writing during the prior year. Those surveyed were asked: "With the exception of work or school, did you do any creative writing such as stories, poems or plays during the last 12 months?" Whereas 12.7 percent of 18-24 year-olds indicated that they had done creative writing, only 7.9 percent of 25-34 year-olds and 6.7 percent of 35-44 year-olds reported doing so. As people age, the number of creative writers falls even further. Only 5 percent of 55-64 year-olds and 4.1 percent of 65-74 year-olds do creative writing. Instead of developing and improving writing skills over time, many people, it seems, simply give up on writing as they grow older.[10]

The reasons people stop writing or come to dislike writing are varied and complex. Many people, no doubt, abandon writing because they let themselves believe that it is a skill that is not useful to them. Instead, they see writing as the province of academics, journalists and published writers. Others conclude that writing takes too much time or perceive that effective writing is—and forever will be—beyond their grasp. Bottom line: many people never train themselves to process information like writers. They fail to observe people or places long enough to see what writers see; they dash off a series of sentences and call it a day, not realizing the importance of revision; or they fail to use simple tools (e.g., a dictionary or thesaurus) that any talented writer knows need to be used to write effectively. When writing needs to be done, it is often done sloppily, with too little revision, without the necessary commitment to quality, and without a coherent understanding of the writing process. Whereas Edwards addresses underdeveloped artistic skills, I am interested in remedying poor writing skills. That's why I like to talk to people about the craft of writing. And that's why I wrote this book.

In *Art Objects*, Jeanette Winterson emphasizes that "art takes time." That is certainly true, at least with respect to high-quality writing or visual art. What I learned in 1991 as I drove eastward toward Québec, reading bits of Edwards's book as I stopped at rest areas and camping sites along the way, is that the basic skills needed to create visual art are actually quite simple. As Edwards writes: "These skills are not drawing skills. They are *perceptual* skills, listed as follows: (1) the perception of edges, (2) the perception of spaces, (3) the perception of relationships, (4) the perception of lights and shadows, and (5) the perception of the whole, or *gestalt*." Edwards notes that "the fifth skill, the perception of the whole, or *gestalt*, is neither taught nor learned but instead seems to emerge as a result of acquiring the other four skills." "Progress," Edwards writes, "takes the form of practice, refinement of technique, and learning what to use the skills for." For writing, progress is equally dependent upon practice, learning useful writing techniques, and learning when and how best to use those techniques.[11]

My skepticism of Edwards's book—I never imagined I'd really be able to draw well by book's end—remained with me throughout the first chapter, particularly after reading this line: "Learning to draw is more than learning the skill itself; by studying this book you will learn *how to see.*" I remember thinking: what kind of crackpot is this author? Doesn't she realize that everybody who is reading this book can already see? Doesn't she know that I have perfectly good eyesight and can probably see haystacks and sunflowers as well as anyone ever has or will, van Gogh, Monet and Renoir included? And other readers at least have corrective lenses, right? It wasn't until later chapters that I fully understood what Edwards, an art professor at California State University, Long Beach, was really saying about *seeing* and I came to appreciate her insights. The only thing that kept me reading beyond chapter one at the time was the extraordinary contrast in quality of pre-instruction versus post-instruction facial portraits of students who'd taken Edwards's drawing course. If nothing else, the side-by-side, before-versus-after facial sketches exhibited in the book kept up my ever-so-slight hope that I, too, might learn to draw and that I would not turn out to be Edwards's first hopeless case.[12]

The first pencil sketch I did was the product of a "vase-faces" exercise out of the book—that is, a drawing that, depending on how you look at it, either appears to be a vase or two human faces seen in profile. To facilitate an L-mode to R-mode shift in thinking, Edwards asks readers to draw a one-line profile of a person's head on the left side of a piece of paper, with the facial features facing toward the center. As I drew a single, uninterrupted line from top to bottom I named each of the symbolic shapes—forehead, nose, lips, chin, neck—as I went. After drawing horizontal lines at the top and bottom of the profile, forming the top and bottom of the "vase," I then followed Edwards's instruction to draw a mirror image of the facial profile on the page's right-hand side to complete the vase. This second profile was a reversal of the first image to make the vase symmetrical, but there was a significant shift in the way I drew the second profile. Instead of drawing my own internalized *symbol* for each of the facial features as I worked downward, I found myself—as Edwards predicted—"*scanning* back and forth in the space between the profiles, estimating angles, curves, inward-curving and outward-curving shapes, and lengths of line *in relation to* the opposite shapes." In essence, I was attempting *to copy* an exact, reverse image of the first facial profile.[13]

The second exercise I did out of Edwards's book—copying an upside-down line drawing of a Picasso portrait of composer Igor Stravinsky—was merely intended to reinforce the point that in order to draw realistic-looking replicas of people or objects, the artist simply needs *to copy* what's there to draw. Upside-down images are often difficult to decipher, and Edwards asks that when one is confronted with the upside-down image, no attempt be made to name any of Stravinsky's body parts. Instead, Edwards asks that one merely copy the upside-down image's angles, shapes and lines. By taking thirty minutes to make a replica of the inverted image, I actually ended up creating a pretty fair copy of the Picasso drawing. Once I turned my own hand-drawn image right-side up, so I could see what I'd created, it was striking how much my drawing looked like Picasso's original, non-inverted portrait of Stravinsky sitting in a chair. It didn't have the grace of the Picasso, to be sure, but it had an equal number of lines in roughly the same places, which was what the exercise was all about. By just getting absorbed in replicating the lines and shapes before me instead of creating names and oversimplified symbols for things before I drew them, which—in Edwards's words—prevents one from seeing "the thing-as-it-is," I had created my first realistic-looking drawing. It was a breakthrough. At a café in Toronto, no less![14]

By the time I traveled through Québec City, Maine's Acadia National Park, and had gotten half-way down the eastern seaboard, I'd drawn detailed sketches of birds and human hands and faces. I drew a portrait of Ralph Waldo Emerson in Concord, Massachusetts, and on a whim, I picked up an issue of *People* magazine in West Virginia and drew a sketch of Madonna on my way home. I could *see*. I could finally *see*. It was the "aha" feeling that I could only imagine a young Helen Keller would have felt if she had woken up one morning and her ears and eyes had worked and she'd found that she suddenly had perfect hearing and 20/20 vision. It was *that* good! Sunlight was no longer just sunlight, and a rose was no longer just a rose. Sunlight hitting plants created interesting shadows depending on at what angle it hit, and flowers had uniquely shaped petals and stems and leaves and thorns that I could reproduce with my own hand. Writer Marcel Proust's insight gives a glimpse of what I felt as I observed familiar objects like trees and rocks in a new way: "The voyage of discovery lies not in finding new landscapes, but in having new eyes."[15]

One of the things I found particularly instructive as I learned to draw was Edwards's mention of a sighting device used by sixteenth-century German artist Albrecht Dürer. That device, an upright grid positioned between the artist and the artist's subject, allows the artist to divide an image into small, square parts, thereby allowing the image to be more easily replicated piece by piece. Instead of looking at, say, a nude human figure and seeing the entire body, an artist using Dürer's device might see an eye through one square, a curled finger through another square, and so on and so forth. Good artists learn to sight images "by eye" and without the use of a cumbersome grid. For beginning artists like me, however, the grid allows complex images to be mechanically broken down into more manageable parts. Instead of looking at a person and immediately visualizing a stick figure—the *symbol* for a human figure learned (and, for many, never unlearned) in grade school— the budding artist sees the constituent parts of the person's body in

terms of lines, shapes and shadows that, with time, can be replicated as they appear through the framework of the grid. Writers,
too, can learn to write better, more detailed descriptions by isolating particular aspects of what is seen. The broader perspective—the
gestalt—is still important, but to gain that perspective one must first
be able to describe the smallest of details.[16]

Because of my newfound knowledge and talent, I had a greater
appreciation for all the artwork I saw in the museums I visited on
my trip in Montreal, Philadelphia, and Boston. My simple
sketches, which took hours to finish, weren't bad, at least by my
own don't-be-so-hard-on-yourself-you've-only-been-at-this-for-
a-couple-of-weeks standard, but they paled in comparison to the
rich, textured oil paintings by the modernist and Impressionist
masters that were displayed at the public galleries. What I realized
is that artwork is hard work, but that I could create it if I only put
in the time. By working through the *Drawing on the Right Side of
the Brain* exercises and learning to see as artists see, I at least got an
inkling of the enormous effort that must have gone into the making of masterpieces like Leonardo da Vinci's "Mona Lisa" or Gustav
Klimt's "The Kiss." I was only working in black-and-white lead
with a number 2 pencil, whereas the oil and acrylic paintings
hanging before me had been done in full color with intricate shad-
ing and blending of the most brilliantly selected colors, no doubt
mixed by hand by the artists themselves. Though my artistic talents
were only emerging, I finally understood the artistic process and
was able to grasp the true import of the words of Henry Hoskins,
who said, "The great masterpieces were once only pigments on a
palette."[17]

A good writer, of course, does not *copy* the writing of others.
There is a name for those who do that: plagiarists. To "plagiarize"
is, as *The American Heritage Dictionary* defines it, "to use and pass off

as one's own" the writings or ideas of another person. While novice artists learn by copying what is seen, accomplished artists do more than that, they infuse their drawings, paintings and sculptures with feeling and their own particular styles. That's why most art lovers are easily able to distinguish van Gogh's paintings from those done by Picasso or Georgia O'Keeffe. Admittedly, the line between plagiarism and fair use is sometimes a subjective one and can lead writers into gray areas. As the American writer Wilson Mizner noted before his death in 1933: "When you take stuff from one writer it's plagiarism; but when you take it from many writers, it's research." When in doubt, always err on the side of caution; if you're relying on someone else's words or ideas, attribute what you're saying to that person, with quotes or citations when necessary. It's okay for writers to *imitate* other writers' styles, but it's not okay to just steal another's words or ideas and make them your own. Just as Impressionist painters do more than copy what they see, good writers make their subjects their own by describing or explaining what they see *in a unique way*, infused with personality.[18]

My discovery of art and drawing that summer of 1991 (thanks to one book) literally changed the way I *perceive* objects and people's faces and movements. Even now, I can still feel the influence of Betty Edwards's teachings. I know that I'll never be Matisse or Degas or Jasper Johns and that I'll always be a better writer than portrait artist, just as Jeanette Winterson recognizes that she'll always be a writer first and an art-lover second. But I know this too: knowing something about art and the artistic process is critical—no, indispensable—for those who want to be good at writing. That is because so much of the writing process is about observation and expression. After reading Edwards's book, I can simply *describe* objects better—with more focus and force—for having learned how to draw, how to *see* things for what they really are. What I learned from Edwards is how to perceive things as an artist does and that the more one practices drawing (or anything else, such as writing), the better one becomes at it.

Like the artistic process, the writing process is frequently misunderstood or irrationally feared. Many people—even those who operate on a regular basis in the "L-mode" described by Edwards—believe that only "born writers" or the "naturally gifted" can write well, a myth that deters some people from even trying to write. I remember when I was in high school and read novels such as George Orwell's *1984*, Ernest Hemingway's *For Whom the Bell Tolls*, and John Knowles's *A Separate Peace*. The prose felt so graceful and effortless, but when I tried writing a novel myself, my words sounded awkward and unsophisticated. I felt utter frustration, like I was feeling in the dark for a light switch in an unfamiliar room and was unable to find one. I dreamed of writing a Great American Novel, with the style of Jack London or John Steinbeck, but my writing never seemed to measure up, and I often felt as if I'd only gotten W. Somerset Maugham's advice: "There are three rules for writing the novel. Unfortunately, no one knows what they are." In my lowest moments, I almost convinced myself that I should give up writing, feeling that I lacked even a small dose of the talent of the writers I so idolized.[19]

In truth, however, almost anyone—regardless of age, background or experience—can learn to write well, just as almost anyone can learn to swim, ride a bicycle, or fly a kite. There will always, of course, be those who can write better than others, but that does not change the fact that every person is *capable* of becoming an effective, even extraordinary, writer. Indeed, the writing process itself really just consists of five simple steps that anyone can learn: (1) pre-writing, or preparing to write; (2) writing, which involves putting one's thoughts or ideas down on paper; (3) revision, or improving one's work product; (4) proofreading for errors, such as in capitalization, grammar, punctuation or spelling; and (5) publication, in whatever form—however formal or informal—that might take. Once these steps are understood anyone can use the writing process effectively, just as once the drawing process is demystified anyone can learn to draw. One's style and voice will emerge naturally once you put the steps of the writing process together. The more you learn to see and analyze as a writer sees and analyzes, the better your writing will become.

Pre-writing—the initial step of the writing process—is critical to any writing project because it requires seeing what's out there on a given subject and preparing to write. If the writing project demands research or interviews, that research, or those interviews, must be done first. Failing to prepare properly for a writing session is like hosting a party but not buying any food or beverages beforehand to entertain your guests. For starters, write down what questions you want answered. That way, when you do your research or talk to people, you'll have a rough notion of what information you're looking for or what you need or want to find out. A writer's job is to uncover the truth and reveal it in an enlightening way. Because the truth is often hard to find, a skilled writer needs to be a detective, constantly searching for evidence to shed light on a given topic. The writer needs to delve into that subject before deciding what he or she wants to say or even *can* say while staying true to the facts. There's nothing worse than a writer who either makes things up or, out of laziness, fails to become informed before trying to put pen to paper.

The more a writer becomes immersed in a subject, the better equipped that writer will be to arrive at the truth and find something of significance to say. "The essence of writing," historian

David McCullough notes, "is to know your subject." Research can be done at public libraries, at historical societies, on the Internet, or at government agencies, but research, when necessary, must be done. As you research, think of yourself as a deep-sea diver searching for sunken treasure. The writer Zora Neale Hurston, a leading figure in the Harlem Renaissance, put it succinctly: "Research is formalized curiosity. It is poking and prying with a purpose." As you do it, keep notes of what you're finding. In writing his controversial biography of Ronald Reagan, for example, author Edmund Morris created some 18,000 color-coded notecards documenting various aspects of his subject's life. Writing and research go hand in hand, unless, of course, you're writing fiction or just making entries in a diary or journal. Writing without researching first might be likened to trying to drive a car without any gas in the fuel tank, just as doing research without doing any writing is like filling up the tank but never getting in the car.[20]

This book focuses on the craft of nonfiction writing, a genre that lends itself to different approaches. National Book Award-winner Ron Chernow has described two ways to tackle a typical nonfiction writing project. "You can set out on your journey armed with a thesis and collect supporting facts along the way," Chernow says, or you can surrender all preconceived beliefs and submit to the material itself. Partisan, one-sided exposés certainly have their place Chernow admits, noting that this is "the art of the legal brief and indictment." As a lawyer, I've certainly seen my fair share of those. Chernow, however, favors those writers who "zealously search for facts that contradict their working hypotheses," who like "to stub their toes on hard, uncomfortable facts strewn in their paths"—the kind of writers Herman Melville, of *Moby-Dick* fame, called "divers." Although I often write legal briefs as a zealous advocate for clients, I also prefer (and you should too) approaching any research and writing project with an open mind. As one of my law professors once advised, it is better to go into a situation looking to *disprove* your working hypothesis. If you're only looking for evidence to *confirm* an existing belief, you're more likely to overlook facts that might lead you to a different, more truthful conclusion.[21]

Doing pre-writing research, whether you're approaching it objectively or from a highly subjective perspective, can be eye-opening and exhilarating because you're learning about new things. Actually, that's the best part of pre-writing: it can change your outlook by exposing you to new facts and ideas. The joy of writing is that you're constantly making new discoveries, and the pre-writing phase helps you to make that happen. As writer Anne Lamott explains: "One of the gifts of being a writer is that it gives you an excuse to do things, to go places and explore." If you want to know the truth, you have to go to the source—be that a public official, a book, a newspaper or magazine article, a place, a physical object, or something else. You have to ask yourself, or your inter-view subject, the hard questions. Questions like these: "What biases might the subject of my research have?" "How did you come to hold that belief?" "What are the reasons for that view?" "Why do you say that?" "What am I looking at here?" "What do I find inter-esting about what's in front of me?" If you don't have the right questions, you'll never get the right answers.[22]

When you're doing a writing project, don't be afraid to pick up the phone and call people. More often than not, they'll be flat-tered or happy to talk to you and tell you what they know. Whenever I interview someone, whether for a book I'm writing or for a legal dispute I'm working on, I almost always end up with a new, more enlightened perspective. I learn something I never knew before or go away thinking about a public policy issue, a person, or a legal dispute in a new way. Human beings are unique because they all possess different skills and have different life experiences; take advantage of the knowledge of others because it may be your only chance to get that information or to gain understanding for yourself. Don't hesitate to go on fact-finding missions. Go to the places you want to write about, talk to the people you want to speak with, and take time to study whatever interests you. Basho, a seventeenth-century haiku master, put it this way: "If you want to know about a tree, go to the tree."[23]

But *pre-writing* involves more than research and paying attention to what a subject (or a particular subject matter) has to say to you. It also involves putting yourself in the right frame of mind to write. Because writing is hard and often frustrating, especially for beginning writers, many people find it difficult to get in the right mental state to begin a writing session. Those bumper stickers you often see may come to mind: "I'd rather be fishing," "I'd rather be skateboarding," "I'd rather be surfing," "I'd rather be playing quidditch," "I'd rather be at a Goo Goo Dolls concert," "I'd rather be _____"—just fill in the blank with your favorite sport or activity. To overcome this problem, set up a routine for yourself: a set place and a regular time for writing. Find a place that's conducive to writing—be it at a desk, on a park bench, or in a coffee shop—and make sure that you can stay there long enough to get something done. And then begin, even if you don't feel like writing in the slightest. I like to write at my desk, but what's most important is that you feel comfortable while you write. If you feel out of place, your writing is not likely to go well because you aren't at ease. What you're trying to do is create the right climate for effective writing—a setting where you can listen to what your mind is telling you and where you can observe what you need to see without distractions.

The essayist and naturalist John Burroughs once wrote, "What we love to do, that we do well," and "The eye sees what it has the means of seeing, and its means of seeing are in proportion to the love and desire behind it." In other words, if one is passionate about doing something, one's passion will make it possible to do. Just as Jeanette Winterson became an avid art lover after becoming passionate about art, one's passions—whether old or new—can fuel one's writing and make seeing and learning possible. As Burroughs explained: "The eye is informed and sharpened by the thought. My boy sees ducks on the river where and when I cannot, because at certain seasons he thinks ducks and dreams ducks." "If we think birds," Burroughs wrote, "we shall see birds wherever we go; if we think arrowheads, as Thoreau did, we shall pick up arrowheads in every field." Burroughs's insights have much to do with the art of observation—and writing, which requires keen perceptual and descriptive skills.[24]

It is a simple concept, but one that is often forgotten. If one makes it a point to look for something, it can be seen if it is there to see and it can be artfully described, with care and attention to detail, if the desire is there to do that. Just try it. Look at a physical object and spend fifteen minutes describing it in writing. If you've never done that before, I bet you'll be amazed at all the interesting and descriptive details you'll be able to write down in that short time frame. Now imagine how much your descriptive skills would improve over the course of a year if you did that simple exercise every day with the same kind of focus that you put into your favorite hobby. Revision skills are no different: the more you revise, the better you'll get at it. If one practices and learns to take pride in one's written words, one's writing will improve over time. You must be passionate about writing, but once you make that commitment, your perspective will change and you'll learn to see *as a writer sees.*

Good writing is like a priceless, Impressionist painting. Both are beautiful, but both are created only through painstaking effort—and initial missteps—by their creators. Anne Lamott, author of *Bird by Bird: Some Instructions on Writing and Life*, has described the writing process, using an analogy to art, this way: "Think of a fine painter attempting to capture an inner vision, beginning with one corner of the canvas, painting what he thinks should be there, not quite pulling it off, covering it over with white paint, and trying again, each time finding out what his painting isn't, until he finally finds out what it is." Writing well requires that same kind of search: for a vision, then for execution of that vision through writing and relentless revision. Every great painter, from Rembrandt to Picasso to the pointillist Georges Seurat, made errant strokes, but what they didn't do was settle for mediocrity or refuse to paint over their brush strokes and start anew. Such tenacity—whether in painting or writing—pays off. Once you find out what one corner of your vision is, you're on track. Stumbling upon the right structure and tone for a piece of writing takes time, but if you listen patiently to what your material is telling you, you'll find that structure and tone, just as the painter discovers the right colors for a canvas.[25]

The writing process requires creativity, but that's something all of us possess. To tap your inborn, creative impulses, set aside blocks of time when you plan to do nothing but write. In her book, *The Artist's Way*, writer Julia Cameron recommends (as I do) two specific exercises to awaken your innate creativity: *morning pages* and *artist dates*. *Morning pages*—what she also calls *brain drain*—are daily, three-page ruminations to be written in longhand. These pages, Cameron says, "are meant to be, simply, the act of moving the hand across the page and writing down *whatever* comes to mind."

"Nothing," she notes, "is too petty, too silly, too stupid, or too weird to be included." Their purpose is to make people stop judging themselves, and to show them that, by writing, they can do creative work and find their own bearings and strengths in the process. "It is impossible to write morning pages for any extended period of time without coming into contact with an unexpected inner power," Cameron writes. Obviously, if you're not a morning person (something I can certainly relate to), *afternoon pages* or *late-night pages* are okay, too. *Artist dates* are simply times you set up with yourself, in advance and as often as possible, to allow you to nurture your creativity while you're alone.[26]

Writing, like drawing, requires intense concentration and that precious commodity, time. But if you learn to love using written language, writing can also be one of life's most interesting and engaging activities. As Vincent van Gogh once said, "It's as interesting and as difficult to say a thing well as to paint it. There is the art of lines and colours, but the art of words exists too, and will never be less important." My daughter Abigail, at age eight, once spoke of the need to create "a writing bubble," where calm and silence prevail, to form the ideal atmosphere for writing. I couldn't have said it better myself. Writing is done best when the right ambience is created so that thoughts and words can flow freely. When done well, the result, effective writing—like an artist's masterpiece—can be incredibly moving, capable of conveying the most complex of thoughts, ideas or emotions. If one cares about good writing, as Henry David Thoreau cared about the wilderness or finding arrowheads on his walks, one can become a good writer. All it takes is practice and time and a willingness to be observant so that one may learn the secrets of the craft.[27]

You can write about *anything*, and if you write well enough, even the reader with no intrinsic interest in the subject will become involved. –Tracy Kidder • Only the words break the silence. –Samuel Beckett • How often misused words generate misleading thoughts. –Herbert Spencer • A writer is not so powerless as he usually feels, and a pen, as well as a silver bullet, can draw blood. –Graham Greene • Write what makes you happy. –O. Henry • We are what we pretend to be, so we must be careful about what we pretend to be. –Kurt Vonnegut • Express everything you like. No word can hurt you. None. No idea can hurt you. Not being able to express an idea or a word will hurt you much more. As much as a bullet. –Jamaica Kincaid • A great writer is, so to speak, a second government in his country. And for that reason no regime has ever loved great writers, only minor ones. –Alexander Solzhenitsyn • The more you have thought and written on a given theme, the more you can still write. Thought breeds thought. It grows under your hands. –Henry David Thoreau • It has been said that writing comes more easily if you have something to say. –Sholem Asch • Better to write for yourself and have no public, than write for the public and have no self. –Cyril Connolly • Writing is your form of prayer. You put words together one by one to reach the truth. –Mary Kay Blakely • Words can sting like anything. –Phyllis McGinley • Never forget that writing is as close as we get to keeping a hold on the thousand and one things. –Salman Rushdie • A speech reminds us that words, like children, have the power to make dance the dullest beanbag of a heart. –Peggy Noonan • Technique is only a telephone wire—what's important is the message going through it. –Kent Nagano • Every writer carries in his or her mind an invisible tribunal of dead writers, whose appointment is an imaginative act and not merely a browbeaten response to some notion of authority. This tribunal sits in judgement on our own work. –Robert Hughes • In a way I used up some of my loneliness by writing. –Truman Capote • I wanted to try to build a bridge of words between me and that world outside, that world which was so distant and elusive that it seemed unreal. –Richard Wright • Why not go out on a limb? Isn't that where the fruit is? –Frank Scully • A good essay must have this permanent quality about it; it must draw its curtains round us, but it must be a curtain that shuts us in, not out. –Virginia Woolf • Poetry is a subject as precise as geometry. –Gustave Flaubert • Poetry is the spontaneous overflow of powerful feelings: it takes its origin from emotion recollected in tranquillity. –William Wordsworth • The purpose of language is to express, not to impress. –Patricia Westheimer

E X P R E S S I O N

Nothing stinks like a pile of unpublished writing. –Sylvia Plath • A poem begins with a lump in the throat; a home sickness or a love sickness. It is a reaching-out toward expression; an effort to find fulfillment. A complete poem is one where an emotion has found its thought and the thought has found the words. –Robert Frost • A novel is an impression, not an argument. –Thomas Hardy • I think satire is among the most powerful weapons we have. You can do more with it than any other kind of writing. –Art Buchwald • Poetry is a way of taking life by the throat. –Robert Frost • Genius is the ability to put into effect what is in your mind. There's no other definition of it. –F. Scott Fitzgerald • Not everything that is thought should be expressed. Not everything that is expressed should be expressed verbally. Not everything that is expressed verbally should be written. Not everything that is written should be published. –Israel Salanter • The audience is the reason you're performing. –Darci Kistler • Poetry should begin with emotion in the poet, and end with the same emotion in the reader. The poem is simply the instrument of transference. –Philip Larkin • When a word is so near the right one that a body can't quite tell whether it is or isn't, it's good politics to strike it out and go for the Thesaurus. –Mark Twain • The unpublished manuscript is like an unconfessed sin that festers in the soul, corrupting and contaminating it. –Antonio Machado • If there is a bedrock principle underlying the First Amendment, it is that the government may not prohibit the expression of an idea simply because society finds the idea offensive or disagreeable. –William Brennan • I had written those pages without a specific recipient in mind. For me, those were things I had inside, that occupied me and that I had to expel: tell them, indeed shout them from the roof-tops. –Primo Levi • I'd as soon write free verse as play tennis with the net down. –Robert Frost • Metrical poetry is ultimately allied to song, and I like the connection. Free verse is ultimately allied to conversation, and I like that connection too. –Thom Gunn • It is splendid to be a great writer, to put men into the frying pan of your words and make them pop like chestnuts. –Gustave Flaubert • Sir, more than kisses, letters mingle souls. –John Donne • I have now attained the true art of letter-writing, which we are always told is to express on paper exactly what one would say to the same person by word of mouth. –Jane Austen • Write about what you're most afraid of. –Donald Barthelme • Good writers define reality; bad ones merely restate it. A good writer turns fact into truth; a bad writer will, more often than not, accomplish the opposite. –Edward Albee • The moment a man sets his thoughts down on paper, however secretly, he is in a sense writing for publication. –Raymond Chandler • We write both to express ourselves and to be heard by others, but first we have to learn how to tolerate ourselves as we work at our writing. –Joan Bolker • It don't mean a thing if it ain't got that swing. –Duke Ellington • When talented people write well, it is generally for this reason: they're moved by a desire to touch the audience. –Robert McKee • Writing's greatest reward, for most of us anyway, is the sense of reaching an audience. –Peter Elbow • Good writing is good speaking caught alive. The speaking tones are all there on the printed page. –Robert Frost

The mystery of language was revealed to me. I knew then that 'w-a-t-e-r' meant the wonderful cool something that was flowing over my hand. That living word awakened my soul, gave it light, joy, set it free!

–Helen Keller, THE STORY OF MY LIFE

Words can do wonderful things. They sound purr. They can urge, they can wheedle, whip, whine. They can sing, sass, singe. They can churn, check, channelize. They can be a hup, 2, 3, 4. They can forge a fiery army out of a hundred languid men.

–Gwendolyn Brooks, CONTENDING FORCES

The limits of my language mean the limits of my world.

–Ludwig Wittgenstein, philosopher

Speech is civilization itself. The word, even the most contradictory word, preserves contact—it is silence which isolates.

–Thomas Mann, German writer

CHAPTER THREE

Why I Write

We all want to express ourselves. It is only human to have that desire. We talk. We gesture. We give tokens of affection—cards, gifts and bouquets of flowers—to our friends and the people we love. At a wedding, the bride and groom exchange rings and vows of love and fidelity; at retirement parties, retirees get gold watches, pen sets, or clocks. We communicate through all sorts of mediums: film, television, radio, print media, and high-tech devices such as cell phones, Blackberries, and pagers. People even send one another *emoticons* via e-mails. There's the *standard smiley*, :-), the *sad smiley*, :-(, the *left-handed smiley*, (-:, even the *winking smiley*, ,-), among many others. Not only is expressive behavior perfectly natural, but the ability to express oneself is critical to one's success in life. If you can't communicate effectively, you can't do the things that you want to do. Becoming an effective writer, it turns out, is one of the best ways to learn the art of expression.

Just what exactly can effective writing do for you? That's a question, of course, that only you can answer. There are common reasons why people write, but each person has different goals and motivations and I can only speak for myself. So, I'll tell you why I write, and you can judge for yourself if writing makes sense for you. When all the benefits of writing are considered, I hope you'll see for yourself that writing has much to offer—and that many persuasive reasons exist to improve your writing skills.

When I was a boy, toting around pencils and pens and spiral-bound notebooks in a backpack at Saints Peter and Paul Grade School, I never dreamed of becoming a writer. I liked action-packed *Curious George* stories, that's true, and in fourth grade I read a book called *Custer's Last Stand* at least five times. I laughed aloud at the high jinks of that hilarious little monkey, and I loved reading and re-reading the drama of General Custer's last battle at Little Big Horn. But I didn't hunger to become a storyteller or one who writes. After I crawled into my bunk bed at night and my mother read a chapter of a Nancy Drew or Hardy Boys mystery and shut off the lights, I longed to become somebody important: a rugged expedition leader like Sir Edmund Hillary, a deep-sea explorer like Jacques Cousteau, a rock star or a secret agent like 007. I was too young then to have read the wisdom of Ralph Waldo Emerson: "The writer is an explorer. Every step is an advance into new land." Or to have heard the Japanese proverb: "If you wish to learn the highest truths, begin with the alphabet."[1]

In the first years of my life, I didn't really consider writers to be people of importance, so I never gave much thought to becoming one. Writers merely recorded things or told somebody else's story, and it was the somebody else whom I viewed as truly important. Growing up in a modest-sized, Midwestern town—Mankato, Minnesota, now home to 28,000 people—I longed to be that somebody else. I wanted to escape the confines of my youth and break records and boundaries and make new discoveries and do something truly extraordinary. I wanted to become a Major League Baseball player, an Olympic runner, or perhaps a congressman or mayor. I dreamed of becoming a heroic soldier, a statesman, or a pioneering scientist. I know now that life is not about fame or fortune, but about living in a way that makes living meaningful and worthwhile. Back then, however, I harbored grandiose visions of celebrity and did little more than toy around with writing, never dreaming of becoming a writer who would simply tell others' stories.

It was only later that my ambitions changed and I seriously considered the activity of writing. When I failed to make the Mankato Royals, the all-city Little League traveling team, I realized that I was no Joe DiMaggio. I lost a good deal of respect for my one-time idol, General Custer, while taking a military history course in college, and my political ambitions came crashing down when I placed fifth in a field of six candidates on primary election day for University of Minnesota student body president. The only person I beat, by a mere one vote, was another undergraduate whose platform was to do whatever the student body wanted her to do—a kind of leadership by plebiscite. An acting or musical career seemed far-fetched—in high school, I failed to land a part on stage in *Hello, Dolly* and ended up doing lighting and set design, and my brief stint taking piano lessons attracted more reminders about my fingers drooping over the keys than praise for my musical ability. And I knew early on that I would face long odds in getting the National Geographic Society to finance a deep-sea dive looking for sunken treasure or a dogsled expedition to the North Pole.

So, as my college graduation neared, my childhood dreams—daydreams, really—resembled hordes of documents that had just slipped through a paper shredder. I still knew that I wanted to do something important with my life, but I no longer knew what that would be. As I filled out the paperwork to get my diploma, it suddenly hit me that in my headlong rush to zip through my education and onto bigger and better things, I didn't really know what I was going to do. I'd skipped my senior year at Loyola High School and rushed through college in three years only to discover that my fast-track career plans—not very well thought out, I quickly realized—had been derailed. With graduation day looming closer, my practice of taking course overloads every quarter while working twenty to thirty hours a week to pay for it all, often putting my social life on the back burner, abruptly looked like a senseless act of masochism.

Because I dreaded the prospect of finding a real eight-to-five job in corporate America, I did what almost every other self-respecting political science major did in my graduating class: I applied to law school. I knew attorneys made decent money, and joining the legal profession seemed like a genteel way to pay for rent, groceries, and the occasional movie and night out on the town. I still remember when I found out that I'd been accepted to law school: I was living in Kingston, Jamaica, as part of a University of Minnesota program called Minnesota Studies in International Development. Going to law school, it turned out, was a life-changing experience, just as my three-month stint in Jamaica opened my eyes as never before to dire poverty in developing countries. In the island's capital, Kingston, I saw row after row of tin shacks that families lived in, and in Jamaica's Blue Mountains, I saw kids without shoes and with rotting teeth due to poor dental care. In law school, I learned how to think critically as I read and analyzed statutes and court cases, and as part of my legal education I took copious notes in class as I tried to make sense of everything that I was reading and hearing from my professors. Making written outlines of course materials, I discovered, was the best way to master the large volume of information that I was expected to understand.

I can't say that the practice of law is all that glamorous, but it's always intellectually challenging, and I can say unequivocally that it's greatly improved my writing and intellectual skills, and for that alone—despite all the late nights at the office—I'm grateful. I've worked at big law firms, and now practice at a smaller firm, but one aspect of law firm life has never changed: the need to write. The lawyer's grind of producing briefs and correspondence on an almost daily basis has always been a crucial part of my job, and it certainly provides ample opportunities to hone—if not occasionally dull, if one's not careful—one's prose. Although most pleadings and legal briefs follow the same format and are read by only a handful of people—the client, one's adversary, opposing counsel and the judge—these documents are critical to the functioning of the judicial system, and continual use of the writing process has certainly made me a better writer. Anyone who writes a lot as part of their job has undoubtedly had the same experience: a gradual improvement in writing skills over time due, in part, to the sheer amount of writing that must be done.

You may not be a lawyer or someone who writes a lot now, but that's no impediment to becoming an effective writer. With effort, you, too, can become more proficient with written language—no matter what your vocation or your life experience to date. Your brain's capacity for change—what scientists call *plasticity*—is clear, and if you put in the necessary time and take pride in your work, you'll become a more skilled, even brilliant, writer over time. One thing is clear: practice is key. This is as true for writing as it is for anything else. A study done at the Music Academy of West Berlin found that "superior" students—those most likely to go on to be concert performers—put in an average of twenty-four practice hours per week. In contrast, "good" students—as judged by teachers—practiced an average of only nine hours per week. The more you write, the better your writing becomes. It's that simple. As Michelangelo, who spent four years creating his master-piece paintings on the ceiling of the Sistine Chapel, reminds us, artfulness just takes time and relentless determination. "Genius," he said, "is eternal patience."[2]

I remember doing a little creative writing as a middle-school student; a short story about a leprechaun, if memory serves. However, my interest in writing didn't really blossom until high school, when I took an English class taught by one of my favorite teachers, Chris Thiem, who coached our school's cross-country and track-and-field teams, of which I was a member. Nearly every day after coming home from school, I banged out poetry and sketchy novel outlines on my parents' electric typewriter—in a frenzied, Jack Kerouac-style—that I still keep in a now dusty bin in the basement of my house. I even tried my hand at songwrit-ing. I drank lemonade and played Boggle at Mr. Thiem's house after running five miles on a Saturday, and throughout his course, I stayed up late reading novels such as Kurt Vonnegut's *Slaughter-House Five*, J. D. Salinger's *The Catcher in the Rye*, and Harper Lee's *To Kill a Mockingbird*. It was in that class that I came to appreciate the power of words. And it was in that class that I came to admire writers and first aspired to become one. Although I wrote a lot in high school, I knew very little then about how to write, let alone what inner impulses were driving me to write.

Since that time, I've learned a lot about the discipline of writ-ing and have had more time to explore my motivations for writ-ing. I've gotten law review articles published in academic journals, I've edited newsletters, I've published three books on the subject of capital punishment, and after enrolling in Hamline University's M.F.A. program, I've written short stories, essays, and more poems. I've critiqued the writing of others, agonized over word and punctuation choices in my own writing, and even tried my hand at writing children's stories. After pouring hundreds of hours of work into each of my own law review articles and books, I've gained tremendous confidence as a writer, even though (as far as income goes) I don't make my living as a writer—unless, of course, you count my writing as a lawyer, which I do. After all, if I didn't know how to write, I wouldn't be an attorney and wouldn't have that means of financial support.

Although people who know how to write effectively often have good-paying jobs, the best benefits of effective writing are personal and have nothing to do with money. Writing develops critical thinking skills, and it allows one to reach an audience. For me, publishing itself is gratification enough. Each time I publish a book, I like the feeling when the bound copies arrive and I am finally able to flip through their crisp, newly cut pages. I like knowing that my books end up in libraries across the country and that others might look to my words for guidance. And I like hearing the reactions of others to things that I have written. Publishing—whether in the form of a book, an article, or a blog— turns writing from a solitary act into a social one. Once read, a piece of writing can spark discussion and debate, laughter or dismay, social action, even outrage or anger. The publishing process can be grueling, but there's nothing quite like seeing one's own words in print. I haven't published any fiction or poetry yet, but I'm sure I'll feel the same thrill if I ever get to see one of my short stories or poems in a literary journal or anthology.

Even though I've written a lot since age 16—literally millions of words by now—I never considered myself *a writer* until the early part of 1996. My wife and I were preparing our taxes that year, when I realized I'd incurred research and copying expenses while working on my first book manuscript. I'd been doggedly writing that manuscript since I got involved in working on a death penalty case in Texas through a local organization, Minnesota Advocates for Human Rights. It wasn't until our accountant prepared the 1040 tax form for us, and I saw the word "AUTHOR" typed out next to the phrase "Principal business or profession," that I had the epiphany that I really was a writer. When I saw that word in capital letters next to my name, it caught me off guard at first, but I then quickly realized what should have been obvious to me all along: I am a person who likes sitting in front of a keyboard and expressing myself; I am a person who likes flipping through dictionaries and thesauruses in search of the best words to use; in short, I am a person who likes language. I like perusing newspapers and magazines, and I like reading novels and biographies and all sorts of other nonfiction books.

Most people probably can't pinpoint the exact date when they began to think of themselves as writers; Isabel Allende published three novels before she got up the courage to put "writer" rather than "housewife" in the "Occupation" line on a form. For those who love words, or have a love-hate relationship with them, there is usually no "aha" moment; it is a slow, gradual process. And in a sense, it was that way for me, too. All the writing I did in high school and college, and later in law school and as a practicing lawyer, gave me permission to think of myself as a writer. In truth, becoming a full-fledged writer is a state of mind. The day I put my John Hancock on that 1040 form was the day I first thought of myself as a writer, even though I'd been one all along. And even though my annual income from book sales has never exceeded a few thousand dollars, thinking of myself as a writer has made all the difference in the world. I write more than I used to because I think of myself in that way, and I take the craft more seriously because I've invested more of myself in it.[3]

I know the exact date when I came to think of myself as a writer—the *when* question—but there's one question that's more difficult to answer. It's the *why* question. What compels me to sit in front of my laptop on weekends or late into the night and tap on the keyboard until I've produced a readable essay or finished the chapter of a book? What possesses me to forgo certain social events that I might otherwise have attended so that I can write books or peck out a poem, perhaps producing a few worthwhile pages or lines over the course of three to four hours of work? In short: why do I write?

When George Orwell answered that question in his famous essay, "Why I Write," he listed four great motives for writing: sheer egoism, esthetic enthusiasm, historical impulse and political purpose. Joan Didion, in answering the same question, wrote this: "I write entirely to find out what I'm thinking, what I'm looking at, what I see and what it means." She calls writing the act "of imposing oneself upon other people, of saying *listen to me, see it my way, change your mind*." Like Orwell, I write largely for political and historical purposes, to create something of lasting worth or beauty, and, yes, if I must admit, out of a bit of ego—what Orwell describes as the "desire to seem clever, to be talked about, to be remembered after death." Like Didion, I also write for clarity of thinking, to express myself and to persuade. I know of no better way to test the logic of my ideas than to subject them to the rigor of the written word. I want to express myself effectively and writing helps me do that.[4]

In speech and during our daily lives, people fumble their words all the time. "I collided with a stationary truck coming the other way," one insurance claimant famously reported. "I promise you a police car on every sidewalk," Washington, D.C. Mayor Marion Barry promised, leaving his constituents with a memorable image indeed. Dan Quayle, more than anyone, perhaps, became notorious for his public misstatements. "One word sums up probably the responsibility of any Vice-President, and that one word is 'to be prepared,'" Quayle stammered in December 1989. "Welcome to President Bush, Mrs. Bush, and my fellow astronauts," he remarked on the twentieth anniversary celebration of the Apollo 11 moon landing, a gaffe matched only by Quayle's comment that "Buzz Lukens took that fateful step...." Quayle had confused Astronaut Buzz Aldrin, who stepped onto the moon's surface in 1969 as part of the first manned lunar-landing mission, with Donald "Buz" Lukens, an Ohio congressman who resigned in disgrace after being convicted of contributing to the delinquency of a minor and being accused of fondling a capitol elevator operator.[5]

Presentations and political speeches, even sound bites, should elevate discourse, not muddle thought or butcher the English language. People are fallible, of course, and always will be, and I'll be the first to admit that I've bollixed speech and said stupid things on more than one occasion. But writing improves thinking, meaning the more you write the less likely it is that you'll make verbal flub-ups or say or write something that sounds silly. Illogical lines can make us laugh, as I do every time I read quotes from New York baseball legend "Yogi" Berra. Among Berra's more memorable lines: "Baseball is 90 percent mental—the other half is physical." "Slump? I ain't in no slump. I just ain't hitting." "If you come to a fork in the road, take it." "You should always go to other people's funerals; otherwise, they won't come to yours." Unless humor is the goal, however, one's words (especially those put in writing) should be crafted more carefully than they sometimes are in our day-to-day lives. What writing regularly does is give you practice using words, a better appreciation for how and when they should be used, and prepare you for using words *effectively* in whatever context you find yourself.[6]

If we don't strive to be articulate citizens, we risk slipping into what George Orwell called *doublethink*, "the power of holding two contradictory beliefs in one's mind simultaneously, and accepting both of them." It's confused thought that leads some leaders to say the most incoherent or baffling things. "That's not a lie; it's a terminological inexactitude," U.S. Secretary of State Alexander Haig said in a 1983 television interview. "It is clear our nation is reliant upon big foreign oil. More and more of our imports come from overseas," George W. Bush noted in 2000; "I understand small business growth. I was one," Bush told the *New York Daily News* that same year. Because I oppose the death penalty, one of my personal favorites comes from U.S. Senator Orrin Hatch, who disagrees with me on that subject. "Capital punishment," Hatch said, "is our society's recognition of the sanctity of human life." Say what? Although misstatements in oral speech are forgivable, when illogical thinking or sloppy writing lead to bad public policy decisions or poorly drafted legislation, it is nothing short of a tragedy. Writing sharpens the mind; do it.[7]

Everyone has good reasons to write, although even those who identify themselves as professional writers often can't articulate exactly why they feel compelled to write. Columnist George Will describes writing as "a metabolic necessity" for him. "I write all the time," he says, noting, "I have an itch to write. I would explode if I couldn't write." Gloria Naylor, a National Book Award winner, has said this about why she puts pen to paper: "The truth, the unvarnished truth, is that I haven't a clue. The answer to that question lies hidden in the same box that holds the origin of human creativity, our imperative need as a species to communicate, and to be touched." Writing does fulfill a desire we all have to be creative, and that, in my view, is reason enough to take up writing. You, of course, must make up your own mind about how writing fits into your life and your particular circumstances or lifestyle.[8]

For me, it all boils down to this: now that I've discovered the joys and rewards of writing, and know what a valuable dimension it brings to my life, it's an activity I'd never want to live without. I *need* to write at work, but I *want* to write for myself. I know that writing sharpens my thoughts. I know that writing makes me a better, more engaged person and member of my community. And I like it when I have time to write outside of the workplace, and I feel lost almost if I'm not working on some writing project or another. I think everyone can benefit, in one way or another, from making time to write, and the thought of living without writing is, to me, unthinkable.

In her book examining what drives people to write (and what produces writer's block in others), Boston-area neurologist Alice Flaherty notes that there is actually a medical term— *hypergraphia*—for the overwhelming urge to write. The ordinary desire to write, she says, is neither "a core emotion like joy or fear" nor "a biological drive in the sense that hunger or sexual desire is"; instead, the drive to write fits into the category of "secondary emotions" that include complicated states such as guilt or hope. Secondary drives, Flaherty explains, include the urge to buy a house, with the urge to write growing out of the more fundamental drive to communicate. People communicate to get what they want, be it food, shelter, companionship or sex, with scientists such as Steven Pinker noting that we, as humans, have a "language instinct." From eighteen months of age through age eighteen, Pinker writes, children rapidly pick up new words. One neurologist,

Frank Wilson, likens the whole process of language acquisition to giving a child "a labeling gun whose relentless operation compels her to take possession of the world by putting labels on everything she possibly can."9

Flaherty's research is especially intriguing. After outlining the role of the brain's temporal lobes (necessary for understanding meaning) and its limbic system (the seat of emotion and drive) in producing creative writing, Flaherty examines why people write, stop writing, or have trouble writing. Communication can be therapeutic, she notes, citing the work of psychologist Dylan Evans, who calls language the world's first mood-altering substance. Words, Evans says (and I concur from experience), can improve one's mood by consoling, entertaining, or allowing one to vent. "The first two ways benefit the hearer; the third, the speaker," Flaherty explains, adding yet another reason of her own for why people write: "to summon aid from others." Conversely, depression makes people write less, Flaherty observes, as can "too-early editing," whereby "a writer begins criticizing and altering a text before there is enough of a rough draft to evaluate." Again, revision is key, but only after the writer flexes his or her creative muscles and gets enough material on the page to revise. "The drive to write produces a first draft; it is the drive to write well that produces the second, third, twentieth," Flaherty adds.10

At the other end of the spectrum from *hypergraphia* lies *agraphia*, the selective loss of the skill to write (typically caused by strokes)—not to be confused with *writer's block*. All "blocked writers," Flaherty says, "share two traits: they do not write despite being intellectually capable of doing so, and they suffer because they are not writing." A perceived inability to write, Flaherty reasons, "reflects the sufferer's feeling that he or she cannot contribute to the world, cannot communicate with others in any meaningful way." Writing is helpful, Flaherty explains, because it allows people, through self-expression, to gain a sense of relief. "The activity of writing changes everything," author Joyce Carol Oates has said, explaining how writing, all by itself, lifts her spirits. "When I don't write, I feel like shit," Ernest Hemingway once said, putting it more bluntly. "The kaleidoscope of reasons why writers think they write remains hard to fit into any one theory," Flaherty concludes, noting that people often write to give their lives meaning.[11]

I certainly do not *love* writing, at least not in the ordinary sense of that word. I love my parents and brothers. I love my wife and daughter. I love pepperoni-and-green-olive pizza and movies and traveling. The writing process, by contrast, is frequently frustrating, and I always find it especially hard to write that first sentence. But writing is something that I could never give up. It's something that I enjoy, if only for the challenge of it, like the feeling of accomplishment I get from putting in the last piece of a 1,000-piece puzzle. Writing helps me figure things out, it makes me feel connected to the world. It also gives me an outlet for trying to make social change. "It is not possible," George Orwell said, "for any thinking person to live in such a society as our own without wanting to change it." If you see injustice in the world (as I do), writing can be your weapon to combat that injustice.[12]

By day, I write principally to analyze or convey information, whether it's in a legal brief, a memo to a client, or a letter to opposing counsel. When I write at night or on weekends, however, I write principally to articulate my own beliefs, to unwind, or out of simple compulsion and nothing more. I want to express myself on the page, and I want to express myself as well, and as artfully, as I am able. The subjects that interest me most are people, the concepts of equality, freedom and justice, and human rights—the right to live without fear of persecution, the right to be free from discrimination, the right to be educated, the right to enjoy the natural world, and the right to speak, write and express oneself freely, wherever one happens to be. I agree with George Orwell, who said his "starting point" for a writing project was always "a sense of injustice"; "I write," he said, "because there is some lie that I want to expose, some fact to which I want to draw attention, and my initial concern is to get a hearing."13

It's when I don't feel pressured to write, when I'm writing poetry, on a subject I care passionately about, or when I'm deep in the revision process and have lost track of time, that I most enjoy writing. At such times, I write for "the joy of mere words" or "the sounds and associations of words"—to borrow Orwell's phrases. Indeed, Orwell himself said that he could not write a book, or even a long magazine article, if writing were not also "an aesthetic experience" for him, a process by which "a work of art" is produced. I only know that I feel most alive when I'm writing or when I read my own typeset words in print. I like the feeling of knowing that my words may change the way someone thinks about a subject or will alter, at least in some small way, the political landscape in which I live. Like an astronaut planting a flag on the moon, I want future generations to take notice of my ideas and to remember: I was here, I lived on the planet, I had something of importance to say.14

Words are all we have. –Samuel Beckett • Syllables govern the world. –John Selden • Without language, there is no way to understand the passage of time. –Lou Ann Walker • No word has the exact value of any other in the same or in another language. –George Santayana • These ten English words are used far more frequently than any others: a, and, I, in, is, it, of, that, the, to. –Hugh Walpole • It takes five hundred small details to add up to one favorable impression. –Cary Grant • We are walking lexicons. In a single sentence of idle chatter we preserve Latin, Anglo-Saxon, Norse; we carry a museum inside our heads, each day we commemorate peoples of whom we have never heard. –Penelope Lively • Punctuation ought to be exact. –Marianne Moore • Do not be afraid of the semicolon; it can be most useful. –Ernest Gowers • A word, in a word, is complicated. –Steven Pinker • Perfect grammar—persistent, continuous, sustained—is the fourth dimension, so to speak; many have sought it, but none has found it. –Mark Twain • Third person and first person are at least as different as major and minor keys in music. –Norman Mailer • I think in sounds. –Maurice Ravel • Life is like playing a violin solo in public and learning the instrument as one goes on. –Samuel Butler • The ultimate goal of all research is not objectivity, but truth. –Helene Deutsch • Self-confidence is the first requisite to great undertakings. –Samuel Johnson • To treat your facts with imagination is one thing, but to imagine your facts is another. –John Burroughs • A society whose intellectual leaders lose the skill to shape, appreciate, and understand the power of language will become the slaves of those who retain it—be they politicians, preachers, copywriters, or newscasters. –Dana Gioia • The polymorphic visions of the eyes and the spirit are contained in uniform lines of small or capital letters, periods, commas, parentheses—pages of signs, packed as closely together as grains of sand, representing the many-coloured spectacle of the world on a surface that is always the same and always different, like dunes shifted by the desert wind. –Italo Calvino • Language grows and evolves, leaving fossils behind. The individual words are like different species of animals. Mutations occur. Words fuse, and then mate. –Lewis Thomas • Language is fossil poetry. –Ralph Waldo Emerson • English is the great vacuum cleaner of languages: it sucks in anything it can get. –David Crystal • If language is to lead at all to understanding, there must be rules. –Albert Einstein • When I feel inclined to read poetry I take down my Dictionary. The poetry of words is quite as beautiful as that of sentences. The author may arrange the gems effectively, but their shape and lustre have been given by the attrition of ages. –Oliver Wendell Holmes

FUNDAMENTALS

Adjectives are the sugar of literature and adverbs the salt. –Henry James • Writing is a physical activity. The pen gives voice to the hand. Each written word is connected to the writer both through the immediate physical relationship of fingers and pen. In the art of writing there is a part of the self that is invested in and so identified with the thing written. –Shoshana Zuboff • If I feel the need for inspiration I read the OED. –Anthony Burgess • The writer's only responsibility is to his art. He will be completely ruthless if he is a good one. He has a dream. It anguishes him so much he must get rid of it. He has no peace until then. –William Faulkner • The greatest masterpiece in literature is only a dictionary out of order. –Jean Cocteau • Language is grammatically complex because we are, our thoughts and feelings and relationships are, because life is. –Nancy Malone • The English language is the sea which receives tributaries from every region under heaven. –Ralph Waldo Emerson • There's not much to be said about the period except that most writers don't reach it soon enough. –William Zinsser • Once the grammar has been learned, writing is simply talking on paper and in time learning what not to say. –Beryl Bainbridge • I am interested in detail. I enjoy decoration. By accumulating this mass of detail you throw light on things in a longer sense. –Patrick White • Details fascinate me. I love to pile up details. They create an atmosphere. –Muriel Spark • All the great things are simple, and many can be expressed in a single word: freedom; justice; honor; duty; mercy; hope. –Winston Churchill • A writer needs three things, experience, observation and imagination, any two of which, at times any one of which, can supply the lack of the others. –William Faulkner • If you're a writer, the assimilation of important experiences almost obliges you to write about them. Writing is how you make the experience your own, how you explore what it means to you, how you come to possess it, and ultimately release it. –Michael Crichton • I would rather be ashes than dust! I would rather that my spark burn out in a brilliant blaze than it should be stifled by dryrot. I would rather be a superb meteor, every atom of me in magnificent glow, than a sleepy and permanent planet. The proper function of man is to live, not to exist. I shall not waste my days in trying to prolong them. I shall use my time. –Jack London • If you want to be a writer, you have to write every day. –Walter Mosley • Everybody is talented, original and has something important to say. –Brenda Ueland • Sentence structure is innate but whining is acquired. –Woody Allen • If the only tool you have is a hammer, you tend to see every problem as a nail. –Abraham Maslow • Like a superhighway, the sentence is a triumph of engineering: the stately capital letter, the procession of words in their proper order, every arch and tunnel, bridge and buttress perfectly fitted to its job. –Patricia T. O'Conner • Transitions act like railroad switches, smoothing the turn from one track to another. –Thomas Kane • Language is a part of our organism and no less complicated than it. –Ludwig Wittgenstein • Craft certainly can be taught, even if genius cannot. –Scott Russell Sanders • What do I mean by a phrase? A clutch of words that gives you a clutch at the heart. –Robert Frost • Language is our meeting place, the sea we all live in. –Tobias Wolff

He who would learn to fly one day must first learn to stand and walk and run and climb and dance; one cannot fly into flying.

−Friedrich Nietzsche, German philosopher

A whole is that which has beginning, middle, and end.

−Aristotle, ancient Greek thinker and scientist

The use of language is all we have to pit against death and silence.

−Joyce Carol Oates, novelist

By words the mind is winged.

−Aristophanes, Greek dramatist

CHAPTER FOUR

A Writer's Tools

In one sense, writing *is* easy. All you need to write is something to write with, something to write on, and something to say. The first two are straightforward and easy to tackle. You can write with a pen or pencil or type on a keyboard, and you can compose on loose-leaf paper, in a notebook or on a computer, whatever feels most comfortable. Writing instruments and paper are inexpensive—as are most computers these days—so very few barriers of entry exist to writing practitioners. The words—the last thing you need—cost nothing at all and come from the mind itself. And once one starts writing, words can and should flow as freely as tap water from a faucet. Because everyone also has the ability to revise those words, everyone has the tools at his or her disposal to write effectively. The only other must-have item needed to produce high-quality writing is a commitment to excellence.

We all have continuous streams of thoughts—what language experts call *mentalese*—and writing is about translating those thoughts into written form. Some writers go to extremes to capture the spontaneity of their minds at work. Jack Kerouac, for example, spun out the first draft of his novel, *On the Road*, in only three weeks at a friend's apartment in New York City in 1951. To create the manuscript, he used a typewriter and a continuous, 120-foot-long roll of paper so as to free himself of the burden of changing sheets of paper while he typed. Although he kept detailed notes of his travels, which helped fuel his burst of creative energy, Kerouac drank coffee and hurriedly recorded his story on the scroll of paper he'd taped together, not even pausing to divide his text into paragraphs. Regardless of how it's done, author and woman's suffragist Mary Heaton Vorse disclosed what it really takes to write well: "The art of writing is the art of applying the seat of the pants to the seat of the chair."[1]

While some people express themselves with words so well that their communication skills seem natural or almost effortless, it is generally because they have had a lot of practice. Members of Congress are usually good at giving speeches because they give a lot of them, and successful TV talk show hosts are gifted communicators and interviewers because they talk to people all the time and are experienced at engaging guests and listeners. David Letterman and Conan O'Brien are good at telling jokes because they regularly tell them in their monologues, just as PBS's Jim Lehrer and Ray Suarez and CNN's Anderson Cooper and Larry King are good at asking questions because they've become adept at it. Again, studies show that it's *the amount of accumulated practice* that distinguishes top performers—chess grand masters, concert violinists, professional ice skaters, and the like—from lesser performers. Although most people can't deliver a speech as well as Ronald Reagan or Bill Clinton could during their presidencies, anyone, no matter how inarticulate or shy, can learn to speak articulately and write effectively over time.[2]

Words, obviously, are a writer's sole means of expression. Gestures and non-verbal cues, such as winks or raised eyebrows, are meaningful in face-to-face conversation, but in writing their significance can only be described on paper. A person who intends to be an effective writer must, therefore, learn how to use language to clearly convey concepts and information. If something is said well, effective communication occurs; if something is not put just right, however, miscommunication transpires. Just consider Vice President Dan Quayle's infamous speech to the United Negro College Fund, whose motto is "A mind is a terrible thing to waste." Quayle's take: "What a waste it is to lose one's mind. Or not to have a mind is very wasteful. How true that is." Or ponder yet another of Quayle's public gaffes: "It isn't pollution that's harming the environment. It's the impurities in our air and water that are doing it." If Quayle had just stuck to carefully crafted written remarks, his speeches might have drawn far less disparaging news coverage than they did.[3]

When composing text, it must never be forgotten that words are slippery creatures, often capable of conveying multiple meanings or of being misused or misinterpreted. These real newspaper headlines could be read more than one way: "Drunk Gets Nine Months in Violin Case," "Iraqi Head Seeks Arms," "Queen Mary Having Bottom Scraped." The sheer complexity of the English language makes for pitfalls galore. The word *fine* has fourteen definitions as an adjective, six as a noun, and two as an adverb; *set*—one of English's most versatile words—has 126 uses as a verb and 58 as a noun, among others. The meanings of *set* are so varied that the *Oxford English Dictionary* uses 60,000 words just to recount them. Some words actually have contradictory meanings. *Cleave* can mean stick together or cut in half, depending on its context, and *sanction* can either signify permission to do something or a measure forbidding that it be done. As Richard Lederer points out in *Crazy English*, our mother tongue doesn't always make sense: we drive on parkways but park in driveways. Go figure.[4]

Because language is subject to so much ambiguity, it must be used with precision or it will only obfuscate what the user of it wants to say. The twenty-volume, second edition of the *Oxford English Dictionary*, spanning 21,730 pages, defines 615,100 words, and the in-progress revision of that dictionary, in the making for many years now, ultimately may define one million words. If scientific and technical terms, medical conditions, chemical substances, and the names of flora and fauna are added into the mix, the number of words grows exponentially. There are 1.4 million named insect species alone. Obviously, with so many words in circulation, a complete command of the English language is impossible. However, the sheer number of words available to us makes using language fun and full of surprises. To be a skilled writer, you must become passionate about words and pay attention to what words are available and what they mean in particular contexts.[5]

With new technologies and increasing globalization of the world's economies, the opportunities to communicate across borders have exploded. People's exposure to other cultures and communities, accelerated by the availability of television, telephones, airline travel and e-mail, have led to an explosion in cross-cultural, often international communications. We see foreign films. We surf the Internet and find links to Web sites run by people half-way around the world. And families sponsor foreign exchange students and salespeople travel the globe to sell their products and services, with foreign words and American slang transmitted daily through cyberspace and TV shows. There are oppressive regimes that try to suppress what their people can read or write or hear or do; they exist in places such as China, Iran, North Korea and Sudan. But because of emerging technologies, people's ability to communicate with one another around the globe—whether they live in urban centers or in remote villages or farmhouses—increases with every passing year. No longer are we isolated from once-distant peoples; e-mails can be sent to someone in Geneva, Switzerland, or Tokyo, Japan, just as easily as they can be sent to someone down the hall at a company's offices.

In fact, computers and the Internet have given us a vast array of new opportunities, not to mention a plethora of new words and phrases, all entering the language almost overnight. In the United States alone, there are more than 200 million Internet users, with the world's Internet population estimated to be more than 880 million. In the frenetic pace of the twenty-first century, not only are strangers able to connect online, but language itself changes at a dizzying pace. Existing words suddenly take on new meanings, two short words are ingeniously joined to create a longer compound, nouns abruptly morph into verbs, or totally new words appear without warning. When Random House produced a second edition of its twelve-pound, unabridged dictionary in 1987, it added 50,000 new words—among them, *preppy* and *sunblocker*—that were not listed twenty-one years earlier. That dictionary also included 75,000 new definitions of old words; of its 315,000 entries, 210,000 needed revision. To *webmasters* and *bloggers*, two new occupations, a *port* can mean something totally different than what it meant to seafarers in England or ship-building American cities just decades ago. If you were living in the 1960s and you'd told someone that you'd been *slammed* or *spammed*, or that you *googled* someone, you'd undoubtedly have gotten the most quizzical look imaginable.[6]

Indeed, the English language—having borrowed words from over 120 languages—grows daily, welcoming into the lexicon new words, as it always has. *Shampoo* originated in India, *caucus* comes from the Algonquin Indians, *potato* hails from Haiti, *prairie* is French, *rodeo* and *coyote* came from early Spanish settlers, *sauna* is of Finnish origin, *polka* is Czech, and *oasis* has Egyptian roots. English has pilfered words such as *pizza, spaghetti, macaroni* and *espresso* from Italian, adopted *jambalaya* and *praline* from the New Orleans tradition, and modified German words to create *cookbook, delicatessen, hoodlum* and *nix*. The Yiddish tradition has given us *chutzpah, kibitzer, kosher* and *schmooz*, and Spanish has given Americans more words—among them, *enchilada, plaza, stampede* and *tornado*—than any other language. The pace of change is staggering. In medieval times, new words entered the language each year, but much more slowly than they do today. Nowadays, the number of words coined each year is approximately 15,000 to 20,000, with people all over the world making up words to suit their fancies. Indeed, new *sniglets*—words that don't appear in the dictionary, but should—appear daily, giving writers more choices than ever before. The creative ways in which words can be used is nowhere more apparent than in the advertising industry, where double-entendres and wordplays are as common as pharmaceutical ads and beer commercials.[7]

The English language is thus ever evolving, as are its rules. This means that speakers and writers are always innovating and remaking the language in a process that has gone on for centuries. Just one English playwright, William Shakespeare, coined approximately 2,000 new words, among them *accommodation, apostrophe, assassination, bedroom, critical, dislocate, dwindle, excellent, expose, frugal, gust, hurry, impartial, leapfrog, lonely, majestic, monumental, obscene, pell-mell, premeditated, radiance, sanctimonious, submerged, summit* and *useless*. The famous bard also invented compounds like *cold comfort, fancy free, hotblooded, laughing-stock, long-haired, love affair, sea change* and *tongue-tied*, not to mention phrases like *one fell swoop, to be in a pickle, vanish into thin air, play fast and loose* and *foul play*. It's hard to imagine the English language today without those words and phrases in it, though Shakespeare had a particularly good excuse: the concept of a dictionary was not invented until 1538, just a couple of decades before his birth in 1564. English is malleable, yet enduring, with Shakespeare's quotable lines still in use today, either on stage or in everyday conversation: "The better part of valor is discretion." "Nothing will come of nothing." "How long a time lies in one little word!"[8]

Consequently, writers will always have many versatile words, as well as many types of words, at their disposal. There are *nouns*, used to name a person, place, thing, quality or idea; *proper nouns*, identifying a specific person, place or thing, as in Adam Smith, the Eiffel Tower or Rome, Italy; and *verbs*, that part of language that expresses action or existence. Many words can actually function as both nouns and verbs: *bear, drink, fight, run, fund* and *cut*, among them. There are *adjectives* (such as *happy, sad* and *lucky*), which modify nouns; *pronouns* (such as *I, you, he, she, they* and *it*), which take the place of nouns; *articles* (such as *a, the* or *this*), which tell us whether a noun refers to a particular thing or just one of many of those things; *adverbs* (such as *slowly* or *very*), which modify verbs, adjectives or adverbs themselves; and *prepositions* (such as *in, among* or *with*), which show how a noun or pronoun relates to another word in a sentence. There are also words such as *and* that connect other words or phrases—*conjunctions*—and words that condense two words into one—*contractions*. And let's not forget *interjections*, those words or phrases that express strong emotion or surprise. A couple from my generation: "Awesome!" "Cool!"[9]

When you write, sound is all important. Words themselves are made up of sounds that allow us to give voice to them. There are *vowels*—"a," "e," "i," "o," "u," and, yes, let's not forget that oft-neglected, sometimes "y"—and *consonants*—consisting of all the letters of the alphabet that are *not* vowels. Although most words contain both kinds of sounds, it is a mere twenty-six letters of the alphabet—and their phonetic characteristics, both hard and soft—that form the basis for the entire English language. The International Phonetic Alphabet differentiates between fifty-two sounds used in English, while *The American Heritage Dictionary* lists forty-five English sounds. So variable are the ways in which letters are pronounced that dictionaries have to resort to symbols—"ā", "â", "ä", or, "ō", "ô", "ö", to list just a few—simply to give people a common reference point for how to say particular words. Again, it's all part of the fun. Certain words, known as *homophones*, actually have differently spellings but the same pronunciation, as writer Jan Venolia points out in her illustratively titled book *Write Right!* The word *syllable* itself was thought up to describe a unit of spoken language consisting of a single uninterrupted sound.[10]

The importance of sound to shaping thoughts—and to effective writing or speechwriting—can't be underestimated. If your words sound dull or shrill, you'll come off as dull or shrill; on the other hand, if your words are elegant or graceful, you'll be perceived that way. Your words set a tone. It's almost impossible, in fact, to separate how you feel about a passage of text from how it reads or sounds, whether you're reading it aloud or silently. Sounds shape perceptions, or thoughts, about words and what they stand for—their meaning. As writer Ben Yagoda notes in *The Sound on the Page*, "content does not exist separate from the words in which it is expressed." Saying someone is a *buffoon* conjures up a different image than labeling someone a *clown*. The founder of modern linguistics, Ferdinand de Saussure, who saw thoughts and sounds as intertwined with one another, compared language to a sheet of paper. "Thought is one side of the sheet and sound the reverse side," he said. "Just as it is impossible to take a pair of scissors and cut one side of the paper without at the same time cutting the other," he said, "so it is impossible in language to isolate sound from thought, or thought from sound."[11]

If words are the basic unit of all writing (and they are), vivid and concrete details are what give writing its vitality and life. It's much more descriptive and engaging to read about a *tulip*, *rose*, or *daisy* than to read about a generic *flower*, just as it is more evocative to hear about *a rusty '69 Chevy* or *a little red Corvette* than it is to try to conjure up what a nondescript *car* looks like. The German-born architect and designer, Mies van der Rohe, put it succinctly, "God is in the details." In other words, beauty and meaning are uncovered through specifics—anecdotes or revealing facts or statistics—and the use of descriptive language. "It has long been an axiom of mine," the famed Arthur Conan Doyle wrote in "A Case of Identity" in *The Adventures of Sherlock Holmes*, "that the little things are infinitely the most important." How true. The lesson to be learned by any aspiring writer: when using language, it's almost always best to be specific, to use concrete details. Sweeping generalities or non-descriptive words can hide meaning, whereas precise language can convey information or ideas in a much more meaningful way.[12]

There are certainly times when you'll want or need to use words that are not so specific. You may want to vary the way you're describing something, or you may be unable to be more precise when describing someone. For example, if a police officer is taking down the description of a rapist, and the sexual assault victim doesn't know the perpetrator's name and can't remember his facial features, but does recall his height and what he was wearing, the most accurate description to write down would not name *a specific person* who might conceivably fit that physical description. Instead, the best description the officer could truthfully record might describe the suspect as a "masked 5'10" white male wearing a gray sweatshirt and torn blue jeans." A DNA test or diligent police work might later identify the rapist, but the police officer's initial intake report couldn't do that under the circumstances. Language should reflect reality and only be as specific as the facts allow that language to be. Whenever you can, however, use evocative details to make your writing clear and to give it pizzazz. You want readers to be engaged, not perplexed or bored, by your writing.

A detail is most effective and evocative when it appeals to one of the senses: hearing, sight, smell, taste or touch. As best-selling author Diane Ackerman explains in her book, *A Natural History of the Senses*: "There is no way in which to understand the world without first detecting it through the radar-net of our senses. We can extend our senses with the help of microscope, stethoscope, robot, satellite, hearing aid, eyeglasses, and such, but what is beyond our senses we cannot know." Good writers thus pay attention to readers' senses. To realistically convey the sights and sounds of a New York City streetscape, a writer had better know what typical readers would see if they were standing on a street corner in the Big Apple: a pretzel or hot dog vendor's stand, steam coming up out of a manhole cover, lovers embracing in Central Park, yellow cabs honking their horns and careening through traffic. Writing that "Manhattan was great" tells readers almost nothing; only the use of concrete details can transport readers to that place and explain why the writer felt that way.[13]

Vivid description conveys sights, sounds and feelings, even tastes and scents, by letting us visualize objects and people and what's happening to them. Readers can conjure up, through well-crafted written description, a bustling Chicago pizzeria where customers, jabbering on their cell phones, are waiting impatiently in line to place their orders. Readers can be made to see college kids, dressed in flour-coated aprons, shaping handmade dough by tossing it into the air. Readers can be made to almost taste the pepperoni, sausage and mushroom pizzas slathered with basil-laden tomato sauce and thick layers of mozzarella cheese as they are pulled from industrial-sized stone ovens. As Diane Ackerman notes, "There is much more to seeing than mere seeing. The visual image is a kind of tripwire for the emotions." "When we see an object," she writes, "the whole peninsula of our senses wakes up to appraise the new sight." A good writer can make our mouths water just by describing what's being grilled or baked or eaten. If you neglect your readers' senses, you'll be committing writing malpractice.[14]

If you want to be a gifted writer, the best place to start is a household dictionary; spend time browsing through it, seeing what choices you have. Reading—and looking up words you don't know—is another useful exercise. With a dictionary as your companion, you'll learn more and more words as time passes, and that increased vocabulary will give you a much better chance of being able to say precisely what you want to say when you have the need or want to say it. A good thesaurus (providing synonyms and antonyms for words), a "descriptionary" (a glossary of terms by theme so you can put a word at your fingertips even if you don't remember the word you're looking for), and a "visual" or "picture" dictionary (labeling the constituent parts of pictured objects) also can help you find the best words to use. If you discover that you like writing poetry—what American writer Louis Untermeyer called "the power of defining the indefinable in terms of the unforgettable"—a rhyming dictionary is a must-have, at least if you decide to work in the more traditional forms of verse.[15]

When writing, never forget that the purpose of words is to convey information or to impart feelings or emotions. Words themselves are merely symbols for objects, beliefs, types of action or states of mind. If thrown together in a random or haphazard fashion, words are about as helpful to people as a fireplace in a freezing, unheated house in Siberia without any wood or matches to make a fire. To write most effectively, you need to put your words together as carefully as someone building a tall bonfire made of hundreds of logs. In his book, *Keys to Great Writing*, syndicated columnist Stephen Wilbers emphasizes the importance of making a text meaningful and clear and putting personality into one's writing. "Make every word count," "Use natural language," "Avoid a bureaucratic style," he says. In one of his columns, Wilbers writes about Stan, an old college friend whose writing had become so bogged down with excess verbiage that nobody would even read his e-mails anymore. "I deem it imperative that we commence work on resolving this pressing issue at our earliest possible convenience," Stan wrote in asking Wilbers for help. Wilbers quickly put Stan back on track, noting that in the old days his friend would have said something along the lines of "Let's get started" or "Time's a-wasting."[16]

Think of words as pieces of firewood. If used properly, both words and wood can create tremendous heat and can light up a room (or those in it). Well-written prose attracts readers just as campers are drawn to a warm campfire on a cold night. Different types of wood certainly have unique grains and burn differently, creating distinct scents or colors of flame, and individual words are just as distinctive. Though many words have close synonyms, no other word can do exactly what a given word can do in the context of a given sentence. Another word might be suitable perhaps, but only a certain word can deliver the meaning or punch the writer wants to deliver. Sometimes, writers get so frustrated searching for the right word that they find it desirable to invent a new one, perhaps by fusing together two existing words. *Airport, flowerpot, footwear, seashore, sunflower* and *wristwatch* were undoubtedly formed in just that way. Confucius, the Chinese thinker, believed that wisdom actually comes by learning to call things by their right name. It's hard to say what new words may be dreamed up in the future. In his disturbing novel, *A Clockwork Orange*, Anthony Burgess uses the word *cancer* to describe what we all know as a *cigarette*. Truth-telling at its best, perhaps.[17]

Even the smallest of details matters. The placement (or misplacement) of punctuation marks, for instance, can dramatically shape meaning. "Proper punctuation is both the sign and the cause of clear thinking," writes Lynne Truss in her best-selling book *Eats, Shoots & Leaves: The Zero Tolerance Approach to Punctuation*—a book that gets its name (believe it or not) from a punctuation-related joke about a panda. In the joke, a panda walks into a café, orders and eats a sandwich, and then draws a gun and fires shots into the air. "Why?" the confused waiter asks as the panda heads for the door. "I'm a panda. Look it up," the panda replies, tossing a badly punctuated wildlife manual over his shoulder. The relevant entry reads: "Panda. Large black-and-white bear-like mammal, native to China. Eats, shoots and leaves." The errant placement of the comma after the word "eats" turns the panda from a mammal who eats bamboo shoots and leaves into an animal that wields a gun and then, in the joke, exits stage left.[18]

Thus, a writer must continuously think and vigilantly analyze, even while punctuating a sentence. If the writer is not careful, readers can take away the exact opposite meaning of what the writer really wants to convey. Just consider the difference between the following sentences: "A woman, without her man, is nothing."

"A woman: without her, man is nothing." Or compare these two sentences: "The convict said the judge is mad." "'The convict,' said the judge, 'is mad.'" Even the use of hyphens can avoid ambiguity or confusion in meaning, as the distinction between *reformed* and *re-formed* or *remark* and *re-mark* illustrates. If you're going to say something, make sure you're punctuating it correctly, lest you lose or lessen its impact on your audience. When in doubt, ask a more experienced writer or look up the rule in a reference book. Sometimes all you need is a period at the end of a sentence. That's easy. Other times, however, more punctuation marks are needed, with some complex sentences requiring multiple commas—maybe even a couple of dashes or a semi-colon—before what the English call the "full stop," the period.[19]

A good writer must therefore know how to punctuate so that the writer's prose is as clear and unambiguous as possible. There's a lot to learn, but the basics are pretty easy to articulate. A *colon*, writes Lynne Truss, "theatrically announces what is to come," be it a list, a quotation, or that part of a sentence that serves some other function. *Commas* separate clauses or series of things, *ellipses* indicate that words have been left out, and *parentheses* are used to mark off explanatory or qualifying remarks or to enclose digressions (such as this one). *Dashes*, meanwhile, can be used in pairs to enclose an aside, or singly to place emphasis on a point that follows. "The dash is like a detour; it interrupts the sentence and inserts another thought," writes author-grammarian Patricia O'Conner. A *semicolon*, on the other hand, is placed between two related sentences where there is no conjunction, as in "You take the high road; I'll take the low road." If a comma is a yellow light and a period is a red light, O'Connor notes, "the semicolon is a flashing red—one of those lights you drive through after a brief pause."[20]

Let's take the word-firewood analogy as far as it will go. If a person stranded in the wilderness knows how to build and light a fire, firewood becomes more than twigs or the branches of a downed tree; it becomes fuel for cooking and heating, capable of warming hands and feet and giving hope for survival. Similarly, where words and punctuation are deftly used, they become more than mere arrangements of letters, spaces and little marks; they become endowed with special characteristics and capabilities and—put to good use—can warm the human heart and connect us to one another. "As I watched and listened," environmentalist Sigurd Olson wrote in *The Singing Wilderness,* "I became conscious of the slow, steady hum of millions of insects and through it the calling of the whitethroats and the violin notes of the hermit thrushers." When we read those words, we almost feel that we are sitting next to Olson on the eastern shore of Robinson Lake where he wrote them.[21]

Bear in mind, just because you have good material to work with, your firewood, does not mean that you'll be able to light a fire on your first or second or even third or fourth attempt. Building well-crafted sentences and paragraphs takes time, just as it takes time and effort to light a fire by striking flint against steel— particularly if you've never done it before. But if you keep trying, keep striving for that sometimes elusive flame, you'll eventually create a spark and ignite that fire—a fire that will burn bright and never go out. Good phrases will turn into good sentences, which will become good paragraphs, and you'll soon be building the kind of fire—the kind of artful prose—that you once thought only your favorite author could build. As you work, just remember to set your sights high, never settling for mediocre writing and always revising what you write until you feel you're communicating effectively—and with style. You may not achieve all you hoped to accomplish, but you'll probably come close. As the poet Henry Wadsworth Longfellow put it, "If you would hit the mark, you must aim a little above it."[22]

No book on the art of writing would be complete without at least passing reference to everyone's favorite (or should I say least favorite?) subject: *grammar*. Although the rules of grammar are often misunderstood and frequently ignored, every grade-school student comes to know—and often dread—that topic. Grammar gets a bad rap, I suspect, because its rules are so often associated with our failed attempts to comprehend, memorize and use them. Parents and English teachers drill young people on the rules of good grammar, yet often find themselves correcting children's speech, perhaps in a condescending or ineffectual manner. I'm sure everyone can remember an instance—more than likely quite a few—in which one's grammar was corrected in a way that caused embarrassment or made one feel stupid. "What did you just say?" "The proper word to use in that sentence is 'can' not 'may.'" "That's not how you say it." "'Ain't' isn't a word." These are just some of the ways in which parents and teachers regularly correct speech to try to put a stop to bad grammar or slang.

In truth, *grammar* is just a fancy word for the system of rules for the use of language. Those rules, developed over time, are important. If we didn't have them, we'd have no shared system articulating how words and punctuation should be strung together to create meaning. There is, of course, a vast difference between the rules of grammar and how people talk in the real world. "The rules people learn (or, more likely, fail to learn) in school," notes language expert Steven Pinker, "are called *prescriptive* rules, prescribing how one 'ought' to talk." Those prescriptive rules, developed by style manual, handbook and textbook writers, are enforced on an *ad hoc* basis by a loose network of writers, copyeditors, English teachers and parents. As Pinker points out, the variance between how people talk and "ought" to talk represents the divide between the *prescriptive* rules and the *descriptive* speech patterns actually found by linguists in a given community. Those who break the rules can be innovators, moving our ever-evolving language forward, but writers who want to reach an audience must know how to use the language in the same way that their audience presently uses it and has been trained to speak and write it.[23]

It may be tedious, but to become a more effective writer, you'll need to spend time learning the rules of grammar and proper usage. You need to know how to correctly use words within sentences. You need to know when to use brackets or ellipses and when to capitalize words. And you need to know how to indent paragraphs and use italics, underlining and quotation marks. If you think of grammar rules as that handy book of matches that will allow you to easily light the fire you hope to build, perhaps learning those rules will not seem so burdensome after all. Who knows, pretty soon you may find yourself holding strong opinions on even the most minute of grammar or usage subjects. The more you learn, the better off you'll be. And the more you write, the more you'll learn. "I believe that eventually quantity will make for quality," science-fiction writer Ray Bradbury explains. "Quantity gives experience," he says, noting that "from experience alone can quality come."[24]

So what exactly are the elements of good grammar? Along with the rules about how words are used and strung together in complete sentences, there are rules dealing with specific points of grammar—the use of pronouns and prepositions, singular versus plural forms, subordinate clauses, etc.—and rules dealing with capitalization, punctuation, spelling, and how numbers are expressed in writing. Who could forget, for example, that most famous rule:

"i" before "e" except after "c." Some grammatical rules are simple: a period goes at the end of a declarative sentence, a comma separates numerals in numbers with four or more digits (as in 1,000), an apostrophe denotes possession (as in "the child's doll") or forms a contraction. Other "rules" are more complex, as they seem to lack any particular logic or rationale. Nouns ending in "o," for instance, form their plurals by adding "s" or "es." Some generalizations are possible—most nouns ending in "o" preceded by a *vowel* form their plurals by adding "s" to the singular, whereas most nouns ending in "o" preceded by a *consonant* form their plurals by adding "es"—but exceptions clearly exist (as in *pianos, solos,* or *sopranos*). In the end, a dictionary or usage manual must be consulted to know what's right, making the "rules" seem like total nonsense, which they sometimes are. Even the "i"-before-"e"-except-after-"c" directive has multiple exceptions: *foreign, height, neighbor, reign, their, weight,* to name just a few.[25]

The rules of English grammar, of Latin origin, are so difficult to master because there are so many of them to learn and because they have such varied and multiple exceptions. *Father* and *mother,* for example, are capitalized when used in an address (as in "Yes, Mother, I am going."), but not capitalized when a possessive pronoun is used with them (as in "My father went to the store."). Likewise, smaller numbers are usually spelled out, except when used in a series of related numbers (as in the sentence, "The boys ate 5 burgers, 2 bags of potato chips, and 4 pieces of pie."). Oftentimes, people just forget the rules altogether. I couldn't tell you how many times I've seen *it's* (the shortened form of *it is*) confused with *its* (the possessive form of *it*), even by lawyers, or words put in an illogical or misleading order within a sentence. Many grammar rules are not hard-and-fast "rules" at all, but simply guidelines or conventions for connecting concepts to one another.

Applying these guidelines and conventions requires the exercise of discretionary judgment—judgment that is only gained by lots of experience.[26]

Conventions of spelling can be equally confusing, as I can attest from helping my daughter prepare for her spelling tests at school. How do you explain to a grade-school student that a word is *not* spelled just as it sounds? Although spelling is completely predictable from regular rules for about 84 percent of English words, the way some words are spelled—take *colonel* or *island*—frequently has nothing to do with how they are pronounced. One must often resort to mnemonic devices to teach a child how to memorize and spell certain words. "When you eat 'dessert,' you always want to come back for the second 's'," goes one memory trick—a quick way to remember the difference between a barren "desert" and what may be your favorite part of a meal. "When you 'assume' something you make an 'ass' of 'u' and 'me'," goes another. Practice tests and rote memorization, as well as repeatedly writing out words that have been misspelled in the past, are often the only ways for people to learn how to spell. Thankfully, spell-checkers have made writers' lives easier, though they are not a panacea, because they won't catch everything for you.[27]

If you don't learn about grammar and usage, how to spell, and how to distinguish between particularly troublesome words (e.g., *advice* and *advise*, *affect* and *effect*, *capital* and *capitol*, *complement* and *compliment*, *ensure* and *insure*, *farther* and *further*, *prescribe* and *proscribe*, *principal* and *principle*, *stationary* and *stationery*, and *than* and *then*), you are likely to appear sloppy or uneducated. To pick on Dan Quayle again: just think how much credibility he lost when, as a sitting U.S. vice president, he told William Figueroa, a 12-year-old boy, that *potato* was spelled "potatoe," causing the boy (against his own better judgment) to misspell the word on the classroom blackboard. And if you lose your credibility, you've lost everything, for no one will trust (or will less likely listen to) what you have to say, even if what you have to say is of the utmost importance. Knowing the difference in meaning between *already* and *all ready* and between *altogether* and *all together*, it turns out, is consequential; it can mean the difference between effective writing and ineffective prose. Knowing the rules of grammar and proper usage is, in fact, the best way to help you become a more polished and effective communicator in all facets of your life.[28]

This book—as I said—is not intended to be a grammar book. Yet, to write well, I cannot emphasize enough that you need to learn the rules of proper grammar and usage. To do this, I would recommend that you read three short books: Margaret Shertzer's *The Elements of Grammar*, L. Sue Baugh's *Essentials of English Grammar: A Practical Guide to the Mastery of English*, and Patricia O'Connor's *Woe Is I: The Grammarphobe's Guide to Better English in Plain English*. These books (the first two containing a straightforward list of the rules and dos and don'ts, and the third, using humor to make its points) will tell you almost everything you need to know about the English language and how best to express yourself. Obviously, many other good books are widely available, but the important thing is that you read *some* books about grammar and usage to learn the rules. Regular use of a dictionary and a spell-checker can help you spell words correctly, though you must still know when to use *their* as opposed to *there* or *they're*. Grammar- and spell-checkers are supplementary tools, not substitutes for learning how to spell and learning the rules of grammar themselves.[29]

To address the finer points of English usage, you can consult the voluminous standard-bearer, *The Chicago Manual of Style*. That book, now in its fifteenth edition, is 956 pages long and addresses a whole host of topics ranging from abbreviations to such minutia as the use of zeros in decimal fractions. Writing with style takes much more than knowing grammar and usage rules, but learning those rules (or at least as many of them as you can) is a prerequisite to effective writing. No matter how hard you try, you won't be able to write with true style until you have a basic grasp of the rules. But lest you get too discouraged or intimidated by everything there is to know, you should keep in mind that you should learn the rules *as you write*, not try to memorize all of them (which you'll never be able to do anyway) before you begin writing. I've botched my own fair share of sentences as I've learned the craft of writing, and it has sometimes been embarrassing or, I'm sure, cost me a better grade in a class I was taking. But mistakes are part of life, so don't be too hard on yourself. If you mess up, just try harder the next time. Bottom line: if you look up the rules when faced with particular issues that arise in your own writing projects, you'll gradually learn the rules of grammar and how to use words effectively. As Ralph Waldo Emerson explained, "Skill to do comes of doing."[30]

Oftentimes, there are no right or wrong answers. Some writers, for example, like to use lots of dashes, parentheses or semicolons in their writing, which is perfectly fine, while others frown at their use, which is okay, too. Or take exclamation marks, which some writers despise. "Cut out all the exclamation marks. An exclamation mark is like laughing at your own joke," F. Scott Fitzgerald advised. "[T]he exclamation mark is the big attention-deficit brother who gets overexcited and breaks things and laughs too loudly," quips Lynne Truss in *Eats, Shoots & Leaves*. Though frequently overused, exclamation marks—in my opinion, at least—can be effective if used sparingly, such as for apologies, excited utterances, or to express drama, irony or astonishment. Author

Karen Elizabeth Gordon gives these examples of when exclamation marks are warranted and perfectly acceptable: "Wham! Bang! Thwack!" "You're really something!" and "How exciting to see you in traction again!" Deciding what's best—or most appropriate—is all part of the fun. It's all, in the end, a matter of choice or taste.[31]

Other kinds of punctuation marks can be equally subject to a writer's subjective judgments. "This morning I took out a comma and this afternoon I put it back again," Oscar Wilde famously remarked, a recognition of the fact that commas are sometimes optional in particular places within a sentence. What's known as the *Oxford comma*—that is, the second comma in editor Harold Ross's example, "The flag is red, white, and blue"—is optional, though its use can sometimes improve a sentence by making the sentence less ambiguous. Court cases, in fact, have hinged upon the placement or omission of a single comma or semi-colon. For example, where the drafter of a will joined two separate beneficiaries with a conjunction but separated the rest with semi-colons, a Kentucky appellate court had to decide whether the estate had to be divided into nine equal parts or into eight parts with one additional part shared by two parties. Indeed, when using the English language, it's more an issue of personal preference or assessing the particular needs of a specific situation. Although the placement of punctuation marks can matter a great deal, sometimes the words of Gertrude Stein seem appropriate or particularly apt: "There ain't no answer. There ain't gonna be any answer. There never has been an answer. That's the answer."[32]

It's a given, of course, that no one will be able to follow all of the standard conventions of grammar and usage all of the time; that would not be humanly possible or even desirable, as it would curb innovation and creativity (notice that I just quoted an authority figure who said "ain't," which is typically a no-no). People forget rules or make mistakes, whether inadvertently or through ignorance; they disagree about what's best or right or wrong; or they are simply rebellious and don't want to always adhere to custom or conventions, which is all the rules of grammar really articulate in the first place. In writing, absolutes are rare. "The golden rule is that there are no golden rules," Irish dramatist and writer George Bernard Shaw famously remarked. "If you obey all the rules you miss all the fun," Katharine Hepburn warned (in a different context, mind you). Though there are kernels of truth in such admonitions, I personally like T. S. Eliot's advice: "It's not wise to violate the rules until you know how to observe them." If you use bad grammar when you don't know what you're doing, you're more likely to look foolish or ignorant than to gain the respect of your classmates, your colleagues, or your peers. As you work, just do your best, which is all you can do.[33]

Ironically, a good way to learn proper English may be to study a *foreign* language. Because we learn the rules of grammar largely through oral speech, we come to know the difference between good and bad grammar through hearing it in use. We may recognize what sounds right and what doesn't, but sometimes we are unable to articulate *why* the grammar is good or bad. "You should say it like this," a parent might say in correcting a child's speech. If the child asks why, the parent might respond, "That's just the way it is. I can't tell you why, it's just always been that way. And that's the way you need to say it, too." When I studied German in high school and college, I learned many rules of English grammar for the first time because I actually needed to know those rules to understand the rules of the foreign language. Studying a foreign language can also give you insight into a totally different perspective on the world. "The immense value of becoming acquainted with a foreign language is that we are thereby led into a new world of tradition and thought and feeling," writer Havelock Ellis once wrote. As a Czech proverb goes: "Learn another language, get a second soul."[34]

In the end, the foundation for good writing skills is a good education—whether formal or informal. The better educated one becomes, through whatever means, the better writer one becomes. A person learns a lot in kindergarten and grade school, even more in middle school and high school, even more in college, and even more in graduate school or when one enters the working world. A person can be self-taught, as famous inventors such as Benjamin Franklin and Thomas Edison were, but one's grasp of information and ideas is the key to becoming an effective communicator. Becoming better educated, whether by reading, increasing your vocabulary, or studying the rules of language, is not a burden and should never be considered one. Instead, it is a great, life-changing opportunity. Writer-educator Edith Hamilton put it forcefully: "It has always seemed strange to me that in our endless discussions about education so little stress is laid on the pleasure of becoming an educated person, the enormous interest it adds to life. To be able to be caught up into the world of thought—that is to be educated."[35]

The writing process is, fundamentally, about exploration, discovery, and self-improvement, with writing itself making possible scientific advances and human progress, including in the areas of civil rights and human rights. And learning to write well is all about committing oneself to becoming a more effective thinker and communicator. "Language grows out of life, out of its needs and experiences," Helen Keller's teacher, Anne Sullivan, observed, noting the close relationship between words and one's understanding of the world and one's participation in it. "Language and knowledge are indissolubly connected; they are interdependent," she said, explaining, "Good work in language presupposes and depends on a real knowledge of things." In other words, the more you know, the better writer you'll become, and the more you write, the more knowledge you'll gain about writing and life itself. If you want to become a more effective thinker and communicator, read on and take the next step: learning how to better draft and compose your words.[36]

The faster I write the better my output. If I'm going slow I'm in trouble. It means I'm pushing the words instead of being pulled by them. –Raymond Chandler • It's appropriate to pause and say that the writer is one who, embarking upon a task, does not know what to do. –Donald Barthelme • I assumed the burden of a profession, which is to write even when you don't want to, don't much like what you are writing, and aren't writing particularly well. –Agatha Christie • Just get it down on paper, and then we'll see what to do with it. –Maxwell Perkins • I used to sit in the bathroom with the running water in the sink and write because the echo against the tile was nice. –Paul Simon • I write again to-day, or at any moment, as things come into my head. –Thomas Hardy • If we knew what it was we were doing, it would not be called research, would it? –Albert Einstein • All good writing is *swimming under water* and holding your breath. –F. Scott Fitzgerald • In skating over thin ice our safety is in our speed. –Ralph Waldo Emerson • If there is no wind, row. –Latin proverb • I put a piece of paper under my pillow, and when I could not sleep I wrote in the dark. –Henry David Thoreau • I think I did pretty well, considering I started out with nothing but a bunch of blank paper. –Steve Martin • It doesn't have to be the truth, just your vision of it, written down. –Virginia Woolf • Write while the heat is in you. –Henry David Thoreau • The only good piece of advice that I ever read about play-writing was from John Van Druten, who said, "Don't outline everything, because it makes the writing of the play a chore." –Neil Simon • People who can't afford to have writer's block don't get it. That tells you every-thing you need to know about writer's block. –Marshall J. Cook • I feel that one's verse must be as direct and natural as spoken words. –W. B. Yeats • A writer is, on the whole, most alive when alone. –Martin Amis • All I know is that if I sit there long enough, something will happen. –Anne Lamott • I am in the world only for the purpose of composing. –Franz Schubert • Writing is easy: all you do is sit staring at a blank sheet of paper until the drops of blood form on your forehead. –Gene Fowler • One of these days is none of these days. –H. G. Bohn • The young writer would be a fool to follow a theory. Teach yourself by your own mistakes; people learn only by error. –William Faulkner • Shun idleness. It is a rust that attaches itself to the most bril-liant metals. –Voltaire • You can't wait for inspiration. You have to go after it with a club. –Jack London • Write what you know. Write what interests you. If you're fascinated, the work will go faster and be more pleasant. –Robert Bly • A man may write at any time, if he will set himself doggedly to it. –Samuel Johnson

COMPOSITION

All writing comes by the grace of God. –Ralph Waldo Emerson • Inspiration usually comes during work, rather than before it. –Madeleine L'Engle • I write when I'm inspired, and I see to it that I'm inspired at nine o'clock every morning. –Peter De Vries • The moment I took up the pen, I began to be afraid. –Fyodor Dostoevsky • First I write one sentence: then I write another. That's how I write. But I have a feeling writ-ing ought to be like running through a field. –Lytton Strachey • To write is to write is to write is to write is to write is to write is to write. –Gertrude Stein • Don't get it right, get it written. –James Thurber • A writer wastes nothing. –F. Scott Fitzgerald • You separate yourself from your family, from your friends, from your social obligations—it's between you and the page. –Sigurd Olson • If one waits for the right time to come before writing, the right time never comes. –James Russell Lowell • You can always write something. You write limericks. You write a love letter. You do something to get you into the habit of writing again, to bring back the desire. –Erskine Caldwell • The impulse to write a novel comes from a momentary unified vision of life. –Angus Wilson • I must write. I cannot live and not write. –Sigurd Olson • I tend to write in a fragile, edgy, doubtful sort of way, trying things out all the time, never confident that I've got something right. –William Trevor • Write freely and as rapidly as possible and throw the whole thing on paper. Never correct or rewrite until the whole thing is down. –John Steinbeck • The art of writing, like the art of love, runs all the way from a kind of routine hard to distinguish from piling bricks to a kind of frenzy closely related to delirium tremens. –H. L. Mencken • Freewriting is the easiest way to get words on paper and the best all-around practice in writing that I know. To do a freewriting exercise, simply force yourself to write without stopping for ten minutes. –Nikki Giovanni • Rage is to writers what water is to fish. –Nikki Giovanni • When I am working on a book or a story I write every morning as soon after the first light as possible. There is no one to disturb you and it is cool or cold and you come to your work and warm as you write. –Ernest Hemingway • For me, writing—*the only possible writing*—is just simply the conversion of nervous forces into phrases. –Joseph Conrad • What every poet starts from is his own emotions. –T. S. Eliot • The one great rule of composition is to speak the truth. –Henry David Thoreau • Think before you speak is criticism's motto; speak before you think creation's. –E. M. Forster • The goal of freewriting is in the process, not the product. –Peter Elbow • Writing is the process by which you explain to yourself what happened to you. –Arlene Croce • Write fast, write close to the bone. –Bonnie Friedman • First thoughts are the strongest. –Allen Ginsberg • You are free to write the worst junk in the universe. –Natalie Goldberg • Censorship, like charity, should begin at home, but, unlike charity, it should end there. –Clare Boothe Luce • I never know when I sit down, just what I am going to write. I make no plan; it just comes, and I don't know where it comes from. –D. H. Lawrence • Most beginning writers think that if they had any real talent, they would be writing well from the first. They have to learn that they will fail in a number of ways for a considerable time. –Carol Bly

As long as you can start, you are all right. The juice will come.

—Ernest Hemingway, author of *A Farewell to Arms*

As the tennis player rallies before the game begins, so must the writer. And as the tennis player is not concerned with where those first balls are going, neither must the writer be concerned with the first paragraph or two. All you're doing is warming up; the rhythm will come. The first moments are critical. You can sit there, tense and worried, freezing the creative energies, or you can start writing something, perhaps something silly. It simply doesn't matter what you write; it only matters that you write. In five or ten minutes the imagination will heat, the tightness will fade, and a certain spirit and rhythm will take over.

—Leonard Bernstein, Laureate Conductor, New York Philharmonic

A voice is a human gift; it should be cherished and used, to utter as fully human speech as possible. Powerlessness and silence go together.

—Margaret Atwood, Canadian writer

There is no substitute for hard work.

—Thomas Edison, inventor

CHAPTER FIVE

The Writing Process: From Freewriting to Form

At book signings, book buyers often ask authors about the writing process. "When do you write? In the morning, the afternoon, or late at night?" "Where do you write?" "Do you write in longhand or on a computer?" "Do you write every day?" "How do you come up with ideas for your writing?" "Do you prepare an outline before getting started?" These are just some of the more common, process-oriented questions that published writers are asked over and over again, as if there were a magical method to becoming a writer or to being published. "How do you find the time to write?" is another common question—one implying, quite erroneously, that those who write have some super-human ability to manage their time efficiently. Believe me, that's not the case. Anyone who writes has to juggle competing activities just like everyone else.

In truth, no special formula exists for becoming an effective wordsmith. It simply takes hard work and a willingness to accept that one's initial efforts—those first, second and third drafts—are almost sure to be less successful than you might like. Good writing takes time, but all of us can fit writing into our lives. To be a talented writer, you must find the time to write—and then find the time to revise what you first wrote. No matter how busy you are, you must make writing a priority, keeping in mind that the more writing you do, the quicker and more easily you'll be able to write. You're bound to hit speed bumps and potholes and encounter roadblocks and detours on your way, but once you make the commitment to write, only a failure to follow-through will stop you from achieving your goals. "Perseverance," noted film actress Julie Andrews, the legendary star of the Academy Award-winning adaptation of Rodgers and Hammerstein's *The Sound of Music*, "is failing nineteen times and succeeding the twentieth."[1]

For artists, *composition* refers to the way the components of a drawing or painting are arranged—how the whole picture looks. When composing text, writers need to be equally concerned with the way thoughts and ideas are organized on the page. A piece of writing should be coherent; it should have a sense of unity and wholeness; and it should leave the reader with a sense of satisfaction. This is hard to do, but is doable if the writer is willing to take risks, experiment, and laboriously work with the text to construct a piece of high-impact writing. Well-crafted compositions don't come together overnight or all by themselves. They take planning, then execution. They require drafting, then dogged revision. Because ideas often come slowly, all of this takes time, as does the writing process itself. Brenda Ueland, author of the wondrous book, *If You Want to Write*, explains why this is so, calling the act of writing *a thinking process*, "just as drawing is the action of seeing and composing music is the action of hearing."[2]

In many ways, composing text is like composing music, at least as far as the creative process is concerned. One starts with an idea, what the German composer Johannes Brahms called a seed corn that at first grows imperceptibly in secret, only later germinating into the beginnings of a song. That idea is then tossed around in the composer's head, taking shape only after a process of trial and error, with a heavy emphasis on the error. "I have learned throughout my life as a composer chiefly through my mistakes and pursuits of false assumptions," Igor Stravinsky emphasized. Only through determined effort, the kind of effort that requires almost constant devotion to the task at hand, is a piece of beautiful music produced. "Songwriting is about getting the demon out of me," John Lennon once explained, describing what it takes to write music: "It's like being possessed. You try to go to sleep, but the song won't let you. So you have to get up and make it into something, and then you're allowed to sleep." Writing, too, is like making music: you're trying to produce the best composition you can and, while you're writing, you're focused on little else.[3]

Whereas the *pre-writing* phase of the writing process *prepares* you to write, the actual writing or drafting is the real test of one's nerve. Here, a single approach does not suit all, as people vary greatly in the way they like to compose. When I write, I like to be alone and in a quiet place so that I can concentrate on what I'm doing. That's because I (like so many writers I know) like solitude and freedom from distractions so I can stay on task. Studies of distracted drivers, such as those who use cell phones as they navigate through traffic, confirm that it's hard to do more than one thing at a time. Multitasking may be a fact of life in the modern era, but research shows it generally decreases the level of one's performance. One study of 1,000 officeworkers found that interruptions at work consume an average of 2.1 hours per workday, and that the recovery time associated with getting back on task greatly decreases worker productivity. I often write under less than ideal circumstances, such as in my office with a constantly ringing phone, but I do my best writing when I can focus intensely, not only on the writing itself, but on all my assembled research materials. If I'm distracted, writing is much harder.[4]

But everybody is different, and I know others prefer listening to music whenever they write and are unfazed by noisier environments. I myself sometimes listen to jazz or classical music while I write, but I find music with lyrics too distracting. Indeed, research shows that, for some, music can actually *block out* distractions, making it easier to concentrate on the task to be done. A study of surgeons, for example, found their performances improved when they listened to music, with concertos working the best. The most popular pick: Vivaldi's "Four Seasons." Thus, if you like listening to rap, rhythm and blues, rock and roll, classical music, or even easy listening songs while you write, that's okay—so long as you don't feel it's impairing the quality of your work. Whatever works best for you *is* best for you. Writing requires that you get in a groove, and if you need music to do that, by all means turn on the radio or hit the play button.[5]

The writing process itself actually transforms one's mental state. You go from being fully aware of all of your surroundings to being singularly focused on the page or screen in front of you. When I write, I often lose track of time. I may be typing away at my keyboard, or working intently on rewriting a piece of writing, only to look at my wristwatch and see that two or three hours have elapsed. If that happens to you, you know you're doing something right—that you're using the writing process effectively—because you *should* lose track of time when you write. "Writing moves you into a place of intense concentration similar to the concentration of chess and other complex games but more richly colored with feeling," writer Richard Rhodes explains in his book, *How to Write*. That observation, I'd say, is dead-on; it captures the essence of what the writing process is all about, and explains why writing so aids creativity.[6]

As you compose, writing can be rejuvenating, too. Spending time alone in contemplation—whether in a church pew, at home, or by walking in the woods or along a beach—can reinvigorate your senses and lead to profound insight, and that is precisely what time spent writing should seek to achieve. The essayist and nature writer Paul Gruchow, in his thought-provoking book, *Boundary Waters*, describes the effect one is looking to achieve in a writing session. "Writing—any art—happens in a peculiar state of mind," he says, "more subconscious than deliberate, that the handbooks on the subject are always hard-put, and a bit embarrassed, to describe: a kind of trance, it is often said, but really an induced and alert dreaming." In your own writing life, pay attention to the conditions that help you write most effectively and then try to replicate them as often as possible. Following a set routine can be especially conducive to producing a large quantity of high-quality writing.[7]

Whenever you write, you'll be—as writer William Styron puts it—"tapping unconscious sources." You'll be drawing upon memories, the brain's vast storage banks of data, and your mind's innermost (and most private) thoughts. You'll also find yourself focusing intensely on the page or screen in front of you—if not right away, then shortly thereafter. That's because the writing process demands one's attention. Author Doris Lessing describes the writing process this way: "At first it's a bit jagged, awkward, but then there's a point where there's a click and you suddenly become quite fluent." It may not happen immediately, but as your writing session goes on, it will happen. Writing can actually produce a calming effect, where distractions, worries and anxiety dissipate or disappear. One's quest to find the right words must be relentless, and might be likened to the process of putting together a difficult puzzle; after finding the edge pieces and building the frame, one's mind becomes singularly focused on fitting the oddly shaped pieces together. Just as you can lose track of time while working on a puzzle, what may seem like minutes of writing may turn out to have been hours of writing time when you look at the clock.[8]

Effective writers begin by getting something down on the page, however rough, random or incoherent in form. This technique is known as *freewriting*. You can write about the weather, a family member, the past, or really anything at all. You can explore personal experiences, someone else's experiences, or a relationship, place, object, image or emotion—anger, jealousy or love, for example. You may even jot down a series of loosely connected words or scraps of information on a given subject (say, work, cooking, sports or friendship) that, to an outside observer, might appear to be gibberish. All you are trying to do is download information from the mind to the page—without worrying about the content or order of what's there. The German poet, novelist and playwright Johann Wolfgang von Goethe said it well, "Once you feel the urge and the need to write, you must put whatever comes to your lips or your pen straight down without hesitating or selecting." You must refrain from all self-criticism; otherwise, you'll lose your finest inspiration, what he called the richest flowerings of the imagination.[9]

When freewriting, avoid perfectionism or letting your conscious mind intrude on the workings of your unconscious mind. Trying to achieve perfection or being overly critical of yourself while you're writing will only inhibit your ability to keep putting new words on the page. The goal of first drafts is to build a mass of material and to reveal your mind at work by writing down what William James, in *The Principles of Psychology*, called "the stream of thought, of consciousness." Don't hesitate to linger over words, but try to keep your pen or fingertips moving. The poet Walt Whitman—one of the great masters of language—spoke of trying to capture "the very heartbeat of life" by writing "at the instant." "The secret of it all," Whitman said, "is to write in the gush, the throb, the flood, of the moment—to put things down without deliberation—without worrying about their style—without waiting for a fit time or place." Even if you can't immediately think of something to write about, just keep sitting there. When an idea comes or a word pops into your head, get it down right away. The longer you write, the more thoughts and ideas will come to you.[10]

First drafts are meant to be just that, so you should not get frustrated or discouraged by the fact that your first words do not read well or as well as you think they should read. Ernest Hemingway was particularly blunt about what he expected from his initial efforts. "All first drafts are shit," he said. "The only thing that matters about your first draft," he declared, "is that you finish it." The faster you write, the less self-conscious you'll be about what you're putting down on the page and the more material you'll have to rework later. Experienced writers know that writing quickly puts usable material on the page and that usable material is what makes good writing possible. "The faster I can write," says newspaper columnist and novelist Russell Banks, "the more likely I'll get something worth saving down on paper." On a first draft, another writer, Raymond Carver, urged, you must have faith that something's going to come of your efforts and just barrel on through, saving any thoughtful reflections for later, after your initial draft is done.[11]

In her book, *Writing Down the Bones: Freeing the Writer Within*, Natalie Goldberg urges the use of writing exercises to hone one's writing skills. "The basic unit of writing practice," she says, "is the timed exercise"—a commitment to write "for ten minutes, twenty minutes, or an hour." I agree. By following Goldberg's suggestions for freewriting exercises—"Keep your hand moving," "Don't cross out," "Don't worry about spelling, punctuation, grammar," "Lose control," "Don't think. Don't get logical."—a person will write *something* and become comfortable writing. Errors in logic or grammar, punctuation or spelling always can be ironed out later, but if a person doesn't get at least something on the page, she or he will have nothing to work with later. *After* you're done freewriting is the time to begin building your composition. Freewriting is about letting loose your creativity. The third and fourth stages of the writing process—revision and proofreading—allow ample time for language to become more polished and for mistakes to be corrected.[12]

Although freewriting helps you get underway, the making of an artful composition requires much more than recording your thoughts as they first occur to you. As Linda Trichter Metcalf and Tobin Simon explain in *Writing the Mind Alive*: "Expression isn't enough; reflection is also required." The act of writing, by capturing thoughts on paper, allows us to analyze and ruminate over them, giving us as much time as we need to examine them from all angles. Indeed, unrecorded ideas, however good, may vanish forever as they are subject to the frailties of human memory. "A disappearing target like spoken thought is not good enough for reflection, but written thought stays put," Metcalf and Simon emphasize. By writing, one freezes one's thoughts, though those thoughts can always later be thawed—and take on a different form and texture—through revision. Why are reflection and analysis so important? Because we see things we didn't see right away; we may look at things differently after we think twice.[13]

In giving form to material produced by freewriting (and I'll say more about that momentarily), every writer has false starts. When that happens, don't let it discourage or deter you from continuing on with your writing project. Every bit of writing is time well spent, if for no other reason than because the writing you do will inform your work as you go on. Even if you end up at a dead end and can't use what you've written because it doesn't fit or turns out to be all wrong, at least you know what *won't work*. That itself is new knowledge. As writer Brenda Ueland explains, no writing is a waste of time. "With every sentence you write," she notes, "you have learned something. It has done you good. It has stretched your understanding." Writing makes you think (and think critically), which is precisely the point. Your writing may take you down winding roads, or even force you to make some U-turns, but you are enriched and enlightened by the experience.[14]

Before discussing drafting and composition techniques, I feel compelled to say a few words to those who fear writing and all that it entails. For some, I'm aware, the prospect of writing a ten- or twenty-page paper or a lengthy document, such as a grant or sales proposal, may instill a sense of apprehension, even extreme anxiety. In college, I myself often waited until the last minute to start working on papers for class. It wasn't necessarily that I dreaded writing them; it was more that I didn't know quite how to begin and approach each one—and feared I wouldn't be able to come up with an interesting topic and write a stellar paper within the allotted time. I know now that such fears are misplaced. Pre-writing jitters are normal, but starting to write helps put those jitters at bay. If anything, a person confronted with a writing project should welcome the challenge it poses, not be intimidated by it. All you have to do is begin. As President Franklin D. Roosevelt famously remarked, "the only thing we have to fear is fear itself—nameless, unreasoning, unjustified terror which paralyzes needed efforts to convert retreat into advance."[15]

The first step toward overcoming fear of the writing process is to better understand that process. Writer and traveler-adventurer Gerald Brenan, a twentieth-century literary figure who fought in World War I and once shipped 2,000 books to a remote Spanish village to educate himself as a writer, aptly explained why that is so. "Words are as recalcitrant as circus animals," he noted, "and the unskilled trainer can crack his whip at them in vain." "It is by sitting down to write every morning," Brenan said, "that one becomes a writer." What I've come to know is this: *writing itself* brings greater understanding of the writing process, less fear of it, and will, in the end, produce consistently better writing over time. The time of day you write is not the key, for you can write whenever it suits you, according to your specific needs or preferences. It *is* important, however, *that you write.* There is just no substitute for the act of writing where learning to write effectively—or any fear of writing—is concerned. If you don't write, you'll never learn how to do it and you'll always harbor unjustified fears about the writing process.[16]

The only thing that stands in your way of becoming a better writer is procrastination—the thing, I submit, that should be feared more than fear itself. Procrastination only produces anxiety, and the time spent worrying about how to complete a project could be spent actually doing it. If you feel overwhelmed by a writing project, *start it. Begin* the research, *begin* the first draft, *begin* revising. The longer you wait to start a project, the more mentally arduous it will become. If you don't start, you'll never see progress and you'll never get to the revision, proofreading and publication stages of the writing process; it's just a fact of life. And trust me, no matter how daunting the task, you can do it if you just apply yourself. Just think for a second. How many times have you put off a school or work assignment, thinking you'd never get it done, only to finish it at the last minute when the pressure was on and you knew you *had* to do it? Perhaps it wasn't as *well-written* as you would have liked, but I bet it usually—if not always—got done. If it didn't get done, then it's time to turn over a new leaf, especially now that you're armed with new information about the writing process.

To keep yourself writing, and to make sure you always have something to write about outside of compulsory writing projects, keep a journal or a running list of things you'd like to explore in your writing. What are your interests or obsessions? What places or memories can't you forget? Who are the people or historical figures you are most drawn to? Then sit down and write about them. If you just can't seem to think of anything worthwhile to write about, get ideas from friends or family members or check out books such as Jack Heffron's *The Writer's Idea Book*, which contains over 400 prompts and exercises that can get you started with a writing session. The ideas it suggests range from writing about a person you know to reading a newspaper or a page from a favorite book. The idea is to practice enough so that writing becomes a habit, something done on a routine, if not daily, basis. As your writing gets better and better and writing becomes a habit for you, you'll look forward to writing as much as you look forward to eating meals, seeing friends, or showering after a hard workout.[17]

When you write, no subject should be considered off-limits. Good writers don't shy away from controversial subjects, and they use whatever techniques they can to get themselves going and complete their compositions. John Gardner, a renowned writing teacher, advocates writing regularly, coupled with experimentation. "One of the best ways of learning to write," he said, "is by doing exercises." Write a three-page monologue, write dialogue between two characters who have secrets, describe how a bird sees a landscape, he suggested as possibilities. Other techniques are useful, too. *Clustering*—grouping together circled words or ideas and then connecting the circles with lines to see how they relate to one another—is a proven way to generate good ideas, as is *brainstorming*, either alone or with others. Jot down ideas in quick succession, just as a CEO might fill up a white board in a corporate boardroom with jottings in a determined effort to solve a perplexing distribution problem. One technique I've found helpful to generate good ideas is to write a series of sentences beginning with "I wish...," "I believe...," or "I remember..."; this will give you a ready-made list of things to write about later.[18]

By writing frequently, you'll also fend off *writer's block*, what writing consultant Cathleen Rountree calls "a temporary or chronic inability to put words on paper" and what author Ralph Keyes calls "the unconscious mind exercising its right to remain silent even as the conscious one wonders what in the heck is going on." Writing practice keeps your mind limber and ready to capture its insights when they arrive—as they inevitably do. And by writing on a regular basis, you'll prove to yourself that you *can* write—and can write even when you don't feel like writing. You'll even discover that writing at times when you don't particularly feel like it can lead to *a desire to write* as a writing session, only reluctantly begun, progresses. As neurologist Alice Flaherty, of Harvard Medical School, explains in her book, *The Midnight Disease: The Drive to Write, Writer's Block, and the Creative Brain*: "writing regularly, inspiration or no, is not a bad way to eventually get into an inspired mood; the plane has to bump along the runway for a while before it finally takes off." Indeed, accomplished writers know that if you wait for inspiration, for some magical moment to occur when one's fear of writing suddenly disappears and one feels like writing, you may never find yourself in the mood to write.[19]

People's fear of writing is real and certainly cannot be minimized or brushed aside. Even the most experienced writers are not immune. "All my life, I've been frightened at the moment I sit down to write," award-winning, Columbian-born writer Gabriel García Márquez notes. "Blank pages inspire me with terror," famed novelist Margaret Atwood concedes. Such fears are understandable. Again, writing is hard. A little self-doubt is to be expected, and is healthy even. Those who have no apprehension at all about the writing process simply may not appreciate how hard it is to write well, or may just have low standards for their writing. If fear of writing is common, then freewriting is the antidote to writer's block. In fact, writer Tom Wolfe calls writer's block a "misnomer" for what's really just ordinary fear. What freewriting does is help you overcome that fear. As you start filling up that first page, any fear of writing will subside as you realize that you're doing the very thing that you thought you couldn't do—or couldn't do well. Freewriting, Flaherty explains, loosens up the writer and decreases one's fear of writing. Similarly, the more you revise and proofread, the more familiar and less anxious you'll feel about those processes.[20]

In his book, *The Courage to Write: How Writers Transcend Fear*, Ralph Keyes describes writing as both frightening and exhilarating. "Trying to deny, avoid, numb, or eradicate the fear of writing is neither possible nor desirable," he says, calling anxiety an inevitable and necessary part of the writing process. I agree. Because writing has permanence and brings with it the risk of criticism, even ridicule, it naturally makes people reticent to reveal on paper what they believe. "A writing block," Keyes concludes, "is little more than the brain's sensible section flashing: DANGER AHEAD. STOP!" Noting that putting words on paper *but not for public consumption* can help relieve writing anxiety, Keyes, too, advocates the regular use of freewriting to cope with any fear of writing one may have. He likens the product of freewriting to "a sculptor's wet clay." The use of the technique gives writers a dose of confidence and essential materials to work with before the real work begins: fashioning a coherent, readable text from material created by freewriting, as a sculptor molds a beautiful statue from a pile of slippery clay. The freewriting you do can remain private, so there's no need to have anxiety about how your initial efforts look. It's what you do with the mass of material that freewriting generates that matters the most.[21]

Writers, of course, differ widely in their approaches to building a composition. I heard a talk some time ago by Scott Russell Sanders, an essayist, nature writer and teacher at Indiana University, my alma mater. He says there are two kinds of writers: those who spill everything out onto the page at once and then organize it later, and those who write one sentence at a time, always looking back after each sentence is written to make sure that all the preceding sentences and paragraphs are well-written and still make sense. I do both. I always know I can revise what I write, so I often freewrite at the beginning of a writing session. Writing with speed and a lack of precision helps me form a rough sketch of what I want to cover or say, and writing quickly also brings to the fore my most creative and intuitive thoughts. But now that I've been writing for so many years, I sometimes like to find the precise word I'm looking for when I'm in the moment thinking about a particular word choice. If I can feel the right word or phrase coming, I may wait until it's arrived before moving on. I realize that it's important to get down on the page a *quantity* of words, but I also know that it's important not to forget *quality*. Thus, I now tend to revise my work as I go along, sometimes even while I'm sketching out a first draft.

Some people view the writing process as a strictly linear process. Pre-writing, then freewriting, comes first; revision follows; then proofreading is done before publication. Properly understood, however, the writing process is not that rigid or inflexible. Researchers studying the writing process, in fact, have found that the stages of writing are not always clear cut or done sequentially. The process of composing text is much different for beginning writers than it is for, say, experienced journalists and editors. The way in which text is created and revised is just one example. Whereas inexperienced writers often view the first draft as being close to a final draft, and see the revision step as simply a "rewording" activity, experienced writers know that many drafts will be necessary and view the main goal of revision as discovering the form or shape of their argument or composition. Likewise, studies have found that experienced writers had more concern for their audience and their reader's expectations throughout the writing process. While college freshmen tend to view their first drafts as needing only mechanical corrections, more experienced writers routinely make changes to initial drafts that alter the structure and content of a text, using the writing process to discover meaning.[22]

What I'm saying is this: as a writer gains confidence and experience and learns the tricks of the writing process, the way in which that process is used will evolve. At first, it's advisable to separate the freewriting and revision steps. If you neatly divide the writing process, Peter Elbow explains in *Writing with Power*, you can exploit the "opposing muscles" of creativity and critical thinking one at a time; "fast early writing" allows you to be "loose and accepting," while revision allows you to be "critically toughminded." But experienced writers tend to mix it up: a little freewriting here, a little revision there, more freewriting, more revision, and so on till the project is sufficiently ready for proofreading. Be practical, let your brain work as you see fit. Just be cognizant of your objective in writing. "If you have a deadline," Elbow says, analogizing the writing process to an elliptical, orbiting voyage, "divide your total available time: half for raw writing, half for revising." As Elbow explains: "For the first half, *the voyage out*, you do pieces of almost-freewriting during which you allow yourself to curve out into space—allow yourself, that is, to ignore or even forget exactly what your topic is. For the second half, *the voyage home*, you bend your efforts back into the gravitational field of your original topic as you select, organize, and revise parts of what you produced during the voyage out." Once the writing process is understood, it's all really a matter of personal preference as to how you use it.[23]

Because people write in such individualized ways, the craft of writing might be likened to flyfishing. There are proven techniques for writing and catching fish, but every writer and angler works a little differently, albeit *within certain parameters*. Just as the two brothers in Norman Maclean's popular novella, *A River Runs Through It*, each flyfish on Montana's Big Blackfoot River in an individualized way—one selecting a Bunyan Bug No. 2 Yellow Stone Fly and the other constantly switching flies—every writer must discover the method and rhythm that works best for herself or himself. There are certain things every successful angler must know, but how that knowledge is translated into use varies by individual. Having pen and paper or a fishing pole and tackle box enables one to write or fish, but one needs a guide—at least at the beginning—to learn the scope of potential techniques that can be employed. "It is an art that is performed on a four-count rhythm between ten and two o'clock," the boys' father, wearing a glove on his casting hand, instructs his sons on how to fly cast in Maclean's famous story. Similarly, the art of writing is about using well-known techniques *within a prescribed range of acceptability* to reach one's audience. One should always choose a workable structure and process, but beyond that one is free to develop a writing process and style that best suits the writer and the writing task at hand.[24]

Let's turn now (as promised) to the difficult issues writers face as part of the composition or drafting process. When writing, a writer must grapple almost immediately with four fundamental issues: topic, theme, form and perspective. The topic is the specific subject of a piece of writing. The theme is the central idea of a composition, though longer writings may, of course, have more than one theme. The form—what painter Ben Shahn calls "the shape of content"—is simply the pattern or format in which the writing is organized, whereas perspective, or point-of-view, deals with the angle or position from which a story is told or information is delivered. A writer must consider all of these things carefully, as they are integral components of effective writing. What you present, how you present it, and from what vantage point all influence the entire written work and how it will be perceived. The objective is to create highly readable, thought-provoking prose, though how you get there is up to you. Content, by definition, will have a form; the writer's role is to put the content in the best possible form so it has the maximum effect.[25]

As to the first issue, the writer's topic, a writer always prefers an engaging subject, not only to keep the audience's interest but to hold the writer's interest over the course of the writing project. (Sometimes, obviously, the writer has no such luxury, as the topic is assigned, not chosen.) As to the second issue, a thoughtful, clear theme is crucial if you want readers to understand what you're saying and to take away something meaningful from your writing. If you can't articulate your main theme in a single, declarative sentence, you probably don't have one. That means you'll need to do more research or go back to the drawing board and re-tool your thinking on your topic before you will be able to articulate what you really want to say. I've seen this particular problem with law students I've taught over the years in my death penalty seminar. As they struggle with paper topics or draft their papers, they often spend too little time *framing the issue*. If one's topic and theme, as framed, are too general or vague, one's writing on whatever subject is chosen will seem that way too. Only concisely framed issues will uncover the right questions and generate reasoned, understandable answers to those questions. Of course, it's often necessary to do a rough draft—or multiple drafts—before your ideas, and a clear topic and theme, emerge.

In deciding how best to convey information or tell a story, the writer must consider lots of questions, many of which are tied up with the issues of audience and format of presentation. What form will be used? A diary entry, a letter or e-mail, a book, a magazine article, an essay, a poem, a fictional story? And how will that form be used? Who will speak? The writer, using "I" and "me" and speaking in the first-person; a second-person voice, in which the writer uses "you" as if talking to the reader; or a narrator, speaking in the third-person, created by the writer? Likewise, at whom will the writing be directed? Are you writing for yourself? A family member, a friend, a boss, a group of total strangers? Is your audience made up of Ph.D.'s or junior-high students? Are the members of your audience of a particular religious or ethnic background, or do they have something in common, such as AIDS, breast cancer or a commitment to protecting the environment? The writer's task is to carefully choose the form and approach that best fits the occasion and objective at hand.[26]

Readers' expectations should be considered carefully in selecting the form. That's because writing is typically done for readers, and different forms each have their own quirks and benefits and limitations. An e-mail or letter, for example, allows spontaneity and intimacy, whereas a memo for work requires more formality and precision and is likely to be less entertaining than, say, a missive to a friend or a joke written by a comedian. If you're looking to reach a wider audience, newspaper or magazine articles offer writers a degree of flexibility, but publications usually restrict the number of words, forcing content to be condensed. Books give writers much more space in which to work, but not everyone always has the time to read them (let alone write them). Poems—often short and sweet and full of imagery—require rigorous attention to issues of rhythm and sound, but may not be suitable for conveying certain types of information such as statistical data or the kind of information usually found in charts or bar graphs. When you write, try to put yourself in your readers' shoes and choose your form wisely because the success of your writing depends upon it.[27]

The point-of-view decision you make is particularly critical (and should not be an afterthought) because it shapes the entire way in which a piece of writing is put together. "Rather than thinking of point of view as an opinion or belief," explains writer Janet Burroway, "begin with the more literal synonym of 'vantage point.' *Who* is standing *where* to watch the scene." As Burroway advises, ask yourself these questions: "*Who speaks? To whom? In what form? At what distance from the action? With what limitations?*" A first-person account puts you, as narrator, front and center, whereas second- and third-person accounts are not restricted by the "I" perspective. If it didn't happen in front of the narrator, the writer of a first-person account will only be able to report hearsay or rumors about what happened. Use of the second-person form, which turns readers into participants, is more uncommon, though it's a staple of how-to guides, as this book demonstrates. Third-person accounts give you freedom, but they also distance you, as the writer, from the prose. Therefore, think hard about what you want to achieve with your writing—and what information you have to convey—before selecting your point-of-view.[28]

After choosing a topic and theme, and settling on a form and an appropriate point of view, the writer must then decide what to say and how best to say it. All of these things are subject to change in the midst of a writing project, but when you write, you must start somewhere—with at least a provisional approach in mind. Once you've gathered your research materials and laid them out in front of you, try to discern what those materials are telling you. "The discipline of the writer," environmentalist Rachel Carson said, "is to learn to be still and listen to what his subject has to say." Wilderness advocate Sigurd Olson used the term "creative silence," which, he said, brings about "the awakening of ideas and thoughts normally hidden when one is with others, the emergence of concepts often lost owing to interruptions and responsibilities." Oftentimes, you'll only find your ideas, or the right words to express yourself, in the thick of the writing process when your mind is freed from other distractions. Sigurd Olson actually had a special, shoreline rock he loved to go to in northern Minnesota, a place he called Listening Point, where he so often found inspiration for his writing. "Everyone has a listening-point somewhere," Olson wrote, emphasizing that "only when one comes to listen, only when one is aware and still, can things be seen and heard."[29]

To guide you, either before you write or after you've already done some freewriting, craft an outline of what you want to say (or perhaps more accurately, what you *think* you want to say). This can be extremely important, at least if you're dealing with a writing project of any complexity. Visualizing the structure of a draft—whether you plan to write a continuously flowing essay or use Roman numeral headings and subheadings to break up the text—gives you at least a skeletal conception of what you plan to say before you try to say it. An outline will also help you define your topic and theme and help you assess if your ideas are structured—and will therefore be presented—in a logical order or progression. As Peter Elbow explains in *Writing with Power*: "An outline, by its nature, almost forces you to figure out what you really mean. And because of its compressed visual form, it permits you to see your whole train of thought or narrative in one glance and thereby detect problems you miss when you go through your writing more slowly." I create outlines all the time, and I find them extremely useful for almost any writing project.[30]

The building blocks of good prose are well-crafted sentences and paragraphs. In an article, essay or other composition, each paragraph should generally have a topic sentence, and the sentences in that paragraph should normally support that topic sentence. In addition, all of the sentences and paragraphs within a composition should further the overarching theme of the piece of writing. As you create topic sentences and lay out the supporting evidence, beware of sweeping generalizations and vague or ambiguous language. Whereas undocumented and vaguely worded generalizations are bland and weak (and may not even be true), logical statements and conclusions supported by specific, verifiable information make for lively and compelling prose. As you add particulars and specificity, you use spacing and pacing to give your ideas grain and texture. Paragraph breaks separate the larger ideas of a composition, giving readers a little white space between them. As the constituent parts of paragraphs, of course, sentences must do the heavy lifting when it comes to expressing ideas and supporting those ideas with concrete facts and persuasive arguments.

If a writer makes a sweeping generalization, such as "space exploration is important for the advancement of science," then the writer should back up that generalization with facts or arguments, preferably both. For example, it might be emphasized that experiments conducted at the international space station or on shuttle missions have increased our scientific knowledge of weightlessness and lightning. Did you know that low-light level TV cameras on shuttle missions have recorded a total of nineteen images of upward, vertical discharges of lightning moving out from the top of thunderstorms? Or that on the shuttle mission Endeavor in December 2001, scientists, looking for ways to save cork oak trees in the Maamora forest in Morocco, studied the effects of weightlessness on the development of gypsy moths? A writer might further note that the Spirit and Opportunity rovers, which landed on Mars, discovered that water once flowed across that planet's surface, giving us new insight into the question of whether Mars was ever capable of supporting life.[31]

When writing, always put your best foot forward and don't hold anything back, unless you're doing so out of tactfulness or to be polite, which, of course, are valid and honorable reasons. As Annie Dillard explains in her best-selling book, *The Writing Life*: "Write as if you were dying. At the same time, assume you write for an audience consisting solely of terminal patients. That is, after all, the case. What would you begin writing if you knew you would die soon? What could you say to a dying person that would not enrage by its triviality?" Dillard emphasizes that writers should never hoard good material for later, and I wholeheartedly concur. "One of the few things I know about writing," she writes, "is this: spend it all, shoot it, play it, lose it, all, right away, every time." Something better will arise for later, she wisely explains, adding, "These things fill from behind, from beneath, like well water." If you have faith in yourself and continue to write, you'll find new words each time you pick up a pen or go to your computer keyboard. "When you write," Dillard says, "you lay out a line of words. The line of words is a miner's pick, a woodcarver's gouge, a surgeon's probe. You wield it, and it digs a path you follow. Soon you find yourself deep in new territory."[32]

Endings, of course, are often the most difficult to write. Ideally, a good ending provides closure for readers even as it creates a passageway—a new way of thinking—for readers to follow after leaving the text. If you're trying to influence people, an ending is your last chance to do that. One way to create a good ending is to come back to an image or detail that you used as an attention-getting device at the beginning, giving the piece of writing a satisfying sense of unity. In *On Writing Well*, William Zinsser speaks of good endings providing a "sense of symmetry" and "resonance" and says this: "The perfect ending should take your readers slightly by surprise and yet seem exactly right." It's hard to create that kind of ending, but it can be done if you put enough thought into it. Re-reading what you've written after you think you've finished it is one way to help you discover that perfect ending—as well as the best beginning. "The last thing one discovers in composing a work," the French mathematician Blaise Pascal said from experience, "is what to put first."[33]

Writing a lengthy piece of writing can be a daunting task, but only if one thinks of it that way. What good writers know is that almost any project, when broken down into small tasks, becomes manageable. The novelist John Steinbeck, author of such classics as *The Grapes of Wrath*, *Of Mice and Men* and *Cannery Row*, put it well: "When I face the desolate impossibility of writing five hundred pages a sick sense of failure falls on me and I know I can never do it. This happens every time. Then gradually I write one page and then another." Eventually, Steinbeck's novels got finished. Most writing projects, of course, do not involve hundreds of pages of words; but even if they do, the important thing to remember is that the work will get done if the job is broken down and tackled one item at a time. If you're writing about the Vietnam War, don't try to write about the whole war, as well as its historical consequences and cultural impact, all at once; instead, break up your research and writing into smaller segments, tackling, say, one specific battle or firefight at a time. Your compositions will get done, but only if you keep your composure, don't allow yourself to get overwhelmed, and *compose*.[34]

To create a composition that you will be proud of, you need to start, then keep going—even when it all looks hopeless or you start to think that you've only created a big mess. The best advice I can give to aspiring writers—or those who just want to be more effective communicators—is to make time to write and then use that time efficiently. Set aside periods of time to write, daily if possible, and make writing a part of your life and something you look forward to doing. And whether you're writing for yourself or for publication, set realistic, concrete goals—300 or 400 words a day, 1,500 or 2,000 words per week, or even more if you can spare the time. Once you've set those goals—call them word quotas, if you like—strive to meet them and do meet them. Don't dawdle. You can create a masterful composition if only you put in the time it takes to do so. As the Roman philosopher Epictetus long ago proclaimed, "If you wish to be a writer, write." It's simple advice, but it also happens to be true. Only by writing does one become a better writer. And only by writing are compositions ever born.[35]

Imagination is not enough. Knowledge is necessary. –Paul Scott • I have always been puzzled by the idea that we writers should lay down our sense of good and evil before we take up our pens. –Bjørnstjerne Bjørnson • I call upon the intellectual community in this country and abroad to stand up for freedom of the imagination, an issue much larger than my book or indeed my life. –Salman Rushdie • The test of a first-rate intelligence is the ability to hold two opposed ideas in the mind at the same time, and still retain the ability to function. –F. Scott Fitzgerald • When you are writing you will probably think harder than you ever have in your life and more clearly. –Brenda Ueland • In the long run of history, the censor and the inquisitor have always lost. The only sure weapon against bad ideas is better ideas. –Alfred Whitney Griswold • Now is the time to thrust forward new leaders with new ideas. This is no time for timidity. –Paul Wellstone • Words are like money; there is nothing so useless, unless when in actual use. –Samuel Butler • Delay is natural to a writer. He is like a surfer—he bides his time, waits for the perfect wave on which to ride in. Delay is instinctive with him. He waits for the surge (of emotion? of strength? of courage?) that will carry him along. –E. B. White • Inspiration, then, is the impulse which sets creation in movement: it is also the energy which keeps it going. –Roger Sessions • Creation begins typically with a vague, even a confused excitement, some sort of yearning, hunch, or other preverbal intimation of approaching or potential resolution. –Brewster Ghiselin • Do not fire too much over the heads of your readers. –Anthony Trollope • Writing teachers invariably tell students: Write about what you know. That's, of course, what you have to do, but on the other hand, how do you know what you know until you've written about it. Writing is knowing. What did Kafka know? The insurance business? –E. L. Doctorow • All thought is a feat of association: having what's in front of you bring up something in your mind that you almost didn't know you knew. Putting this and that together. That click. –Robert Frost • A classic is a book that has never finished saying what it has to say. –Italo Calvino • There are three kinds of readers: one, who enjoys without judging; a third, who judges without enjoying; another in the middle, who judges while enjoying and enjoys while judging. The last class truly reproduces a work of art anew; its members are not numerous. –Johann Wolfgang von Goethe • Books bring with them detachment and a critical attitude that is not possible in a society dependent on the spoken word. –David Riesman • Keep reading books, but remember that a book's only a book, and you should learn to think for yourself. –Maxim Gorky

IDEAS

If you believe everything you read, better not read. –Japanese proverb • In reading, when I come upon an unfamiliar word or phrase I have a sensation of derailment. –Roger Brown • I like the provisional nature of unprinted material held in the computer's memory—like an unspoken thought. –Ian McEwan • Sometimes you can lick an especially hard problem by facing it always the very first thing in the morning with the very freshest part of your mind. This has so often worked with me that I have an uncanny faith in it. –F. Scott Fitzgerald • A poem doesn't exist till it's written. –Randall Jarrell • Writing is a long process of introspection; it is a voyage toward the darkest caverns of consciousness, a long, slow meditation. I write feeling my way in silence, and along the way discover particles of truth, small crystals that fit in the palm of one hand and justify my passage through this world. –Isabel Allende • Many times I just sit for three hours with no ideas coming to me. But I know one thing: if an idea does come between nine and twelve, I am there ready for it. –Flannery O'Connor • All words are pegs to hang ideas on. –Henry Ward Beecher • Sound sense is the first principle and source of writing well. –Horace • The telephone book is full of facts, but it doesn't contain a single idea. –Mortimer J. Adler • But words are things, and a small drop of ink, falling like dew, upon a thought, produces that which makes thousands, perhaps, millions, think. –Lord Byron • A great flame follows a little spark. –Dante Alighieri • It is impossible for a muddy thinker to write good English. –William Zinsser • To write jargon is to be perpetually shuffling around in the fog. –Sir Arthur Quiller-Couch • I disapprove of what you say, but will defend to the death your right to say it. –S. G. Tallentyre • Reading furnishes the mind only with materials of knowledge; it is thinking that makes what we read ours. –John Locke • What spectacle can be more edifying or more seasonable, than that of liberty and learning, each leaning on the other for their mutual and surest support. –James Madison • Good writing is making yourself a clear transparency for an idea worth writing about. –Janet Aiken • Each writer is born with a repertory company in his head. –Gore Vidal • It is a good thing for an uneducated man to read books of quotations. –Winston Churchill • Grasp the subject, the words will follow. –Cato the Elder • Real education consists in drawing the best out of yourself. What better book can there be than the book of humanity? –Mahatma Gandhi • If there is anything worse for a writer than missing the bus, it is being thought twenty years later, to have got on the wrong one. –Paul Scott • When an old man dies, a library burns down. –African proverb • The discipline of the written word punishes both stupidity and dishonesty. –John Steinbeck • Good books are the warehouses of ideas. –H. G. Wells • If we had to say what writing is, we would define it essentially as an act of courage. –Cynthia Ozick • Writing is a way to explore a question and gain control over it. –Joan Countryman • An idea can have value in itself, but its usefulness diminishes to the extent that you can't articulate it to someone else. –Kevin Byrne • Our life is what our thoughts make it. –Marcus Aurelius • It is by logic that we prove, but by intuition that we discover. –Henri Poincaré • Words are the small change of thought. –Jules Renard

If you can't write your idea on the back of my calling card,
you don't have a clear idea.

—David Belasco, theatrical producer

The act of writing is the act of discovering what you believe.

—David Hare, British playwright

Words set things in motion. I've seen them doing it.
Words set up atmospheres, electrical fields, charges.

—Toni Cade Bambara, American writer

No army can withstand the strength of an idea whose time has come.

—Victor Hugo, French author

CHAPTER SIX

Substance Matters

Ideas are rooted in thoughts, and those thoughts and ideas drive human progress and our communications with one another. We are all capable of thoughts and thus all capable of coming up with good ideas—ideas that can help others as well as ourselves. Inventors and creative thinkers study the ideas of others and then come up with something new. Eli Whitney invented the cotton gin, the Wright brothers pioneered flight and the field of aviation, and other innovators have made our lives easier, safer or more productive by translating their ideas into actions. Some breakthroughs have literally allowed us to see better. Mary Anderson patented the windshield wiper in 1905 after seeing New York City streetcar drivers opening their windows when it rained; her invention became standard equipment on American cars by 1916. Dr. Patricia Bath, an ophthalmologist, became the first African-American woman doctor to patent a medical device when she developed a probe to allow cataracts to be painlessly vaporized from patients' eyes. Physician and humanitarian Albert Schweitzer believed that every new idea is in some way embedded in older ones, a recognition that we must first learn before we can innovate. Bath's patented device, for example, came about only after years of study in her quest to treat and prevent blindness.[1]

If you want to accomplish something, whether in science, in the arts or humanities, or through your writing, you need to come up with good ideas through reflection. As Ralph Waldo Emerson said, "Thought is the seed of action." This means developing your mind and making it receptive to new ideas—something writing does quite well. In our daily lives, we think in what MIT professor and brain researcher Steven Pinker calls "mentalese" or the "language of thought." This mental process is unlike English or any other spoken language, but everyone does it. "People without a language would still have mentalese," Pinker explains, noting that "if babies did not have a mentalese to translate to and from English, it is not clear how learning English could take place." Spoken and written language, when acquired, thus supplement our mentalese, giving us greater mental capacity and enabling us to articulate thoughts and ideas and to communicate more effectively with one another. "Knowing a language," as Pinker says, "is knowing how to translate mentalese into strings of words and vice versa."[2]

The mind, which makes mentalese and human language possible, is uniquely engineered to allow us to act, speak and write. Made up of one hundred billion nerve cells, or *neurons*, the human brain has two mirror-image halves, known as the *cerebral hemispheres*. These hemispheres sit atop the *brain stem*, the major route by which information is sent to (and received from) the spinal cord and cranial and peripheral nerves. Both hemispheres are themselves divided into four lobes, all of which serve specialized functions, thus enabling human activity. The *temporal lobes* are concerned with emotions, hearing and aspects of visual perception; the *occipital lobes*, with vision; the *parietal lobes*, with creating three-dimensionality; and the *frontal lobes* with mysterious aspects of ambition, judgment and behavior. Particular subparts of the brain also play key roles. The *hippocampus* is associated with learning and memory; the *hypothalamus* regulates the activities of internal organs and controls the pituitary gland; and an area called *V4* helps us see colors. There are even particular regions of the brain, known as *Wernicke's area* and *Broca's area*, that are responsible for language comprehension and the production of speech.[3]

Writing is a sophisticated activity, but fortunately, the brain's operating system is as complex and efficient as a supercomputer. Each neuron makes approximately one thousand to ten thousand contacts with other neurons at points of contact called *synapses*. These networks of neurons store information and use electrical signals to communicate via wire-like structures called *axons*, which are up to a meter in length, and *dendrites*, shorter, branch-like extensions of the neuron cell bodies. At the junctures between neurons—the synapses—neurons interact with one another through neurotransmitters in a process whereby proteins concentrate chemicals into packages and then release them to receptor proteins on the receiving cells. The receiving cells selectively bind to the chemicals and convert the signal back into an electrical form. Because of the small gap between neurons, it takes only a fraction of a millisecond for the receiving neuron to detect the chemical transmission from the sending neuron. So far, more than a hundred different chemicals, such as glutamate and serotonin, have been identified as being used by the brain. It is this sophisticated organ that you put to work when you write. The biochemistry of the brain, of course, is not something you need to know a lot about; all you need to know is that *it works!*[4]

I am not a scientist, let alone an expert on brain function, but I do know this: the more I use my mind, the better equipped I am to handle new information or novel situations. By reading and actively participating in the affairs of life, I become better able to comprehend things and navigate the complexity of the world. And by writing, I journey deep into the workings of my mind, causing synapses to fire and axons to flow with activity like oil in a pipeline. I've learned that if I don't understand something, I can always consult experts, whether through books, articles, or one-on-one conversations. And by writing things down for myself—by assimilating information from a variety of sources and then putting it in a logical order—I can gain even greater understanding than when I'm just wrestling with the words in my head or in a book without the aid of my own notations. When students take notes in class and make course outlines, they are using powerful, time-tested methods of learning. Notes capture information, allowing one to go back and access that information at any time, and outlines help us organize the complexity of that information.

And the brain is far from static, especially when put to use—as writing requires. Neurons emit a weak electrical signal when activated, and oscilloscopes and sensitive electrodes are able to capture this electrical activity. Researchers at the Salk Institute for Biological Studies recently found that stimulating environments actually spur the development of new brain cells in the brain's hippocampus. "This is intriguing," scientists Steven Quartz and Terrence Sejnowski emphasize, "since the hippocampus is used for forming long-term memories for facts and events and its destruction is implicated in the memory loss that accompanies Alzheimer's disease." "We now believe," they write, "that new challenges throughout life can spur new brain cell growth as the brain responds to the demands you place on it." Other studies confirm that finding. Just as animals, such as rats and mice, develop more complex brain circuitry when placed in cages with toys and frequently rearranged obstacles (as opposed to those put in simpler environments), people who actively use their minds on a regular basis—as writers and readers do—reap great intellectual rewards. Reading ability, it should come as no surprise, is one of the best predictors of educational success.[5]

Until the advent of reading and writing, the only way humans could communicate with one another was through speech, non-verbal gestures, or the most rudimentary of symbols, whether etched on cave walls or scratched in the dirt or sand with sticks. As far as anyone knows, written language is only about 5,000 years old. Writing likely originated in Sumer, a collection of city-states centered along the banks of the lower Tigris and Euphrates Rivers, sometime between 3500 and 2800 B.C., with written forms of language appearing later in Egypt, China and Mexico. Early Sumerian writings developed as a convenient way to keep track of trade and consisted of clay tablets of hieroglyphics or cuneiform, wedge-shaped characters with pictographic origins. Written languages, however, developed steadily and later found non-commercial uses, such as the recording of history, as they allowed any kind of information to be encoded and preserved. Although the first known use of a symbol to stand for a word or number occurred in the vicinity of 8000 B.C., the creation of alphabets—the building blocks of language—did not occur until much later. John and Deborah Darnell, archaeologists at Yale University, found carved inscriptions along an ancient Egyptian desert road, placing the invention of the earliest known phonetic alphabet at around 2000 B.C. Even today, some of the world's languages have no written form at all.[6]

The availability of books—which hold and transmit ideas and

which now line library and bookstore shelves—is itself a fairly recent phenomenon. Although early Roman citizens had access to over 25 public libraries, during the Dark Ages—between 400 and 900 A.D.—books were scarce and unaffordable to all but European society's richest members. According to medieval historian Thomas Brown, during that time frame "a manuscript of 400 leaves could cost half the annual salary of a high-ranking civil servant." Between 1200 and 1500, Paris gained renown for its thriving artistic workshops, which produced finely illuminated manuscripts, such as Bibles, psalters, and secular books. But again, these were made largely for wealthy patrons. It took the invention of the printing press to revolutionize the book trade. The printing press and movable metal type allowed the first printed book, the Gutenberg Bible, to be published and distributed in 1455, and with that new technology, it wasn't long before books became more widely available. Between 1455 and 1500, more than 35,000 books were published in Europe, and by 1640, more than 20,000 different titles were available in just England alone. One need only walk through any modern-day bookstore or public library to realize how much has changed since medieval times and to see the exponential growth of written forms of communication. By writing, you'll be participating in an exciting human activity that has the capacity to change the world—and that already has in countless ways.[7]

Just as sound recordings allow us to experience first-hand the brilliance of Bach's, Beethoven's or Mozart's compositions, be they concertos, symphonies or sonatas, written language allows us to know others' thoughts and ideas. This, in turn, allows for the development of more complex thoughts and ideas—all built upon the foundation laid down, in writing, by past generations of thinkers. Indeed, scientists in this century must study prior research if they ever hope to make new scientific advances in their fields of study. It is, in fact, the engine of written language, used for centuries to document scientific discoveries, that makes innovation and new technologies possible. In 1687, Isaac Newton described gravity in his masterwork *Principia Mathematica*; in 1735, Swedish naturalist Carolus Linnaeus published an enduring system of nomenclature in *Systema Naturae*; in 1859, in *On the Origin of Species*, Charles Darwin described the principles of evolution and natural selection; in 1971, Jane Goodall documented the behavior of primates in Africa in her best-seller *In the Shadow of Man*; and physicist Albert Einstein, when he was alive, defined energy as being equal to an object's mass times the speed of light squared in his famous equation $E=mc^2$. The advancement of science without the aid of writing is almost inconceivable. If we didn't have writing, I doubt very much that computer games, the iPod, or laptops would ever have been invented. Computer code itself is a written form of communication.[8]

In the realm of law and individual and human rights, written texts, more than anything else, have established, and then served to guarantee, rules of conduct or important freedoms. The Code of Hammurabi, inscribed on eight-foot stone markers placed around the ancient kingdom of Babylon, is the earliest known set of written laws. Its 282 clauses regulated nearly every aspect of Babylonian life. The most famous document in English history, the Magna Carta, was negotiated over a five-day period in 1215 in a meadow beside the Thames. Among other things, that charter—granted by King John of England to dissident barons at Runnymede—guaranteed the right to a trial by jury, a right to leave and re-enter the country (except in times of war), and the right to be free from arbitrary confiscation of property. "No widow shall be compelled to marry, so long as she wishes to remain without a husband," read one of the charter's provisions. The Ten Commandments—among them, "Thou shalt not kill" and "Thou shalt not steal"—rank as the best-known example of the written laws of Christianity.[9]

Today, the notion of living without written laws and regulations is unthinkable. We rely on laws and regulations to fight crime, to protect the environment, and to ensure the safety of workers. Just imagine what life would be like in the United States without the protections of the First Amendment: "Congress shall make no law respecting an establishment of religion, or prohibiting the free exercise thereof; or abridging the freedom of speech, or of the press; or the right of the people peaceably to assemble, and to petition the government for a redress of grievances." Or just imagine how different American history would be if President Abraham Lincoln had not issued his Emancipation Proclamation in 1863. "I do order and declare that all persons held as slaves," Lincoln proclaimed, "are, and henceforward shall be free." Writing, which has already transformed the world, can change lives, too.[10]

Instruments of international law contain some of the world's most aspirational language. The Universal Declaration of Human Rights, adopted by the United Nations General Assembly in 1948, proclaims in Article 1 that "All human beings are born free and equal in dignity and rights." "Everyone has the right to life, liberty and security of person," "No one shall be subjected to torture or to cruel, inhuman or degrading treatment or punishment," "No one shall be subjected to arbitrary arrest, detention or exile," and "Everyone has the right to freedom of opinion and expression," read other key provisions of that declaration, drafted by a U.N. commission chaired by Eleanor Roosevelt. A series of treaties— among them, the International Covenant on Civil and Political Rights, the Geneva Conventions, the Convention against Torture, the Convention on the Rights of the Child, the Convention on the Elimination of All Forms of Discrimination against Women, and the Vienna Convention on Consular Relations—have established other important human rights standards on the international level. When new international agreements are negotiated and signed, they, too, will be in writing.[11]

And words matter. Throughout human history, it is words—both spoken and written—that have challenged us, moved us, informed us, and shaped our future. One of my own political heroes, Hubert H. Humphrey, penned an influential autobiography, *The Education of a Public Man*, and had this to say in his last speech before Congress: "The moral test of government is how it treats those who are in the dawn of life, the children; those who are in the twilight of life, the elderly; and those who are in the shadows of life, the sick, the needy and the handicapped." I find those words, like so many of Humphrey's speeches, incredibly inspiring. In fact, the words and writings of our civic and political leaders, whether liberal or conservative, indisputably help define society's agenda and the way we look at ourselves, not to mention the way we live our lives as citizens. Written instruments actually facilitate the Rule of Law—the idea that governmental authority may only be exercised in accordance with laws that are adopted through established procedures.[12]

Whatever your political views, never underestimate the power that ideas and words—including your own—can have, either in your own life or in your community or country. In 1960, U.S. Senator Barry Goldwater, of Arizona, published *The Conscience of a Conservative*, a book that sold over 3.5 million copies and helped mold modern American conservatism. Over 40 years later, in *The Conscience of a Liberal*, U.S. Senator Paul Wellstone, of Minnesota, gave this advice, which has stuck with me: "We should never separate the lives we live from the words we speak. To me, the most important goal is to live a life consistent with the values I hold dear and to act on what I believe in." Goldwater and Wellstone are no longer with us, but their ideas live on in their books and in their published speeches. That is the great thing about publishing what you write: through your writings, your ideas can be perpetuated.[13]

With writing, depending on the scope of one's project, it can take hours or days or weeks or months—sometimes even years—before your thoughts gel and crystallize into a gem worthy of publication. "I once scribbled 'hobbit' on a blank page of some boring school exam paper in the early 1930s," recounted J. R. R. Tolkien, the Oxford professor who published *The Hobbit* in 1937. "It was some time before I discovered what it referred to," he said. That book has now sold over 42 million copies and been translated into 26 languages. In the late nineteenth century, the German physiologist and physicist Herman Helmholtz—in a helpful way of thinking about it—described discoveries as the product of three stages: *saturation*, connected with research or information gathering; *incubation*, or the mulling over of that information; and *illumination*, the discovered solution. The poet Paul Valéry, who grappled mightily with words, described such inspiration and insight (which is all part of the writing process) in a slightly different way: "Sometimes I have observed this moment when a sensation arrives at the mind; it is as a gleam of light, not so much illuminating as dazzling." In 1908, French mathematician Henri Poincaré put forward a fourth stage—*verification*, or checking one's solution for usefulness and error—that might be likened, for our purposes, to citechecking and proofreading.[14]

Above all else, the creative process requires keeping an open mind. By avoiding premature judgments on what you write, which is what freewriting does, you spur rather than stifle creativity. As the German poet and philosopher Friedrich von Schiller wrote to a young writer in 1788: "It seems a bad thing and detrimental to the mind if reason makes too close an examination of the ideas as they come pouring in—at the very gateway, as it were." As Schiller explained in his letter, a thought looked at in isolation may seem trivial or fantastic, but may be made sensible by another thought that comes thereafter. In conjunction with other thoughts that, at first, may seem equally absurd, Schiller wrote, even a seemingly trivial thought may turn out to form a key link in a chain of logic. Reasoning, he noted, cannot take place unless the mind "retains the thought long enough to look at it in connection with the others." And the best way to retain thoughts is by writing them down. Ideas "rush in pell-mell," Schiller noted, emphasizing that it is only after they've been recorded that the mind is able to "look them through and examine them in a mass."[15]

Just as writing can transmit powerful ideas, the writing process itself can help you unleash those ideas. By sitting down to write, you'll be compelling yourself to think. And by writing down what you think, you'll be putting down on paper your mind's thoughts as they occur to you, giving you the chance to interact with them and to be inspired. "Inspiration is not the exclusive privilege of poets or artists," the Polish poet Wisława Szymborska said in accepting the Nobel Prize for Literature at age 73. As she said in her acceptance speech: "There is, has been, and will always be a certain group of people whom inspiration visits. It's made up of all those who've consciously chosen their calling and do their job with love and imagination. It may include doctors, teachers, gardeners—and I could list a hundred more professions." It's all about inquiry. "Difficulties and setbacks never quell their curiosity," Szymborska noted, explaining how inquiry aids in problem solving and how problem solving leads to further inquiry. "A swarm of new questions emerges from every problem they solve," she said, adding that whatever inspiration is, it's born from a continuous "I don't know." When you write, you'll sometimes generate more questions than answers, but at least you'll have discovered the right questions, which you'll still have the opportunity to answer later.[16]

As a general matter, those who write enjoy inquiry, exploration and coming up with creative solutions. Pat Conroy, the author of *The Great Santini* and *The Prince of Tides*, put it this way: "Good writing is the hardest form of thinking. It involves the agony of turning profoundly difficult thoughts into lucid form, then forcing them into the tight-fitting uniform of language, making them visible and clear." As Conroy writes: "Exactness is a virtue in even the most word-possessed writer. There is enormous power in stating something simply and well." Observation is paramount, with writers constantly probing for new insights and understanding—not only as to matters of substance, but as to matters of style. Good writers take pride in their prose. Conroy again: "I try to notice everything, and if I take the time to write it, I would simply like to write it better than anyone else possibly could. If I am describing the Atlantic Ocean, I want to make that portion of the high seas mine forevermore, and I do not want the reader daydreaming about Herman Melville's ocean while getting a suntan on poor Conroy's."[17]

If you can describe or explain something with language, perhaps in a novel way, you will have done something worthwhile, even extraordinary. You may not be William Shakespeare, but if you can clearly articulate thoughts or ideas with words, it means that you are able to understand something. It also means that you are able to share that understanding with others. Those are not small things, particularly in a world that is as complex as the one in which we live. Just as surely as another person's writings, when read, can change one's thinking on a particular topic, the development of writing skills can improve one's intellectual prowess and allow you to communicate more effectively with others. "The pen is the tongue of the mind," the Spanish writer Miguel de Cervantes wrote. A pen, of course, certainly can be that, but only if you know how to use it and make the commitment to devote yourself to the craft of writing.[18]

I myself enjoy finding the right words to give voice to what I know or believe. Before publishing my first book, *Death in the Dark: Midnight Executions in America*, I spent several years researching the history of American death penalty laws. I discovered that many of those laws mandated that executions take place "before sunrise," and that laws in Delaware and Louisiana actually required executions to occur between midnight and 3:00 a.m. Of the 313 American executions carried out from 1977 to 1995, I found out, more than 82 percent of them took place between 11:00 p.m. and 7:00 a.m., when most people are asleep. More than 50 percent of the executions actually took place between midnight and 1:00 a.m. I also learned that, in 1907, the Minnesota Supreme Court upheld the constitutionality of a Minnesota gag law, dubbed the "midnight assassination law" by its contemporaries because it required non-public, nighttime executions and criminalized newspaper coverage of hangings. Executions "must take place before dawn, while the masses are at rest," the court ruled, for the "purpose of avoiding publicity." That is interesting information—as is the fact that the U.S. Supreme Court actually upheld the constitutionality of that law. Writing *Death in the Dark* gave me the opportunity to impart what I had learned to others—and to influence people's thinking on the subject of capital punishment.[19]

Ultimately, writing hones thought as a rock polisher shines agates. There's just something about putting down your thoughts on the page, and then being forced to relate them to one another, that exposes weaknesses in one's thought process or any frivolous or fallacious arguments. Novelist George Orwell saw good prose as a window pane, capable of clarity and truth-seeking. Revision, obviously, must be part of the equation, as it is the reshaping of language that brings clear-mindedness. Whereas well-chosen words and well-crafted sentences lead to quick comprehension of complex ideas, sloppily constructed sentences easily confuse readers. It's not enough to have good ideas; you need to organize and refine them. As the nineteenth-century writer Anne-Sophie Swetchine put it, "To have ideas is to gather flowers; to think, is to weave them into garlands."[20]

As a practicing lawyer, I myself regularly spend enormous amounts of time writing and revising so that I capture complexities with carefully sewn nets of words. A judge or a client needs to know what the facts are and what the law is, and in a way that quickly allows a client to grasp the pros and cons of a particular course of action or that gives a judge the information needed to make a reasoned decision. As a former law clerk, I certainly saw lawyers who filed poor quality motion papers and then stood up in court and, in effect, "winged it." I can tell you, when that happens it's not a pretty sight. Such lawyers get caught off-guard by hard questions, even softballs—questions they could have anticipated if only a better, more polished brief had been written. The lawyers who've prepared in advance do best, and that means they've spent quality time *before* a hearing deciphering the often complicated facts of a case, researching the law, and then mustering the facts and the law into a coherent whole through a well-written brief. It's not always possible to anticipate every question, but there's no substitute for good preparation, and that means using the writing process to vet arguments from every possible angle.

There's no question: the writing process can be chaotic and messy. But writer Patricia Hampl explains precisely what the writing process can do for you if you use it. "I don't write about what I know," she says, "but in order to find out what I know." In her memoir, *I Could Tell You Stories*, Hampl describes what her own writing process looks like after she gets under way: "I sit before a yellow legal pad, and the long page of the preceding two paragraphs is a jumble of crossed-out lines, false starts, confused order. A mess. The mess of my mind trying to find out what it wants to say." Sound familiar? It should. "For me," Hampl says, "writing a first draft is a little like meeting someone for the first time. I come away with a wary acquaintanceship, but the real friendship (if any) is down the road." Intimacy with a text, as with a friend, she writes, only comes from paying attention. "It is always a thrilling risk," Hampl says, "to say exactly what you mean, to express exactly what you see." Obviously, it helps to have at least *some* notion of what you want to say before you start writing, but the revision process will always enable you to refine your thoughts and ideas no matter how jumbled your initial drafts may be.[21]

When writing, build the best case you can using your mental prowess and the factual evidence you've gathered. This is just as critical for the writing process as it is for any trial lawyer preparing a case. Let me give you an example. When I meet with a new client, I always ask a series of questions to identify any viable claims or defenses. There are many kinds of causes of action that can be brought in a lawsuit—breach of contract, breach of warranty, and fraud claims, to name just a few—and each type of claim requires that certain factual predicates be met. Legal defenses—such as waiver, estoppel, or statutes of limitations—are no different: they, too, require an application of the law to the facts. Asking questions allows me to gauge the client's chances of success, though drafting a written legal opinion is often the best way for me to get my arms around whatever factual or legal issues I'm examining. Some lawyers actually like to draft their closing arguments long before trial—just so they can focus on the strengths and weaknesses of their case. By writing, one gains greater understanding.

One of the smartest things a litigator can do after opening a new file—and I recommend the technique for all writers—is to create a chronology of the facts. Sometimes just by organizing all of the relevant facts into chronological order, one is able to see how facts relate to one another in significant ways. For example, two events may appear at first to be totally unrelated. Upon noticing that they happened just minutes apart, however, the lawyer or writer may find a connection or discover that one motivated or caused the other. Making a chronology of relevant dates, times and facts can be helpful in more ways than one. Chronologies reveal the sequence of events, as the 9/11 Commission's written report did so dramatically in tracking the events of September 11th and the four hijacked planes. But more importantly, chronologies allow the writer to see how—and perhaps why—something happened. Chronologies can be tricky, though. Oftentimes, what's *missing* from a chronology is just as important as what's on it. Just consider the Sherlock Holmes anecdote about the significance of absence. "Did you notice anything about the dog barking in the night?" Holmes famously asked his sidekick Watson. "I didn't hear the dog bark," Watson replied. "Precisely," Holmes said. "It was the fact that the dog did *not* bark that was significant."[22]

As you write, stay focused. A common problem with any piece of writing is that it can easily become rambling or too long without any legitimate purpose. Thus, after you've downloaded your thoughts rather randomly onto the page or your computer, go back and try to boil down what you're trying to say into a single, concise sentence. That carefully articulated, declarative sentence (subject to revision, of course) becomes your theme, forming the axis around which your main points, sub-points, and supporting evidence then spin. Busy judges, for example, need to know right away what's at issue in a case. A lawyer might tell a judge that A, B and C happened and that the lawyer's client was injured in X, Y and Z ways, but before doing so, the judge needs to know why A, B and C and X, Y and Z are important in the first place. The judge needs to know the *context* in which the facts and any relevant laws are being presented. If the lawyer points out up-front—in an introductory paragraph—that the case involves a salesman's fraudulent misrepresentations that cost the plaintiff $100,000 and caused a bankrupty, the judge will then be able to easily put A, B and C and X, Y and Z in proper perspective. An up-front roadmap, which lets readers see what's ahead, lets readers know where the writer plans to take them, just as car headlights enable a driver to see at night.

Also, when writing something, always remember to play the devil's advocate. A good piece of writing—a personal essay or a legal brief, for instance—will take on, and meet, the opposing side's best arguments head-on. In this respect, a good writer is like a good debater. The skilled debater is able to forcefully articulate the points favoring a particular position, but that debater is also able to anticipate, and then refute, the other side's main points. If a political candidate has no comeback to an opponent's argument, that candidate will have lost that portion of the debate. The next time you write, pick an issue that you feel passionate about, but then try to consider it from the opposite perspective. Write down the best three or four arguments you can think of favoring the opposing side, and then try to beat back, as best you can, each of those arguments in writing. If you can't, you're either on the wrong side of the issue or you need to think harder or do more research to find out why the particular point under consideration is not persuasive after all. Effective writing does not run away from "bad" facts or try to sweep them under the rug; on the contrary, it articulates and then addresses them. As writer Aldous Huxley, the well-known essayist and author of *Brave New World*, said, "Facts do not cease to exist because they are ignored."[23]

Although words are to writers what horses are to jockeys, the whole world—full of concepts, thoughts, objects and people—is the writer's domain. "The writer," essayist Ralph Waldo Emerson once said, "believes all that can be thought can be written." Human beings, he noted eloquently, possess "the faculty of reporting, and the universe is the possibility of being reported." Emerson was right. A writer can take on any topic or subject matter and, through clearly expressed language, describe the most tangible physical object or the most abstract thought or idea. And it can be done with style. Novelist Virginia Woolf, who used her imagination to create much-loved novels such as *Mrs. Dalloway* and *To the Lighthouse*, once beautifully described "a book" as "not made of sentences laid end to end, but of sentences built, if an image helps, into arcades or domes." In other words, artfully sequenced sentences do not just make for a flat picture or narrative, but can bring characters, events or ideas to life in a colorful, three-dimensional way, much like an IMAX film or a Broadway musical does.[24]

Ultimately, writing can and should—and often does—bring ideas to life. A writer can put an idea on paper, and the next thing you know that idea has been turned into action, be it in the form of a new law, a publication, the formation of a small business, or the creation of a non-profit organization. A college student, Fred Smith, turned a school paper conceptualizing an overnight delivery system into Federal Express, a successful, worldwide enterprise that now employs over 200,000 people. And Betty

Edwards's book, *Drawing on the Right Side of the Brain*, has sold more than 2.5 million copies and been translated into thirteen languages, turning non-artists into artists and giving its readers a whole new outlook on life. And I could go on and on with such examples, for writing has touched and moved so many people in so many different contexts. Never forget: words charge the mind, connect us to one another, and are valuable tools for introspection, expression and problem-solving, capable of shaping and enriching our lives in meaningful ways.[25]

What we play is life. –Louis Armstrong • If I don't write it's because I'm writing. –Colette • Writing is done away from the typewriter, away from the desk. I'd say it occurs in the quiet, silent moments, while you're walking or playing a game, or even talking to someone you're not vitally interested in. You're working, your mind is working, on this problem in the back of your head. –Henry Miller • Never write about a place until you're away from it, because it gives you perspective. –Ernest Hemingway • Books are good enough in their own way, but they are a mighty bloodless substitute for life. –Robert Louis Stevenson • Summer afternoon—summer afternoon...the two most beautiful words in the English language. –Henry James • Everything that I have written is closely related to something that I have lived through. –Henrik Ibsen • When I am, as it were, completely myself, entirely alone, and of good cheer—say, travelling in a carriage, or walking after a good meal, or during the night when I cannot sleep; it is on such occasions that my ideas flow best and most abundantly. –Wolfgang Amadeus Mozart • In order to really appreciate rest we must first experience fatigue and without experiencing fatigue we cannot ever hope to know the complete mental relaxation that comes from muscular effort. –Sigurd Olson • Man does not live by words alone, despite the fact that he sometimes has to eat them. –Adlai Stevenson • No great work has ever been produced except after a long interval of still and musing meditation. –Walter Bagehot • If I had to live my life again, I would make a rule to read some poetry and listen to some music at least once a week; for perhaps the parts of my brain now atrophied would thus have been kept active through use. –Charles Darwin • My formula for living is quite simple. I get up in the morning and I go to bed at night. In between I occupy myself as best I can. –Cary Grant • I think it's important for a writer to keep in shape. –Norman Mailer • All things can tempt me from this craft of verse. –W. B. Yeats • The history of my life is the history of the struggle between an overwhelming urge to write and a combination of circumstances bent on keeping me from it. –F. Scott Fitzgerald • For me, writing means having one foot in one world, and the other in the real one. –Carol Shields • One cannot think well if one has not dined well. –Virginia Woolf • After reading Thoreau I felt how much I have lost by leaving nature out of my life. –F. Scott Fitzgerald • Books are a world in themselves, it is true; but they are not the only world. The world is a volume larger than all the libraries in it. –Thomas Hardy • At no time am I a quick thinker or writer: whatever I have done in science has solely been by long pondering, patience and industry. –Charles Darwin

INTERMISSION

Joys come from simple and natural things, mists over meadows, sunlight on leaves, the path of the moon over water. Even rain and wind and stormy clouds bring joy, just as knowing animals and flowers and where they live. Such things are where you find them, and belong to the aware and alive. –Sigurd Olson • How important it is to take the time to read literature, to look at art, to go to concerts. If all parts of your brain aren't nourished, you become really limited—less sensitive. It's like food. You'd get pretty strange if you ate ice cream all the time. –Kent Nagano • I wrote many poems. I always put them away new for several weeks in a bottom drawer. Then I would take them out and re-read them. If they seemed bad, I would throw them away. They would all seem good when I wrote them and, usually, bad when I would look at them again. So most of them were thrown away. –Langston Hughes • Generosity is the soul of writing. You write to give something. To yourself. To your reader. To God. –Erica Jong • I have always secretly admired people who could read a newspaper while eating. –Robert Benchley • By the time one has finished a piece it has been so often viewed and reviewed before the mental eye, that one loses, in a good measure, the powers of critical discrimination. Here the best criterion I know is a friend. –Robert Burns • I want to live other lives. I've never quite believed that one chance is all I get. Writing is my way of making other chances. –Anne Tyler • Poets are like baseball pitchers. Both have their moments. The intervals are the tough things. –Robert Frost • Writing is an adventure. To begin with, it is a toy and an amusement. Then it becomes a mistress, then it becomes a master, then it becomes a tyrant. The last phase is that just as you are about to be reconciled to your servitude, you kill the monster and fling him to the public. –Winston Churchill • I've mostly written about sex by means of the space break. –Barbara Kingsolver • The man who adds the life of books to the actual life of everyday lives the life of the whole race. The man without books lives only the life of one individual. –Jessie Lee Bennett • Reflection is the beginning of reform. –Mark Twain • Art is energy shaped by intelligence. –Gore Vidal • Let us read and let us dance—two amusements that will never do any harm to the world. –Voltaire • Writing is like getting married. One should never commit oneself until one is amazed at one's luck. –Iris Murdoch • I should have no objection to go over the same life from its beginning to end; requesting only the advantage authors have, of correcting in a second edition the faults of the first. –Benjamin Franklin • The reality is more excellent than the report. –Ralph Waldo Emerson • It is not enough to think, one also has to breathe. Dangerous are the thinkers who have not breathed enough. –Elias Canetti • All work and no play makes Jack a dull boy. –Jack Nicholson • Weekends are a good working time because people think you've gone away and don't disturb you. –Julian Barnes • The art of living is more like wrestling than dancing, in as much as it, too, demands a firm and watchful stance against any unexpected onset. –Marcus Aurelius • Life is what happens to us while we're making other plans. –John Lennon • For everything that lives is holy, life delights in life. –William Blake • Distance has the same effect on the mind as on the eye. –Samuel Johnson

I love living. I have some problems with my life, but living is the best thing they've come up with so far.

–Neil Simon, playwright

Time gives good advice.

–Maltese proverb

The way to learn a language is to breathe it in. Soak it up! Live it!

–Doris Lessing, THE SUMMER BEFORE DARK

Life can only be understood backwards, but it must be lived forwards.

–Søren Kierkegaard, Danish philosopher

CHAPTER SEVEN

Rest and Relaxation

"To keep a lamp burning we have to keep putting oil in it," advised Mother Teresa, winner of the Nobel Peace Prize for her work with India's destitute and poor. That is sound advice, especially for writers, who always need new energy, or fresh material, to fuel their writing lives. A new experience or a break from writing can reenergize the writer and produce new ideas and insights —a fresh outlook that is only possible because of the passage of time and what has been learned while *not* writing. And when I use the term *writers*, I'm not just referring to journalists, published authors, and those who earn their living solely by writing. Anyone who writes is a writer and those who write anything at all—even e-mails—should consider themselves to be writers.[1]

The goal of writing is to express yourself as best as you can, and you won't be able to do that unless you are able to objectively judge what you've already written. Taking time off from writing— which brings greater objectivity—is often just what you need to achieve that new perspective. If you are too close or too attached to the words you've written, you may find it difficult to delete or change words or re-structure your text in the revision process. Objectivity is hard to achieve in evaluating your own work, but the passage of time allows you to judge your ideas and word choices more dispassionately—something effective writers have realized (and used as a technique) for centuries. The Roman poet Horace waited eight years before deciding if he liked a poem he wrote. That's an extreme example, but it makes a point: you can't always judge the quality of your writing right after you craft your words.[2]

In editing my third book, *Legacy of Violence: Lynch Mobs and Executions in Minnesota*, I came to know why putting distance between myself and my writing is so important. I had signed a book contract with the University of Minnesota Press calling for a manuscript of no longer than 90,000 words; my completed manuscript, however, contained more than 140,000 words. I had done a tremendous amount of research for that book, and I wanted to tell all of the stories that I'd unearthed—never mind the fact that I'd agreed to write a much shorter text. I still remember the first reaction of my editor, Todd Orjala, after I turned in the manuscript. In an e-mail, he paraphrased astronaut James Lovell's famous words: "Houston, we've had a problem."[3]

I first fantasized about telling my publisher to just arbitrarily cut every third word in the manuscript, a fanciful idea rooted more in anger than in reality. I then went into denial, refusing to cut anything at all—after all, I'd written those extra 50,000 words and I liked what I'd written. After stewing over what to do and failing to persuade my editor to publish the entire manuscript, I finally let it sit untouched for about six months. Only after that time did I realize that significant cuts really should be made; the text, I saw, would actually read better if they were. The edits were difficult to make, but once I got going, the revision process was actually easier to finish than I had anticipated. And as much as I hate to admit it, the finished product—now in bookstores—is a much better book because of the editorial process. The writing is tighter, and so is the narrative flow.

Why is it that we need time away from our words in order to write more effectively? The answer: When we speak or write, a natural reaction is to stand by what we first say, no matter if it makes sense or not. Nobody likes to look foolish or to be proven wrong, but the fact of the matter is that what first comes to one's mind or mouth is often muddled, rambling or perhaps even dead wrong. In conversation, extemporaneous speeches or written drafts, words may be ill-chosen or have the wrong connotation for the job at hand. Only by stepping back, and then looking at what is there (and as if someone else, and not you, had written it), can a piece of writing be re-worked to truly accomplish its intended purpose. So, take breaks from writing. You deserve them and, in the end, they will improve your writing.

Taking time off from writing can generate new ideas, too. While you're doing the dishes, taking a shower or walking down the street, you may have an epiphany or solve a problem within your text that has stumped you. I often think of my own writing, if only intermittently, when I'm away from it. People who write, in fact, usually carry their ongoing writing projects with them wherever they go (if not physically, then mentally). I myself like to keep a little notebook by my bedside so that I can jot down any ideas I have before I go to sleep or in case I wake up with a thought I don't want to lose. During the day, I also like to scribble short reminder notes to myself—whether in my calendar or on Post-it® notes—whenever I get good ideas. That way, I'll have them when I begin a new writing session. I know that ideas can

come at anytime, so I try to capture them when they do, no matter how far away my computer keyboard may be.

One of the things I like best as an escape from work (and from
writing) is to travel. I love seeing new things and going new places
and meeting new people. There's nothing like hopping on a plane
or taking a cross-country car trip and ending up in New Orleans
or San Francisco or Glacier National Park or the Florida Keys; taking a long hike in the Tetons or the Canadian Rockies; or, with
work far, far away, walking through the bustling streets of
Manhattan and stumbling upon a great pastry shop or Thai restaurant. I often work long hours as a practicing lawyer, and I get
burned out if I work too long without a break. Getting away for a
week or two can do wonders for one's outlook on life, just as taking a break from writing can refresh the writer. A well-timed vacation—perhaps as low-key as a quick weekend getaway to a nearby
campground—can rejuvenate your senses, your judgment, and
your sense of perspective. Long trips to distant places are rare, mind
you, but whenever I fly or drive somewhere, even for a couple of
days, it's almost always relaxing.

Sometimes, of course, it is neither feasible nor possible to head
out of town for the weekend or fly away to some exotic destination. Things may be too busy at work or at school; money may be
tight or unavailable; or you may have family or other obligations
closer to home. If that is the case, just make the best of your situation. A walk to a park or coffee shop, a couple hours spent ice
skating or playing tennis, or just going out to a new restaurant or
deli in your neighborhood may be just what you need for a little
break. Even a walk around the block can help. Getting stuck in a
rut is a terrible fate, and doing something fun or a little out of the
ordinary is a terrific way of ensuring that life stays interesting.
Play volleyball. Study Spanish. Take up birdwatching. Talk to a

neighbor. People who want to write well cannot afford to be hermits; they need to know what's going on in the world. Seeing movies and plays, reading, spending time with family and friends, bicycling, or going running keep the writer fresh and up-to-date. Just ask award-winning novelist Richard Ford, who recommends "lavish periods away from writing"—"so much time," he says, "that my writing life sometimes seems to involve not writing more than writing, a fact I warmly approve of."[4]

Good writers try to understand the world, and that means—indeed, necessitates—regularly getting away from work and out of one's house or apartment. In fact, writers usually find their inspiration from periods of contemplation or leisure, whether spent alone or interacting with others. It is almost inconceivable that Robert Frost would have found the words for his famous poem, "The Road Not Taken," had he not spent a lot of time walking in the woods. "Two roads diverged in a yellow wood/And sorry I could not travel both/And be one traveler, long I stood/And looked down one as far as I could/To where it bent in the undergrowth," Frost's evocative poem begins. The famed American poet and his English friend Edward Thomas, to whom Frost originally sent the poem, did, in fact, take long walks in the English countryside discussing Shakespeare's sonnets and World War I before Thomas (later killed in action) enlisted in the army and Frost returned to New Hampshire to write the poem. It shows. "Two roads diverged in a wood, and I—/I took the one less traveled by/And that has made all the difference," Frost's poem ends.[5]

Not writing, to enjoy a sunny, summer day or a bright, winter morning, may seem unproductive if you're working on a piece of writing. That time, however, may turn out to be precisely what you need to refine or finish it. Time and distance can re-invigorate both you *and* your writing. Never think that to be a good writer you must write constantly; that is simply not the case. I try to write every day, but I don't always do that. Some days are simply too beautiful to spend indoors in front of a computer screen; other days I just don't get to writing. Some people write compulsively, as if there is nothing else in the world to do, and that can lead to extremes. You certainly don't have to be like Isaac Asimov, who wrote 477 books before he died at age seventy-two, to be a talented writer. Let me assure you: not writing some days is perfectly okay. As Socrates advised, "In all things be moderate."[6]

Eating well, exercising regularly, and getting enough sleep will also help you write more effectively. It's hard to concentrate when you're hungry, tired or feeling lousy, and to write well you need to be able to think clearly. "The task of writing a sentence," neurologist Alice Flaherty explains, with a touch of humor, "requires the ability to generate an appropriate idea, to translate it from 'mentalese' into English, to generate the words in their written form, to find a pen, to hold it correctly on the paper, to respond to the fact that at first nothing comes out of the pen by shaking it a few times, to do so without getting ink on your clothes, to form the letters correctly, and to simultaneously read the sentence for errors." The writing process, in other words, requires hand-eye coordination, as well as the ability to cogently put ideas together and then express those ideas intelligibly through written language. If you're too distracted or don't feel right, you'll have problems doing what's necessary to write well.[7]

Exercise—even if it's just taking a long, brisk walk—is very important to one's physical and mental health. Because writing is a sedentary, principally intellectual endeavor, physical exertion is all the more essential. It's been documented that schoolchildren who spend an hour a day in gym class do better on tests than those who are inactive, and research shows that college students who exercise do better academically, too. Other studies show a direct connection between exercise and intelligence. Fifty-year-olds who did a four-month walking program improved their mental performance by 10 percent over their pre-walking levels, and the MacArthur Studies of Successful Aging found a similar increase in performance for the over-65 age group. In studies done at the University of Illinois, it has been discovered that rats placed on an exercise regimen grew more capillaries, carrying more oxygen-rich blood to brain cells. Here's the deal: the brain needs oxygen, and physical conditioning thus helps the brain's performance.[8]

Exercise, notes Dr. David Snowdon of the University of Kentucky Medical Center, is "one of the most reliable ways to preserve cardiovascular health, and its benefits apply at every age." In his book, *Aging with Grace: What the Nun Study Teaches Us About Leading Longer, Healthier, and More Meaningful Lives*, Dr. Snowdon explains how exercise "improves blood flow, bringing the brain the oxygen and nutrients it needs to function well." The brain, he notes, "accounts for only about 2 percent of the body's weight but demands 15 to 25 percent of the available oxygen." Exercise, Dr. Snowdon emphasizes, "also reduces stress hormones and increases chemicals that nourish brain cells"; changes that ward off depression—a cause of writer's block—and even some kinds of damage to brain tissue. In other words, when you're stressed out about your life or your writing, get out and *do something*; you'll feel better afterward and you'll be better able to cope with the challenge confronting you. The Nun Study—a study of 678 Catholic sisters, ranging in age from 74 to 106—found that the risk of developing Alzheimer's disease, which afflicts up to 45 percent of Americans aged 85 or over, may be lessened through an active, optimistic, and intellectually engaged lifestyle.[9]

That ground-breaking study, in which the brains of Notre

Dame sisters from all over the United States were autopsied immediately following their deaths, is also notable because it found that writing ability correlates with longevity and well-being. By examining autobiographies written by the nuns decades earlier (at age twenty-two, on average) when they were novices, Dr. Snowdon and his colleagues found that 90 percent of the nuns with Alzheimer's disease had "low idea density" in those autobiographies, as compared to only 13 percent of healthy sisters. The "idea density" measure, tied to vocabulary, quantity of ideas, and complexity of sentence structures, enabled Dr. Snowdon and his colleagues to predict, just from studying the content and style of the autobiographies, which nuns would live longer, more productive lives and be Alzheimer's-free. Those who used multisyllabic words in their autobiographies were more likely to have healthy minds, whereas the nuns who later developed Alzheimer's had used monosyllabic words more frequently. The study's finding that those whose autobiographies contained the most positive emotional content lived, on average, 6.9 years longer than nuns who had used the fewest positive-emotion sentences, paralleled those of a Mayo Clinic study of 839 patients, published in 2000, finding that optimists (as classified by standardized personality tests) lived longer than pessimists. Because of the importance of linguistic ability on the outcome of the aging process, Dr. Snowdon now gives this advice to expectant parents: "Read to your children."[10]

With writing, the importance of sleep cannot be overemphasized either. Imaginative thinking and problem-solving ability are linked to adequate sleep. Yet, seventy million Americans, studies show, are sleep-deprived. Although the recommended daily amount of sleep is eight hours for adults and at least an hour more for adolescents, 71 percent of American adults and 85 percent of teens fail to get the suggested amount. "In both school and work environments," recounts Dr. William Dement, the director of the Stanford University Sleep Research Center, "well-slept people are much more engaged, can keep more ideas in their head simultaneously, and can think through new ideas more clearly." At the University of Luebeck, German researchers asked volunteers to work math problems involving eight-digit numbers and two rules. Hidden in the pattern, however, was a third rule. The group that got eight hours of sleep discovered the hidden rule three times more often than those who had stayed up all night. "If you're sleep-deprived you're less creative than you would be if you had adequate sleep," confirms Dr. Jeffrey Durmer, a sleep specialist at Children's Healthcare of Atlanta. Indeed, the mind itself is at work while you sleep, so sleeping is time well spent. "For a long time," Durmer notes, "people thought of sleep as a period when you were not existing." "Now," he adds, "we know sleep is an active process, not just unplugging your brain."[11]

Nighttime dreams—or daydreams, for that matter—can be especially beneficial to your writing life because the things you dream about are often the things most worth writing about. Your daydreams often reflect your hopes or aspirations, and your dreams at night can illuminate as well, shedding light on what's bothering you, for example. As part of a good night's sleep, dreaming can be restorative and generate new thoughts and ideas for you, all while you're unconscious. Periods of brain activation occur during REM, or rapid eye movement, sleep, a 1953 discovery made possible through the invention of the electro-oculogram, which measures eye movement, and the electroencephalograph, or EEG, which records brain waves from the surface of a patient's head through amplification. Dreams are common, with 95 percent of sleepers studied in laboratory settings reporting dreams when awakened during clusters of rapid eye movements. More modern, brain-imaging technologies—such as positron emission tomography (PET) scans, which record how tissue density is altered by blood flow—reveal that, during REM sleep, brain regions associated with hallucination are more active, while those associated with memory and directed thought are less active. Though dreams can be difficult to decipher (if they make any sense at all), one's unconscious mind should never be overlooked as a source of writing material.[12]

Indeed, the brain, which makes dreams possible, regularly generates new ideas, either while you're awake or as you sleep, thus continuously nourishing your writing life. Scientists have discovered that active neurons, which pump ions such as chloride, potassium, and sodium to transmit electrical charges through their semi-permeable membranes, require more oxygen than non-active cells. That oxygen—which fuels thought—is supplied by increased blood flow, making visible the brain at work, at least to doctors and research scientists using PET scans and functional magnetic resonance imaging (fMRI) technology. Sleep researcher J. Allan Hobson, a professor of psychiatry at Harvard Medical School, notes that thinking can be inspired by (indeed, be the product of) the brain activity that is observed during REM sleep. Lack of sleep, Hobson warns, can impair your creativity and your ability to read and write, talk and listen, and organize your thoughts. I've noticed the same thing: my ability to reason and write effectively diminishes as I become sleep-deprived. I can pull an all-nighter and still write the next day, but I write faster and much better when I'm well-rested.[13]

Life, even in its earliest stages, is a delicate balancing act for any human being. Children love to play, but even grade-school students must develop good study habits and prepare for tests, just as high school and college students must worry about grades and their plans after graduation. For adults, it is no different: work schedules must be juggled with leisure and family time. You don't want to be a workaholic, but you also want to reach your full potential so that your life is as meaningful and as fulfilling as possible. I've worked at pretty intense jobs most of my adult life, but hard work also brings a sense of dignity and purpose. Even retirees, we all know, often pursue hobbies and volunteer work to stay engaged and so they can continue to be active, productive members of society in their later years. "To write or not to write?" is not the right question to ask yourself. "How much to write?" is the proper question because your answer to that question deals with finding balance in one's life. My suggestion: work hard at your writing, but play hard too. That way, you'll get things done, have the opportunity to achieve your goals, yet still have fun. "Let us endeavor so to live," Mark Twain once wrote, "that when we come to die even the undertaker will be sorry."[14]

Obviously, anyone who writes must learn to manage his or her writing life. The writer must spend time alone, for it takes solitude and intense concentration to write well. But the writer must also spend time interacting with others and *not* writing, for life, after all, is about living, not just sitting in front of a notebook or a computer screen. It is, in the end, human relationships that make our lives most meaningful—though writing can and does enhance the quality of those relationships and the quality of life itself. Even extremely productive writers such as Louisa May Alcott, who wrote the classic novel *Little Women*, saw the need—as I do—for plenty of downtime and leisure. As Alcott advised: "Have regular hours for work and play; make each day both useful and pleasant, and prove that you understand the worth of time by employing it well. Then youth will be delightful, old age will bring few regrets, and life will become a beautiful success."[15]

Reading, the love of reading, is what makes you dream of becoming a writer. –Susan Sontag • We read to know we're not alone. –C. S. Lewis • I do not read a book: I hold a conversation with the author. –Elbert Hubbard • Who often reads, will sometimes wish to write. –George Crabbe • A room without books is like a body without a soul. –Cicero • Just the knowledge that a good book is waiting one at the end of a long day makes that day happier. –Kathleen Norris • Read, read, read. Read everything—trash, classics, good and bad, and see how they do it. Read! You'll absorb it. Then write. –William Faulkner • God be thanked for books! They are the voices of the distant and the dead. –James Baldwin • When we read, we start at the beginning and continue until we reach the end; when we write, we start in the middle and fight our way out. –Vickie Karp • Outside of a dog, a book is a man's best friend. Inside of a dog, it's too dark to read. –Groucho Marx • It should be self-evident that a man who wants to write well must learn his craft from other writers. –Roger Sherman Loomis • Books are messengers of freedom. –Daniel Boorstin • A well-composed book is a magic carpet on which we are wafted to a world that we cannot enter in any other way. –Caroline Gordon • Some books are to be tasted, others to be swallowed, and some few to be chewed and digested. –Francis Bacon • Books are a form of immortality. –Wilfred Peterson • I would be most content if my children grew up to be the kind of people who think decorating consists mostly of building enough bookshelves. –Anna Quindlen • One must be an inventor to read well. –Ralph Waldo Emerson • I've never known any troubles that an hour's reading didn't assuage. –Charles de Montesquieu • A memorandum is written not to inform the reader but to protect the writer. –Dean Acheson • Perhaps no place in any community is so totally democratic as the town library. The only entrance requirement is interest. –Lady Bird Johnson • I ransack public libraries, and find them full of sunk treasure. –Virginia Woolf • To be truly literate, citizens must be able to grasp the meaning of any piece of writing addressed to the general reader. –E. D. Hirsch • Were it left to me to decide whether we should have a government without newspapers, or newspapers without a government, I should not hesitate a moment to prefer the latter. –Thomas Jefferson • Dictators are as scared of books as they are of cannon. –Harry Golden • A great book should leave you with many experiences, and slightly exhausted at the end. You live several lives while reading it. –William Styron • At first it was a longing to read. Later it became a longing to write. –Ethan Canin • I grew up in a house crammed with books. –Kurt Vonnegut

READING

Sooner or later the life of our time is summarized in its books. –Malcolm Cowley • All modern American literature comes from one book by Mark Twain called *Huckleberry Finn*. –Ernest Hemingway • All writers learn from the dead. As long as you continue to write, you continue to explore the work of writers who have preceded you; you also feel judged and held to account by them. –Margaret Atwood • Writers have to start out as readers, and before they put pen to paper, even the most disaffected of them will have internalized the norms and forms of the tradition from which they wish to secede. –Seamus Heaney • Losing yourself in a book, the old phrase, is not an idle fantasy but an addictive, model reality. –Susan Sontag • Books brought me the greatest satisfaction. Just to be alone, reading, under the house, with lizards and spiders running around. –Jamaica Kincaid • A great library contains the diary of the human race. –George Dawson • A family library is a breeding-place of character. –Graham Greene • I enjoy my library. It is a sort of large secretion of coral around a living organism. I can see chalky banks of books which reflect my interests. –Jonathan Miller • Books are…funny little portable pieces of thought. –Susan Sontag • One reads to know other people's thoughts. –Philip Stanhope • When I want to read a good book, I write one. –Benjamin Disraeli • There are two motives for reading a book: one, that you enjoy it; the other, that you can boast about it. –Bertrand Russell • The true university of these days is a collection of books. –Thomas Carlyle • A good book is the precious life-blood of a master spirit, embalmed and treasured up on purpose to a life beyond life. –John Milton • A good news-paper, I suppose, is a nation talking to itself. –Arthur Miller • I opened Shakespeare at the age of nine and was electrified. –Melissa Green • From your parents you learn love and laughter and how to put one foot before the other. But when books are opened you discover that you have wings. –Helen Hayes • I took a speed read-ing course and read *War and Peace* in twenty minutes. It's about Russia. –Woody Allen • Always read stuff that will make you look good if you die in the middle of the night. –P. J. O'Rourke • There are worse crimes than burning books. One of them is not reading them. –Joseph Brodsky • We shouldn't trust writers, but we should read them. –Ian McEwan • We all know that as the human body can be nourished on any food, though it were boiled grass and the broth of shoes, so the human mind can be fed by any knowledge. –Ralph Waldo Emerson • I love reading another reader's list of favorites. Even when I find I do not share their tastes or predilections, I am provoked to compare, contrast, and contradict. It is a most healthy exercise, and one alto-gether fruitful. –T. S. Eliot • I write that I may read, and so contemplate what I have written. –Aidan Chambers • What is reading but silent conversation? –Walter Savage Landor • When you start reading in a certain way, that's already the beginning of your writing. You're learning what you admire and you're learning to love other writers. The love of other writers is an important first step. –Tess Gallagher • We read fine things but never feel them to the full until we have gone the same steps as the author. –John Keats • In reality, people read because they want to write. Anyway, reading is a sort of rewriting. –Jean-Paul Sartre

What really knocks me out is a book that,
when you're all done reading it, you wish the author
that wrote it was a terrific friend of yours and you
could call him up on the phone whenever you felt like it.

–J. D. Salinger, THE CATCHER IN THE RYE

Books must be read as deliberately and reservedly as they were written.

–Henry David Thoreau, essayist and poet

I read my own books sometimes to cheer me when it is hard
to write, and then I remember that it was always difficult,
and how nearly impossible it was sometimes.

–Ernest Hemingway, Pulitzer Prize winner

Language tethers us to the world; without it we spin like atoms.

–Penelope Lively, English novelist

CHAPTER EIGHT

A Bookshelf of Friends

Every good writer is a reader first. The reason for that is simple: one cannot become an effective writer or thinker without reading the works of others. One learns about science by reading books about astronomy, biology, chemistry and physics; about law by reading casebooks and legal treatises; about algebra and calculus from math texts; and about writing *by reading* (and, of course, by writing on your own). Written texts not only teach us, they show us, by example, what can be done with words, and they start us down new paths, toward greater awareness and understanding. As Sven Birkerts writes in *The Gutenberg Elegies: The Fate of Reading in an Electronic Age*, "To read, when one does so of one's own free will, is to make a volitional statement, to cast a vote; it is to posit an elsewhere and to set off toward it." When we read, Birkerts explains, "we not only transplant ourselves to the place of the text, but we modify our natural angle of regard upon all things; we reposition the self in order to *see* differently."[1]

Words and books reveal life, even as they transmit information.

That is because words come from life and books are written as a result of life. As historian Barbara Tuchman aptly notes, "Books are the carriers of civilization. Without books, history is silent, literature dumb, science crippled, thought and speculation at a standstill." "They are engines of change, windows on the world," she said, calling books "companions, teachers, magicians, bankers of the treasures of the mind" and "humanity in print." Were he alive, President Abraham Lincoln—himself a gifted writer—would have agreed. Reading gives us access to others' discoveries, Lincoln observed, saying elsewhere, "The things I want to know are in books. My best friend is the man who will give me a book I have not read."[2]

Many people exercise regularly at a gym or health club. They lift weights, they do laps in the pool, they run or jog around a chalk-lined track, all for the purpose of staying in shape. They also play competitive or recreational sports—tennis or soccer, football or softball, or racquetball, basketball or volleyball, among others— and walk, bicycle or rollerblade, all to make themselves feel good about their bodies. If physical fitness is a national craze, it's understandable, for obesity is a major public health issue and one's well-being and self-esteem are not laughing matters. Yet, many people who pump iron or workout on a regular basis read only infrequently, preferring instead to use their leisure time to watch television or play video games for hours at a time. Growing up, I watched a lot of MTV, played lots of Atari and hand-held video games, and frequented arcades (and I can't say I was harmed by it). However, I discovered in college that there is a lot more to life than sitting in front of a TV screen or playing Asteroids or Pac-Man. Reading builds one's mind as much as push-ups or pull-ups strengthen one's arms.

The decline of reading as a leisure activity is as distressing as it is well-documented. A 2004 report of the National Endowment for the Arts, titled "Reading at Risk," reported the results of a Census Bureau survey of over 17,000 adults on the national trends in adult literary reading. The report found that the percentage of U.S. adults reading literature—loosely defined as any novels, short stories, plays or poetry—dropped from 56.9 percent in 1982 to 46.7 percent in 2002. More disturbingly, only 56.6 percent of American adults reported that they had read *any* kind of book in the prior twelve months, excluding books required for work or school. The trend for teenagers, who *see* less reading in the home than they did previously, is similar. The National Institute for Literacy found that a smaller percentage of 13- and 17-year-olds read for pleasure daily in 1999 than in 1984 and that fewer 17-year-olds saw adults reading in their homes in 1999 than in 1984. While more than 80 percent of adults read daily newspapers in 1964, only 55 percent of adults read them in 2002.[3]

Although watching TV or documentaries or listening to the radio can be educational, any learning that occurs is very passive. As Dana Gioia, chair of the National Endowment for the Arts, explained in his preface to the NEA report: "most electronic media such as television, recordings, and radio make fewer demands on their audiences, and indeed often require no more than passive participation." Other gadgets, while entertaining, also have their drawbacks. Interactive electronic media, such as the Internet and video games, Gioia notes, "foster shorter attention spans and accelerated gratification." Reading, on the other hand, requires active, often prolonged engagement with the text, just as a wilderness hike in the mountains or a long-distance canoe trip require that you break a sweat as you interact with your surroundings. In short, reading makes you work—at least if you're doing it properly. As British dramatist and essayist Sir Richard

Steele said long before television was invented: "Reading is to the mind what exercise is to the body."[4]

Actually, reading works wonders. It allows you to appreciate and comprehend things, and it allows you to make connections between ideas and concepts, or persons or events, you've never connected before. Reading explains. It allows you to almost step into the shoes of the writer and see the world from the writer's perspective. And reading is empowering and pleasurable. E. B. White, author of children's classics *Charlotte's Web* and *Stuart Little*, was particularly emphatic about the benefits of reading. "Reading," he said, "is the work of the alert mind, is demanding, and under ideal conditions produces finally a sort of ecstasy. This gives the experience of reading a sublimity and power unequalled by any other form of communication." Because reading, like writing, requires thinking, it also fosters new ideas and sets our minds in motion. Scientist Carl Sagan likens the brain to a muscle; when you use it, you feel good. "Understanding is joyous," he said.[5]

Reading books, in fact, not only improves one's quality of life, but can be a life-changing experience. In college and law school, I worked at public libraries and saw first-hand how people thirst for—and benefit from—the knowledge that is found in books. In working at the circulation desk at the University of Minnesota's Walter Library, in the History and Travel Department at the Minneapolis Public Library, and at a public affairs/environmental studies library at Indiana University, I learned just how useful books can be, not to mention the many mysteries they can unlock. During my schooling, I also read countless books that changed the way I look at the world—and at myself. I read a geology textbook, *The Earth's Dynamic Systems*, that explained everything from minerals and plate tectonics to volcanoes and the formation of rivers. I read a book by Scott Turow, called *One L*, that prepared me for my first-year of law school. And among many other books, I read John F. Kennedy's Pulitzer Prize-winning *Profiles in Courage*, which taught me about what it means—and what it takes—to stand up for what is right.[6]

For me, reading has always been an important part of my life. As a boy, I remember going to the Blue Earth County Library, taking down books from my parents' bookshelves, and reading under the covers late at night with a flashlight. I remember being intrigued and inspired by the lives of the characters and personalities that I encountered in novels and biographies. And I remember, when I was in high school, wandering around B. Dalton's at the local shopping mall to pick out a good book to buy and take home. The money I earned as a newspaper carrier was meager, but it was enough to buy books. As an adult, I've given many books as gifts, but selling books—the texts I've learned from—is not in my nature. Books are so important to me that I chose the Hungry Mind Bookstore in St. Paul, Minnesota, as the locale where I got engaged to be married. I proposed in the bookstore's nonfiction aisle, and my marriage, to a fellow writer and reader, has endured, though, lamentably, the independent bookstore has not, having gone out of business.

Today, reading is just as important to me as ever. In the morning, I read the local newspaper to find out what's going on in the world, whether in business, national or international affairs, or in politics in Minnesota, my home state. At the Minneapolis law firm where I work, I read every day as part of my job, and to do that job well, I need to know what laws or regulations are in place and what rulings have been issued by judges. Consulting and reading the proper sources—and then writing about what I've read—allows me to earn a living. Before I go to bed at night, I often read books or magazines such as *The Atlantic Monthly* or *The New Yorker* just for pleasure. To be honest, I cannot imagine a life without lots of reading; reading is simply a part—and a major part, at that—of who I am. I still go to libraries and buy books on a regular basis, and I firmly believe that everyone should own books and build a personal library, however modest or large that may be.

Many others feel much the same way, as perhaps you do. Writer Anne Lamott goes so far as to call books "as important as almost anything else on earth," echoing the sentiments of novelist Anatole France, a Paris book dealer's son who once called words "a magic finger that sets a fibre of the brain vibrating like a harp string." Lamott writes: "What a miracle it is that out of these small, flat, rigid squares of paper unfolds world after world after world, worlds that sing to you, comfort and quiet or excite you." "Books," she says, "help us understand who we are and how we are to behave," "show us what community and friendship mean," and "show us how to live and die." As someone who loves both reading and writing, Lamott knows just how critical reading is to writing and vice versa; reading improves writing skills, for new writing styles and approaches are encountered through reading, and writing makes one better appreciate what one reads. "Becoming a writer," Lamott adds, "can also profoundly change your life as a reader. One reads with a deeper appreciation and concentration, knowing now how hard writing is, especially how hard it is to make it look effortless. You begin to read with a writer's eyes."[7]

The process of acquiring proficiency with words is a long one—though it begins at a time when we may not even be cognizant of it. From the time we are infants, the sounds and words of others continually shape us. At first, babies cry and grunt and then coo and laugh. But pretty soon language blossoms exponentially. Between five and seven months, infants begin to play with sounds, as opposed to just using them to express hunger, pain, surprise or

joy. Babbling—repeating the same syllables over and over again—
starts between seven and eight months, and by the end of their first
year infants produce sound variations, with many producing their
first words, such as *ba-bee* or *da-dee*. In the second year of life, toddlers rapidly acquire and use words—*car, dog, juice, up, go, no* and
bye-bye, to name a few—which are first used in isolation, but later
combined with others to form two-word directives. Eventually,
more complicated sentences take shape. The acquisition of new
words, often learned through pointing at objects, is sped up
through reading, first by parents or siblings or grandparents, and
then, at around age five, by the child alone.[8]

Learning to read is hard, especially for some. A child must learn
that series of letters stand for particular concepts or objects and
that these printed symbols—the words—connect to one another
to create meaning. Films of eye movements show that young or
untrained readers "fixate" as many as five to six times while reading a single line. People with dyslexia—a disorder affecting five to
ten percent of the populace and impairing one's ability to recognize and comprehend written words—face particular difficulties.
But once a child learns to read, the world suddenly becomes a
much more manageable place. Children can see for themselves
what a stop sign is for, can find their own names on masking tape
affixed to cubbies or lockers on the first day of school, and can
occupy themselves reading *Scholastic News* or magazines such as
American Girl, *Highlights*, *Boys' Life*, or *National Geographic*.
Teenagers and adults alike can transport themselves to other places
or times, even fantasy lands, by reading Laura Ingalls Wilder, J. K.
Rowling, or J. R. R. Tolkien novels, or can stay abreast of current
events by reading *Newsweek*, *TIME*, *USA Today* or *U.S. News &
World Report*.[9]

Along with children's parents and guardians, reading molds

character and values as one gains intelligence through the act. C. S. Lewis, the author of *The Chronicles of Narnia*, admits to being the product of "endless books." As Lewis describes it: "My father bought all the books he read and never got rid of any of them. There were books in the study, books in the drawing room, books in the cloakroom, books (two deep) in the great bookcase on the landing, books in a bedroom, books piled as high as my shoulder in the cistern attic, books of all kinds reflecting every transient stage of my parents' interest, books readable and unreadable, books suitable for a child and books most emphatically not." It is like that with books: they offer endless possibilities. As Lewis relates his childhood experience: "In the seemingly endless rainy afternoons I took volume after volume from the shelves. I had always the same certainty of finding a book that was new to me as a man who walks into a field has of finding a new blade of grass."[10]

Other well-known figures—writers, scientists and politicians alike—have repeatedly noted the tremendous influence that words and books have had on their lives. Eudora Welty, one of the twentieth century's greatest literary figures, spoke of the gratitude she felt toward her parents for introducing her "into knowledge of the word, into reading and spelling, by way of the alphabet." Nobel laureate Alexander Solzhenitsyn called literature and art the only substitutes for experiences we've not had ourselves, and comedian Will Rogers said that people only learn through two things: reading or associating with smarter people. Thomas Jefferson, in an 1815 letter to his friend, John Adams, said simply: "I cannot live without books." His contemporary, Benjamin Franklin, thought books so critical to life that he urged those who wished to be remembered after death to "either write things worth reading or do things worth writing." Books can positively influence anyone.[11]

The impact books can have is demonstrated by the age-old

desire of some people to try to censor them. In 35 A.D., Caligula banned Homer's *The Odyssey* for expressing Greek notions of freedom; Dante's work was burned fourteen centuries later; and Toni Morrison's *The Bluest Eye* was removed from the eleventh-grade curriculum at Lathrop High School in Fairbanks, Alaska, following parental complaints. The rationales offered for censorship are common, if predictable. Books are labeled, among other things, as immoral, obscene or politically subversive. James Joyce's *Ulysses*, D.H. Lawrence's *Lady Chatterly's Lover*, Margaret Sanger's *My Fight for Birth Control*, and Theodore Dreiser's *An American Tragedy* have all been banned (as have many other books) at one time or another. Often books have been removed from libraries or school classrooms, with the most frequently attacked books including classic titles such as Mark Twain's *The Adventures of Huckleberry Finn*, Anne Frank's *The Diary of a Young Girl*, J.D. Salinger's *The Catcher in the Rye*, Maya Angelou's *I Know Why the Caged Bird Sings*, and *Our Bodies, Ourselves* by the Boston Women's Health Book Collective.[12]

Some writers actually risk their lives, or lose them, because of what they write. Perhaps the most famous case is that of Salman Rushdie, who wrote a controversial novel, *The Satanic Verses*, that angered Islamic fundamentalists. The book was banned in several countries with predominantly Muslim populations, and a religious edict, or *fatwa*, was issued in 1989 by Iran's leader, Ayatollah Khomeini. That edict called for Rushdie's execution and forced the Indian-born, British author into hiding. In violent demonstrations over the book in Pakistan, six people died and one hundred people were wounded; riots in India led to more than a dozen other deaths; and the 15 Khordad Foundation, an Iranian charity, offered a $2.5 million reward for Rushdie's murder. And it did not stop there. The American publisher of the book, Viking Penguin, received bomb threats and thousands of menacing letters; two major bookstore chains temporarily pulled the book from their shelves; two independent booksellers in Berkeley, California, were firebombed; and Hitoshi Igarashi, the book's Japanese translator, was stabbed to death. The *fatwa* was officially lifted in 1998, but Rushdie still lives in fear for his life. Other writers have been threatened or attacked, driven into exile, or even shot, hanged or burned at the stake.[13]

If writing entails risk-taking, people read books because of their content, often going to great lengths to obtain them—even at great risk to themselves. Take the case of legendary writer Richard Wright. The son of a Mississippi sharecropper, Wright grew up in abject poverty and was often hungry and without adequate clothing or shelter. Abandoned by his father, Wright, at age eighteen, had to resort to using a forged note and the library card of a friendly white man just to get his hands on books—books that were forbidden to him, yet that meant his salvation, his way out of shacks, low-rent housing and malaise and hopelessness. Wright's forged note—his ticket to knowledge and a better life—read, with great irony given the racism Wright fought, "Dear Madam: Will you please let this nigger boy have some books by H. L. Mencken." "I hungered for books," Wright wrote later in his famous autobiography, *Black Boy*, explaining how he longed for "new ways of looking and seeing." Whenever you pick up a book, you should thus feel immense gratitude that you have that option.[14]

In *Books and Islands in Ojibwe Country*, the award-winning writer Louise Erdrich explains why authors write books and why people like to read them: "So we can talk to you even though we are dead," "So I can talk to other humans without having to meet them," "So that I will never be alone." I like what Erdrich has to say. Books allow their readers to gain the wisdom and knowledge of others, even those who have died, perhaps centuries ago. A person, through his or her writings, is able to leave a valuable legacy, to pass something down from one generation to the next. Best of all, reading and writing keep one company if one is lonely or alone. As Anne Lamott relates, "Writing and reading decrease our sense of isolation. They deepen and widen and expand our sense of life: they feed the soul." Just as I read books to my daughter Abigail to instill in her a passion for reading, John Adams, the second U.S. president, passed down his love of books to his son, the future and sixth U.S. president. "You will never be alone with a poet in your pocket," he told his son John Quincy Adams in a particularly memorable letter.[15]

Writing and reading allow us to converse with one another. The writer and the reader may not see—or even know—each other, but the writer reaches an audience, and readers react to the writer's words as they are read. The writer's words provoke questions, and the reader seeks answers to those questions out of personal experience or from the text itself. Good writers try to anticipate such questions and, if they have answers, provide them. Not only does reading connect us to the past, but it allows information to be transmitted and received in a sort of dialogue—with the writer on one side and the reader on the other. "Language is fossil poetry," Ralph Waldo Emerson said, and that's true. Just as dinosaurs left behind bones in the form of fossils, so too do writers leave marks or impressions, both on the world and on their readers. But it must never be forgotten that language is also a living creature—an exchange of views that takes place in real time. "There may be no more pleasing picture in the world," explains essayist Roger Rosenblatt, "than that of a child peering into a book—the past and the future entrancing each other."[16]

Deciding what to read can be extremely difficult given the

sheer number of books published every year—164,609 titles in 2003 in the U.S. alone. Yet, the vast amount of available reading material is a blessing, not a curse, for books and other written materials were not always so readily at hand. The Library of Congress, authorized in 1800, began with a modest, $5,000 appropriation approved by President John Adams. The first books, intended for "the use of Congress," came from London the very next year. The entire collection consisted of 740 volumes and three maps. When the U.S. Capitol, including the new library, was burned down by British troops in 1814, Thomas Jefferson—to reconstitute the library—sold his personal library at Monticello to the federal government for $23,940. The collection of 6,487 books included literature and works on a range of different subjects, written in English, French, German, Greek, Latin, Russian and Spanish. Today, the Library of Congress is the largest library in the world and contains nearly 128 million items on approximately 530 miles of bookshelves. The massive collection includes more than 29 million books and other printed materials, 12 million photographs, 4.8 million maps, 2.7 million recordings, and 57 million manuscripts. Much of the material is actually available online. With such an array of choices, it's no wonder people have a hard time deciding what to read.[17]

I myself subscribe to my local newspaper, a couple of national-circulation magazines, and the *New York Times*. Through the *New York Times Book Review* and other publications, I am able to sift through what is being published and keep an eye out for new books that may be of interest to me. I like to read books on a wide variety of subjects, and many times I pick up books I just happen to run across or ones that come recommended by people I know. Consulting friends and acquaintances about what they're reading, and checking out the best-seller lists or past book-award winners, are especially good ways to find worthwhile books to read. Just one reminder: best-seller lists are not lists of the *best* books; they list the books that *sold* the best. So, follow your own instincts in deciding what to read.

I deliberately try not to limit my reading to those subjects that I already understand or that I'm already interested in. As the poet T. S. Eliot explained, "No one can become really educated without having pursued some study in which he took no interest. For it is part of education to interest ourselves in subjects for which we have no aptitude." To stretch your mind, you need to read books that go beyond your current reservoir of knowledge and understanding. If you don't know much about history or law, read some books on those subjects, however painful it might be at first. If you're fascinated by plants and animals but have never studied botany or zoology, read field guides or books about mammal behavior or bird identification. Browse library or bookstore shelves, pay attention to what's being published, and attempt to identify and then read the very best books you can, using your time wisely. As Henry David Thoreau said, and as I now commend to you, "Read the best books first, or you may not have a chance to read them all."[18]

Again, reading and writing are interrelated skills. The more one reads, the more one becomes interested in writing. And the more one writes, the better reader one becomes. When I write, I almost always need to do research and that research inevitably involves reading. And as I read, I pay attention to how the writing I'm reading is put together and to the techniques in use. Over the course of writing my first three books, for example, I spent time at the Library of Congress, the Minnesota History Center, and a host of local libraries. In researching the history of capital punishment, I read lots of books on the subject as well as countless nineteenth-

and early twentieth-century newspaper articles on microfilm. I analyzed these sources carefully, then wrote, then re-read what I'd written to see if I liked what I'd written and to figure out what else I still needed to research, read or revise to complete my writing projects. Reading and writing, it seems to me, are part of the same circle.

In a sense, writing *is* reading. As novelist, playwright and film-maker Susan Sontag notes in her essay, "Directions: Write, Read, Rewrite. Repeat Steps 2 and 3 as Needed," the art of writing is really just "to practice, with particular intensity and attentiveness, the art of reading." "You write," Sontag explains, "in order to read what you've written and see if it's OK and, since of course it never is, to rewrite it—once, twice, as many times as it takes to get it to be something you can bear to reread." For Sontag, "the rewriting—and the rereading—sound like effort," but are "actually the most pleasurable parts of writing." Beginning to write, Sontag adds, is intimidating, akin to the prospect of plunging into an icy lake. The "warm part," she reminds us, comes "when you already have something to work with, upgrade, edit." Even if your writing is a mess, she says, you'll be able to fix it. "Reading usually precedes writing," Sontag emphasizes, noting how "the impulse to write is almost always fired by reading."[19]

One's love of language and its possibilities, I would argue, is directly proportionate to one's exposure to language. A person with little or no access to books—someone who is illiterate, per-haps—may not see the value of reading or writing. That person may have had no exposure to the magical quality of written language and may not have experienced the sheer power of a good book. To those in the know, however, books can open minds and doors, lead to greater understanding and success, and can, at their best, actually transform lives. Books can help you solve a difficult problem or fix a household appliance; they can fuel your imagination or help you get your personal finances in order; they can even transport you, through description, to faraway lands or the high seas, to places such as Mongolia, Iceland or the Galápagos Islands. If you read Adam Gopnik's *Paris to the Moon* or Sarah Turnbull's *Almost French*, you suddenly find yourself strolling through the City of Light or sipping coffee at Parisian cafés.[20]

The more you read, in fact, the broader your worldview and interests will become. As journalist and religious leader Lyman Abbott explained, "A broad interest in books usually means a broad interest in life." If you read about a place, you become intrigued by that place. If you read a biography, you become interested not only in the subject of it, but in the era in which that person lived. Whenever I read a good book or a well-written newspaper or magazine article, I find myself drawn to the subject matter. It's almost impossible to read good prose and not be moved or entertained or informed by it. It's just the nature of reading. Although there's much more to life than reading, a life without reading—without books and newspapers and magazines—would be pretty drab. Reading makes you aware of what's going on in the world, and that, in turn, makes you want to be engaged in your country and community all the more.[21]

If one reads enough, a desire inevitably follows to learn more about how those words came into being in the first place. My own fascination with writing came about after I had encountered great novels and immersed myself in books. I remember reading books such as *The Hobbit, The Ugly American*, and George Orwell's *Animal Farm* and wondering how published novelists were able to craft their novels so skillfully. Reading thus led to inquiry. Just as some study artistic techniques to gain a better appreciation for art, avid readers often study writing so that they, too, can have a greater respect for the books they're reading and for the writers who wrote them. Indeed, that's why people join book clubs, to discuss and take stock of works of art. And for the dedicated writer, reading is just as important—if not more so. That's because reading is what writers do. As novelist James Michener described his own experience: "In the unbroken chain of which I am a part, reading breeds writing, which breeds more reading."[22]

Because reading helps one learn to write, I cannot commend it enough. Just as babies learn to speak by imitating sounds they hear, kids and adults learn how to write well by reading the writing of others. "I never presume to give advice on writing. I think the best way to learn to write is to read books and stories by good writers," says columnist Maureen Dowd. "It's a hard thing to preach about," Dowd says of writing, invoking what jazz musician Thelonious Monk once said about his field, "Talking about music is like dancing about architecture." You need to dig in as you might with dirt in a garden; you need to read, you need to experience words for yourself. The legendary writer, William Faulkner, for example, saw no substitute for reading where the art of writing was concerned. "Read, read, read. Read everything—trash, classics, good and bad, and see how they do it," he advised, making an analogy to carpenters who must work as apprentices to learn their craft. "Read!" Faulkner said. "You'll absorb it. Then write."[23]

When reading, it's important to read for information, but equally important to read with a critical eye, analyzing and questioning what you're reading. In particular, you want to synthesize what you're reading with other things you already know. In their classic, if oddly titled tome, *How to Read a Book*, Mortimer Adler and Charles Van Doren emphasize that there are different levels and types of reading. Elementary school children use basic reading skills, going from one word to the next, often very laboriously, as they work to build vocabulary and intuit meaning. In contrast, teens and adults read in different ways depending on the circumstances: they may read for pleasure, read analytically to figure something out, or skim a text to save time. Though illiteracy is still a problem in many places, once people learn to read, reading is easy, at least for those who don't suffer from dyslexia. As satirist James Thurber said: "I always begin at the left with the opening word of the sentence and read towards the right, and I recommend this method." If one reads enough in the way one should, reading critically becomes second nature.[24]

The best readers learn to read *syntopically*—what Adler and Van Doren call the most sophisticated kind of reading. "When reading syntopically," they say, "the reader reads many books, not just one, and places them in relation to one another and to a subject about which they all revolve." "With the help of the books read," Adler and Van Doren write, "the syntopical reader is able to construct an analysis of the subject that *may not be in any of the books.*" In other words, the reader is able to assimilate information and independently evaluate and process that information in order to arrive at a new insight or conclusion. A reader with that ability will always find novel things to say, including in writing. Writers, in fact, fully expect readers to interpret the text, make judgments for themselves, and then go beyond the text. This is all part of the fun. As author-publisher Elbert Hubbard said: "The best service a book can render you is not to impart truth, but to make you think it out for yourself." In this respect, readers seek clarity, just as writers do when they write.[25]

A reader's goal—be it information, entertainment, understanding, or a combination thereof—may determine how a text should be read. If you're sunbathing on the beach in Miami, Florida, maybe reading a Tom Clancy or Ann Patchett novel, read as closely or as casually as you like. But if you're reading for understanding or to improve your writing skills, you shouldn't blow by things you don't comprehend at first or skip over words you don't know. Instead, carefully study what's there before you, paying close attention to the writer's message, technique and style. Ask yourself: Do I agree or disagree with the writer or do I need more information before deciding? What works and what doesn't? If something works, why? If something doesn't, why not? Benjamin Franklin actually advised any reader to read with a pen in hand and "enter in a little book short hints of what you find that is curious or that might be useful." Not bad advice. Browsing a book's table of contents, or flipping through a book's pages in advance of reading the text, can also give you a preview of what's ahead, what path the book will take. That, too, can be helpful.[26]

Optimally, the effective reader is always absorbing ideas, assimilating them into his or her repertoire of thoughts, looking to come up with new ideas that go beyond the thoughts of others. Whatever one's purpose, reading—like writing—always involves the use of one's mind. A punch line needs to be grasped; the relevance of a statistic needs to be considered; a written argument needs to be understood and analyzed. As Adler and Van Doren write: "Since reading of any sort is an activity, all reading must to some degree be active. Completely passive reading is impossible; we cannot read with our eyes immobilized and our minds asleep." Listening and reading, they point out, are sometimes misperceived as largely passive activities in which one is "thought of as *receiving* communication from someone who is actively engaged in *giving* or *sending* it." But as Adler and Van Doren write, if writers and speakers are thought of as baseball pitchers, readers and listeners resemble catchers, who also play an active role on baseball diamonds. Catching a ball, Adler and Van Doren explain, "is just as much an activity as pitching or hitting it."[27]

In the final analysis, reading not only entertains (an important thing in and of itself), but constitutes an indispensable form of self-improvement that nourishes one's mind and spirit. Reading educates. It literally drives mental impulses and has the capacity to alter human behavior. And books do change people. For the author of more than a dozen books on natural history, it was Aldo Leopold's *A Sand County Almanac*. As Scott Wiedensaul described that book in a personal essay: "It is a book about connections—ecological connections, to be sure, but it also gave me my first sense of connection to a wider community, a validation of the passion I'd devoted to 'things natural, wide and free,' and the first recognition that such devotion could be the work of a lifetime." For me, all the books that have influenced my life just thus far are too numerous to list or count; I've read hundreds of books in my nearly forty years of life, and my thinking has been influenced by their words in thousands of different ways, if only subtly at times. Reading, like other sensory activities, fires the brain's neurons and allows us to make connections between concepts and ideas and connects us to one another.[28]

Though it should come as no surprise, readers are actually more likely to participate in their communities. Statistics from the 2002 Survey of Public Participation in the Arts show that readers are much more likely than non-readers to play sports and are also much more likely to visit art museums and attend performing arts and sporting events. According to the NEA's 2004 report, "Reading at Risk," readers of novels, short stories, poetry and plays are almost three times as likely to attend a performing arts event, nearly four times as likely to visit an art museum, and over one-and-a-half times as likely to attend sporting events or participate in sports activities. The NEA report also shows that literary readers are over twice as likely to do volunteer or charity work as those who do not read literature. Frequent book readers—those who read 12 to 49 books per year—are the most likely segment of the population to volunteer or do charity work. By reading, one acquires new information, and one becomes a better citizen, a better writer, and a more educated and influential person. Chicago educator Marva Collins may have said it best: "Readers are leaders."[29]

Revise a *lot*. You can usually make it funnier. –Dave Barry • When I was twenty I was in love with words, a wordsmith. I didn't know enough to know when people were letting words get in their way. Now I like the words to disappear, like a transparent curtain. –Wallace Stegner • The first attempts are absolutely unbearable. I say this because I want you to know that if you see something worthwhile in what I am doing, it is not by accident but because of real intention and purpose. –Vincent van Gogh • I know my stuff all looks like it was rattled off in twenty-three seconds, but every word is a struggle—every sentence is like pangs of birth. *The Cat in the Hat* ended up taking well over a year. –Dr. Seuss • A perfectly healthy sentence, it is true, is extremely rare. –Henry David Thoreau • Remember: what lasts in the reader's mind is not the phrase but the effect the phrase created: laughter, tears, pain, joy. If the phrase is not affecting the reader, what is it *doing* there? Make it do its job or cut it without mercy or remorse. –Isaac Asimov • Of every four words I write, I strike out three. –Nicolas Boileau • Nothing you write, if you hope to be any good, will ever come out as you first hoped. –Lillian Hellman • Writing is adding; editing is subtracting. –Michael Larsen • Easy reading is damned hard writing. –Nathaniel West • I struggle to be brief, and become obscure. –Horace • Good editors are really the third eye. Cool. Dispassionate. They don't love you or your work; for me that is what is valuable—not compliments. Sometimes it's uncanny; the editor puts his or her finger on exactly the place the writer knows is weak. –Toni Morrison • Nothing is a waste of time if you use the experience wisely. –Auguste Rodin • The chief difference between good writing and better writing may be measured by the number of imperceptible hesitations the reader experiences as he goes along. –James Kilpatrick • Writing means summoning oneself to court and playing the judge's part. –Henrik Ibsen • When you say something, make sure you have said it. The chances of your having said it are only fair. –E. B. White • Writing is one of the easiest things: erasing is one of the hardest. –Rabbi Israel Salanter • I hate to see a parcel of big words without anything in them. –William Hazlitt • The wastepaper basket is the writer's best friend. –Isaac B. Singer • There are days when the result is so bad that no fewer than five revisions are required. In contrast, when I'm greatly inspired, only four revisions are needed. –John Kenneth Galbraith • I love revisions. Where else in life can spilled milk be transformed into ice cream? –Katherine Paterson • If I don't rewrite them it's because I don't see how to write them better, not because I don't think they should be. –Robert Louis Stevenson

REVISION

The last act of writing must be to become one's own reader. It is, I suppose, a schizophrenic process. To begin passionately and to end critically, to begin hot and to end cold; and, more importantly, to try to be passion-hot and critic-cold at the same time. –John Ciardi • Nobody gives a damn about a writer or his problems except another writer. –Harold Ross • In order to read properly what one has written, one must think it again. –Jules Renard • I haven't quite reached the ruthless artistry which would let me cut out an exquisite bit that had no place in the context. –F. Scott Fitzgerald • The most essential gift for a good writer is a built-in, shockproof shit detector. This is the writer's radar and all great writers have had it. –Ernest Hemingway • If it can't be read aloud, it's no good. –John Braine • The writer does the most, who gives his reader the most knowledge, and takes from him the least time. –Charles Caleb Colton • In baseball, you only get three swings and you're out. In rewriting, you get almost as many swings as you want and you know, sooner or later, you'll hit the ball. –Neil Simon • It's okay if you mess up. You should give yourself a break. –Billy Joel • Writing is very improvisational. It's like trying to fix a broken sewing machine with safety pins and rubber bands. A lot of tinkering. –Margaret Atwood • Even Noble Laureates can benefit from the comments of a good editor. –Colleen McCullough • Writing is a two-person job. Even if you are a skilled editor of your own work, a second skilled editor will make suggestions you will inevitably miss, simply because, as the author, you lose a certain amount of objectivity. –Susan Page • The business of selection and revision is simply hell for me—my efforts to cut out 50,000 words may sometimes result in my adding 75,000. –Thomas Wolfe • I published it in the waste-paper basket. –Rudyard Kipling • I often covered more than a hundred sheets of paper with drafts, revisions, rewritings, ravings, doodlings, and intensely concentrated work to construct a single verse. –Dylan Thomas • I constantly rewrite—an incinerator is a writer's best friend. –Thornton Wilder • A writer is unfair to himself when he is unable to be hard on himself. –Marianne Moore • Editing is the same as quarrelling with writers—same thing exactly. –Harold Ross • Sentences and words are a passion and they do not just happen they evolve gradually. –Marty Martin • The pleasure of the first draft lies in deceiving yourself that it is quite close to the real thing. The pleasure of the subsequent drafts lies partly in realizing that you haven't been gulled by the first draft. –Julian Barnes • I rewrite endlessly, sentence by sentence; it's more like oxywelding than writing. –Patrick White • The last thing one knows in constructing a work is what to put first. –Blaise Pascal • An author of talent is his own best critic—the ability to criticize his own work is inseparably bound up with his talent. It *is* his talent. –Graham Greene • Brevity is the sister of talent. –Anton Chekhov • You want to write a sentence as clean as a bone. That is the goal. –James Baldwin • Writing is more like a sculpture where you remove, you eliminate in order to make the work visible. –Elie Wiesel • Does anybody learn writing, or do they just touch someone who lets them see the power of the deleted word? –Richard Bach • If we knew everything beforehand, all would be dictation, not creation. –Gertrude Stein

*The difference between the almost-right word and
the right word is really a large matter—it's the difference
between the lightning bug and the lightning.*

–Mark Twain, American writer

*Read and revise, reread and revise, keep reading and revising
until your text seems adequate to your thought.*

–Jacques Barzun, educator and historian

*One must not hold one's self so divine as to be unwilling
occasionally to make improvements in one's creations.*

–Ludwig van Beethoven, composer

*As every writer worth his salt very well knows, there is only one
specific irreplaceable term that fits into a certain situation. It is
the knack of hitting upon such terms continually, often by dint
of laborious effort, which distinguishes the great stylist
and helps dress the truth in beautiful garb.*

–Emile Cailliet, biographer and theologian

CHAPTER NINE
The Revision Process

The process of revision is about organizing your thoughts, then fine-tuning them and finding the right words to express exactly what you want to say. This thinking process takes time, and it's not easy. It involves contemplation and concentration, re-reading your writing several times, adding or deleting words or sentences or even whole paragraphs or pages, moving text around within your writing, fixing errors, and perfecting your word choices. "What is written without effort," eighteenth-century writer and lexicographer Samuel Johnson correctly recognized, "is in general read without pleasure." I share that sentiment, as have other writers throughout history. Ernest Hemingway rewrote the last page of *A Farewell to Arms* thirty-nine times before he was satisfied with it. When asked "What was it that had you stumped?" Hemingway replied, "Getting the words right." Henry David Thoreau, searching for the right words to express himself, laboriously wrote seven drafts of *Walden*—now a classic—over eight years. Biographer Edmund Morris once spent seven hours just trying to perfect a single sentence.[1]

These examples may sound extreme. However, what sets good writers apart from others is a willingness to revise the writing and perfect, as much as possible, one's arrangement and choice of words. When I write a letter to opposing counsel, for example, I often dictate a first draft using a dictaphone. After my assistant transcribes my dictation, I pull up the draft letter on my computer and revise it, often extensively. I modify the substance and structure of the letter, make sure the paragraph breaks make sense, and repeatedly go over and revise my selection of words. Dictating onto an audiotape is akin to freewriting, but sending out a letter as "dictated but not read" (as some people do) is a risky thing to do. Even a short letter may need substantial revision before it's ready to be mailed or faxed (or these days, put in a PDF file), and if something is hastily dictated it is unlikely to express exactly what needs to be said. Many times, I take the time to compose letters on my own keyboard without even using dictation because I know that writing effectively involves much more than typing up what first comes to mind—and that I will need to work with the words a great deal on my own anyway.

Above all else, the revision process requires attention to detail. After you have put all of your thoughts—however fragmentary—down on the page, you need to assess whether your writing is as logical, readable and engaging as possible. My own experience is that initial drafts of what I write can almost always be improved upon by doing more work. What I like to do is re-read what I've written and then step back and ask myself a series of questions: Is everything there that needs to be there? Or, are there gaps or leaps in logic in the text? Is the writing well-organized and complete? Does the structure work? When you revise, try asking yourself those same questions. And as you revise, make sure that your points flow logically. After you've done a draft, outline your main points to see if you've put them in the right order or if you need to add a section or take one out. To test the strength of a given idea or conclusion, build a syllogism: if A equals B and B equals C, then A better equal C. If your reasoning doesn't make sense, go back and rethink or refine your ideas. If your words are imprecise, add more precision.

When I'm editing, I like to work on the computer first and then later by hand—with a pen or pencil—after printing out what I've written. It's convenient to edit using a computer because text can be so easily added, deleted or moved—all right on the screen in front of you. However, it's also nice to be able to sit in a comfortable chair and read through a hard copy of a draft and be able to flip back and forth between pages. That gives me the chance to ask myself—and seek answers to—important questions. Have I said exactly what I want to say? Does the writing, as is, flow gracefully from one idea to the next, with seamless transitions? Have I used the best voice and the best tone for the task at hand? Have I misspelled anything? If I see that improvements can still be made, I continue on with the revision process until I'm satisfied with whatever it is that I'm writing.

Revision is about much more than tinkering with words; it is also about remaining open to changing *your thinking*. Until your thoughts are crystal clear—and those thoughts are articulated clearly on the page—you haven't finished the revision process, a process that makes you carefully consider, and then reconsider, thoughts and ideas. Writer Raymond Carver, who studied under John Gardner, the legendary fiction-writing teacher, believed strongly, as his teacher did, in continual revision. Here's how Carver—one of my favorite poets and writers—described Gardner's approach: "It was a basic tenet of his that a writer found what he wanted to say in the ongoing process of seeing what he'd said. And this seeing, or seeing more clearly, came about through revision. He *believed* in revision, endless revision; it was something very close to his heart and something he felt was vital for writers, at whatever stage of their development." If what you wrote doesn't sound right, your thinking or your words probably aren't right, though, through effort, they can be made so.[2]

Perfection is impossible to attain, but clear and intelligible writing is possible if one puts in enough time. The writer-naturalist Henry Beston, best known for his classic book, *The Outermost House: A Year of Life on the Great Beach of Cape Cod*, sometimes spent an entire morning on a single sentence, "unable to go on," his wife recalled, "until he was completely satisfied with both words and cadence, which he considered equally important." What you are trying to do when you revise is give more meaning and life to your words. "The more you zero in on the precise meaning you have in mind," writes Peter Elbow in *Writing with Power*, "the more you can strip away unnecessary words and thereby energize your language." In the end, you want your writing to pop and sizzle.[3]

The revision process is not a one-step procedure. It's not about reading through a draft once, fixing whatever you happen to see is wrong on that read-through and then stopping. Don't think of revision as going in once for a dental appointment to get your teeth cleaned and perhaps a couple of cavities filled. Instead, think of revision as going in for a series of major surgeries as well as a succession of regular check-ups. In fact, I tend to revise in what might be thought of as waves or layers. I might first revise for accuracy of content. I might then revise for completeness, then for overall structure. Later, I might revise for issues of voice, tone and style. At the end, I revise for grammar and spelling errors. Sometimes I revise in a more haphazard fashion, but I never just do one read-through. Because there's so much to do, it's actually hard to revise a piece of writing for everything at once. There are simply too many issues to consider at one time when revising, and breaking down the revision process into stages—with each stage concerned with a different issue—thus proves to be a much more efficient and effective way to get the job done.

Revising is not meant to be drudgery; it is intended to clarify and organize ideas, polish thought, and eliminate flat, confusing, or uninteresting prose. And it can be a satisfying process—if done right. Don't just take my word for it—listen to what other writers have had to say. "Revision is one of the exquisite pleasures of writing," novelist Bernard Malamud said; "Half my life is an act of revision," novelist John Irving once quipped, no doubt only half-joking. Indeed, there is a certain thrill in seeing words, sentences and paragraphs take shape, and that can only happen through revision. Without revision, writing can be bland and boring or, worse yet, muddled or misleading, leaving readers unsatisfied and rendering the writer's words ineffective. That is precisely why good writers do so much revision. Revising your writing line-by-line, and over and over again, is the best way—if not the only way—to make sure that you're saying what you really want to say.[4]

One proven technique for improving the quality of your work through revision is to read aloud what you've written. This allows you to hear what the reader will hear. If something sounds awkward when you read it aloud, it needs to be re-written. "Listen even for the tiniest jerk or stumble in your reading, the tiniest lessening of your energy or focus or concentration as you say the words," Peter Elbow advises. Ask yourself some specific questions as you re-read and revise. Does the writing make sense? Would a total stranger—someone with a totally different background than your own—understand the text? Is the writing authentic? Too wordy? Cumbersome? If something sounds odd or strained, fix it. Aim for accuracy and clarity, and try to strike the right note. Now try it. Take something you've written before and try to make it better by using this time-tested technique. If you find it too awkward to read in your normal voice, just mouth the words quietly to yourself. It will still help.[5]

In fact, silent reading is a modern phenomenon. Few people in ancient times could read or write, so they relied upon hearing words read aloud. According to Alberto Manguel's *The History of Reading*, not until the tenth century did reading silently become usual. Even as late as the eighteenth century, reading aloud was seen as the best way to enjoy literature. Silent reading, Manguel notes, gave readers "an unrestricted relationship" with printed words. "The words," he writes, "no longer needed to occupy the time required to pronounce them. They could exist in interior space...could echo just as well within as without." Silent *revision* is common, but reading aloud while you revise can produce better writing because so much of writing is about the sound of what you say. Good writing is pleasing to the ear; it's musical. "If it sounds good," Duke Ellington said, "it is good." Famed storyteller Robert Louis Stevenson went so far as to offer this suggestion: "Read every sentence aloud to yourself. Nothing which your own ear is dissatisfied with should stand."[6]

In the revision process, you need to make sure that every word counts. Pare down your writing so it effectively conveys ideas and information with clarity and elegance. Your readers will appreciate it if you condense your writing to include only what's necessary. If you don't edit, your writing may be rambling and unreadable, perhaps even full of errors in logic. "Brevity is the soul of wit," William Shakespeare famously remarked, expressing sentiments shared by others. "I have made this letter longer than usual," Blaise Pascal wrote, "because I lack the time to make it short." If you can say what you want to say in fewer words, do so. Author E. B. White's former English teacher, William Strunk Jr., put it succinctly in *The Elements of Style*: "Omit needless words."[7]

Only one caveat: don't eliminate so much text that your ideas become hidden, oversimplified or impossible to decipher. If you do, your writing may be misunderstood. Novelists like their readers to read between the lines, to interpret dialogue or events for themselves, but good nonfiction usually fully articulates the writer's ideas, blow by blow, without ambiguity. As a lawyer, part of my job is to communicate information to the court, and when I write a legal brief I must adhere to court-imposed page limitations. Federal district courts, for example, restrict litigants to 35-page briefs, which seems like a lot of space. But in really complicated cases, putting all the necessary facts and legal arguments in that number of pages is hard, and lawyers aren't permitted to just shrink the font size or reduce the margins. I've sometimes had to get a judge's permission to submit a longer brief than allowed by the rules. If you leave out too much, you risk omitting critical facts of interest to readers. Enough said.

As you revise, remember that descriptive details and word choices are particularly important. Consider the difference in meaning, some subtle and some not, among *cabin, house, home, manse, mansion, shack, tenement,* and *trailer.* Fancy words, such as *altercation* or *egress,* may slow readers down, whereas simpler alternatives, such as *fight* or *exit,* will not. If you choose the wrong word, or use the wrong detail, your writing will be less effective than it could be. What you need to do is put yourself in the reader's shoes and consider all of the writing that has turned you off over the years: all the writing you had to wade through as if you were trying to walk through a mosquito-infested swamp with thick undergrowth. Every kind of writing can benefit from revision. In 2004, the *Wall Street Journal* reported that New York personal-ad coaches, including a former writer for HBO's *Sex and the City*, actually command up to $150 per hour to help singles edit their ads so that the ads read better and generate responses. Single women and eligible bachelors, it seems, know that word choices matter, and so should any self-respecting writer. Indeed, if you don't eliminate awkward or clumsy phrasing in your writing, you risk bogging down your readers.[8]

Be particularly wary of redundant words or wordy phrases. Lawyers, I must admit, are frequent culprits, often using age-old catchphrases—*assault and battery, null and void, first and foremost* and *cease and desist*—even though one word alone would do just fine. Try to avoid such phrases and re-read your writing carefully to ferret them out. Instead of saying "I repeat again," say, "I repeat." Instead of "absolutely necessary," "honest truth" or "join together," write "necessary," "truth" or "join." As Robert Harris explains in his book, *When Good People Write Bad Sentences: 12 Steps to Better Writing Habits*, quantity of words shouldn't be confused with quality. "Because" is less wordy than "owing to the fact that" or "for the simple reason that"; "except for" is shorter than "with the exception of"; "after" is more concise than "after the conclusion of"; and "round" conveys the same information as "round in shape."[9]

The revision process—part of the writing process itself—takes intense concentration. In his book *Mind Wide Open: Your Brain and the Neuroscience of Everyday Life*, Steven Johnson writes about how he feels when he's in the midst of writing. "When I'm truly locked in working on a passage," he says, "a 747 could be taking off in the room and I wouldn't notice." To prove his point, Johnson paid a visit to Columbia University's Brain Imaging Group to have a head exam done with a five-ton, $2 million GE Twin-Speed fMRI scanner. That piece of equipment captures brain activity within a three-dimensional model of the brain by measuring levels of oxygenation in the blood of nerve cells. Johnson notes that, though roughly 500,000 neurons must be active in an area for the scan to register them, the fMRI scan "is as close to pure vision of the mind's inner life as current technology allows us." Just as the brain-imaging technique known as magnetoencephalography, or MEG, shows what regions of the brain are stimulated when various parts of the body are touched, PET scans and functional Magnetic Resonance Imaging pinpoint those regions of the brain that are active or inactive while we do specific things.[10]

Johnson's experiment called for him to read a passage from someone else's prose, as well as a passage from one of his own in-progress manuscripts, during his fMRI exam. The results—depicted on roughly forty color printouts, with images of Johnson's brain at "rest" and while reading—showed that Johnson's brain looked much different when he was reading and considering his own writing. "Look at this," Joy Hirsch, the program's director, told Johnson as she explained the recorded images. "The same areas are working, but they're working much harder with your own words. It's amazing." What struck Johnson about the image taken while he concentrated on forming a new sentence for his own passage of text was how brain activity was so centralized in one area. As Johnson described the microscopic patterns of blood flow and electrical activity he observed: "perhaps the most telling thing about my brain map was what didn't show up on the images." When he was focused, he noted, "there was almost no activity in areas that weren't related directly to the task at hand."[11]

One of the best ways to learn how to revise is to edit the

writings of others. When you're not revising your own words, you'll be more objective as you examine the quality of the structure, content and style of what's before you. A favorite exercise in writing classes—and for good reason—is to critique other students' work. This allows students to give feedback to one another so that everyone, through the resulting comments, can develop a critical eye for what works and what doesn't. Try it yourself with a friend or fellow writer. Exchange comments with one another and then talk through your respective critiques. You'll likely make discoveries that you wouldn't be able to make if you only looked at your own writing. Over time, practice with critiquing others' work will help you become a better judge of the quality of your own writing. If nothing else, you'll get valuable practice at identifying spelling, grammar and usage errors. Just make sure you're always respectful as you're giving your comments. Writing is personal, so suggestions to another must be packaged with care.[12]

In actuality, the revision process is a lot like a sculptor's work in that both revision and sculpting require similar skills and the same kind of intellectual absorption. A sculptor, Elbert Hubbard once noted, creates a beautiful statue by chipping away the unneeded parts of a marble block. It is, he said, a process of elimination. With writers, it's much the same: you start out with a mass of material and you're trying to shape what's there. Linda Pastan, a two-time National Book Award finalist, puts it this way: "I start with a lot of material, a kind of hunk of marble somehow excreted onto the page, and my job seems to be to chisel at it and chisel at it until everything that doesn't belong has been removed." Writer Joyce Carol Oates similarly likens writing and re-writing to sculpting. Just as the writer works diligently to execute a vision, Oates explains, the sculptor, too, envisions a sculpture that already exists within the piece of marble. All the sculptor has to do, Oates says, is "to chip away and sand away to release what's already there."[13]

Revising, admittedly, can be a daunting task, particularly if you're struggling with what you want to say. Oftentimes, entire sections of text must be re-worked or deleted for a piece of writing to take proper shape. This can be painful, as you may have spent hours or days (or even weeks or months) on what's in your text. However, restructuring of text and major changes, often involving wholesale deletions of what you originally wrote, are sometimes the only way to make your writing read well and make sense. The sheer number of words that may have to be jettisoned can be mind-boggling. In writing one of his plays, Chekhov reportedly wrote a page-long speech, then reconsidered and crossed out everything except for "Yes." Simon & Schuster editor-in-chief Michael Korda once famously told an author to turn more than seventy pages of text into "one very good sentence."[14]

Good writers are really just dedicated *revisers*. They take time to polish their words and how they are presented, and they resist the temptation to believe that what they said first was said best. They don't delude themselves, but believe that with more exertion, they'll be able to express themselves more effectively than they did on their first or second or even third or fourth tries. They are not (nor should be) perfectionists—though some try to be. They simply recognize that more effort will produce better writing, and that writing without revision almost always produces a poor quality text. In returning to the writer-sculptor comparison, I should point out that, in at least one respect, writers actually have it much better than sculptors. Whereas sculptors may chisel too deep and chip off an important piece of work—forcing the sculptor to begin anew with a new block of stone—writers can just "undo" a change or "cut" and "paste" text to the bottom of a document while considering whether to include it or exclude it.

When you revise, you need to consider the whole of your text even as you hone particular portions of it, one section at a time. Consider what Joyce Carol Oates says about how she works: "My method is one of continuous revision; while writing a long novel, every day I loop back to earlier sections, to rewrite, in order to maintain a consistent, fluid voice; when I write the final two or three chapters of a novel, I write them simultaneously with the rewriting of the opening of the novel, so that, ideally at least, the novel is like a river uniformly flowing, each passage concurrent with all the others." The same method should be used with non-fiction. If you want your writing to read smoothly, you'll need to take the time to revise so that creases and kinks disappear, just as they do at a dry cleaner after you drop off a wrinkled shirt or blouse.[15]

And make no mistake, time spent on re-structuring and re-working your writing will pay off. If it helps, try to think of creating a readable composition as building a house. First you need a rough sketch, your vision; then you need blueprints, the refinement of that vision; then there are the necessary raw materials, the lumber and shingles, the bricks and concrete, the windows and doors. This is followed by the labor, what it takes to build the foundation and the structure itself, with its beams and joists. Household appliances, a furnace, wiring, and gas and water hook-ups must be installed next to make the house functional, and there are, almost always, the inevitable change orders, the alterations to the original plans, either to deal with unforeseen circumstances or to accommodate a homebuilder's last-minute, impulsive desire to add some new feature. Only after all that is there a finished, habitable home—a place to put furniture and personal items. One can't expect to go, overnight, from rough architectural drawings and a messy construction site to a warm and fully furnished house.

And so it is with writing. Constructing a piece of writing takes painstaking effort; well-crafted paragraphs and sentences don't just materialize, they take time to construct.

No matter what kind of writing project you're working on, whether it be work-related or purely personal in nature, your satisfaction with the final product will be directly related to your investment of energy in it. The more time you spend on your writing, the better it will become. My first three books—*Death in the Dark: Midnight Executions in America*, *Kiss of Death: America's Love Affair with the Death Penalty*, and *Legacy of Violence: Lynch Mobs and Executions in Minnesota*—took countless hours to research, write and revise, as did the book you're reading now. Although it was a long process to go all the way from initial concept to the final bound books (many hundreds of hours per book), when I think of all the things of which I am most proud, my published books most readily come to mind. You, too, will be pleased with your writing if you put in the time it takes to make your prose readable, memorable and stylish.[16]

When revising, keep in mind your objective, your audience, and any constraints you are facing. "Each discipline has its own climate, its own expectations in written material," explains Donald Murray, author of *The Craft of Revision*. As Murray writes: "A writer, to be effective, needs to know the limitations of the assignment and then discover how to be creative within those limitations. Every art—the business letter, the poem, the research grant—is created from the tension between freedom and discipline." The writer has considerable latitude with any writing project, but that freedom must be exercised in a reasonable fashion given the nature of the task at hand. Obviously, the more time spent trying to strike the right chord, locating that delicate balance between a form's limitations and one's boundless creativity, the more likely one is to succeed at the task. "The writer has to control the material, to make sense of it," Murray writes, "by shaping the information into a form that gives the material meaning and carries that meaning to the reader."[17]

Words and phrases, of course, can obscure meaning or illuminate it. As Murray writes: "Writers write with information: accurate, specific, significant information. It is essential to the craft of revision to consider the information communicated in the draft. Words are the symbols for information, and when there is no information behind the words, the draft is like a check with no money in the account: worthless." Indeed, the use of a particular word in a particular sentence can either ruin that sentence or create a masterful one. Just consider President John F. Kennedy's word choices at his 1961 inaugural address:

> Let the word go forth from this time and place, to friend and foe alike, that the torch has been passed to a new generation of Americans, born in this century, tempered by war, disciplined by a hard and bitter peace, proud of our ancient heritage, and unwilling to witness or permit the slow undoing of those human rights to which this nation has always been committed, and to which we are committed today at home and around the world.

"And so, my fellow Americans," Kennedy said in that historic speech, "ask not what your country can do for you; ask what you can do for your country." The way Kennedy's words were put together shows just how powerful and moving individually linked words can become.[18]

On the other hand, words that are carelessly put together are apt to be less than rousing to listen to or read. Consider what two U.S. presidents had to say on the subject of unemployment.

Herbert Hoover, while campaigning for the presidency in 1928: "When a great many people are unable to find work, unemployment results." And Calvin Coolidge, while discussing the economic climate in the United States in 1931: "When more and more people are thrown out of work, unemployment results." With statements such as these, which state the obvious but fail to inspire or use language creatively, it's no wonder (if such statements are representative) that JFK ranks as a much more revered president than either Hoover or Coolidge on presidential surveys which consider, among other things, communication skills. As another American president, Franklin D. Roosevelt, once said, "Things depend so much on the way they are put."[19]

Because good writing requires the use of effective details, the revision process also entails making one's writing more vivid and specific. Writer Charles Johnson, a National Book Award winner and a fiction-writing teacher at the University of Washington, puts it this way: "When I'm writing, my whole process of revision is largely devoted to increasing the specificity of everything that is there, to try to see more vividly and with more detail in my imagination." "I tell my students all the time," he says, "You've got to be generous in the details that you give in your writing—and the best way to be generous is to be specific." Johnson, also a gifted cartoonist, compares what he does when he writes to what he does when he draws, which I think is a useful analogy. "I do think about things like the quality of light as it strikes the characters and creates shadows around them," he says, emphasizing, "I think about detail as minutely as I do when I'm drawing." Indeed, the study of other disciplines is a key to becoming an effective writer. "Music can prepare one for writing prose that is very metrical and cadenced and musical," Johnson notes, adding that one creative endeavor "cross-fertilizes" another.[20]

When you're revising, don't be afraid to elicit the opinions of others, whether for content or style. Your friends or colleagues may see things that you missed or that need further clarification or explanation. At the law firm where I work, it's common for lawyers to show one another their work prior to a particular letter or legal brief being sent out of the office. This way, any errors—whether in logic, grammar or spelling—are caught so that they don't diminish the credibility of a client's case or the firm's reputation. Although writing is a solitary activity, showing your work to others gives writing an interactive component and can alert you to flaws that can be corrected to make your writing stronger and better. One must learn, of course, to accept criticism (ideally, constructive criticism) of one's work. Try not to be defensive, even if you start feeling like a fool for something that you missed or did wrong. And don't just shrug off suggestions. Try to be open to revising your work if, upon analysis and reflection, it's clear that your writing could be improved.

Editors (and I don't just mean editors at publishing houses or magazines) serve a valuable role for writers, and all writers should have them, even if they are simply trusted friends or colleagues. "What a good editor brings to a piece of writing is an objective eye that the writer has long since lost," explains William Zinsser in his classic book *On Writing Well*. As Zinsser notes:

> [T]here is no end of ways in which an editor can improve a manuscript: pruning, shaping, clarifying, tidying a hundred inconsistencies of tense and pronoun and location and tone, noticing all the sentences that could be read in two different ways, dividing awkward long sentences into short ones, putting the writer back on the main road if he has strayed down a side path, building bridges where the writer has lost the reader by

not paying attention to his transitions, questioning
matters of judgment and taste.

A good editor is sometimes a luxury, but if one is available, don't
hesitate to take advantage of his or her comments or suggestions.
The writer may decide not to follow them, or may decide to follow only some of them, but a second (or even third or fourth)
opinion on one's own words never hurts.[21]

When editing your writing, another tip to keep in mind is that
effective writers typically use the active voice. In the active voice,
the subject of a sentence *performs* the action described by a sentence's verb. "She spilled the milk," is an example of the active
voice in use. "The milk was spilled by her" is a passive construction in which the subject *receives* the action. A passive voice weak-
ens prose and distances the reader from the action, and (you'll
notice) is both longer and more cumbersome. William Zinsser, the
reigning dean of the art of nonfiction writing, puts it succinctly:
"Use active verbs unless there is no comfortable way to get around
using a passive verb. The difference between an active-verb style
and a passive-verb style—in clarity and vigor—is the difference
between life and death for a writer." Good writers don't want
readers yawning through their prose, and using the active voice
will help you make sure that doesn't happen.[22]

There are, of course, situations where you'll want to use a passive voice. If the receiver of the action is more important than the
performer of it, or if you want to de-emphasize the role of that
performer, a passive construction may be optimal. Also, use of the
passive voice can help vary sentence structures or, less honorably,
avoid responsibility. "I lost your money gambling" is a much
more direct and informative statement (and more accepting of
blame) than "Your money was lost at a casino," which tells readers

nothing at all about who actually lost the cash or how. It's okay to use the passive voice, but use it sparingly. You don't want your writing to read like this famous example: "It was midday. The bus was being got into by passengers. They were being squashed together. A hat was being worn on the head of a young gentleman." The tortured passage continues: "A long neck was one of the characteristics of the young gentleman. The man standing next to him was being grumbled at by the latter because of the jostling that was being inflicted on him by him. As soon as a vacant seat was espied by the young gentleman, it was made the object of his precipitate movements and it became sat down upon."[23]

The most difficult question to answer: how do you know when your piece of writing is finished? That's a tough one because one's writing can almost always be improved. "A poem is never finished, only abandoned," believed the poet Paul Valéry. Writing instructor Anne Lamott offers only this, which I think makes good sense: you'll know when it's time to move on. "What happens," she says, "is that you've gone over and over something so many times, and you've weeded and pruned and rewritten, and the person who reads your work for you has given you great suggestions that you have mostly taken—and then finally something inside you just says it's time to get on to the next thing." Bottom line: when your writing gets so polished that you (or others) no longer find fault with it, even after searching for minor errors following multiple readings, you'll know that it's time to stop work on one writing project and start work on the next one.[24]

An integral part of the writing process (and one not to overlook) is proofreading—the fourth stage of the writing process. This involves making sure your writing contains no grammatical, spelling or factual errors. If you need to double-check your sources to make sure you've correctly cited, referenced or paraphrased them, do so. If you've typed "100 percent" when you meant to type "10 percent" and you don't catch your mistake, you'll look foolish. The revision process takes raw materials and transforms them into a usable product, just as iron ore is refined to make metal. The proofreading process is akin to polishing a finely crafted object into something of great beauty, like a bronze sculpture, a silver plate or a gold ring. If you don't proofread, you may send something out into the world that, later, you won't be proud of or may regret. A misspelled name or a thoughtless remark can be embarrassing; an important, improperly transcribed phone number can cause a major headache for the reader, who may need to reach someone right away, but will be unable to because of a writer's sloppy proofreading. Proofreading is your last best defense against such errors.

As you proofread, *assume* that typographical errors are in the text; they probably are, and only a word-by-word examination will reveal things that need fixing. Remember, the omission of a single word, even a hyphen, can totally change meaning. Language expert Bill Bryson uses the example of "the twenty-odd members" of a government's cabinet versus "the twenty odd members" of a cabinet. I myself was once interviewed by a newspaper reporter about my opposition to the death penalty, with the interviewer's questions and my answers then transcribed for a Q&A piece for St. Paul's Sunday morning paper. Luckily, I picked up an early edition of the *St. Paul Pioneer Press* at a nearby gas station on Saturday evening before the final edition of the Sunday paper was printed and distributed. The paper's early edition had a headline that mistakenly read: "A lawyer and author of a history of the death penalty in Minnesota argues that a problem of violence can be solved by violent means." The headline writer had erred by using the word "can" instead of "cannot," leading readers of the paper's early edition to believe (if they didn't read the text of the Q&A) that I somehow advocated capital punishment (which I don't). A quick telephone call to the paper's newsroom saved the newspaper from running a headline in its Sunday morning edition that contained a huge error, which should have been caught by someone other than me. What a difference a word makes, and what a difference proofreading can make to your final work product.[25]

To summarize, always remember to revise and proofread what you write. Don't just sit down, hammer something out, and then click send or ship it out, whether to a supervisor at work or to a publication's editor. Write something, but then take the time to go back and work on it and improve it. Try to shorten it. Try to make the prose tighter. Try to write better transitions between paragraphs. The more you do it, the better you'll get at it. If it's helpful, think of the revision process as a filter: you start out with a mass of rough material and endless possibilities, but by the time you're done you've winnowed out that material and are left only with the finest language that allows you to reach your targeted audience in the best way possible. If everything you send out is a first draft, everything you write, for the most part, will read like a first draft. Try to polish what you write and be relentless in your quest to find the right words to express exactly what you want to say, even if your words are just in the form of an e-mail to a friend or coworker. And be positive about the revision process. Revising can be fun, for—like the writing process—the revision process is about venturing into unknown territory and making new discoveries.

Nothing is as important as a likeable narrator. Nothing holds a story together better. –Ethan Canin • The task of the nonfiction writer is to find the story—the narrative line—that exists in nearly every subject, be it the life of a person or the life of a cell. –Russell Freedman • There is no longer any such thing as fiction or nonfiction; there's only narrative. –E. L. Doctorow • The trial lawyer's job and the novelist's were, in some aspects, shockingly similar. Both involved the reconstruction of experience, usually through many voices, whether they were witnesses or characters. –Scott Turow • The beginning is the most important part of the work. –Plato • I have decided to keep a full journal, in the hope that my life will perhaps seem more interesting when it is written down. –Sue Townsend • Writing fiction is a solitary occupation but not really a lonely one. The writer's head is mobbed with characters, images and language, making the creative process something like eavesdropping at a party for which you've had the fun of drawing up the guest list. –Hilma Wolitzer • The idea of writing down my memories rather smiles upon me. It is pleasant to wander down the lanes of yesterday into the land of long ago and to bring back tales. –W. Graham Robertson • Plot is to literature what individual holes are to miniature golf. –Stanley Elkin • The writer is like a person trying to entertain a listless child on a rainy day. –John D. MacDonald • Surrounded by my memories that night, I took my pen and I began to write. –Kuki Gallmann • The unread story is not a story; it is little black marks on wood pulp. The reader, reading it, makes it live: a live thing, a story. –Ursula K. Le Guin • If something comes into a writer's or painter's mind the only thing to do is to try it, to see what one can do with it, and give it a chance to show if it has real value. Story-telling is always experimental. –Sarah Orne Jewett • When we read a story, we inhabit it. –John Berger • There are several kinds of stories, but only one difficult kind—the humorous. –Mark Twain • The difference between a mountain and a molehill is your perspective. –Al Neuharth • How does one know which is the final version of a story? In the same way the cook knows when the soup is ready, this is a trade secret that does not obey the laws of reason but the magic of instinct. –Gabriel García Márquez • Storytelling is as innate to human experience as music, and some of us may feel a fundamental responsibility to recognize that and to seek as wide an audience as is possible. –Scott Turow • I always stopped when I knew what was going to happen next. That way I could be sure of going on the next day. –Ernest Hemingway • An author must learn the principles of good storytelling only in order to write better from the heart. –Uri Shulevitz

NARRATIVE

Originality does not consist in saying what no one has ever said before, but in saying exactly what you think yourself. –J. F. Stephens • Any sorrow can be borne, if you can turn it into a story. –Isak Dinesen • The more a picture has to give, the greater it is. –Henri Matisse • One should never write up or down to people, but out of yourself. –Christopher Isherwood • Writing has laws of perspective, of light and shade just as painting does, or music. If you are born knowing them, fine. If not, learn them. Then rearrange the rules to suit yourself. –Truman Capote • I see every thing I paint in this world, but everybody does not see alike. To the eyes of a miser a guinea is more beautiful than the sun, and a bag worn with the use of money has more beautiful proportions than a vine filled with grapes. –William Blake • Every good story is of course both a picture and an idea, and the more they are interfused the better the problem is solved. –Henry James • The purpose of narrative is to present us with complexity and ambiguity. If life's lessons could be reduced to single sentences, there would be no need for fiction. –Scott Turow • Poetry is the opening and closing of a door, leaving those who look through to guess about what is seen during a moment. –Carl Sandburg • The things I like to find in a story are punch and poetry. –Sean O'Faolain • A short story is like a stripped-down racer; there's no room for anything extra in there. –Robert Asprin • Your tale, sir, would cure deafness. –William Shakespeare • Stories are like genes, they keep part of us alive after the end of our story. –A. S. Byatt • Yes— oh dear yes—the novel tells a story. –E. M. Forster • I want the reader to turn the page and keep on turning to the end. This is accomplished only when the narrative moves steadily ahead, not when it comes to a weary standstill, overloaded with every item uncovered in the research. –Barbara Tuchman • You must try a thousand themes before you find the right one, as nature makes a thousand acorns to get one oak. –Henry David Thoreau • Action is eloquence. –William Shakespeare • He did not speak to them without a parable. –Gospel of St. Mark, 4:34 • If you're a writer, a real writer, you're a descendant of those medieval storytellers who used to go into the square of a town and spread a little mat on the ground and sit on it and beat on a bowl and say, "If you give me a copper coin I will tell you a golden tale." –Robertson Davies • An honest tale speeds best being plainly told. –William Shakespeare • The key to successful writing in finance and economics is storytelling. Tell stories and you'll never be accused of writing boring stuff about Wall Street or the dismal science. –Mark Skousen • Narration is as much part of human nature as breath and the circulation of the blood. –A. S. Byatt • Story-telling is an instinct to come to terms with mystery, chaos, mess. –Graham Swift • In all my work what I try to say is that as human beings we are more alike than we are unalike. –Maya Angelou • Show, don't tell. –Henry James • Tell me the story as it lies in your head. –Rudyard Kipling • There's something in a writer that lets us know when something works, a click of recognition. If the story were a person, it would come to life at that moment; it would start to breathe. –Alice Walker • Whenever there's something wrong with your writing, suspect that there's something wrong with your thinking. –Patricia T. O'Conner

No tears in the writer, no tears in the reader.

–Robert Frost, American poet

A word after a word after a word is power.

–Margaret Atwood, from the poem "Spelling"

All good books are alike in that they are truer than if they had really happened and after you are finished reading one you will feel that all that happened to you and afterwards it all belongs to you: the good and the bad, the ecstasy, the remorse and sorrow, the people and the places and how the weather was. If you can get so that you can give that to people, then you are a writer.

–Ernest Hemingway, author of THE OLD MAN AND THE SEA

Writing, when properly managed (as you may be sure, I think mine is), is but a different name for conversation.

–Laurence Sterne, eighteenth-century novelist

CHAPTER TEN

Storytelling

We all grow up listening to stories, and we all like to hear or tell them. Parents and grandparents tell stories around the dinner table; a scout leader tells a ghost story around a campfire; a comedian tells a series of jokes on stage; a boyfriend and girlfriend swap stories about old flames. I still remember listening to comedy albums of Bill Cosby in high school and laughing aloud; exchanging stories with college and law school roommates; and hearing stories about how my parents first met in a beginning social dance class at Ball State Teachers College in Muncie, Indiana. Stories are all around us, and they make life interesting. When I think about the past, I think about it in terms of stories. I bet you do, too.

Before discussing the pertinence of storytelling to the craft of writing, I should add that stories are no less important to me today than they were years ago. I go to movies and plays to watch stories unfold and to be entertained, and I tell stories to friends and neighbors and they, in turn, tell stories to me. Radio personality Garrison Keillor has fashioned a whole career, and become famous, by telling intricately woven and detailed stories about the fictional characters who live in Lake Wobegon. Stories are important to people, including me, because they allow us to experience other perspectives. They guide our lives, and they connect us to the world and to one another. As novelist Charles Baxter puts it, "We understand our lives, or try to, by the stories we tell."[1]

We all know people, certainly, who are better storytellers than others. Some people just have good timing and delivery skills, adept, perhaps, at using dramatic pauses or gestures. All of us, I bet, can think of a family member, a friend, or a friend of a friend who can make a story come alive like almost no one else. For some, it's an uncle or aunt, a brother or sister, or a grandparent. For me, it's my wife, Amy. As an elected official, she gives lots of speeches, and she has a knack for telling funny stories. One of her favorites is about the day she overheard our daughter, Abigail, then age five, talking to a friend in her room. Abigail and her friend were playing with dolls when Abigail's friend unexpectedly announced that, one day soon, she was going to have a baby. Amy leaned closer, listened anxiously for Abigail's response, and was relieved and delighted when Abigail told her friend in a loud, confident voice, "I'm going to have a baby, too, someday. But you can't have a baby until you run for office and win an election!"

The great thing about writing—as opposed to oral communication—is that you have ample time to make a story great, to get it just right, even if you're not the kind of person who, in conversation, can spin out a story with little or no advance notice. What the freewriting process allows you to do is put all your raw material—the facts of what happened—down on paper without requiring that you actually tell your story to anyone in an interesting or coherent form, at least initially. The revision process then enables you to work with the facts or details you have, or the events you've experienced, and shape and re-shape them until your story comes to life. It may take three drafts or it may take twelve drafts, but eventually you'll find a way to make your story work well on the page. By revising, you'll be able to make readers feel like they were right there, watching it all happen.

If you learn to tell good stories in your writing, your writing will get read and you will unleash a power that has been with us for centuries: the power of stories. "If you speak with passion," writer Richard Rhodes explains, "many of us will listen. We need stories to live, all of us. We live by story. Yours enlarges the circle." Well-crafted stories build bridges; they help connect you with your subject matter, and they help you, as a writer, connect with readers. In working out your story, you learn something, and once you've found that nugget others will want to read it. Award-winning biographer David McCullough puts it succinctly, in what rings true to me: "I'm always drawn to a good story—that's foremost. I'm very much interested in the power of the fundamental narrative of what happened."[2]

Good writing, I've discovered, usually tells a compelling story. The story can be in the form of a scientific discovery, the plot of a novel, or the real-life story of an individual, a group of friends, the origins of a company, or the aftermath of a tsunami or a California mudslide. Poetry is often less about narrative than it is about imagery or the sheer sound of words, but other writing, be it fiction or nonfiction, typically involves storytelling to one degree or another. Just think about it. The great American novels—John Barth's *The Floating Opera*, Ralph Ellison's *Invisible Man*, Jack London's *The Call of the Wild*, Harper Lee's *To Kill a Mockingbird*, and Mark Twain's *The Adventures of Huckleberry Finn*, to name just a few—all tell memorable stories. The great fables and fairytales—"The Ugly Duckling," "Cinderella," "The Hare and the Tortoise," and "The Sleeping Beauty"—are great because storytellers such as Hans Christian Andersen told enchanting or captivating tales that can be read or told again and again. And the great short stories—such as Raymond Carver's "What We Talk About When We Talk About Love," John Cheever's "The Swimmer," Franz Kafka's "Metamorphosis," and Flannery O'Connor's "Good Country People"—are anthologized and taught in schools because they tell dramatic and unforgettable stories.[3]

Though people tend to associate storytelling with fiction, storytelling techniques are equally important to nonfiction writing. Someone reading a magazine article, a biography or a memoir expects to encounter a good story as much as does a devotee of science fiction, literary or crime novels, or short stories. By storytelling, I don't mean that the nonfiction writer should exaggerate, embellish, or make up facts to entertain readers. Telling lies or half-truths in nonfiction is a big no-no; if you lose readers' trust, you've lost everything. What I mean by storytelling is that the material you use—whether it be facts, statistics or quotations—should be put together and conveyed in an interesting, moving fashion. Good stories often involve dramatic action—something happens, to someone or to something—and that action has, or is given, meaning in the text. A well-told story or piece of nonfiction not only holds readers' concentration, but it sparks readers' imaginations, perhaps even moving them to act themselves. "The storyteller shares the story," notes explorer Ann Bancroft, explaining how stories in themselves have the power "to ignite people to their own possibilities."[4]

To tell a good story, the first thing you need to do is get readers' attention. The use of an attention-getting device—a personal anecdote, the telling of a dramatic event, or a joke, for example—is a particularly effective way to draw readers into a narrative. If you don't get readers' attention right away, you're likely to lose them entirely or be unable to maintain their focus on what you have to say. There's a lot of writing out there in the world to read, and you want your writing to stand out. You certainly don't want readers to put down your writing after they've only gotten through the first paragraph or first page. And you certainly don't want your readers to be paraphrasing what American film producer Samuel Goldwyn once said, "I read part of it all the way through." If your writing is bland, confusing, or poorly organized, the reader may stop reading or simply skim your writing, missing the key points you wanted to get across.[5]

The elements of a good story—whether intended for children or adults—are universal. There is the opening or set-up: what draws readers into the story. There is the plot or story line, which must be told in a way that holds readers' attention. And there is the ending: the part of the story that wraps up loose ends and delivers the punch or the "aha" moment to readers. Good fiction normally has a conflict, a crisis, and a resolution, and nonfiction often does too, though a dramatic telling may be enough to carry readers to the last word even if there is no tidy resolution to the telling of real-life events. Conflict is what (or who) prevents a person from getting what is wanted, with the crisis prompting the resolution, if there is one. The stronger you can make your beginning, middle and ending, the stronger your story will be.

What holds virtually any good story together, of course, is its content, its compelling scenes or vignettes, and its compelling characters—the actors who perform the action, or are acted upon, in the story. When a story is told well, it has a certain *gestalt*—a wholeness to it—that is, perhaps, hard to define, though we seem to know it when we see it (or read it). The character of Huckleberry Finn, floating on a log raft down the Mississippi

River, is memorable; so, too, are the narratives I've read of those who narrowly survived the New York City terrorist attacks and the collapse of the World Trade Center towers. If a story captures the drama of what happened, how, and to whom, it can paint a picture as moving as any Academy Award-winning film or any of the finest oil paintings or sculptures in the Louvre Museum or the Musée d'Orsay in Paris.

Finding the right form for your story—the form that will best allow you to tell the story and connect with your audience—is a matter of trial and error. "There is only one right form for a story, and if you fail to find that form the story will not tell itself," Mark Twain wrote. "You may try a dozen wrong forms," he emphasized, "but in each case you will not get very far before you discover that you have not found the right one—and that the story will always stop and decline to go further." A good writer knows that a story, to be effective, must be appropriate for the audience, and must be told in an appropriate form. One particular form may work best, but in truth a story can be told in many ways; you just need to find *a* form that works well for you—and that the audience will appreciate. Again, your goal is to connect with your readers. Just as opposable thumbs allow humans to grab objects, librarian Carol Birch and educator Melissa Heckler write in an essay on storytelling, a well-told story is "a mental opposable thumb, allowing humans to grasp something in their minds—to turn it around, to view it from many angles, to reshape it, and to hurl it even into the farthest reaches of the unconscious."[6]

As you write and tell your story, the issue of perspective becomes particularly important. Perspective comes into play from two different vantage points: the *writer's* perspective and the *reader's* perspective. At the outset, then, the writer must carefully consider from what point of view a story, essay or article will be written, who it will be directed at, and whether it will be written in the past tense or the present tense. The writer—who always has an audience of at least one, himself or herself—especially needs to consider the make-up of the intended audience before deciding how best to tell a story or convey information. If you're writing for yourself, feel free to let loose; if you're writing for others, though, you need to pay attention to your likely readers and what they need or will want to know. Martin Luther King Jr.'s greatness as a communicator, writer James Baldwin once wrote, was "in his intimate knowledge of the people he is addressing, be they black or white, and in the forthrightness with which he speaks of those things which hurt or baffle them." If a writer does not consider the audience, that audience may be perplexed or even offended by the writer's words.[7]

Good stories can be told in many different ways. As a writer, you can be direct and to the point, like the no-nonsense sports-caster who calls plays from the press box or the blunt friend who is always the first to tell you when you need a haircut. You can tell it like it is, with as much spontaneity as you like, though the more you revise, the more polished (or even spontaneous) you can make your writing look. A direct approach—particularly with nonfic-tion—is often the best, because then there's no confusion about what you're trying to get across. On the other hand, you can also employ more subtle means to communicate an idea or get across a message—and that can work, too. Perhaps you want to leave readers lingering over a question or a series of questions. If you want readers to find their own way, an indirect approach—akin to painting an abstract work of art, but not titling it, leaving viewers to wonder what it portrays—may work best. There may, in fact, be multiple forms and approaches that work for your story, but you just need to find a form—and an approach—that is effective.

Storytelling is a judgment call, really, with little to guide you except your own intuition. Writer Margaret Atwood, for one, feels uncomfortable whenever she's asked what constitutes a "good" story, or what makes one story "better" than another. "Once you start making lists or devising rules for stories, or for any other kind of writing," Atwood writes, "some writer will be sure to happen along and casually break every abstract rule you or anyone else has ever thought up, and take your breath away in the process." As Atwood explains: "We don't judge good stories by the application to them of some set of external measurements, as we judge giant pumpkins at the Fall Fair. We judge them by the way they strike us. And that will depend on a great many subjective imponderables, which we lump together under the general heading of taste." All she wants from stories is what children want from them, which, she says, is quite a lot. "They want their attention held, and so do I," Atwood writes. "They want to feel they are in safe hands, that they can trust the teller." Children are longing to hear stories, she says, but only if the teller is longing to tell them. As Atwood writes: "If you want their full attention, you must give them yours. You must hold them with your glittering eye or suffer the pinches and whispering. You need the Ancient Mariner element, the Scheherazade element: a sense of urgency. *This is the story I must tell; this is the story you must hear.*"[8]

In her book, *Negotiating with the Dead: A Writer on Writing*, Atwood notes that "a writer is not the same thing as a tale-teller." The oral storyteller can improvise in the midst of a story, responding to the audience as the performance proceeds, while the writer composes alone and must "scratch" through "draft after draft," trying to anticipate the audience's reaction and perfect the story before releasing it in final form to an audience the writer "may never see or know." Atwood's comments are insightful, as is her description of the writer-audience relationship as "an upside-down V," with the writer and the reader "at the two lateral corners" with "no line joining them." Between them is a third point, the "text" or "written word," Atwood says, describing that point as "the only point of contact" between writer and reader. It is *that* point of contact that writers must keep in focus as they write—and as they read and revise their own work. If you absorb the techniques of other writers at that point of contact, you'll discover techniques that you can use in your own writing, even if the writers you're reading are faraway or buried in distant cemeteries.[9]

A look at how children's authors write for kids is instructive for any writer because the same narrative techniques that work for children also work with adults. Russell Freedman, the Newbery Award-winning author of *Lincoln: A Photobiography*, has this to say about writing nonfiction for a young audience: "I believe that a book of history or a biography can carry within its pages a magical power. It can convey all the vividness and immediacy of great fiction while retaining the authenticity, the additional power, of lived experience." Freedman's secret: "Whether I'm writing a biography of Abraham Lincoln or an account of child labor, I think of myself first as a storyteller and I do my best to give dramatic shape to my subject, whatever it may be." Storytelling devices associated with fiction, he explains, can also be used to add drama to nonfiction; two of the most effective techniques being the use of vivid, detailed scenes and character development. To bring President Lincoln to life, Freedman used plenty of concrete details, such as the fact that the commander-in-chief would say "Howdy" to visitors and invite them to "stay a spell." "It's important for the reader to picture people and events," Freedman notes, "but it's also important to hear those people talking." Through a writer's portrayal of a character's appearance, mannerisms, and dialect or manner of

212 Writing for Life

speaking, we come to know the personalities of the characters in our stories.[10]

When writing a narrative, be specific. The use of actual names and real places is almost always more effective than using generic descriptions or characterizations. If you read that "a man and a woman" walked down the "street" of a "city" or "large metropolitan area," very little imagery comes to mind, and you've actually learned very little. But if the writer reports that she once saw John Lennon and Yoko Ono stroll hand-in-hand through New York City's Central Park, the reader learns something concrete. Likewise, if one reads that someone is a "good athlete," what does that tell you, exactly? At what sport? In comparison to whom? Wouldn't it be better to tell readers, for example, that "Bill can run a 4-minute mile" or that "Anne has a .400 batting average in softball." Only by using specificity is one's writing brought to life. Every time you use a concrete detail, you enrich a sentence. In contrast, the use of vague language may only fill up space without adding meaning or evoking feeling or engaging the readers' senses.

The use of concrete, well-constructed narrative throughout a piece of writing is what will move readers, perhaps even to tears of joy or sorrow. "When you write," Ernest Hemingway advised, "your object is to convey every sensation, sight, feeling, emotion, to the reader. So you have to work over what you write." Your objective as a writer is to transport readers to a different place or realm, to put them in a different state of mind. You do this by writing in a way that your readers can relate to and by using words that they can take in as naturally as they inhale or exhale. Some types of writing—appliance instruction booklets or computer software manuals, for instance—will contain fewer stories and not be nearly as exciting to read as an award-winning novel or book of essays. But even technical writing, business letters or legal briefs, which must follow certain conventions, can still be written in an interesting and lively manner. Purposeful narrative can make learning how to use a cell phone or a computer fun, just as well-written corporate sales proposals can be both informative and engaging. Even the law, with all of its arcane statutes and lengthy regulatory codes, can be presented in an inviting fashion. The law, after all, affects people's lives in real and dramatic ways, and people's lives are inherently interesting.[11]

When it comes to storytelling, writing differs from other mediums in significant ways. Three major art forms that we encounter on a regular basis are film, prose and theater. Movies and television programs often evoke quick laughter, even tears, because we receive information and images through our eyes and ears. "Film images are even more intense than those in reality," playwright Stuart Spencer writes, "because they have been selected and deliberately distilled into a purer form in order to achieve greater impact." Theater also has strong visual and aural dimensions to it, with actors themselves all contributing to an instantaneous, visceral effect on the audience. In comparison, written texts, which can also move us, generally evoke a more contemplative response. "When we read a line of prose," Spencer writes, "the brain is required to go through certain analytical processes that are not required of it when watching a film." Watching TV or a movie— or a theater performance—allows viewers to be completely passive during the experience. Writing, by contrast, requires the reader's full participation, and is an interactive experience requiring that readers actively use their minds as they read and respond to the writer's words. To keep readers engaged, the writer must thus use artful storytelling techniques.[12]

When telling stories, writers have many arrows in their quivers, from personal experiences and memories to statistical facts and opinions. James Baldwin, the Harlem-born writer, believed, as I do, that all writing grows out of life itself. "One writes out of one thing only—one's own experience," Baldwin wrote. "Everything depends on how relentlessly one forces from this experience the last drop, sweet or bitter, it can possibly give," he said. You've had experiences in your life and you've learned things: use those experiences and that knowledge in your writing. If you take what you've learned and fashion it, through drafting and revision, into authentic prose that has meaning for others, then you will have become a first-rate storyteller and performed a valuable service in the process. As writer Andrew Greeley explains: "The storyteller invites the members of the audience to enter his world for a brief time, to meet his creatures, to love them, if only just a little, and to learn from them and their lives possibilities for their own lives. Thus it becomes possible that the readers will leave behind the world of the author with a richer understanding of who they are and who they might become."[13]

Although words can bluntly communicate emotions or information, writers can also let words *reveal* through the use of description. This is often a particularly effective technique, as writer Natalie Goldberg explains:

> There's an old adage in writing: "Don't tell, but show."…It means don't tell us about anger (or any of those big words like honesty, truth, hate, love, sorrow, life, justice, etc.); show us what made you angry. We will read it and feel angry. Don't tell readers what to feel. Show them the situation, and that feeling will awaken in them.

In other words, instead of using abstract characterizations, use descriptive language that makes people *feel* what you're trying to get across. If you use words to show people crying in a church pew at the funeral of a teenage drunk-driving victim, you don't need to tell readers that those people are "sad"; if you show someone jumping up and down after winning the lottery, you don't need to tell us that the person is "happy." Readers are smart; if you show them the right details, they will get what you intend to convey without being explicitly told it.[14]

Sometimes, a writer needs to show *and* tell. It's okay to do both, but just remember that words can be even more moving and powerful if readers are allowed to see for themselves what *led* the writer to a particular conclusion. If you tell readers that someone was "mad," you will have conveyed an important piece of information, but done little more than that. Showing the reader what made that person mad is usually much more effective because it allows the reader to empathize with that person or the situation. *Show* the underlying circumstances: the details of a car accident or lost job, the thing that hurt or angered that person. And *show* the person's reaction as the car crashed or upon hearing the bad news. Was there blood on the dashboard? Was a fist pounded on a table? If you *show* readers what happened, they'll go away knowing more and be more satisfied (or better able to visualize what actually transpired) in the process.

When telling (or showing) your story, try to write it up with the same unique voice you use in ordinary conversation—only better. Don't try to write in a way that is different from how you normally communicate, but use the kind of language you normally would, keeping in mind the particular circumstances that are compelling you to write. If you try to write in a way that you think will make you sound "literary" (whatever that is), you'll only sound pretentious or use words improperly if you're not familiar with how to use them. Instead, be yourself, although you should try as hard as possible—as writer Les Edgerton suggests—to eliminate "the warts." If you constantly say "y'know" or "like" or "um" when you talk, those expressions, or fillers, don't belong on the page (unless, of course, you're trying to capture someone's particular dialect or pattern of speech in a piece of writing). If you just be yourself, your writing will have personality, originality and force. Truman Capote, the author of *In Cold Blood*, gave especially good advice. "What I am trying to achieve," he said, "is a voice sitting by a fireplace telling you a story on a winter's evening."[15]

To write well, you must do much more than transcribe what you might say to someone orally. Ordinary speech or dialogue usually makes for dry reading if simply transcribed, as I can attest from reading trial and deposition transcripts that record lawyer's questions and the word-for-word testimony of witnesses. People speak in sentence fragments, skip from one thought to the next, and repeat themselves. Your speaking voice is what gives your writing distinctive personality, and that voice should not be ignored. After all, your individuality and unique perspective—forged by your own life experiences—are your greatest assets as a writer. "Writers seldom write just as they speak," Kingsley Amis reminds us in *The King's English*, "but they move away from their speaking voice at their peril." That said, only revision brings writing to life. Oral speech and good writing differ in that written words are chosen and crafted more carefully, with written texts typically going through several rounds of revision before entering the world. United States Supreme Court Justice Stephen Breyer describes the ideal, saying his aim is to write "not the way I speak, but how I would like to speak."[16]

When trying to tell a story, don't worry if, at first, you don't get it quite right. As writer Patricia Hampl writes: "[A]s with any attempt to tell a story, it is necessary to put something first, then something else. And so on, to the end. That's a first draft." Beginning a story is hard, as Hampl explains: "The first thing I usually notice at this stage of composition is the appalling inaccuracy of the piece." And telling a story well all the way through is even harder—though it can be done—because you have to fit all the details together in a compelling way. Indeed, writer E. L. Doctorow likens the process of writing a story to crossing a dark forest with only a flashlight to light the way. The writer, he notes, cannot see the final destination, but can see enough to take the next step and, by walking, can eventually get there. If it helps, think of revision as a Sherpa guide: a trusted companion who, even in the dark, can lead a climber, at high altitudes, from base camp—over ice falls and through treacherous weather—to the top of Mount Everest.[17]

What I can tell you is this: if you take the time you need to write and then adequately revise the story you want to tell, you won't regret it. You'll be proud of what you've created, and your story, if shared with others, will make a valuable contribution, regardless of whether your story informs or merely entertains. That is because stories give our lives meaning and help us get through life, no matter what twists and turns life has in store for us. As writer Anne Lamott reflects on the importance of stories: "We are given a shot at dancing with, or at least clapping along with, the absurdity of life, instead of being squashed by it over and over again. It's like singing on a boat during a terrible storm at sea. You can't stop the raging storm, but singing can change the hearts and spirits of the people who are together on that ship."[18]

Style is character. –Joan Didion • As for style of writing, if one has anything to say, it drops from him simply and directly, as a stone falls to the ground. –Henry David Thoreau • English is a stretch language: one size fits all. That does not mean anything goes; in most instances anything does not go. –William Safire • This diary writing has greatly helped my style; loosened the ligatures. –Virginia Woolf • The adjective is the banana peel of the parts of speech. –Clifton Fadiman • The greatest possible mint of style is to make the words absolutely disappear into the thought. –Nathaniel Hawthorne • You have to write a million words before you find your voice as a writer. –Henry Miller • Irony is that little grain of salt which alone renders the dish palatable. –Johann Wolfgang von Goethe • Prose = words in their best order; poetry = the *best* words in the best order. –Samuel Taylor Coleridge • Style, of course, is what every good young author looks to acquire. –Norman Mailer • Styles, like everything else, change. Style doesn't. –Linda Ellerbee • Reading your work aloud, even silently, is the most astonishingly easy and reliable method that there is for achieving economy in prose, efficiency of description, and narrative effect as well. Rely upon it: if you can read it aloud to yourself without wincing, you have probably gotten it right. –George Higgins • A good writer is one you can read without breaking a sweat. –Patricia O'Conner • There is a great mystery in the way words meet each other in rhymes and puns, like amorous couples of the most diverse origin. –Harold Acton • Self-plagiarism is style. –Alfred Hitchcock • What's another word for *thesaurus*? –Steven Wright • Fashion passes, style remains. –Coco Chanel • Make everything as simple as possible, but not simpler. –Albert Einstein • First have something to say, second say it, third stop when you have said it, and finally give it an accurate title. –John Shaw Billings • The business of literature is to reveal life. –Maxwell Perkins • I am convinced that writing prose should not be any different from writing poetry. In both cases it is a question of looking for the unique expression, one that is concise, concentrated, and memorable. –Italo Calvino • I keep telling young writers I meet that if they want the sure road to success, for heaven's sake, write something that will make people laugh. –Bennett Cerf • Humor is the secret weapon of the nonfiction writer. It is secret because so few writers realize that it is often their best tool—and sometimes their only tool—for making an important point. –William Zinsser • A humorist entertains his readers. A satirist makes them think. –Richard Armour • Finding one's own manner is elusive. While it certainly helps to develop a unique style, first you have to learn how to write. –Norman Mailer

STYLE

Words have weight, sound and appearance; it is only by considering these that you can write a sentence that is good to look at and good to listen to. –W. Somerset Maugham • Word-carpentry is like any other kind of carpentry: you must join your sentences smoothly. –Anatole France • A good title should be like a good metaphor: It should intrigue without being too baffling or too obvious. –Walker Percy • Don't try to be witty in the writing, unless it's natural—just true and real. –F. Scott Fitzgerald • One can cure oneself of the *not un-* formation by memorizing this sentence: A not unblack dog was chasing a not unsmall rabbit across a not ungreen field. –George Orwell • It is hard to utter common notions in an individual way. –Horace • Great literature is simply language charged with meaning to the utmost possible degree. –Ezra Pound • Let's have some new clichés. –Sam Goldwyn • The test of good prose is that the reader does not notice it any more than a man looking through a window at a landscape notices the glass. –W. H. Auden • Language is more fashion than science, and matters of usage, spelling and pronunciation tend to wander around like hemlines. –Bill Bryson • Don't tell me the moon is shining; show me the glint of light on broken glass. –Anton Chekhov • Commas in *The New Yorker* fall with the precision of knives in a circus act, outlining the victim. –E. B. White • Have no unreasonable fear of repetition. –James J. Kilpatrick • The word *glamour* comes from the word *gram-mar*. –Steven Pinker • Always be a poet, even in prose. –Charles Baudelaire • Have something to say and say it as clearly as you can. That is the only secret of style. –Matthew Arnold • A simile must be as precise as a slide rule and as natural as the smell of dill. –Isaac Babel • I know it's finished when I can no longer stand working on it. –Bernard Malamud • The adjective is the enemy of the noun. –Voltaire • In conversation you can use timing, a look, inflection, pauses. But on the page all you have is commas, dashes, the amount of syllables in a word. When I write I read everything out loud to get the right rhythm. –Fran Lebowitz • Don't say it was "delightful"; make *us* say "delightful" when we've read the description. You see, all those words (hor-rifying, wonderful, hideous, exquisite) are only like saying to your readers "Please will you do my job for me?" –C. S. Lewis • Forward motion in any piece of writing is carried by verbs. Verbs are the action words of the language and the most important. Turn to any passage on any page of a successful novel and notice the high percentage of verbs. –William Sloane • In writing, punctuation plays the role of body language. It helps readers hear the way you want to be heard. Careful use of those little marks emphasizes the sound of your distinctive voice and keeps the reader from becoming bored or confused. –Russell Baker • Arguments over grammar and style are often as fierce as those over IBM versus Mac, and as fruitless as Coke versus Pepsi and boxers versus briefs. –Jack Lynch • If it takes a lot of words to say what you have in mind, give it more thought. –Dennis Roth • I don't wish to sign my name, though I am afraid everybody will know who the writer is: one's style is one's signature always. –Oscar Wilde • Style is a very simple matter; it is all rhythm. –Virginia Woolf • Writing style is like clothing—the decorative covering we put over the content. –Jack Rawlins

It's not what I do, but the way I do it.
It's not what I say, but the way I say it.

—Mae West, film star

When I was twelve, people told me that if I want to be
successful, I must change my grip, give up this two-handed backhand.
I said I would change, but I knew I wouldn't. The truth is I am a very stubborn
person. I was hitting the ball and it felt good to me, so I said to myself, why
change? It is important to find your own personality in the game, your own style.
You have to find it, no one else can find it for you.

—Björn Borg, Swedish tennis player

Style is something peculiar to one person; it expresses one
personality and one only; it cannot be shared.

—Freya Stark, travel writer

Style is a simple way of saying complicated things.

—Jean Cocteau, writer and filmmaker

CHAPTER ELEVEN

Effective Communication

Style is an elusive concept. In the world of fashion, for example, what is fashionable one year may not be the next. Long skirts may be all the rage, then shorter skirts, but then mini-skirts or pants suddenly become trendy. Polyester is hot in one decade, then it's decidedly not in the next; wool and cotton, as opposed to synthetic fabrics, take over as what everyone wants to be seen in and wearing. And, needless to say, we all have different views about what looks good and what doesn't, just as we all have different conceptions of beauty. One need only look around at people, or talk to them, to come to this realization. Although we all have different conceptions of what style is, style, however loosely defined, is, undeniably, a desirable, much sought after quality.[1]

With writing, style also depends largely upon who is defining it. "Proper words in proper places make the true definition of style," author Jonathan Swift advises. "The greatest thing in style is to have a command of metaphor," Aristotle tells us. In her essay "What Is Style?" Mavis Gallant puts it this way: "Style in writing, as in painting, is the author's thumbprint, his mark." We all want our writing to be stylish, of course, but just how does one go about acquiring that intangible, often elusive quality? It's an issue writers have grappled with since they began writing centuries ago, and it's what humorist Garrison Kellior's *Prairie Home Companion* creation, private investigator Guy Noir, might call "one of life's most persistent questions." That's because style is hard to pinpoint and achieve—even though we all know that we want to make the best impression we can in our communications with others.[2]

For many writers, myself included, style is really, at its core, about making the writing the most interesting and readable as is humanly possible. This means using varied sentence constructions with clear language full of interesting details and images, even if the writer uses mostly common, one-syllable words. "Art," the Italian philosopher Saint Thomas Aquinas said, "is the human disposition of sensible or intelligible matter for an esthetic end." Three things, Aquinas said, are needed for beauty: wholeness, harmony and radiance. Well put. Ask yourself: Does your writing flow gracefully as you cover all of your points? Is your writing lively or bland? If it's bland or choppy, then continue to write and revise. You want your writing to pack a punch. At the outset of a writing project, you're tapping feeling, even passion. "Find what gave you emotion; what the action was that gave you excitement," Ernest Hemingway advised, telling writers how to begin. "Then write it down, making it clear so that the reader can see it too," he said. By the end, you want to have built something remarkable, not just have filled up the page with words. Your aim is precision and persuasive, effective prose. "Prose is architecture, not interior decoration," Hemingway noted.[3]

For me, as with many other writers, style is also about saying something of importance. If I don't have something to say, it will be hard for me to write something worth reading by someone else. "Style in writing," notes columnist William Safire, "is not just elegance in phrasing; it should marshal argument and prose to move or persuade." When I write, I want my writing to have an impact on its audience. I want to give readers new information, and I want to move readers to my way of thinking. You should always, of course, pay attention to the esthetics of language—how something is phrased. But you also must be sure that your words, however beautiful they may sound, are conveying real meaning. Content and style, in fact, are closely linked to one another. Until you have a clear idea of what you want to say in terms of substance, selecting the best words to express yourself will be hard. On the other hand, playfully experimenting with language—trying out one phrase and then another—can help you unearth good ideas. Neither content nor style can be separated from one another, with language being the only way to convey anything of beauty or consequence. As the poet Anne Sexton said, "Content dominates, but style is the master."[4]

The writing project you're working on may dictate what is acceptable and what may not be. You need to work within the tradition of a given form to have your writing taken seriously—and to be considered a stylish writer. A lawyer, for example, cannot pen and submit a sonnet or twelve-stanza poem to the U.S. Supreme Court in place of a traditional appellate brief. The nation's highest court has specific rules governing the form and submission of briefs, and those rules don't allow the submission of poetry in lieu of a recitation of procedural history, facts and arguments. But so long as readers' expectations as to form are met, a writer has lots of room *within a given form* to be creative. Indeed, effective speaking and writing often defy the audience's expectations in ways that are not too outlandish to the audience's sensibilities. If an audience expects a sermon or lecture, perhaps a humorous story may work best for an orator; if readers expect to encounter a dry, technical manual, but get a witty, yet informative set of instructions, readers will be thankful and relieved.

Use the revision process to hone your delivery and to create a readable, engaging style. Be creative, but show respect for a form's limitations. "You can work against reader expectation when the draft communicates significant information in the manner most appropriate to that information," explains revision expert Donald Murray, "but it is important, in some way, that you let the reader know—in one way or another—that you know the reader's expectations and are contradicting them on purpose." In other words, let readers know that you know what you're doing. Murray gives a specific example. "The challenge of academic writing," he writes, "is to find a way within the tradition to express your own critical views, to be individual within formal limitations." Whether you need to write a paper for class or a letter for work, you don't want to leave your teacher or audience thinking you're a buffoon or don't know what you're doing. You want to be original, but you also don't want to say something inappropriate or offensive for the occasion. Writing is ineffective if it leaves readers perplexed or disappointed.[5]

You don't need to use long or obscure words to woo your audience. "Short words are best and the old words when short are best of all," Winston Churchill offered; "I never write *metropolis* for seven cents because I can get the same price for *city*. I never write *policeman* because I can get the same money for *cop*," advised Mark Twain, a master stylist who earned his living as a writer, often getting paid by the word. One study shows that just twenty monosyllabic words account for twenty-five percent of all spoken English. The words, in order of frequency, are simple: *I, you, the, a, to, is, it, that, of, and, in, what, he, this, have, do, she, not, on* and *they*. It need not be any different with writing. Short words, like *sun, moon, heat* or *glass*, have strength and grace. Don't be afraid to use them; if you do, and you use them properly and with class, your writing will be powerful, not weak. Long words have their place, but don't try to use them just for the sake of using them. Reserve their use to when such words are called for or needed.[6]

To have style, you need to use proper grammar and carefully connect the words you use, paying attention to issues of tense, clarity, feel and structure. Try to avoid unwarranted tense changes. A shift from the past tense to the present tense can jar readers and lead to confusion about what happened or when it happened. And try to put paragraphs and words in the right order so that they make sense. If you don't pay attention to such things, your writing will not take readers efficiently from point A to point B, but will resemble a train wreck or a pile of bricks. In *Write Right!*, Jan Venolia gives the following example of a misplaced modifier: "Sylvester picked up a girl in a blue jacket named Bonnie." Presumably, the writer is trying to tell us the girl—not the jacket— is named Bonnie, but the sentence, as written, is not clear on that point at all. There is a big difference, Venolia notes elsewhere, between "He told her that he wanted to marry her frequently" and "He frequently told her that he wanted to marry her." Only by carefully proofreading what you write will you be able to avoid such missteps. I personally like the advice of nineteenth-century English essayist Matthew Arnold: "Have something to say and say it as clearly as you can. That is the only secret of style."[7]

Using the right tone and voice are critical components to writing effectively. *Tone* is a musical concept; it has to do with the sound of language. Writer Les Edgerton describes tone as "another way of describing the *mood* of a piece." The tone, he says, "transports you to an emotional place as a reader." A tone can be ironic, sarcastic, melodramatic, excitable, dry, serious, formal, sentimental, just about whatever you want it to be. Whenever I write, I try to strike the right chord for the audience and the occasion. If I'm writing a demand letter, asking a litigant to pay my client money, I try to take a confident and firm tone about the merits of my client's case. In contrast, in writing an e-mail to a close friend, I always try to be witty, so my tone tends to be flippant or whimsical. What you don't want is to sound discordant or off-key.[8]

Voice is a much more intangible quality. It consists of who you are and all of the influences that have shaped your life. "A writer's voice," explains Pat Schneider, a well-known writing teacher, "is an incredibly delicate instrument made up of all the places he or she has been, all the persons loved and lived with, all the cultural nuances of original neighborhood, workplace, home, country, continent, historical period, and personal story." We all have a distinct voice, but that voice can sometimes be difficult for a writer to locate, particularly if one has anxieties about the writing process. "Forget that you are writing. Just talk onto the page," advises Schneider, calling your "colloquial speech"—the "language of home" you learned growing up—one of your most valuable assets. "Use it," she says. "Your own first-learned speech is the primary color on your artist's palette. Everything else you learn will add variety, but the language of your own childhood home is your greatest treasure, your primary source." Just remember: after you freewrite, you still need to revise to refine the way your voice sounds on the page.[9]

In writing, deciding on what voice to use—let alone what tone to employ—can be tricky. In his book, *Finding Your Voice: How to Put Personality in Your Writing*, Les Edgerton notes: "There are a thousand different voices you might possess. The important thing is that the voice be yours and no one else's." But what *is* your voice? The truth, of course, is that you have many voices—and can use many tones of voice. You may speak with tenderness to a child, with authority or confidence to a client or coworker, or with vulnerability to a lover. Salespeople often put on an act to make a sale. "This is the best product I've ever used," they say, and they try to mean it. "Voice," writer Richard Rhodes explains, "is a role you put on, as an actor puts on a role when he steps out onto the stage." Your approach should reflect your feelings. If you are angry or irritable and you want to get that across, your tone should show that; if you are cynical, your writing may reflect that; and if you are happy, let that joy show through your voice and the tone of that voice. Above all else, don't be afraid to reveal yourself on the page.[10]

Admittedly, locating and then maintaining your chosen voice and tone can be challenging at times. You may find it difficult to find the exact words you're looking for, either to express an abstract idea or to convey the importance of a specific event. A good way to capture the emotional state you're trying to achieve in your writing is to look at a photograph or an object that will trigger a memory. Even tastes or smells—of, say, baked ham or lilacs—can conjure up particular memories. You want your readers to see or experience what you have, but you also need to retain your judgment and not get too close to your subject (at least while you're writing and analyzing what you're writing about). You need to stay detached from your text as much as possible so that you don't fall in love with what you first write—and so you have the judgment to revise and thus improve your writing. If you've been away from a piece of writing too long and have lost touch with what you were trying to accomplish, re-read what you've written so that you can recapture your voice and tone and keep them consistent as you finish the piece.[11]

The cadence of your writing is critically important. As writer Bonni Goldberg explains, "A piece isn't complete until you're satisfied with how it sounds out loud: the rhythm of the phrasing, the melody of the words grouped together." "It is," she says, "like choreographing a dance: each word is a member of the company and you are in charge of orchestrating their movements." If monotony is hard to take, then varied sentence structures and evocative words keep things interesting. "For me, writing is a question of finding a certain rhythm," notes French writer Françoise Sagan, who wrote her first novel, *Bonjour Tristesse*, at age eighteen. "I compare it," she says, "to the rhythm of jazz." If you want readers to breeze through your writing, use short sentences and short paragraphs. Long sentences and lengthy paragraphs tend to slow readers down and make them linger over (if not put down) your words, while shorter segments of text speed up the pace. Whereas a sentence of fifty words may make the reader feel as if she or he is floating down a meandering river, a sentence of two words can produce a staccato-like effect.[12]

Even punctuation can regulate the way readers read. As writer Lynne Truss explains, "On the page, punctuation performs its grammatical function, but in the mind of the reader it does more than that. It tells the reader how to hum the tune." "Periods punctuate. They create pauses, and pauses create emphasis," Stephen Wilbers, author of *Keys to Great Writing*, writes, noting how other punctuation marks, like commas and semi-colons, serve similar functions. Parentheses are often used to make humorous asides; colons create anticipation; semi-colons, first used in 1494 by Venetian printer Aldus Manutius, suggest a close relationship between two statements; dashes highlight an abrupt interruption in the text and create emphasis; and question marks force readers to ponder things. Indeed, punctuation marks—akin to the notations that guide musicians when playing musical scores—were used by Greek dramatists centuries ago to guide actors in how to read their parts. The earliest known punctuation, dated to around 200 B.C. and credited to Aristophanes of Byzantium, advised actors when to breathe.[13]

How something sounds shapes how the reader perceives, or reacts to, the content of what is said. "That guy's a nerd," will elicit a different response (and has a much different feel to it) than "That man has poor social skills." Likewise, "I planned a candlelight dinner" is not comparable to "We'll be eating without lights" or "I'm going to light something on fire before we eat." Thus, combine your words—and pick your words and punctuation—carefully. "Rhythm," Les Edgerton explains, is "related to breath control." Just ask a poet. Robert Pinsky likens writing to jazz improvisation, and fellow poet Mary Oliver emphasizes the importance of "chosen sounds" in crafting a quality poem. As Edgerton sagely advises: "Read your work aloud. In longish passages, especially, see if you find yourself running short on breath before the natural pauses." If you find you're out of breath by the time you reach a comma, a semi-colon or a period, your natural rhythm is being violated. "Rewrite the sentence," he says, "until you can read it easily without straining your lungs."[14]

Writing with style also means revising your text—not only for content and sound, but to eliminate unnecessary verbiage. Again, brevity is desirable. As English professor William Strunk, one of the authors of *The Elements of Style*, wrote: "Vigorous writing is concise. A sentence should contain no unnecessary words, a paragraph no unnecessary sentences, for the same reason that a drawing should have no unnecessary lines and a machine no unnecessary parts. This requires not that the writer make all his sentences short, or that he avoid all detail and treat his subjects only in outline, but that every word tell." Other well-known writers have had similar advice which would be wise to heed. Ernest Hemingway—a master stylist—especially liked the rules he learned early in his career as a reporter for the *Kansas City Star*. Among what he called the best writing rules he ever learned: "Use short sentences," "Use vigorous English," "Be positive, not negative," "Never use old slang," and "Eliminate every superfluous word."[15]

Certain kinds of words—such as adjectives—should be used sparingly. Reserve their use to make your meaning more precise. "As to the adjective, when in doubt, strike it out," Mark Twain advised, reflecting his wariness of this type of word, which sometimes just takes up space without adding a lot or serving any function. The teacher and poet Billy Collins actually asks his students "to take off all the modifiers and see what they have left." This is a particularly good strategy to try with your own writing. Take something you've written in the past, and see if you can make it shorter and crisper by cutting out some adjectives. As Collins says, "The adjective can be a parasite that feeds off the noun and eventually kills it. There's nothing like a good noun standing there on its own. Cup. Hat. Bone. Each one tells its own long story." It's okay to use adjectives, but don't let them overrun your writing. Consider the use of a noun on its own, as adjectives often add little to the meaning of sentences.[16]

Adverbs, too, are often unnecessary. "You will clutter your sentence and annoy the reader if you choose a verb that has a specific meaning and then add an adverb that carries the same meaning," William Zinsser notes in *On Writing Well*. Don't say a radio "blared loudly" or that someone "tightly clenched" his teeth, Zinsser says, explaining that "blare" connotes loudness and that there's no other way to clench one's teeth. Redundant adverbs weaken verbs. And it is strong verbs that make or break prose. As Donald Hall and

Sven Birkerts write in the ninth edition of their book, *Writing Well*: "Verbs act. Verbs move. Verbs do. Verbs strike, soothe, grin, cry, exasperate, decline, fly, hurt, and heal. Verbs make writing go, and they matter more to our language than any other part of speech." When overused, adverbs slow down the action; when verbs are used properly, they make language soar or make prose move at the speed of light.[17]

Getting rid of sexist language, which only perpetuates stereotypes, also makes for more effective writing. Not all doctors or lawyers are men; not all nurses or elementary school teachers are women; and both sexes dance, do gymnastics and play soccer and basketball. Your writing should reflect such realities. It's not much more work to write *firefighters* as opposed to *firemen*, and it's less likely to offend your readers. To write more inclusively, you can alternate between using *he* or *she* in specific examples or you can convert nouns or pronouns from singular (e.g., *she* or *he*) to plural (*they* or *their*). It's okay to call a male member of Congress a *congressman* or a female member of Congress a *congresswoman*, as it would be political correctness at its worst for writers to deny themselves the use of common words. But use good judgment when you write. Although *The American Heritage Dictionary* now lists *waitron* as a neutral substitute for a *waiter* or *waitress*, no one I know uses *waitron* to ask for service in a restaurant. *Server* maybe, but not *waitron*. In your writing, you don't need to ignore the gender of people, but you should always be sensitive to the fact that sexist language reinforces negative stereotypes.[18]

More than anything else, effective nonfiction writing is precise, not obtuse. In his famous 1946 essay, "Politics and the English Language," writer George Orwell lamented that "the English language is in a bad way." After citing a number of ineptly worded passages he'd read before, Orwell noted that what they shared in common was "staleness of imagery" and a "lack of precision." "The writer either has a meaning and cannot express it, or he inadvertently says something else, or he is almost indifferent as to whether his words mean anything or not," Orwell wrote, condemning the passages at issue as being full of abstract generalizations or ambiguous phrases. "This mixture of vagueness and sheer incompetence is the most marked characteristic of modern English prose," Orwell warned, saying that all too frequently "prose consists less and less of *words* chosen for the sake of their meaning, and more and more of *phrases* tacked together like the sections of a prefabricated henhouse." People use "worn-out metaphors which have lost all evocative power," Orwell noted, "because they save people the trouble of inventing phrases for themselves." Foreign words and expressions are used "to give an air of culture and elegance," he said, adding that writers often use "pretentious diction" to "dress up" what would otherwise be simple statements.[19]

To illustrate the problem, Orwell translated a well-known verse from Ecclesiastes into what Orwell derided as "modern English." The verse: "I returned and saw under the sun, that the race is not to the swift, nor the battle to the strong, neither yet bread to the wise, nor yet riches to men of understanding, nor yet favour to men of skill; but time and chance happeneth to them all." The translation, Orwell's parody: "Objective consideration of contemporary phenomena compels the conclusion that success or failure in competitive activities exhibits no tendency to be commensurate with innate capacity, but that a considerable element of the unpredictable must invariably be taken into account." Whereas the Biblical verse uses crisp, vivid images and contains just sixty syllables, the parody, with its long words, has ninety syllables and—in Orwell's words—"contains not a single fresh, arresting phrase."[20]

The lesson: the concrete is more effective than jargon or the vague and abstract. "As I have tried to show," Orwell wrote, "modern writing at its worst does not consist in picking out words for the sake of their meaning and inventing images in order to make the meaning clearer." "It consists," he said, "in gumming together long strips of words which have already been set in order by someone else, and making the results presentable by sheer humbug." At a 1977 conference of sociologists, *love* was defined as "the cognitive-affective state characterized by intrusive and obsessive fantasizing concerning reciprocity of amorant feelings by the object of the amorance." The concept of love is complex, but come on, can't we do better than that? Even today, many politicians speak of *revenue enhancers* or *user's fees* instead of *taxes*; *shock and awe* instead of *bombing*; and *anti-personnel devices* instead of *land mines*. During the Vietnam era, the term *pacification* was used in place of *invasion* or *war* and the phrase *silent majority* was coined to describe those who did not oppose the government's policies. Even those killed in action were described as *inoperative combat personnel*.[21]

Fortunately, Orwell pointed out, the misuse of prose "is reversible." That's because people have control over how they write. "Modern English, especially written English," Orwell wrote, "is full of bad habits which spread by imitation and which can be avoided if one is willing to take the necessary trouble." "If one gets rid of these habits," he said, "one can think more clearly, and to think clearly is a necessary first step towards political regeneration." It's important—whether in politics, business or in any other arena—to avoid words that only obscure reality. When auto dealers sell *pre-owned vehicles*, for example, should the buyers of them feel any better than if they bought *used cars*? I don't think so; so writers at least, if not salespeople, should call such cars by what they are: "a beat-up Mustang," "a rusty Toyota truck," or "a Ford with over 100,000 miles on it," as the case may be. A good writer should enlighten, not muddy the waters.[22]

A scrupulous writer, Orwell advised, will ask at least four questions with every sentence written: "What am I trying to say? What words will express it? What image or idiom will make it clearer? Is this image fresh enough to have an effect?" And perhaps two more: "Could I put it more shortly? Have I said anything that is avoidably ugly?" "The great enemy of clear language is insincerity," Orwell wrote, explaining: "When there is a gap between one's real and one's declared aims, one turns as it were instinctively to long words and exhausted idioms, like a cuttlefish squirting out ink." What's needed, he said, is to let one's meaning choose the word, and not the other way around. "In prose," he wrote, "the worst thing one can do with words is to surrender to them." One's words are chosen to make an impression on others, and you want to have a mastery of the language you use so that you can make the best impression possible.[23]

In the end, Orwell came up with the following rules that he felt "will cover most cases":

(i) Never use a metaphor, simile or other figure of speech which you are used to seeing in print.
(ii) Never use a long word where a short one will do.
(iii) If it is possible to cut a word out, always cut it out.
(iv) Never use the passive where you can use the active.
(v) Never use a foreign phrase, a scientific word or a jargon word if you can think of an everyday English equivalent.
(vi) Break any of these rules sooner than say anything outright barbarous.

Orwell saw a need for writers to cut out all "stale" images, "vagueness" and "prefabricated phrases" so that language expresses ideas and does not "corrupt thought." His advice is just as smart today as it was in 1946.[24]

There are times, of course, as Orwell recognized, when you'll want to break the rules. Users of language may choose a passive construction, for example, to de-emphasize the person who performed, or is performing, the action. This happens all the time for various reasons. "Mistakes were made"—Ronald Reagan's famous dismissal of the Iran-Contra scandal—sounds and feels a lot different than a statement such as "I take full responsibility." What specific mistakes? Who made them? When he delivered that line, Reagan was making a deliberate choice, but he certainly wasn't thinking of the motto on President Truman's desk: "The Buck Stops Here." In other instances, a foreign word like *détente* may best express the concept or thought you want to express. But if you're writing for an audience that speaks and reads primarily English, be wary of using any foreign words or phrases that your audience is not likely to understand.[25]

The development of a writer's style, or voice, is critical to that writer's success as a communicator. What the writer has to say may be of the utmost importance, but if the writer cannot say what she or he wants to say in a captivating way, the writer's words may never be read at all. Skill is necessary, but so, too, is vision and execution. Writer Raymond Carver puts it nicely: "Some writers have a bunch of talent; I don't know any writers who are without it. But a unique and exact way of looking at things, and finding the right context for expressing that way of looking, that's something else." Although talent is common, Carver explains, what every good writer delivers—and should deliver—is *a unique perspective*, one that cannot be found someplace else. "It's akin to style, what I'm talking about, but it isn't style alone," he said. "It is the writer's particular and unmistakable signature on everything he writes. It is his world and no other. This is one of the things that distinguishes one writer from another." It's a writer's special way of looking at things and that writer's ability to express that way of seeing, Carver says, that makes any writer truly great.[26]

Although one's style develops only over time, a number of valuable writing techniques can be used at any time to add style to a writer's prose. These techniques include the use of metaphor or simile, suspense or satire, rhyme or alliteration, foreshadowing or hyperbole, repetition or parody, or vivid imagery. A thoughtful comparison can illuminate; intentionally holding something back may pique the reader's interest; understating or exaggerating something can make a point. Also, evocative images may move readers or playful prose can powerfully achieve its principal purpose, particularly if it's not pointless, patronizing, prolix pageantry penned with the parasitic panache of a pathetic, persnickety pawnbroker, a pugnacious, paranoid purveyor of parakeets, partridges and piranhas and protected species of penguins, parrots and pileated woodpeckers, or perhaps a preachy, unpalatable pollster or pamphleteer prone to partisan punditry and pandering in the press replete with perplexing platitudes paired with polarizing political psychobabble and pseudoscientific, psychoanalysis. Phew! But slight of hand is not enough. The writer Kurt Vonnegut emphasizes that a "winning" style begins with "interesting ideas in your head." As Vonnegut writes: "Find a subject you care about and which you in your heart feel others should care about. It is this genuine caring, and not your games with language, which will be the most compelling and seductive element in your style."[27]

To add color, spice and flair (a dash of tabasco sauce, if you will, to liven things up), I find humor to be as disarming as it is effective. Even a simple joke—even a corny one—can break the ice. "A good laugh," Laura Ingalls Wilder once advised, "overcomes more difficulties and dissipates more dark clouds than any other one thing." Humorists such as Dave Barry, who once quipped that "the metric system did not really catch on in the States, unless you count the increasing popularity of nine-millimeter bullets," and who taught writing to business people for eight years and tried, in his own words, to get his students "to stop writing things like 'Enclosed please find the enclosed enclosures,'" know funny lines take discipline and hard work to write, perhaps more so than any other kind of writing. But the payoff is well worth the effort. It's simply hard to beat a well-executed setup followed by a witty punch line. For example, in *Monty Python and the Holy Grail*, a knight says, "'Tis but a scratch," after his adversary cuts off both of his arms. The line generates a laugh because the film audience can plainly see the sheer absurdity of the words. Mark Twain's comment, "Whenever I get the urge to exercise, I lie down and rest until it goes away," is funny for much the same reason; it, too, juxtaposes thoughts you wouldn't ordinarily expect to hear side-by-side. If the form you're using permits humor, use it. Your audience will appreciate the comic relief.[28]

Writing, after all, should be pleasing to read. If you forget that, you've lost your way and may find yourself on the road to nowhere. As writing guru William Zinsser writes: "You must find some way to elevate your act of writing into an entertainment." "Usually," Zinsser explains, "this means giving the reader an enjoyable surprise." "Any number of devices," he notes, "will do the job: humor, anecdote, paradox, an unexpected quotation, a powerful fact, an outlandish detail, a circuitous approach, an elegant arrangement of words." Instead of using clichés such as "the cat's out of the bag" or "the horse is already out of the barn," come up with an original line. Why not try using something along the lines of what President Richard Nixon's assistant, H. R. Haldeman, came up with to describe Watergate disclosures: "Once the toothpaste is out of the tube, it's hard to get it back in." The craft of writing is serious business, but neither your words nor your voice on the page need betray that fact.[29]

Metaphors and analogies are two of a writer's most valuable tools. Metaphors invite categorization and inference. Because they require a mental leap from one thing to another, they also require logic and the use of imagination. Whereas similes compare using "like" or "as," metaphors go a step further. "Metaphor," writes Natalie Goldberg, "is saying the ant *is* an elephant." Metaphors are useful because they explain the unfamiliar in terms of the familiar. Both ancient and modern writers have used metaphors to bring understanding and fresh insight, and you should use them, too. "Ordinary words," Aristotle explained, "convey only what we know already; it is from metaphor that we can best get hold of something fresh." Susan Goldsmith Wooldridge puts it nicely in her book *Poemcrazy: Freeing Your Life with Words*: "Metaphor is a bridge bringing things together. The world is a stage. Life is a dream."[30]

The use of analogies—the drawing of an extended likeness between two things, with the writer showing that a feature or pattern in one is also present in the other—can also help people better understand complex ideas, processes or situations. In legal disputes, for example, lawyers constantly encounter disagreements that, while novel in some respect, may closely resemble legal disputes that were already resolved by a judge. A competent lawyer will find such legal precedents and then, arguing by analogy, try to persuade the judge to rule in a certain manner based on those prior court rulings. Metaphors and analogies demand logical thinking and creativity, but all of us are creative and can reason, making these tools available to everyone.[31]

Of course, to write gracefully and with clarity, you need to know about grammar and proper word usage and gain a command of the language. "Grammar is glamour," writes Peter Elbow in *Writing with Power: Techniques for Mastering the Writing Process*. "Writing without errors doesn't make you anything," he explains, "but writing with errors—if you give it to other people—makes you a hick, a boob, a bumpkin." His point, I think, seems pretty clear. Just as a foul-smelling guy wearing dirty, cut-off shorts and a torn t-shirt at a black-tie affair will have difficulty finding a dance partner, a person using bad grammar will have a problem getting his or her writing taken seriously. If you think grammar doesn't matter, think again: people in the workforce need to communicate effectively, and good grammar facilitates effective communication. That's why businesses spend big bucks on training people to write. And that's why it's particularly disturbing that the National Commission on Writing found that "more than 50 percent of first-year college students are unable to produce papers relatively free of language errors."[32]

William Safire's satirical "Fumblerules of grammar" illustrate just some of the grammar and usage pitfalls to avoid when composing text:

> Don't use no double negatives.
> Proofread carefully to see if you any words out.
> Take the bull by the hand and avoid mixed metaphors.
> If I've told you once, I've told you a thousand times,
>   resist hyperbole.
> "Avoid overuse of 'quotation "marks."'"
> Avoid commas, that are not necessary.
> If you reread your work, you will find on rereading that
>   a great deal of repetition can be avoided by rereading
>   and editing.
> Avoid clichés like the plague.
> Never use a long word when a diminutive one will do.

Avoid colloquial stuff.[33]

Of course, most of these directives are just suggestions disguised as directives. There are times, for example, when you may want to use a cliché to make a point—and that's perfectly okay. If you're writing about someone who is constantly using clichés, you couldn't capture the essence of that person without using them. In the case of double negatives, usage expert Patricia O'Conner (using a cliché, no less) says "Never say never." Double negatives are sometimes handy, she notes, if you want to avoid coming right out and saying something. She gives the following illustrations when people use them for effect: "Your blind date is not unattractive." "I wouldn't say I don't like your new haircut." People use double negatives to be clever or polite or for other reasons. Just be aware that William Safire has good reasons for asking writers to avoid the kinds of pitfalls he warns against in his rules. You may find a valid reason for using a cliché, a double negative, or even a mixed metaphor, but it better be a good one.[34]

If you think you'll never be able to write anything original, let that thought go, too. Because of the sheer diversity of words, every piece of writing—unless plagiarized—is likely to be unlike any other currently in existence. With a "combinatorial system" like language, expert Steven Pinker explains, "there can be an unlimited number of completely distinct combinations with an infinite range of properties." "Go into the Library of Congress and pick a sentence at random from any volume," he says, "and chances are you would fail to find an exact repetition no matter how long you continued to search." The number of unique sentences that a person can produce is breathtaking, he notes. With such limitless possibilities, writing becomes a wondrous opportunity. It may take much revision to find the best way to express yourself, but that's okay. Words are all around you; all you have to do is pluck them from where they hang waiting, like the ripe fruit of an orange or plum tree. As the poet Robert Frost said, "All the fun's in how you say a thing."[35]

The meaningful choices writers possess give them great freedom, but also a responsibility (to their readers) to choose wisely among all those choices. A writer, for instance, can paint a house *green* or *emerald* or *yellow* or *cream-colored* or can describe a lawyer as *zealous* or *overzealous*. These subtle (or not-so-subtle) distinctions matter. The writer's choice of words in a particular context evokes certain feelings or images in readers. When connected, strings of words have the ability to bore, give profound insight, or send a reader soaring to new heights. It all depends on which words are chosen for the job and how well they perform. It's not possible to purge language of all clichés—what William Zinsser calls "the enemy of taste"—but good writers generally enliven their writing when they eliminate lackluster figures of speech such as "bored to tears" and "nip it in the bud." These are the kind of pre-fabricated phrases that George Orwell warned about. Even slang can invigorate writing by conveying intense feeling. Although slang should be used sparingly, here's what Abraham Lincoln's biographer, Carl Sandburg, had to say on the subject: "Slang is a language that rolls up its sleeves, spits on its hands and goes to work."[36]

Words, if wielded properly, can make a difference. They can cajole and persuade, they can move the will of a nation, and they can redeem, even save, lives. When President Abraham Lincoln gave his Second Inaugural Address—just 703 words arranged in twenty-five sentences and four paragraphs—it was heralded by abolitionist and African-American newspaper editor Frederick Douglass as a "sacred effort" and "more like a sermon than a state paper." "With malice toward none; with charity for all," Lincoln began the concluding paragraph, words that so moved Douglass that, at a eulogy for Lincoln, Douglass predicted that Lincoln's words "will live immortal in history," as they have—etched in stone at the Lincoln Memorial in Washington, D.C. Dr. Martin Luther King Jr.'s "Letter from Birmingham Jail" shaped American history, as did Abigail Adams's many letters to her husband. I personally know lawyers whose skillful advocacy and legal briefs have spared death-row inmates' lives. Albert Burrell, Donald Gunsby and David Wilson are alive today because their cases were presented in a persuasive way in habeas corpus proceedings. If the right words are woven together into coherent, vibrant sentences, and those sentences are pieced together into well-crafted paragraphs, the result can be as remarkable as the double-helix in a strand of DNA.[37]

Ultimately, effective writing is clear and engaging, and it brings a fresh perspective to a subject or issue. "Style is a product of highly conscious effort but is not self-conscious," Eudora Welty writes, adding: "Even with esthetic reasons aside, the self-consciousness would not be justified. For if you have worked in any serious way, you *have* your style—like the smoke from a fired cannon, like the ring in the water after the fish is pulled out or jumps back in." A writer's reward for attaining a discernible, effective style is the knowledge that one has said best what had to be said, or that a way has been found to articulate a thought or idea in a novel way. When Muhammad Ali said, "Float like a butterfly, sting like a bee," he was expressing himself with style. All writers should aim to do the same thing when they spar and box with words in the ring of language.[38]

A real writer is always shifting and changing and searching. –James Baldwin • My own best advice to young writers is: follow your curiosity and passion. What fascinates you will probably fascinate others. But, even if it doesn't, you will have devoted your life to what you love. An important corollary is that it's no use trying to write like someone else. Discover what's uniquely yours. –Diane Ackerman • My future is one I must make myself. –Louis L'Amour • What we call the beginning is often an end. And to make an end is to make a beginning. The end is where we start from. –T. S. Eliot • Human progress is neither automatic nor inevitable. –Martin Luther King Jr. • As long as you live, keep learning how to live. –Seneca • The habits of a vigorous mind are formed in contending with difficulties. –Abigail Adams • Craft is a grab bag of procedures, tricks, lore, formal gymnastics, symbolic superstructures—methodology, in short. It's the compendium of what you've acquired from others. –Norman Mailer • Shoot for the moon. Even if you miss it you will land among the stars. –Les Brown • I'm a great believer in luck, and I find the harder I work, the more I have of it. –Thomas Jefferson • Opportunity is missed by most people because it is dressed in overalls, and looks like work. –Thomas Edison • I realized early on that success was tied to not giving up. –Harrison Ford • I studied the lives of great men and famous women, and I found that the men and women who got to the top were those who did the jobs they had in hand, with everything they had of energy and enthusiasm and hard work. –Harry S. Truman • If you risk nothing, then you risk everything. –Geena Davis • Develop interest in life as you see it; in people, things, literature, music—the world is so rich, simply throbbing with rich treasures, beautiful souls and interesting people. –Henry Miller • We must become the change we wish to see in the world. –Mahatma Gandhi • I discovered that writing was a mighty fine thing. You could make people stand on their hind legs and cast a shadow. –William Faulkner • If you lose the power of wonder, you grow old, no matter how old you are. If you *have* the power of wonder, you are forever young—the whole world is pristine and new and exciting. –Sigurd Olson • All writers are quintessentially American—we fear that not to progress is to plunge into the abyss. And we may be right. –Joyce Carol Oates • It's very easy to write when you're a writer; you have the words trained and they come to your hand like birds. –Pablo Picasso • The great writer does not really come to conclusions about life; he discerns a quality in it. –J. Middleton Murry • Today is the first day of the rest of your life. –Abbie Hoffman • I want to do it because I want to do it. –Amelia Earhart

ENDINGS

I can't imagine not needing to write. I should be very unhappy if I couldn't write. –Iris Murdoch • You cannot have a great democracy without great writers. –Norman Mailer • The pen is mightier than the sword. –Edward George Bulwer-Lytton • I really do inhabit a system in which words are capable of shaking the entire structure of government, where words can prove mightier than ten military divisions. –Václav Havel • I've used my talents as a writer to enable the Ogoni people to confront their tormentors. I was not able to do it as a politician or a businessman. My writing did it. –Ken Saro-Wiwa • What lies in our power to do, it lies in our power not to do. –Aristotle • If writing did not exist, what terrible depressions we should suffer from. –Sei Shōnagon • Words are healers of the sick tempered. –Aeschylus • But a man or woman who publishes writings inevitably assumes the office of teacher or influences the public mind. –George Eliot • I must write to keep my sanity. Writing is the insulin of a disease of long standing. I must take my regular dose or go under. –Sigurd Olson • Too many people in the modern world view poetry as a luxury, not a necessity like petrol. But to me it's the oil of life. –John Betjeman • When power corrupts, poetry cleanses. –John F. Kennedy • Success comes to a writer, as a rule, so gradually that it is always something of a shock to him to look back and realize the heights to which he has climbed. –P. G. Wodehouse • He turns not back who is bound to a star. –Leonardo da Vinci • As a general rule television is better than words in newspapers at communicating wars, and words are better than television at communicating peace. –Nicholas Tomalin • To find the psychic energy to pursue a long career, it seems to me, a writer must juggle between a vigorous, recording curiosity about the world and how it works and the ongoing process of self-creation. –Edmund White • Example is not the main thing in influencing others. It is the only thing. –Albert Schweitzer • All the poems I have written were written for love; naturally, when I have written one, I try to market it, but the prospect of a market played no role in its writing. –W. H. Auden • The time is always right to do what is right. –Martin Luther King Jr. • It is the greatest shot of adrenaline to be doing what you've wanted to do so badly. You almost feel like you could fly without the plane. –Charles Lindbergh • You must once and for all give up being worried about successes and failures. Don't let that concern you. It's your duty to go on working steadily day by day, quite steadily, to be prepared for mistakes, which are inevitable, and for failures. –Anton Chekhov • Actually, I'm an overnight success. But it took twenty years. –Monty Hall • The direction in which education starts a man will determine his future life. –Plato • God, what a hell of a profession to be a writer. One is one simply because one can't help it. –F. Scott Fitzgerald • It is essential to remember that the creative end is never in full sight at the beginning and that it is brought wholly into view only when the process of creation is completed. –Brewster Gheislin • The public is the only critic whose opinion is worth anything at all. –Mark Twain • A writer is a vehicle. –John Irving • Writing can be a lot of fun. Nothing beats the feeling you get when you're writing something good—except the feeling you get when you're finished. –Patricia T. O'Conner

Nothing is particularly hard if you divide it into small jobs.

–Henry Ford, automaker

*In the long run we shape our lives and we shape ourselves.
The process never ends until we die. And the choices
we make are ultimately our own responsibility.*

–Eleanor Roosevelt, diplomat and humanitarian

*The discipline of the writer is to learn to be still
and listen to what his subject has to tell him.*

–Rachel Carson, author of SILENT SPRING

No bird soars too high if he soars on his own wings.

–William Blake, English poet and artist

CHAPTER TWELVE
Parting Advice

This book is not meant to be an ending point; it is meant to be a starting point. A person cannot learn to write well in one day, one month, or even one year, or by reading a single book. A book can show you things, as Betty Edwards's book did for me, but only you can put concepts and ideas into use. You certainly can't learn how to write effectively at one sitting, just as you couldn't possibly expect to learn everything there is to know about plants by taking a short fieldtrip at a local nature center. The task of becoming an effective writer is, in truth, more of a journey than a final destination that one reaches, say, at the end of an Amtrak train ride. I've been writing for many years now, yet I still have much to learn. This book simply articulates my understanding of the writing process and the way in which it works. How you use the writing process will be up to you.

The writing process may be frustrating at times, but that does not mean that one should ever fear or avoid writing. Why? Because you *can* write effectively, and because once you do, you'll be glad you did. Writing is not only a valuable skill; it is an uplifting, creative endeavor. And if you have to write—and life, like it or not, is going to require that you do—why not take the initiative and work toward becoming the best writer you can be, starting now, today? Writing, after all, is not an onerous burden; it is something to look forward to in your daily life. It may take discipline to become a better writer, but that's nothing more than hard work—which all of us can handle, even enjoy. "The days you work are the best days," painter Georgia O'Keeffe reminds us. This book has suggested a number of writing exercises and techniques to hone your skills, and I hope you do or use them as a means to improve the quality of your writing.[1]

Learning to write well won't come easy (it doesn't for anyone), and it will take a long time to realize your full potential as a writer. But don't let that deter you. Just as one must learn to add and subtract and multiply and divide before doing algebra or calculus, so, too, must one practice writing before one can become an accomplished writer. All I can tell you is this: the more you write, the better you will become at it. Your writing will improve over time and with each passing month and year, though you should never forget that every writer—even the best of the best—can always do better. As Ernest Hemingway said, "We are all apprentices in a craft where no one ever becomes a master." Write regularly and you'll hone your talent; fail to write regularly and your skills will atrophy.[2]

To improve your writing, you'll certainly need to make time to write, which may mean less television or time for other activities, but trust me, you'll add so much more to your life if you write on a regular basis. The writing process can enrich your life, as well as the lives of others through the words that you write. Words can bring comfort or assistance, and you'll feel more in control of your life if you know how to use them. Indeed, writing itself can bring great personal satisfaction, even pleasure, as I and other writers can readily attest. The British poet John Keats was reportedly less interested in his finished poems than in the joy he felt in writing them, and I, too, have felt the same sensation. That's because writing can be relaxing, enlightening. Writing will actually improve your communication and critical thinking skills—tremendous benefits in and of themselves. But to become a talented writer, you must *start*. You must *write*.[3]

If you prefer sports analogies (or even if you don't), consider this one: before a college athlete can become the starting point guard of a college basketball team, responsible for calling plays and running the offense, that player must develop the requisite skills and master the fundamentals of the game. The point guard must first learn to dribble, shoot free throws, and pass and control the ball. To avoid fouling out and to be effective on the court, the player must also learn what "traveling" and "charging" are, what a "technical foul" is, and how many seconds are on the shot clock. To be a leading scorer, the point guard must habitually practice making lay-ups and jump shots. And before the point guard can lead the team into the Final Four of the annual NCAA tournament, she or he must learn how to coordinate team members' abilities and utilize their differing, yet complementary skills, be they rebounding, blocking out an opponent, or shooting three-pointers. If the point guard doesn't acquire these skills, the basketball team doesn't have much of a chance of winning their homecoming game, let alone a national championship.

A good writer is a lot like a talented point guard. To become an effective writer, a person must first learn the basics of the writing process and what writing tools are available. Knowing what words to use is like knowing what plays to call, and knowing how to string words together into sentences, with proper grammar and punctuation, is like knowing how to diagram and execute those plays. To carry the analogy further, just as lots of court time enhances a basketball player's skills, good writing judgment comes only with steady practice. Dribbling and shooting skills are honed at long workouts and, perhaps, in pickup games with no referees. Likewise, day-to-day practice with words (both guided and unsupervised) is indispensable, for one cannot become a good writer without putting in the time it takes to get there. As you write, keep in mind the advice of Itzhak Perlman, the famed violinist: "If I miss practice one day, I know. If I miss practice two days, the critics know it. If I miss practice three days, everybody knows it."[4]

You're bound to make mistakes along the way. You're going to write sentences that sound terrible when you read them aloud; you're going to make punctuation and spelling errors; and you're occasionally going to feel like giving up when your writing gets critiqued by others. All I can advise is that you persevere and accept that making mistakes is inevitable whenever you learn new skills. Even master artists, as revealed by X-rays of famous paintings, frequently painted over errant brushwork on still-wet canvases. Accordingly, you should never feel bad if at first you don't succeed in your efforts. The writing process is tricky, no doubt about it, especially when you find yourself searching in vain for the right words to express what you want to say. Just don't let words get the best of you. Instead, get the best out of yourself (and others) by learning to use words effectively.[5]

In your quest to become a better writer, never forget the importance of writing mentors. I've had them and you should too. Writing mentors are usually very much alive and present—a teacher, a parent, a writing workshop participant, a friend whose skills surpass your own—but mentors can also be distant or dead, a writer with an e-mail address or one from a different time and place. Look to writers you admire, whether living or dead, and try to learn from them by picking apart what they did to win you over. A good basketball coach can mean the difference between a game lost and a game won, just as a writing mentor—who critiques your work—can help you turn bland, poorly written pages of text into exciting, invigorating ones. Your writing is still yours, but by soliciting help from others, you'll have more ideas and suggestions to consider as you shape your writing. As Ian Jackman notes in his book, *The Writer's Mentor:* "Mentors don't prescribe. They don't have all the answers, but they know the right questions to ask. They nudge and suggest, pointing this way and that, all the while offering a kindly word in your ear."[6]

Having peers who write is important too. I like to get together with fellow writers who are struggling with some of the same craft issues as I am. Such sessions provide inspiration and new ideas, and they also make the writing process more enjoyable. Just as it's more fun to play basketball with friends than to shoot hoops all by yourself, maintaining friendships with other writers will give you access to sounding boards, or valuable feedback or second opinions, as you navigate the often treacherous writing process. By forming a writing group, taking writing courses, or just staying in touch with those who respect written language and spend time grappling with it, you'll also draw energy from those who, like you, have writing lives. Only one caveat: when you're looking for a critical eye to judge the quality of your writing, you need to find people you can trust. You want honesty, not feigned praise.

If one weathers the inevitable hardships that go along with learning any new skill, one can reap great rewards. "The primary benefit of practicing any art, whether well or badly, is that it enables one's soul to grow," writer Kurt Vonnegut notes, in what I would consider a pretty sage assessment. Indeed, former U.S. Senator Bob Kerrey—a member of the National Commission on Writing—has argued that "we must learn to write in order to participate in the range of experiences available to us as human beings." "Our spiritual lives, our economic success, and our social networks," he says, "are all directly affected by our willingness to do the work necessary to acquire the skill of writing." "In a very real way," Kerrey emphasizes, "neither our democracy nor our personal freedoms will survive unless we as citizens take the time and make the effort needed to learn how to write."[7]

So, whatever you do from here, never forget that you *can* write effectively and that the writing process *will* do meaningful things for you. The writing process is, above all else, a process that heightens one's skills of observation and expression and increases one's awareness of the world and of one's innermost thoughts and aspirations. "Writing," Winston Churchill said, "is an adventure." I agree; it is. Writing allows us to explore the unknown, seek the truth, and comprehend and relive events in our lives. This, undoubtedly, is what led writer Anaïs Nin to say that writing allows us to taste life twice. Writing, though, is much more than a recording device; it catalyzes fresh insights and opens doors you've never opened before. Writing, Abraham Lincoln recognized, is nothing less than "the art of communicating thoughts to the mind, through the eye." So again, embrace writing, don't fear it or run away from it.[8]

All of us write in our own unique way—and that's okay, to be expected, actually. After all, every writer is an individual. Although the steps of the writing process are the same for everyone, you need to write (and use the writing process) in the way that best suits you. The place and time you write, as well as the manner and style in which you write, are matters for you to decide. The possibilities are endless. Some people write most comfortably with pen and paper; others work best at a computer; others prefer to draft on a computer but then edit and revise a hard copy. The documented variations among famed writers is itself instructive. Marcel Proust wrote in bed; Virginia Woolf wrote standing up at an artist's desk; Gertrude Stein and Raymond Carver wrote in cars; Edmund Rostand, the author of *Cyrano de Bergerac*, enjoyed writing in the bathtub. Whereas playwright Tennessee Williams wrote early every morning, writer Anthony Burgess thought the afternoon was the best time to write. In contrast, James Baldwin and Jack Kerouac liked writing at night, working at times until 3:00 or 4:00 a.m. or even through the night. The approaches a writer can take are—and should be—as varied as the species of animals and varieties of plants in a thriving rainforest. The important thing is *to write*—at whatever time or place, or by whatever means, you choose.[9]

We all have an innate impulse to express ourselves and to understand what's happening in our lives and around us. The writing process—more than anything else—provides a valuable, expressive outlet and, simultaneously, taps one's unconscious mind to help one's conscious mind make sense of it all. Writing at work may be compulsory, but those truly dedicated to writing will learn to take pride in all of their writing and develop the discipline to write away from work too. No matter what one decides to do in life, learning to write well will make you a more effective citizen and communicator. And once you learn the craft, you'll find yourself toying around with words for the sheer pleasure of it. Writing shouldn't be limited to one's professional life; it should be done to fuel your hopes and dreams. After all, words are gifts. And who, I ask, can resist opening up beautifully wrapped presents and playing with what's inside? So long as you make writing a priority in your life, believe me, you can find the time to do it.

As an added bonus, writing is therapeutic. When you're feeling down in your life, writing can heal, acting as a balm to whatever is bothering you. That's because writing allows you to confront what's troubling you. Henriette Anne Klauser, author of *Writing on Both Sides of the Brain* and *With Pen in Hand: The Healing Power of Writing*, puts it this way: "Writing goes right to the place that hurts." As Klauser explains, "The act of moving the pen across the page can be meditative, creating a calming state. Sometimes we don't even know what came out of our pen until we go back and read it later. And then we are surprised by the wisdom of our own words, and the insight." Writing harnesses your thoughts, an opportunity that may pass you by if you just let your ideas rattle around in your head. "Writing," Klauser concludes, "brings a fullness to ideas which holding them in your mind alone will never accomplish. Because when you write something down, it speaks back to you."[10]

By writing, you get the chance to understand the forces at work in your life and to formulate effective strategies for steering through them. University of Texas psychologist James Pennebaker has reported on the results of clinical studies showing a relationship between disclosure of emotional experience in writing and mental and physical well-being. A study done at the State University of New York-Stony Brook, for example, found that after asthma or arthritis sufferers wrote about stressful experiences they had had, such as car accidents or the death of loved ones, almost half of the study participants experienced a lessening of their symptoms for several months. The study found that for the relief to continue, however, the writing had to be done a minimum of four days a week and for fifteen minutes a day. In other words, sustained writing time actually improves people's quality of life.[11]

The personal stories of how writing has shaped people's lives are a tribute to the craft of writing and its power. "Writing brings me healing," writes U.N. worker Sindiwe Magona, a South African woman who has written about mob violence and who now lives in the Bronx. "Writers write about what they know," she says. "And that knowledge is sometimes far from pleasant. But it is in writing about our disappointments, our failures, our losses, our defeats, and our pain and suffering that we discover the startling fact that we have survived all this and perhaps even thrived." As someone who writes about human rights issues, I might further add: writing can be cathartic because it allows one to give voice to the voiceless or to expose abuses of power. The experience of novelist Russell Banks may be most representative—and the best articulation—of the good that writing can do: "Writing in some way saved my life. It brought to my life a kind of order and discipline."[12]

In geologic time, writing is a recent development. Life, in the form of single-celled organisms, is 3.5 billion years old, with multicellular plants and animals having existed for 600 million years. Yet, until the appearance a few centuries ago of Sumerian clay tablets, which kept track of laborers, lists of raw materials and products such as barley and beer, humans did not write. The Chinese first used paper in 105 A.D.; Pi Sheng invented movable type, made of baked clay, between 1041 and 1049; and until about the twelfth century, the realm of books and manuscript making was largely restricted to a few European monasteries and monks and scribes. Though writing first emerged in Mesopotamia, China, ancient Egypt and Central America in response to expanding commerce, writing in the modern era—on signs and billboards, on the Internet, and in books and periodicals—is now literally all around us. The Bible remains the world's all-time bestseller, having been published in more than 1,000 languages, but books and articles are available today on almost any topic imaginable. An oversized 732-page scientific treatise about ants (of all things), written by Bert Hölldobler and Edward O. Wilson, was published in 1990 and was so well received that it won a Pulitzer Prize. I even bought a copy to find out what the fuss was all about, and found the subject matter fascinating. If you ever want to know anything about the habits, nests or food sources of *Myrmecocystus mimicus*, honeypot ants, just look on pages 406 to 412! Almost anything you want or need to know about can be found in writing; if what you're looking for can't be found, there's an easy solution: *you* can write about it![13]

Although writing has only been used for a few centuries, it has literally transformed—indeed, made possible—human history and human progress. Educated people learned to write, and the creation of universities—first in ancient Egypt with the fifth-century University of Alexandria, then in medieval times in places such as Paris, Oxford, and Bologna, Italy, and later in other cities—led to rapid developments in the arts, the sciences, and the humanities. And the possibilities for the future are limitless. With books from the world's most prestigious libraries now being digitally scanned at a blistering pace, the prospect of an online, universal library—holding all knowledge, past and present, in searchable form—is no longer just a pipe dream. "It is really possible with the technology of today, not tomorrow," notes Brewster Kahle, an archivist overseeing one of the scanning projects. "We can provide all the works of humankind to all the people of the world. It will be an achievement remembered for all time, like putting a man on the moon," he says.[14]

If you think about it, it is writers and gifted orators—who believe words can make a difference—who have made change possible. Slavery was abolished in the United States, but only after the 1852 publication of Harriet Beecher Stowe's *Uncle Tom's Cabin*, the anti-slavery newspaper editorials of abolitionist Frederick Douglass, and Lincoln's Emancipation Proclamation. Lynchings in America were relegated to history, but only after courageous leaders spoke out, anti-lynching laws were passed, and the NAACP led an organizing campaign that included the publication of *The Crisis*, a magazine edited by W. E. B. Du Bois. The international human rights movement itself grew out of the events of World War II, a war that served as a catalyst for the creation of the United Nations and its charter—a written expression of the world's collective aspirations for peace and international security.[15]

The last step of the writing process—publication—is, of course, optional. You can choose to publish what you write, or you can decide to keep your writings private. There are many writers, in fact, who keep journals or diaries, but never share their words with anyone, even close family members. That's fine, obviously, but never forget that it's only through publication that your written words will be able to influence others and bring about change, innovation or social justice. Once you feel at ease writing, you'll be more likely to start thinking about publishing what you write. Again, this is to be expected. If you set your sights on publication—in whatever form that might take—that should certainly come as no surprise; it's a natural response to the generation of good ideas. "To genius must always go two gifts, the thought and the publication," wrote Ralph Waldo Emerson in a famous essay. To make thought available, Emerson emphasized, "it needs a vehicle or art by which it is conveyed" to others because even the "most wonderful inspirations die" with their originator if one "has no hand to paint them to the senses." The oft-heard phrase "publish or perish" has meaning far beyond the halls and world of academia; unpublished ideas are lost to future generations.[16]

Publishing a piece of writing—whether to a single person,

through desktop publishing, or to potential readers via the Internet or through a magazine or book—can be scary. Publishing involves risk-taking and the possibility of criticism. Indeed, the risk of rejection keeps some from ever even trying to get published or from releasing their words to the world. Your audience may not like what you have to say, and some may even take offense—or take issue with your opinions in public. If you do decide to publish, just try not to let such criticism get to you, though you should always listen to what others have to say because their views may, ultimately, shape your own views. If you believe strongly in what you've written, you have no reason to feel ashamed or bad. If the criticism is valid, you've learned something and your thinking and subsequent writing will be all the better for it. Every time someone points out an error, you'll further hone your writing skills, making you an even more effective communicator the next time you write. What's really scary is a *fear* of communication, a fear that can leave one speechless or wordless at a time when important things need to be said or written.

In fact, communicating with anyone, be they friends, family members or total strangers, can be a risky endeavor, no matter what the form of the communication. We worry that we might say the wrong thing. We worry that we'll be misunderstood or not taken seriously. But that does not mean we should surrender or withdraw from the world or from interacting with others. With writing—as with any other activity in life—there is always the risk of failure. But the benefits of writing far outweigh the risks of not writing, meaning that all of us should strive to improve our writing skills in our daily lives. As President John F. Kennedy noted: "There are risks and costs to a program of action. But they are far less than the long-range risks and costs of comfortable inaction." Theodore Roosevelt, one of my personal favorites, framed the issue this way: "It is hard to fail, but it is worse never to have tried to succeed." As Roosevelt said, "The only one who makes no mistakes is one who never does anything!" Good fortune in life is only possible if you work hard and take chances.[17]

For anyone interested in making a difference in a community, writing is much too important a skill to bypass. It has been used effectively—in books and articles, in editorials and opinion pieces, even blogs—to fight AIDS, diseases such as polio and cancer, drug and alcohol abuse, hunger and homelessness, and poverty. Writing can change people's views and perspectives, and even bulk-mailed fundraising letters can be effective. Though direct-mail pieces may look like junk mail, they work. People send in charitable donations to further worthwhile causes, and the world changes, if ever so slowly. Writing, in fact, has been used throughout history to advance the causes of freedom, equality and human rights—be it in Alabama or Mississippi during the era of Jim Crow laws, to end apartheid in South Africa, or to protect the rights of women and minorities through anti-discrimination laws. I myself write to try to make the world a better place than when I entered it. Among other things, I want to convince Americans to abandon the use of capital punishment—a practice that only adds more violence to our already too-violent society.

Of course, if you intend to make a valuable contribution to society, you'll need to do more than just write. You'll need to act. Reading and writing help you gain understanding, and writing can help you persuade others. But writing will never take the place of personal interaction and face-to-face persuasion within our neighborhoods and our communities. Good writing alone, in other words, won't always get the job done. Oftentimes, you'll need to organize people to take collective action to get something accomplished. As human rights activist Erica Bouza forcefully puts it, "When you've written to your president, to your congressman, to your senator and nothing, nothing has come of it, you take to the streets." You get involved in politics and with charities, you volunteer your time, you knock on doors and make phone calls. You may even decide to run for public office. In short, you do what needs to be done to make change. Writer-lecturer Charlotte Perkins Gilman said it nicely: "Life is a verb, not a noun."[18]

In all the years that I've been reading and learning from other writers, one of the most memorable and tragic figures I've ever run across is Bartleby, the main character in Herman Melville's fictional short story, "Bartleby, the Scrivener." A law-copyist in the days before photocopiers, Bartleby works for an aging Wall Street lawyer. The story's narrator, the elderly lawyer, recounts how, at first, Bartleby did "an extraordinary quantity of writing," copying documents "by sun-light and by candle-light." One day, however, Bartleby is asked to perform a small task, to which he replies, "I would prefer not to." That response quickly becomes Bartleby's refrain whenever he's asked to do work of any kind. Eventually, the frustrated lawyer—unable to summon the courage to fire Bartleby, who "prefers not" to leave the lawyer's office—takes the extraordinary step of vacating his own law office so that he can avoid kicking Bartleby out into the streets.[19]

When Bartleby is evicted by a new tenant, the aging lawyer returns to the building's entryway, where Bartleby is sleeping, to try to help Bartleby find a new job. But Bartleby is obstinate; he "prefers not" to do whatever he is asked to do. "No, I would prefer not to make any change," the unemployed Bartleby tells the lawyer. When the building's landlord has Bartleby arrested for vagrancy, the lawyer slips some silver to a prison "grub-man," asking that he take care of his ex-employee. But Bartleby tells the lawyer, "I would prefer not to dine to-day." A few days later the lawyer returns to find Bartleby's lifeless body lying huddled at the base of a wall, his knees drawn up, with his head "touching the cold stones." The story ends with the lawyer's mention of a rumor he's heard that might shed some light on Bartleby's bizarre behavior: that Bartleby used to work as a subordinate clerk in the Dead Letter Office in Washington, D.C. "Dead letters!" the lawyer ponders, lamenting that Bartleby had worked in an office whose business was to burn never-to-be-read letters by the cartload each year.[20]

Bartleby's story is a story of someone who prefers not to express any preference, but who, in failing to do so, ultimately does anyway. Bartleby's creator, of course, was an imaginative and expressive writer of exceptional ability, and Melville's haunting story, in the end, may tell us more about the importance of language as a tool of communication than it does about the details of Bartleby's life, which are sparse. The job of a scrivener is to mechanically copy legal documents, and the job of a bureaucrat in the ominous-sounding Dead Letter Office is to burn letters that were either misdirected or never received by their intended recipients. Whereas Bartleby's jobs entailed manual transcription— word-for-word copying involving little or no creativity—or actually burning words, what Melville liked was lively language, words that brought a story to life. Here's my take: Words are not intended to end up as dead letters or to be mechanically processed without thinking; they should be used to reach people, to give them understanding, to make them think in new and different ways. Don't think of writing as Bartleby apparently did, as a dull pursuit to be done, if at all, for the purpose of earning a meager living; instead, think of writing as a great adventure, the stuff of Mount Everest expeditions or deep-sea dives in the Black Sea for sunken treasure, and as something that will add a new dimension to your life.

Once the magical qualities of the writing process are known and unleashed, a life lived without writing should seem like not living at all. Writer Gish Jen, for example, once gave up writing (as Bartleby did) because she felt, for a time, that she "was writing instead of living." But after spending lots of time gardening and chatting with dog owners and doing other things besides writing, Jen soon realized that life without writing was "strangely lifeless." "It seemed as though someone had disinvented music—such silence," she wrote in an essay on the subject, saying, "I felt as though I had lost one of my senses." "I missed reasoning with history, I missed roaming a large world," Jen admitted, adding, "I missed tangling with language," "I missed discovering what I thought—or rather, watching what I thought I thought dissolve under my pen." "I missed looking hard at things," she said. For her, the magic of the writing process—"the endless surprise of the sentences, and the satisfaction of thoughts taking form"—simply proved too much to abandon.[21]

Again, whenever you write, you are partaking in a creative and dynamic activity that has changed, and can still change, the world for the better. "There is only one corner of the universe you can be certain of improving, and that's your own self," Aldous Huxley once said in advice reminiscent of what Arnold Lowe advised in *Start Where You Are*. If you, like me, want your life to have meaning, if you want to help people and advance the cause of humanity, of truth or human rights, then write and begin in what Eleanor Roosevelt called the "small places, close to home—so close and so small that they cannot be seen on any map of the world." These places, Roosevelt said, are the realm of the individual: a neighborhood, a school or college, a factory or farm or office. "Such are the places," she said, "where every man, woman and child seeks justice, equal opportunity, equal dignity without discrimination." As Roosevelt told a U.N. commission in presenting a human rights booklet called *In Your Hands*: "Unless these rights have meaning there, they have little meaning anywhere. Without concerted citizen action to uphold them close to home, we shall look in vain for progress in the larger world." Never forget: the truth is powerful, words can make things happen, and things will start happening when you write.[22]

Writing effectively is not—and never will be—easy. You need to take risks and experiment. You need to put in the time it takes to generate material through freewriting, then take the time to revise what you first write. You need to develop a tolerance for uncertainty as you sort through facts and seek to illuminate the truth. "The test of a first-rate intelligence is the ability to hold two opposed ideas in the mind at the same time, and still retain the ability to function," F. Scott Fitzgerald once wrote in *Esquire* magazine. "One should, for example, be able to see that things are hopeless," Fitzgerald said, "and yet be determined to make them otherwise." If you're up to the challenge, however, your life will be a lot more interesting for having taken up writing and having learned to do it well. Don't allow yourself to be silent; think, read, speak and write; interact with the world; and, if you're so inclined, be a muckraker. You have a unique voice; use it and do some good with it.[23]

In the end, you and only you can make the necessary commitment to start where you are and to learn to write more effectively. You can do it if you want or you can decide not to pursue a writing life, it's all up to you. In that spirit, I'll end with a thought—a question really—from the German lyric poet Rainer Maria Rilke, who gave this advice to a young poet in a letter written from Paris in 1903: "Go into yourself. Search for the reason that bids you write; find out whether it is spreading out its roots in the deepest places of your heart." "Ask yourself in the stillest hour of your night: *must* I write?" Rilke encouraged the young poet, a stand-in for any aspiring or practicing writer of any time or place. "Delve into yourself for a deep answer," Rilke said, saying that if your answer is yes, "if you may meet this earnest question with a strong and simple 'I must,' then build your life according to this necessity."[24]

Writing is rewriting. A writer must learn to deepen characters, trim writing, intensify scenes. To fall in love with the first draft to the point where one cannot change it is to greatly enhance the prospects of never publishing. –Richard North Patterson • A thought cannot awake without waking other thoughts. –Maria von Ebner-Eschenbach • We write about what it is that we need to know. –Marcie Hershman • Ignorance of English vocabulary and grammar is a considerable liability to a writer of English. The best cure for it is, I believe, reading. –Ursula Le Guin • I love writing. I never feel really comfortable unless I am either actually writing or have a story going. I could not stop writing. –P. G. Wodehouse • The artist does not draw what he sees, but what he has to make others see. –Edgar Degas • Finding the stories is not the hard part. Writing them down is. –E. Annie Proulx • When I write, everything is visual, as brilliantly as if it were on a lit stage. And I talk out the lines as I write. –Tennessee Williams • If you are using dialogue—say it aloud as you write it. Only then will it have the sound of speech. –John Steinbeck • Writing, like every other complex craft, takes most of us years to master. In that apprenticeship period, many of us experience a great deal of frustration, rejection, and failure. Indeed, one thing that successful writers share is their ability to tolerate defeat and soldier on. –Mary Pipher • The style of an author should be the image of his mind, but the choice and command of language is the fruit of exercise. –Edward Gibbon • Style is a relation between form and content. –Cyril Connolly • Those who write as they talk, will write ill, though they speak well. –George-Louis de Buffon • It may be that I am doing something instinctively, a bit the way a coral reef gets made. The little corals do not know, as they cling to the debris of their predecessors, exactly what kind of a creation they are going to make—a barrier reef. –Gore Vidal • In prose, the worst thing one can do with words is surrender to them. –George Orwell • You will have to write and put away or burn a lot of material before you are comfortable in this medium. You might as well start now and get the work done. For I believe that eventually quantity will make for quality. –Ray Bradbury • Writing is not an amusing occupation. It is a combination of ditch-digging, mountain-climbing, treadmill and childbirth. –Edna Ferber • The only certainty about writing and trying to be a writer is that it has to be done, not dreamed of or planned and never written, or talked about (the ego eventually falls apart like a soaked sponge), but simply written; it's a dreadful, awful fact that writing is like any other work. –Janet Frame • Books are never finished, they are merely abandoned. –Oscar Wilde

You shouldn't pay very much attention to anything writers say. They don't know why they do what they do. –John Barth • Art does not reproduce what we see. Rather, it makes us see. –Paul Klee • I understand that this is a course called "How the Writer Writes," and that each week you are exposed to a different writer who holds forth on the subject. The only parallel I can think of to this is having the zoo come to you, one animal at a time; and I suspect that what you hear one week from the giraffe is contradicted next week by the baboon. –Flannery O'Connor • If my doctor told me I had only six minutes to live, I wouldn't brood. I'd type a little faster. –Isaac Asimov • Often the writing process is filled with a sense of jeopardy. –Sue Grafton • I try to go for the detail that lights up in me like a neon light. –Spalding Gray • Fill your paper with the breathings of your heart. –William Wordsworth • By writing an outline you really *are* writing in a way, because you're creating the structure of what you're going to do. Once I really know what I'm going to write, I don't find the actual writing takes all that long. –Tom Wolfe • One writes for oneself in much the same way one daydreams for oneself. –Anita Shreve • To write, you must concentrate long and hard, and being alone is the price of that concentration. –Tobias Wolff • Learning to deal with rejection is absolutely critical for writers because it's part of the territory. The trick is to see rejection as part of the process rather than an insurmountable obstacle. –Travis Adkins • The danger of outlining is that, from the standpoint of writing, once you've outlined a lot of the fun is over. –Michael Connelly • I think I do like to work under the pressure of a deadline. There's something exciting about knowing you have to get something done by a certain time. –Truman Capote • I am a compulsive writer. I not only love to write; I *must* write. –Richard Marius • There are people who have never studied writing who are fully capable of being writers. I know this because I am an example. I was a part-time registered nurse, a wife, and a mother when I began publishing. –Elizabeth Berg • Making writing a big deal tends to make writing difficult. Keeping writing casual tends to keep it possible. Nowhere is this more true than around the issue of time. One of the biggest myths about writing is that in order to do it we must have great swathes of uninterrupted time. –Julia Cameron • The bookmaking process—fussing with the type, the sample heads, the dust jacket, the flap copy, the cover cloth—has perhaps been dearer to me than the writing process. The latter has been endured as a process tributary to the former, whose envisioned final product, smelling of glue and freshly sliced paper, hangs as a shining mirage luring me through many a grey writing day. –John Updike • I'm not sure I understand the process of writing. There is, I'm sure, something strange about imaginative concentration. The brain slowly begins to function in a different way, to make mysterious connections. –Elizabeth Hardwick • I like to compare my method with that of painters centuries ago, proceeding, as it were, from layer to layer. The first draft is quite crude, far from being perfect, by no means finished; although even then, even at that point, it has its final structure, the form is visible. After that I rewrite it as many times—apply as many "layers"—as I feel to be necessary. –Alberto Moravia • Writing is a nerve-flaying job. –Joan Acocella • Nothing great in the world has been accomplished without passion. –Georg Hegel

Writing enables us to find out what we know—and what we don't know—about whatever we're trying to learn. —William Zinsser • Writing is a social institution created over time. —Barbara Tomlinson • We all compose the world we live in every moment of our lives. —E. L. Doctorow • Whatever sentence will bear to be read twice, we may be sure was thought twice. —Henry David Thoreau • The world is the sum-total of our vital possibilities. —José Ortega y Gasset • The greatest writer cannot see through a brick wall but unlike the rest of us he does not build one. —W. H. Auden • You need to trust yourself, especially on a first draft, where amid the anxiety and self-doubt, there should be a real sense of your imagination and your memories walking and woolgathering, tramping the hills, romping all over the place. Trust them. Don't look at your feet to see if you are doing it right. Just dance. —Anne Lamott • The world is but a school of inquiry. —Michel de Montaigne • The only place where success comes before work is in a dictionary. —Vidal Sassoon • Wit is part of the machinery of the intellect. —Walter Bagehot • Words are the only thing which lasts for ever. —William Hazlitt • You will find it a very good practice always to verify your references, sir. —Martin Joseph Routh • Once a word has been allowed to escape, it cannot be recalled. —Horace • I refuse to separate my search for a way of writing from my search for a way of living. —Scott Russell Sanders • A good poem is a contribution to reality. The world is never the same once a good poem has been added to it. —Dylan Thomas • I am sorry for people who can't write letters. —Elizabeth Bishop • You're the first audience to your work, and the most important audience. —Gloria Naylor • Writing is nothing more than a guided dream. —Jorge Luis Borges • Writer's block has never been a problem on the net—far from it. Alone at their computers, tapping away, correspondents report few difficulties getting started, much less continuing. —Anne Eisenberg • Like block-building, writing is a matter of arrangement. It involves combining letters into words, words into sentences, sentences into paragraphs, and paragraphs into documents or finished pieces. —Stephen Wilbers • The purpose of a writer is to keep civilization from destroying itself. —Albert Camus • I write. The longer I live, the more convinced I've become that I cultivate my truest self in this one way. —Tom Chiarella • There is so much about the process of writing that is mysterious to me, but this one thing I've found to be true: writing begets writing. —Dorianne Laux • If you are a genius, you'll make your own rules, but if not—and the odds are against it—go to your desk, no matter what your mood, face the icy challenge of the paper—write. —J. B. Priestly

NOTES

One of the obligations of the writer is to say or sing all that he or she can, to deal with as much of the world as becomes possible to him or her in language. —Denise Levertov • Writing is the only thing that, when I do it, I don't feel I should be doing something else. —Gloria Steinem • I suppose that writers should, in a way, feel flattered by the censorship laws. They show a primitive fear and dread at the fearful magic of print. —John Mortimer • The compulsion to make rhymes was born in me. For those sated readers of my work who wish ardently that I would stop, the future looks dark indeed. —Noël Coward • I write to find out what I'm talking about. —Edward Albee • There's one characteristic that sets writing apart from most of the other arts—its apparent democracy, by which I mean its availability to almost everyone as a means of expression. —Margaret Atwood • Writing is simple: you just jot down amusing ideas as they occur to you. The jotting presents no problem; it is the occurring that is difficult. —Stephen Leacock • I write one page of masterpiece to ninety-one pages of shit. —Ernest Hemingway • If you can't annoy somebody with what you write, I think there's little point in writing. —Kingsley Amis • It does me good to write a letter which is not a response to a demand, a gratuitous letter, so to speak, which has accumulated in me like the waters of a reservoir. —Henry Miller • I don't wait for moods. You accomplish nothing if you do that. Your mind must know it has got to get down to work. —Pearl S. Buck • A work of art is a corner of creation seen through a temperament. —Émile Zola • Nothing can be created out of nothing. —Lucretius • Nothing great was ever achieved without enthusiasm. —Ralph Waldo Emerson • The only way of discovering the limits of the possible is to venture a little way past them into the impossible. —Arthur C. Clarke • I never know what's going to happen when I write. —Kate DiCamillo • I write in different styles because I hear different voices in my head. —Gore Vidal • The basic tool for the manipulation of reality is the manipulation of words. If you can control the meaning of words, you can control the people who must use the words. —Philip K. Dick • If the English language made any sense, lackadaisical would have something to do with a shortage of flowers. —Doug Larson • Words are vehicles that can transport us from the drab sands to the dazzling stars. —M. Robert Syme • Words are as beautiful as wild horses, and sometimes as difficult to corral. —Ted Berkman • Words that open our eyes to the world are always the easiest to remember. —Ryszard Kapuscinski • Writing organizes and clarifies our thoughts. Writing is how we think our way into a subject and make it our own. —William Zinsser • The struggle is my life. —Nelson Mandela • We parted with a contract / To cherish, and to write —Emily Dickinson • There's only one corner of the universe you can be certain of improving, and that's your own self. —Aldous Huxley • No gains without pains. —Benjamin Franklin • Writers like teeth are divided into incisors and grinders. —Walter Bagehot • Work on good prose has three steps: a musical stage when it is composed, an architectonic one when it is built, and a textile one when it is woven. —Walter Benjamin • It's my experience that you first feel the impulse to write in your chest. It's like a heartache. It's like falling in love, only more so. —Carolyn See

As bees take honey from different flowers, so we must take materials from all sorts of different authors and, once they have been systematically collected, store them away, as it were, in the proper combs.

—Richard White, English historian

Notes are often necessary, but they are necessary evils.

—Samuel Johnson, *PLAYS OF WILLIAM SHAKESPEARE*

If an author asserts things without citing his source, the reader has occasion to believe that he speaks only on the basis of hearsay.

—Pierre Bayle, seventeenth-century writer

Notes expressed in good terms, in few words, and where one asserts nothing without proving it, or without at least citing some good author where one can see the assertion verified, indicating the passage in question so well that the reader can easily find it, if necessary: most readers, I say, will find notes like this of the greatest value.

—Jean Le Clerc, Huguenot journalist and theologian

Notes

CHAPTER ONE Start Where You Are

1. Steven F. Hayward, *Churchill on Leadership: Executive Success in the Face of Adversity* (New York: Crown Publishing Group, 1998), 105; National Commission on Writing (The College Board), "The Neglected 'R': The Need for a Writing Revolution" (Apr. 2003), 36.

2. Diane Ravitch, *The Language Police: How Pressure Groups Restrict What Students Learn* (New York: Vintage Books, 2003), 5; Richard Rubin, "Cracking the SAT Code," *Newsweek*, Aug. 22, 2005; "Long-Term Trends in Student Writing Performance," *NAEPFACTS*, Vol. 3, No. 4 (Sept. 1998), National Center for Education Statistics; http://nces.ed.gov/nationsreportcard/writing/results2002/natachieve.asp (last visited July 12, 2004); http://nces.ed.gov/nationsreportcard/writing/achieve.asp (last visited July 12, 2004). Beware: a study of Web citations and undergraduate papers in microeconomics, done by Philip M. Davis and Suzanne Cohen, found that "Web citations checked in 2000 revealed that only 18% of URLs cited in 1996 led to the correct Internet document." *See* Chuck Zerby, *The Devil's Details: A History of Footnotes* (New York: Simon & Schuster, 2002), 148 & n.28. As one scholar notes: "Web sites are going *poof!* left and right." Ibid., 148.

3. National Commission on Writing (The College Board), "Writing: A Ticket to Work…Or a Ticket Out" (Sept. 2004), 3-4, 7, 11, 14; http://www.entlink.net/education/resources/greenoffice.cfm (last visited May 17, 2006).

4. "Writing: A Ticket to Work…Or a Ticket Out," 3-4, 9-10, 15.

5. Ibid., 28; "The Neglected 'R': The Need for a Writing Revolution," 11.

6. Jackie Crosby, "Magistrate Judge Jack Mason Dies," *Star Tribune* (Minneapolis) (June 11, 2002): B8; http://www.macalester.edu/bulletin/archives/2002/061402.html (last visited Sept. 16, 2003).

7. Crosby, "Magistrate Judge Jack Mason Dies," B8.

8. Arnold Lowe, *Start Where You Are* (New York: Harper & Brothers Publishers, 1950), 1-2, 8.

9. http://www.thinkarete.com/quotes/by_teacher/mahatma_gandhi/ (last visited Sept. 1, 2004).

10. "The Neglected 'R': The Need for a Writing Revolution," 20, 28.

11. Linda Trichter Metcalf & Tobin Simon, *Writing the Mind Alive: The Proprioceptive Method for Finding Your Authentic Voice* (New York: Ballantine Books, 2002), 15-16, 33, 133-34 (emphasis in original). If you're wondering what "proprioceptive" means, you're not alone. I looked in *The American Heritage Dictionary* and found "proprioceptive" listed as an adjective in the entry for the noun "proprioceptor." The latter word means "[a] sensory receptor, chiefly in muscles, tendons, and joints, that responds to stimuli arising within the organism." *The American Heritage Dictionary* (Boston: Houghton Mifflin Co., 2nd college ed. 1982), 994. The authors of this quirkily subtitled book use the term "Proprioceptive Writing" to mean the expression of thoughts in writing to allow reflection on them. Metcalf & Simon, *Writing the Mind Alive*, xxi. According to the authors: "It is a self-guided exercise that calls forth your imagination, your intellect, and your intuition all at once to open your heart and clear your mind." Ibid. "You practice it," they say, "in twenty-five-minute sessions while listening to Baroque music, which roughly reflects the steady rhythm of the human pulse." "It can be used," they note, "as a path to self-expression and creativity, as a path to spiritual renewal, and as a path to emotional health." Ibid. But I digress. Take a look for yourself. I just thought you'd want a little explanation—if only a teaser—of why the word "proprioceptive" appears in the subtitle of a book on the craft of writing.

12. *The American Heritage Dictionary of the English Language* (Boston: Houghton Mifflin Co., 3rd ed. 1992), 505; *Bartlett's Familiar Quotations: A Collection of Passages, Phrases, and Proverbs Traced to Their Sources in Ancient and Modern Literature* (Boston: Little, Brown & Co., 1992), 246.

13. Anne Lamott, *Bird by Bird: Some Instructions on Writing and Life* (New York: Anchor Books, 1995), xxvi. Anne Lamott's book gets its title from a memorable event in Lamott's life. Lamott's father, a writer who taught prisoners at San Quentin's creative-writing program, was fond of advising people to just put down a little bit on paper every day. As Lamott tells it:

I also remember a story that I know I've told elsewhere but that over and over helps me to get a grip: thirty years ago my older brother, who was ten years old at the time, was trying to get a report on birds written that he'd had three months to write, which was due the next day. We were out at our family cabin in Bolinas, and he was at the kitchen table close to tears, surrounded by binder paper and pencils and unopened books on birds, immobilized by the hugeness of the task ahead. Then my father sat down beside him, put his arm around my brother's shoulder, and said, "Bird by bird, buddy. Just take it bird by bird."

Ibid., 18-19.

14. Maxine Hairston, John Ruszkiewicz & Christy Friend, *The Scott, Foresman Handbook for Writers* (New York: Longman, 6th ed. 2002). Studies have shown that grammar instruction, all by itself, does very little to improve the quality of student writing. "The Neglected 'R': The Need for a Writing Revolution," 40 n.4. When one *cares* about writing well, however, one naturally *wants* to use—and to learn to use— good grammar. The trick, I think, is to instill in people early on a desire to write effectively so that learning the rules of grammar becomes *a goal*, not a chore.

15. Lowe, *Start Where You Are*, 7.

16. William Zinsser, *On Writing Well: The Classic Guide to Writing Nonfiction* (New York: HarperCollins, 2001), 148-49; Nicholas Wade, "Early Voices: The Leap to Language," *N.Y. Times* (July 15, 2003): D4; http://www.linguistlist.org/~ask-ling/archive-1997.7/msg00250.html (last visited Jan. 30, 2004) (Dennis Baron of the University of Illinois-Urbana's Department of English writes: "Research at the Center for the Study of Reading shows the average American high school graduate has a vocabulary of 40,000 words. Of course, what constitutes a word depends on how you define a word."); *compare* Steven Pinker, *The Language Instinct: How the Mind Creates Language* (New York: HarperCollins, 1994), 144-45 (citing research to show that the average American high school graduate knows 45,000 words, but that if "proper names," "numbers," "foreign words," "acronyms" and "compounds" were included in the total, "the average high school graduate would probably be credited with something like 60,000 words"); http://www.ku.edu/~pyersqr/Ling107/lexi-con.pdf (last visited Jan. 30, 2004) (stating that "estimates of average vocabulary size vary considerably," but concluding that the "average high school graduate" knows 45,000 words).

17. Pat Schneider, *Writing Alone and with Others* (Oxford: Oxford University Press, 2003), 14; Zinsser, *On Writing Well,* 245.

18. Robert I. Fitzhenry, ed., *The Harper Book of Quotations* (New York:

HarperCollins, 1993), 3; Michael Reynolds, *The Young Hemingway* (New York: W.W. Norton & Co., 1986): 27-30; *Having Our Say: The Delany Sisters' First 100 Years* (New York: Dell Publishing, 1994).

19. James Salter, "Some for Glory, Some for Praise," in Will Blythe, ed., *Why I Write: Thoughts on the Craft of Fiction* (Boston: Little, Brown & Co., 1998), 34-35.

CHAPTER TWO   Learning to See

1. Jeanette Winterson, *Art Objects: Essays on Ecstasy and Effrontery* (New York: Vintage Books, 1996), 7-9.

2. Betty Edwards, *Drawing on the Right Side of the Brain: A Course in Enhancing Creativity and Artistic Confidence* (New York: Jeremy P. Tarcher/Perigee Books, 1989).

3. Ibid.

4. Winterson, *Art Objects*, 3-4, 13-14.

5. Ibid., 4-7, 13.

6. Edwards, *Drawing on the Right Side of the Brain*, 2-3, 182, 188.

7. Diane Ackerman, *A Natural History of the Senses* (New York: Vintage Books, 1990), 209; Betty Edwards, *Drawing on the Artist Within: An Inspirational and Practical Guide to Increasing Your Creative Powers* (New York: Simon & Schuster, 1987), 12; Edwards, *Drawing on the Right Side of the Brain*, xi, xiii; Alice W. Flaherty, *The Midnight Disease: The Drive to Write, Writer's Block, and the Creative Brain* (Boston: Houghton Mifflin Co., 2004), 69; Steven Pinker, *The Language Instinct: How the Mind Creates Language* (New York: HarperCollins, 1994), 306-7, 312.

8. Edwards, *Drawing on the Artist Within*, 12; Edwards, *Drawing on the Right Side of the Brain*, 2-3, 27, 35.

9. Edwards, *Drawing on the Right Side of the Brain*, 37, 62-64, 66, 78, 139.

10. Ibid., 64; "Reading at Risk: A Survey of Literary Reading in America," National Endowment for the Arts (Research Division Report #46, June 2004), 1, 4, 18-19.

11. Edwards, *Drawing on the Right Side of the Brain*, xi-xii; Winterson, *Art Objects*, 7.

12. Edwards, *Drawing on the Right Side of the Brain*, 3, 10-13.

13. Ibid., 46-48.

14. Ibid., 36, 50, 52-53, 55.

15. Robert I. Fitzhenry, ed., *The Harper Book of Quotations* (New York: HarperCollins, 1993), 323; Jack Heffron, *The Writer's Idea Book: How to Develop Great Ideas for Fiction, Nonfiction, Poetry and Screenplays* (Cincinnati: Writer's Digest Books, 2000), 25.

16. Edwards, *Drawing on the Right Side of the Brain*, 6, 118-21, 124; Edwards, *Drawing on the Artist Within*, 185-86.

17. Lawrence Gowing, *Paintings in the Louvre* (New York: Stewart, Tabori & Chang, 1987), 161, 163; L. Schmidt, *Gustav Klimt* (Avon, England: Artline Editions, 1988), 78-79; http://brainyquote.com/quotes/authors/h/henry_s_hoskins.html (last visited Sept. 1, 2004). Many sources were consulted to gather the quotations that appear throughout *Writing for Life*. The sources for the quotations in the text are in these endnotes, and various compilations of quotations on the craft of writing appear in the bibliography. Other sources that I consulted to gather quotations included various books, periodicals, Internet sites, and more general quotation guides. The latter category included *Bartlett's Familiar Quotations, Quotationary, The Fairview Guide to Positive Quotations, The Harper Book of Quotations, The International Thesaurus of Quotations, The New Penguin Dictionary of Modern Quotations, The New International Dictionary of Quotations, The Oxford Dictionary of 20th Century Quotations, The Penguin Dictionary of Epigrams, The Women's Book of Positive Quotations*, and many others. *See, e.g., Reader's Digest Quotable Quotes: Wit and Wisdom for All Occasions from America's Most Popular Magazine* (Pleasantville, N.Y./Montreal: Reader's Digest, 1997); *Quote Unquote*, Vols. 1-2 (Encino, Cal.: Autumn Leaves, 2004); William Safire & Leonard Safir, eds., *Words of Wisdom: More Good Advice* (New York: Simon & Schuster, 1989). For quotes about art and design, sources included: Peggy Hadden, *The Quotable Artist* (New York: Allworth Press, 2002); Helen Hale, ed., *The Art & Artists Quotation Book: A Literary Companion* (London: Robert Hale, 1995); Catharine Fishel, ed., *401 Design Meditations: Wisdom, Insights, and Intriguing Thoughts from 244 Leading Designers* (Gloucester, Mass.: Rockport Publishers, Inc., 2005); Eric Maisel, *Affirmations for Artists* (New York: Jeremy P. Tarcher/Putnam, 1996); and *Everything Reverberates: Thoughts on Design* (San Francisco: Chronicle Books, 1998).

18. *The American Heritage Dictionary of the English Language* (Boston: Houghton Mifflin Co., 3rd ed. 1992), 1383; http://www.zaadz.com/quotes/topics/plagiarism (last visited Sept. 1, 2004).

19. Edwards, *Drawing on the Right Side of the Brain*, 40.

20. Leonard Roy Frank, ed., *Quotationary* (New York: Random House, 2001), 956; Edmund Morris, "The Unknowable," *New Yorker* (June 28, 2004): 40; http://en.thinkexist.com/quotations/research/ (last visited June 23, 2004).

21. Ralph Keyes, *The Courage to Write: How Writers Transcend Fear* (New York: Henry Holt & Co., 1995), 64; *The Writing Life: A Collection of Essays and Interviews* (New York: Random House, 1995), 182-83.

22. Anne Lamott, *Bird by Bird: Some Instructions on Writing and Life* (New York: Anchor Books, 1995), xii.

23. Natalie Goldberg, *Writing Down the Bones: Freeing the Writer Within* (Boston: Shambhala, 1986), 54.

24. John Burroughs, "The Art of Seeing Things," reprinted in *Inspired by Nature* (Helena, Mont.: Falcon Publishing, Inc., 2000), 22-23.

25. Leslie Ann Gibson, comp., *The Women's Book of Positive Quotations* (Minneapolis: Fairview Press, 2002), 430; Lamott, *Bird by Bird*, 9.

26. Julia Cameron, *The Artist's Way: A Spiritual Path to Higher Creativity* (New York: Jeremy P. Tarcher/Putnam, 2002), 9-10, 13-14, 18 (emphasis in original).

27. *The Essential Writings of Ralph Waldo Emerson* (New York: Modern Library, 2000), 818-19; Fitzhenry, *The Harper Book of Quotations*, 482.

CHAPTER THREE Why I Write

1. Leonard Roy Frank, ed., *Quotationary* (New York: Random House, 2001), 952; Quentin Reynolds, *Custer's Last Stand* (New York: Random House, 1951); William Safire & Leonard Safir, eds., *Words of Wisdom: More Good Advice* (New York: Simon & Schuster, 1990), 42.

2. *The Fairview Guide to Positive Quotations* (Minneapolis: Fairview Press, 1996), 258; Ross King, *Michelangelo and the Pope's Ceiling* (New York: Penguin Books, 2003); Richard Restak, *The New Brain: How the Modern Age Is Rewiring Your Mind* (Emmaus, Pa.: Rodale, 2004), 15, 17; Richard Restak, *The Secret Life of the Brain* (Dana Press/Joseph Henry Press, 2001), xiii.

3. Ralph Keyes, *The Courage to Write: How Writers Transcend Fear* (New York: Henry Holt & Co., 1995), 19. The first things I published were self-published. In 1988, I started a politically oriented newsletter called *The Bully Pulpit* in which I published opinion pieces on such topics as the need to reform the Electoral College system, grant statehood to the District of Columbia, and end the practice of juvenile executions. Later, I began publishing law review articles in academic journals. *See* John D. Bessler, "Televised Executions and the Constitution: Recognizing a First Amendment Right of Access to State Executions," 45 *Federal Communications Law Journal* 355 (1993); John D. Bessler, "The Public Interest and the Unconstitutionality of Private Prosecutors," 47 *Arkansas Law Review* 511 (1994); John D. Bessler, "The 'Midnight Assassination Law' and Minnesota's Anti-Death Penalty Movement, 1849-1911," 22 *William Mitchell Law Review* 577 (1996). If you ever feel compelled to read everything there is to know (at least as of 1991) about an obscure subsection of a rule of civil procedure and an even more obscure legal issue concerning the interpretation of language used in that subsection, you can check out my first published law review article. *See* John D. Bessler, "Defining 'Co-Party' Within Federal Rule of Civil Procedure 13(g): Are Cross-Claims Between Original Defendants and Third-Party Defendants Allowable?" 66 *Indiana Law Journal* 549 (1991). Just a word of caution: the lengthy footnotes in that article, which are in a tiny font size, often take up almost entire

pages. Two of the pages contain only two lines of actual text. Ibid., 551, 563. Lawyers and law students have become so famous for long footnotes and extensive citations (and their overuse) that parodies and satires of them cropped up, even in legal journals. *See, e.g.*, Aside, "The Common Law Origins of the Infield Fly Rule," 123 *University of Pennsylvania Law Review* 1474 (1975); Abner J. Mikva, "Goodbye to Footnotes," 56 *University of Colorado Law Review* 647 (1985); Fred Rodell, "Goodbye to Law Reviews," 23 *Virginia Law Review* 38 (1936). One tongue-in-cheek article begins, "This [FN1] is [FN2] the [FN3] world's [FN4] greatest [FN5] law [FN6] review [FN7] article. [FN8]." *See* Andrew J. McClurg, "The World's Greatest Law Review Article for Anyone Taking Life Too Seriously," 81 *A.B.A. Journal* (Oct. 1995): 84. German jurists have even sarcastically called for the development of new disciplines such as "Fussnotenwissenschaft" and "Fussnotologie." *See* Anthony Grafton, *The Footnote: A Curious History* (Cambridge: Harvard University Press, 1997), 25. Thankfully, at least lawyers haven't gotten as bad as to create what Anthony Grafton describes as "the most elaborate set of historical footnotes ever written—a set of four layers, footnotes to footnotes to footnotes to footnotes." Such intricate footnotes appeared in an early publication of an organization known as the Warburg Institute. Ibid., 234. I myself find notes useful, both as a place to provide information and to have a little fun.

4. George Orwell, *A Collection of Essays* (New York: Doubleday Anchor Books, 1954), 315-16; Pat Schneider, *Writing Alone and with Others* (Oxford: Oxford University Press, 2003), 2; Joan Didion, "Why I Write," *N.Y. Times Magazine*, Dec. 5, 1976. In his novel, *1984*, George Orwell created "Room 101," an interrogation room and torture chamber where a prisoner's worst fear (for example, having one's face gnawed by rats) would be realized. After one reads *Writing for Life*, it is my sincere hope that no one will ever most fear the act of writing in any circumstance.

5. Laura Ward, ed., *Foolish Words: The Most Stupid Words Ever Spoken* (London: PRC Publishing Limited, 2003), 90, 100, 222, 259; Ken Rudin, "Congressional Sex Scandals in History," http://www.washingtonpost.com/wp-srv/politics/special/clinton/congress.htm (last visited Sept. 19, 2004); http://www.jsc.nasa.gov/Bios/htmlbios/aldrin-b.html (last visited Sept. 19, 2004); http://www.xmission.com/~mwalker/DQ/quayle/qq/hall.of.fame.html (last visited Sept. 19, 2004); http://www.geocities.com/Area51/Zone/7474/blquayle.html (last visited Sept. 19, 2004).

6. Ward, *Foolish Words*, 128-30, 142; *Bartlett's Familiar Quotations: A Collection of Passages, Phrases, and Proverbs Traced to Their Sources in Ancient and Modern Literature* (Boston: Little, Brown & Co., 16th ed., 1992), 754; http://www.yogiberra.com/yogiisms.html (last visited Sept. 19, 2004); http://www.worldofquotes.com (last visited Oct. 1, 2004).

7. William Martin, *The Best Liberal Quotes Ever: Why the Left Is Right* (Naperville, Ill.: Sourcebooks, 2004), 258; Frank, *Quotationary*, 547; Ward, *Foolish Words*, 74, 78, 85, 86, 94, 102.

8. Brian Lamb, ed., *Booknotes: America's Finest Authors on Reading, Writing, and the Power of Ideas* (New York: Times Books, 1997), 172; Anne Lamott, *Bird by Bird: Some Instructions on Writing and Life* (New York: Anchor Books, 1995), xxviii; Diane Osen, ed., *The Book that Changed My Life: Interviews with National Book Award Winners and Finalists* (New York: Modern Library, 2002), 66; *The Writing Life: A Collection of Essays and Interviews* (New York: Random House, 1995), 63, 167.

9. Alice W. Flaherty, *The Midnight Disease: The Drive to Write, Writer's Block, and the Creative Brain* (Boston: Houghton Mifflin Co., 2004), 2, 195-96.

10. Ibid., 4-6, 32, 46, 54, 88, 200-1.

11. Ibid., 80, 83, 205-6, 213-14, 221.

12. Frank, *Quotationary*, 91.

13. Christina Davis & Christopher Edgar, eds., *Illuminations: Great Writers on Writing* (New York: T&W Books, 2003), 73.

14. Ibid.; Orwell, *A Collection of Essays*, 315.

CHAPTER FOUR A Writer's Tools

1. Leslie Ann Gibson, comp., *The Women's Book of Positive Quotations* (Minneapolis: Fairview Press, 2002), 426; Andrew Robinson, *The Story of Writing: Alphabets, Hieroglyphs & Pictograms* (London: Thames & Hudson Ltd., 1995), 39; http://www.npr.org/programs/morning/features/patc/ontheroad/ (last visited Jan. 2, 2005); http://www.cmgworldwide.com/historic/kerouac/viewheadline.php?id=2217 (last visited Jan. 2, 2005); http://partners.nytimes.com/books/97/09/07/home/kerouac-obit.html (last visited Jan. 2, 2005). Writing teacher Roy Peter Clark emphasizes that writing should be thought of as a craft, like carpentry, though he notes that "[u]nlike hammers, chisels, and rakes, writing tools never have to be returned." "As you gain proficiency with each tool, and then fluency," he says in his book on the subject, "the act of writing will make you a better student, a better worker, a better friend, a better citizen, a better parent, a better teacher, a better person." "You need tools, not rules," he notes. *See* Roy Peter Clark, *Writing Tools: 50 Essential Strategies for Every Writer* (New York: Little, Brown & Co., 2006), 4. The goal of *Writing for Life*—as is the goal of Clark's book—is to give you the tools you need to write effectively. You then have the freedom to use those tools as you best see fit.

2. Atul Gawande, "The Learning Curve," reprinted in *The Best American Essays* (New York: Houghton Mifflin Co., 2003), 90.

3. *Bartlett's Familiar Quotations: A Collection of Passages, Phrases, and Proverbs Traced to*

Their Sources in Ancient and Modern Literature (Boston: Little, Brown & Co., 16th ed. 1992); Steven Pinker, *The Language Instinct: How the Mind Creates Language* (New York: HarperCollins, 1994), 337-38.

4. Bill Bryson, *The Mother Tongue: English & How It Got that Way* (New York: William Morrow & Co., 1990), 69-70; Pinker, *The Language Instinct*, 69-70, 75.

5. Bryson, *The Mother Tongue*, 13, 147; Simon Winchester, *The Meaning of Everything: The Story of the Oxford English Dictionary* (Oxford: Oxford University Press, 2003), 247, 249. Simon Winchester also published another book about the creation of the *Oxford English Dictionary. See* Simon Winchester, *The Professor and the Madman: A Tale of Murder, Insanity, and the Making of the Oxford English Dictionary* (New York: HarperCollins, 1998). The creation of the first edition of the *Oxford English Dictionary*, which took more than 70 years to compile, utilized the volunteered services of readers from around the world who tried to identify the earliest known uses of words. One of the most prolific readers, Dr. William Chester Minor, was a Civil War veteran, former U.S. Army officer, and surgeon. Minor contributed more than 10,000 quotations to the *OED* over the course of two decades, though it was eventually discovered that Minor was an inmate at the Broadmoor Criminal Lunatic Asylum. A disturbed man, Minor had been adjudged not guilty of a murder on the grounds of insanity and had been directed by the British judicial system to be held in custody as a "certified criminal lunatic." Ibid., xi-xiii, 13-17, 20-21.

6. Bryson, *The Mother Tongue*, 151; Susie Dent, *The Language Report: The Ultimate Record of What We're Saying and How We're Saying It* (Oxford: Oxford University Press, 2003), 28; http://www.internetworldstats.com/top20.htm (last visited Apr. 13, 2005).

7. Bryson, *The Mother Tongue*, 73, 76, 151, 162-63; Dent, *The Language Report*, 16, 20, 28; Richard Lederer, *The Miracle of Language* (New York: Pocket Books, 1991), 25-26; Robert McCrum, William Cran & Robert MacNeil, *The Story of English* (New York: Penguin Books, 1992), 77, 106-7, 256, 258-59, 320; Winchester, *The Meaning of Everything*, 15; Peg Meier, "A Wordy Dervish," *Star Tribune* (Minneapolis) (Apr. 17, 2004): E1.

8. Bryson, *The Mother Tongue*, 64-65, 76; *Bartlett's Familiar Quotations*, 170, 179, 187, 208; Lederer, *The Miracle of Language*, 93-95; McCrum, Cran & MacNeil, *The Story of English*, 81-82; Winchester, *The Meaning of Everything*, 17, 19-20; Michael Wood, *Shakespeare* (New York: Basic Books, 2003), 15, 17, 49-50, 63-64, 160, 205.

9. *The American Heritage Dictionary* (Boston: Houghton Mifflin Co., 2nd college ed., 1982), 78, 82, 850, 1342; Bill Bryson, *Bryson's Dictionary of Troublesome Words: A Writer's Guide to Getting It Right* (New York: Broadway Books, 2002), 236-37, 239; Bryson, *The Mother Tongue*, 15-16; Michael C. Corballis, *From Hand to Mouth: The Origins of Language* (Princeton, N.J.: Princeton University Press, 2002), 8; Frederick

Crews, *The Random House Handbook* (New York: Random House, 2nd ed. 1977), 441–42, 449, 459; Margaret Shertzer, *The Elements of Grammar* (New York: Macmillan Pub. Co., 1986), 4–6.

10. *The American Heritage Dictionary of the English Language* (Boston: Houghton Mifflin Co., 3d ed. 1992), xliv, 1817, 2004; Bryson, *The Mother Tongue*, 86; Patricia T. O'Conner, *Woe Is I: The Grammarphobe's Guide to Better English in Plain English* (New York: Riverhead Books, 1996), 207, 216; Jan Venolia, *Write Right!: A Desktop Digest of Punctuation, Grammar, and Style* (Berkeley, Cal.: Ten Speed Press, 2001), 124.

11. Ben Yagoda, *The Sound on the Page: Style and Voice in Writing* (New York: HarperCollins, 2004), xx; Robinson, *The Story of Writing*, 17.

12. Margaret Miner & Hugh Rawson, eds., *The New International Dictionary of Quotations* (New York: Signet, 3rd ed. 2000), 101; *The Oxford Dictionary of 20th Century Quotations* (Oxford: Oxford University Press, 1998), 267.

13. Diane Ackerman, *A Natural History of the Senses* (New York: Random House, 1990), xv.

14. Ibid., 281–82.

15. *The American Heritage Dictionary of the English Language*, 1960; Lederer, *The Miracle of Language*, 181; Marc McCutcheon, *Descriptionary: A Thematic Dictionary* (New York: Facts on File, Inc., 1992); *The Macmillan Visual Dictionary* (New York: Macmillan Pub. Co., 1992); *The Oxford Dictionary of 20th Century Quotations,* 318.

16. Stephen Wilbers, *Keys to Great Writing* (Cincinnati: Writer's Digest Books, 2000), 106–7; Stephen Wilbers, "Put Your Verbiage on a Diet," *Star Tribune* (Minneapolis) (May 28, 2004): D2.

17. Bryson, *The Mother Tongue*, 82; Susan Goldsmith Wooldridge, *Poemcrazy: Freeing Your Life with Words* (New York: Three Rivers Press, 1996), 35; http://www.clockworkorange.com/nadsat.shtml (last visited July 17, 2004).

18. Lynne Truss, *Eats, Shoots & Leaves: The Zero Tolerance Approach to Punctuation* (New York: Gotham Books, 2003), 202. Although Truss bills herself as a stickler for proper punctuation, a scathing (and amusing) review of her book in *The New Yorker* pointed out numerous punctuation errors in Truss's own book. *See* Louis Menand, "Bad Comma: Lynne Truss's Strange Grammar," *New Yorker* (June 28, 2004). Nobody's perfect, just keep that in mind when you write—and when you punctuate!

19. Truss, *Eats, Shoots & Leaves*, 9, 97, 171.

20. Bryson, *Bryson's Dictionary of Troublesome Words*, 227, appendix (suggesting uses for semicolons); O'Conner, *Woe Is I*, 137, 139, 144, 205; Truss, *Eats, Shoots & Leaves*, 118, 120–21; Venolia, *Write Right!*, 52.

21. David Backes, ed., *The Meaning of Wilderness: Essential Articles and Speeches* (Minneapolis: University of Minnesota Press, 2001), xxi. If you want a real wilderness

experience, take a canoe trip in the roadless Boundary Waters Canoe Area Wilderness. Over one million acres in size, northern Minnesota's BWCAW is full of lakes, rivers and portages and forests, plants and abundant wildlife, including bears, moose and beavers. You'll need a permit, but you can reserve one online. *See* http://www.bwcaw.org (last visited Sept. 13, 2006).

22. Leonard Roy Frank, ed., *Quotationary* (New York: Random House, 2001), 27.

23. Pinker, *The Language Instinct*, 383-85; Shertzer, *The Elements of Grammar*, 1.

24. Ray Bradbury, *Zen in the Art of Writing: Releasing the Creative Genius Within You* (New York: Bantam Books, 1992), 53, 131.

25. Shertzer, *The Elements of Grammar*, 8-9, 137; Bryson, *Bryson's Dictionary of Troublesome Words*, 111.

26. Shertzer, *The Elements of Grammar*, 49, 125.

27. Bryson, *Bryson's Dictionary of Troublesome Words*, ix; Bryson, *The Mother Tongue*, 37; Pinker, *The Language Instinct*, 187; http://www.fun-with-words.com/mnem_ explain.html (last visited Aug. 25, 2005).

28. Bryson, *Bryson's Dictionary of Troublesome Words*, 7, 34, 164-65, 190; Robert W. Harris, *When Good People Write Bad Sentences: 12 Steps to Better Writing Habits* (New York: St. Martin's Griffin, 2004), 109-10; Venolia, *Write Right!*, 124; Paul Mickle, "1992: Gaffe with an 'e' at the End," *The Trentonian*, at http://www.capitalcentury. com/1992.html (last visited July 18, 2004).

29. L. Sue Baugh, *Essentials of English Grammar: A Practical Guide to the Mastery of English* (Lincolnwood, Ill.: Passport Books, 2nd ed. 1993); *The Fairview Guide to Positive Quotations* (Minneapolis: Fairview Press, 1996), 276; O'Conner, *Woe Is I*; Shertzer, *The Elements of Grammar*; Mary Ruth Yoe, "The CMS Syndrome," *University of Chicago Magazine* (Aug. 2003): 39-41.

30. *The Chicago Manual of Style: The Essential Guide for Writers, Editors, and Publishers* (Chicago: University of Chicago Press, 15th ed. 2003); Frank, *Quotationary*, 455. *The Chicago Manual of Style* contains all sorts of useful information on style issues and the editorial and publication processes. It also contains a useful bibliography that lists works on topics such as research, writing, editing, grammar and usage, and publishing. I've never seen it used for weightlifting, but it's a thick, hefty tome that weighs in at over three pounds. Every serious writer should have a copy, even if one uses it only infrequently.

31. Karen Elizabeth Gordon, *The New Well-Tempered Sentence: A Punctuation Handbook for the Innocent, the Eager, and the Doomed* (New York: Houghton Mifflin, 2003), 2-3; Cathleen Rountree, *The Writer's Mentor: A Guide to Putting Passion on Paper* (Berkeley, Cal.: Conari Press, 2002), 190; Truss, *Eats, Shoots & Leaves*, 138.

32. Robert I. Fitzhenry, ed., *The Harper Book of Quotations* (New York:

HarperCollins, 1993), 378, 493; Truss, *Eats, Shoots & Leaves*, 30, 84-85; Ronald Goldfarb, "Books in the Law," *Washington Lawyer* (Mar. 2004): 39; *see also* Heaslip v. Freeman, 511 N.W.2d 21, 23 (Minn. Ct. App. 1994).

33. William Safire & Leonard Safir, comps., *Good Advice on Writing: Great Quotations from Writers Past and Present on How to Write Well* (New York: Simon & Schuster, 1992), 214; *The Oxford Dictionary of 20th Century Quotations*, 284; http://www.womenof.com/Articles/cb93002.asp (last visited June 23, 2004).

34. Peter J. Silzer, comp., "Quotations about Language," June 2001 (available online), 33, 57.

35. Lewis D. Eigen & Jonathan P. Siegel, *Dictionary of Political Quotations* (London: Robert Hall, 1993), 152.

36. *Great Quotes from Great Teachers* (Great Quotations Pub. Co., 2003), 25.

CHAPTER FIVE The Writing Process: From Freewriting to Form

1. Leslie Ann Gibson, comp., *The Women's Book of Positive Quotations* (Minneapolis: Fairview Press, 2002), 426; *The Sound of Music* (CBS/FOX Co., 1991).

2. Betty Edwards, *Drawing on the Right Side of the Brain: A Course in Enhancing Creativity and Artistic Confidence* (New York: Jeremy P. Tarcher/Perigee Books, 1989), 98; Leonard Roy Frank, ed., *Quotationary* (New York: Random House, 2001), 45.

3. Frank, *Quotationary*, 159, 160, 449.

4. Richard Restak, *The New Brain: How the Modern Age Is Rewiring Your Mind* (New York: Rodale, 2003), 56-58; Claudia Wallis & Sonja Steptoe, "Help! I've Lost My Focus," *TIME* (Jan. 16, 2006): 74.

5. Linda Trichter Metcalf & Tobin Simon, *Writing the Mind Alive: The Proprioceptive Method for Finding Your Voice* (New York: Ballantine Books, 2002), 48; Restak, *The New Brain*, 60-61.

6. Richard Rhodes, *How to Write: Advice and Reflections* (New York: Quill, 1995), 13.

7. Paul Gruchow, *Boundary Waters: The Grace of the Wild* (Minneapolis: Milkweed Editions, 1997), 11.

8. Cathleen Rountree, *The Writer's Mentor: A Guide to Putting Passion on Paper* (Berkeley, Cal.: Conari Press, 2002), 32, 132; Ralph Keyes, *The Courage to Write: How Writers Transcend Fear* (New York: Henry Holt & Co., 1995), 181.

9. Janet Burroway, *Writing Fiction: A Guide to Narrative Craft* (New York: Harper Collins, 4th ed., 1996), 4-5; William Safire & Leonard Safir, eds., *Words of Wisdom: More Good Advice* (New York: Simon & Schuster, 1989), 37; Pat Schneider, *Writing Alone and with Others* (Oxford: Oxford University Press, 2003), 35. The craft of fiction writing is beyond the scope of *Writing for Life*, though I have included a few references to fiction writing guides in the bibliography (in case you want to learn more

about that particular subject). Studying the writing techniques used by fiction writers is always a useful exercise for any writer.

10. Frank, *Quotationary*, 957; Metcalf & Simon, *Writing the Mind Alive*, 57-58.

11. Rountree, *The Writer's Mentor*, 82; Stephen Wilbers, *Keys to Great Writing* (Cincinnati: Writer's Digest Books, 2000), 228; Will Blythe, ed., *On Being a Writer* (Cincinnati: Writer's Digest Books, 1989), 18.

12. Natalie Goldberg, *Writing Down the Bones: Freeing the Writer Within* (Boston: Shambhala, 1986), 8; Rountree, *The Writer's Mentor*, 86; Brenda Ueland, *If You Want to Write: A Book About Art, Independence and Spirit* (St. Paul: Graywolf Press, 1987), 26.

13. Metcalf & Simon, *Writing the Mind Alive*, 18.

14. Ueland, *If You Want to Write*, 15-16, 58. I highly recommend Brenda Ueland's book, and not just because she was born and lived in Minnesota, my home state. And I'm not alone in that regard. National Public Radio's Andrei Codrescu calls it "an inspirational tract aimed at those who would write but are prevented from so doing by shyness, fear or humility." *See* http://graywolfpress.org (last visited Sept. 13, 2006). Ueland's well-written book is a classic and well worth the read.

15. Suzy Platt, ed., *Respectfully Quoted: A Dictionary of Quotations Requested from the Congressional Research Service* (Washington, D.C.: Library of Congress, 1989), 116.

16. Robert I. Fitzhenry, ed., *The Harper Book of Quotations* (New York: HarperCollins, 1993), 484; Frank, *Quotationary*, 952; http://www.mantex.co.uk/ou/a319/brenan.htm (last visited July 20, 2004).

17. Jack Heffron, *The Writer's Idea Book: How to Develop Great Ideas for Fiction, Nonfiction, Poetry and Screenplays* (Cincinnati: Writer's Digest Books, 2000), 25-26, 35, 38-39, 123.

18. John Gardner, *The Art of Fiction: Notes on Craft for Young Writers* (New York: Vintage Books, 1991), 195, 198, 202-4.

19. Alice Flaherty, *The Midnight Disease: The Drive to Write, Writer's Block, and the Creative Brain* (Boston: Houghton Mifflin Co., 2004), 86; Keyes, *The Courage to Write*, 90; Rountree, *The Writer's Mentor*, 160.

20. *The Literary Almanac: The Best of the Printed Word, 1900 to the Present* (Kansas City: Andrews McMeel Publishing, 1997), 202; Flaherty, *The Midnight Disease*, 95; Keyes, *The Courage to Write*, 24, 90.

21. Keyes, *The Courage to Write*, 3, 13-14, 22-23, 32, 39, 90, 94, 149.

22. National Center for Education Statistics, "National Assessment of College Student Learning: Identifying College Graduates' Essential Skills in Writing, Speech and Listening, and Critical Thinking" (1995), 7, 58-59.

23. Peter Elbow, *Writing with Power: Techniques for Mastering the Writing Process* (Oxford: Oxford University Press, 1998), 9, 30, 60 (emphasis in original).

24. Norman Maclean, *A River Runs Through It and Other Stories* (Chicago: University of Chicago Press, 1976), 1-2, 4, 86, 97-98, 101. I've tried my hand at fly fishing, but fly casting is not at all an easy thing to master. (Ice fishing on Leech Lake at the International Eelpout Festival in Walker, Minnesota, in Cass County Attorney Earl Maus's fishhouse required no casting technique whatsoever, though other skills were obviously required as I caught no fish that day.) I say this only to point out that most everything in life has a craft—even an art—to it. In the retail sales and the real estate business, it's location, location, location (in particular, finding the right one); in politics, U.S. Senator Paul Wellstone was fond of saying that the key is to "organize, organize, organize." In writing, the key is practice, practice, practice.

25. Schneider, *Writing Alone and with Others*, 17; *Writers Inc: A Student Handbook for Writing and Learning* (Boston: Write Source, 1996), 133-34; Ben Yagoda, *The Sound on the Page: Style and Voice in Writing* (New York: HarperCollins, 2004), 23.

26. Burroway, *Writing Fiction*, 199; Heffron, *The Writer's Idea Book*, 181-83; William Zinsser, *On Writing Well: The Classic Guide to Writing Nonfiction* (New York: Harper Collins, 2001), 21.

27. Lewis D. Eigen & Jonathan P. Siegel, *Dictionary of Political Quotations* (London: Robert Hale Ltd., 1993), 30.

28. Burroway, *Writing Fiction*, 199 (italics in original).

29. Heffron, *The Writer's Idea Book*, 226; Sigurd Olson, *Listening Point* (Minneapolis: University of Minnesota Press, 2001), 8; Sigurd Olson, *Reflections from the North Country* (Minneapolis: University of Minnesota Press, 1998), 33.

30. Elbow, *Writing with Power*, 39.

31. http://marsrovers.jpl.nasa.gov/newsroom/pressreleases/20040401a.html (last visited Apr. 7, 2004); http://science.nasa.gov/headlines/y2003/16jan_sts107.htm (last visited Apr. 7, 2004); http://thunder.msfc.nasa.gov/shuttle.html (last visited Apr. 7, 2004); http://www.ghcc.msfc.nasa.gov/skeets.html (last visited Sept. 13, 2004); Wail Benjelloun, Zineb Atay-Kadiri & Mohammed Benzakour, "Effect of weightlessness on the development cycle in gypsy moth," NASA Mission STS-108, Endeavor (launch during 5-17 Dec. 2001).

32. Annie Dillard, *The Writing Life* (New York: HarperCollins, 1989), 3, 68, 78-79.

33. Heffron, *The Writer's Idea Book*, 213-14; Keyes, *The Courage to Write*, 148; Zinsser, *On Writing Well*, 65, 67.

34. William Safire & Leonard Safir, comps., *Good Advice on Writing: Great Quotations from Writers Past and Present on How to Write Well* (New York: Simon & Schuster, 1992), 71.

35. Ibid., 72.

CHAPTER SIX Substance Matters

1. Leonard Roy Frank, ed., *Quotationary* (New York: Random House, 2001), 382; http://inventors.about.com/library/inventors (last visited July 7, 2004) (entries for Eli Whitney, Wright brothers, Mary Anderson and Patricia Bath).

2. Frank, *Quotationary*, 7; Steven Pinker, *The Language Instinct: How the Mind Creates Language* (New York: HarperCollins, 1994), 45, 72-73.

3. V. S. Ramachandran, *A Brief Tour of Human Consciousness: From Imposter Poodles to Purple Numbers* (New York: Pi Press, 2004), 4, 25, 159-62, 164, 166, 170; Steven R. Quartz & Terrence J. Sejnowski, *Liars, Lovers, and Heroes: What the New Brain Science Reveals About How We Become Who We Are* (New York: HarperCollins, 2002), 35.

4. Ramachandran, *A Brief Tour of Human Consciousness*, 2-3, 166; Quartz & Sejnowski, *Liars, Lovers, and Heroes*, 23-25, 33.

5. Quartz & Sejnowski, *Liars, Lovers, and Heroes*, 42, 110, 235-36.

6. Jon E. Lewis, ed., *A Documentary History of Human Rights: A Record of the Events, Documents and Speeches that Shaped Our World* (New York: Carroll & Graf Publishers, 2003), 3; Charles Murray, *Human Accomplishments: The Pursuit of Excellence in the Arts and Sciences, 800 B.C. to 1950* (New York: HarperCollins, 2003), 210-11, 599; Merritt Ruhlen, *The Origin of Language: Tracing the Evolution of the Mother Tongue* (New York: John Wiley & Sons, 1994), 4, 17; Elizabeth J. Himelfarb, "First Alphabet Found in Egypt," *Archaeology*, Vol. 53, No. 1 (Jan./Feb. 2000); Julie Walton Shaver, "We Get Letters: An Invention that Changed the World Has Only 26 Very Small Parts," *N.Y. Times Book Review* (Feb. 15, 2004): 21 (reviewing David Sacks, *Language Visible: Unraveling the Mystery of the Alphabet from A to Z* (New York: Broadway Books, 2003)).

7. Michelle P. Brown, *The British Library Guide to Writing and Scripts: History and Techniques* (Toronto: University of Toronto Press, 1998), 64-65; Bill Bryson, *The Mother Tongue: English & How It Got that Way* (New York: William Morrow & Co., 1990), 126-27; George Holmes, ed., *The Oxford History of Medieval Europe* (Oxford: Oxford University Press, 2001), 51, 98, 315-16; Murray, *Human Accomplishments*, 26, 47, 412; Michael Olmert, *The Smithsonian Book of Books* (Washington, D.C.: Smithsonian Books, 1992), 113-14, 117, 119. Notes have their own historical origins. For centuries, scholars have used notes to persuade and to indicate the sources that have been consulted. Chuck Zerby, *The Devil's Details: A History of Footnotes* (New York: Simon & Schuster, 2002), 1; Anthony Grafton, *The Footnote: A Curious History* (Cambridge: Harvard University Press, 1997), 22. "The first footnote," writes Chuck Zerby, "drifts somewhere in a universe of manuscripts and books, eluding our discovery the way the original bright star of the skies eludes astronomers." Zerby, *The Devil's Details*, 17. Richard Jugge, of sixteenth-century London and the man in charge of printing the Church of England's Bishops' Bible, stands as "a plausible candidate

for the person who first conceived the idea of a footnote," Zerby writes, noting how Jugge placed lettered notes at the bottom of the page. Ibid., 19-28. By the eighteenth century, historical footnotes were a literary art form. Grafton, *The Footnote*, 1, 111, 221, 229. Historian Edward Gibbon (1737-1794) devoted approximately one-fourth of his massive, multi-volume *The Decline and Fall of the Roman Empire* to footnotes. Zerby, *The Devil's Details*, 1-2, 60. In 1743, one Gottlieb Wilhelm Rabener published a dissertation, *Hinkmars von Repkow Noten onhe Text*, which, to the amusement (or chagrin) of readers, consisted entirely of footnotes. Grafton, *The Footnote*, 120. Endnotes, of course, have now also become fashionable, though they are not without their detractors. "Notes," Chuck Zerby writes, "should be reader-friendly; a book should not emulate a supermarket in which the bread is at one end of the store and another common purchase—say, cheese—is at the other." Zerby, *The Devil's Details*, 91 n.3.

8. *The Science Book* (London: Weidenfeld & Nicolson, 2001), 78, 88, 176, 244; James Gleick, *Isaac Newton* (New York: Pantheon Books, 2003), 129; *Jane Goodall: 40 Years at Gombe* (New York: Stewart, Tabori & Chang, 2000), 36; Randal Keynes, *Darwin, His Daughter & Human Evolution* (New York: Riverhead Books, 2001), 274-75; Murray, *Human Accomplishments*, 168-69, 180, 185. According to Umberto Bartocci, a mathematics historian at the University of Perugia, an Italian industrialist, Olinto De Pretto, published the equation $E=mc^2$ two years before Albert Einstein used it to develop the theory of relativity. *See* http://www.guardian.co.uk/international/story/0,,253524,00html (last visited Aug. 16, 2006). The life of Olinto De Pretto, of course, remains as obscure as the scientific magazine, *Atte*, that published De Pretto's work in 1903.

9. Lewis, ed., *A Documentary History of Human Rights*, 7, 12, 23, 140-50, 351, 418-19.

10. *Black's Law Dictionary* (St. Paul, Minn.: West Publishing Co., 5th ed. 1979), 858.

11. Office of the United Nations High Commissioner for Human Rights, "Status of Ratifications of the Principal International Human Rights Treaties," http://www.unhchr.ch/pdf/report.pdf (last visited Feb. 15, 2004).

12. Hubert H. Humphrey, *The Education of a Public Man: My Life and Politics* (Minneapolis: University of Minnesota Press, 1992); http://www.dsba.ie/News/defaultarticle.asp?NID=129&T=N (last visited Sept. 21, 2004).

13. Paul Wellstone, *The Conscience of a Liberal: Reclaiming the Compassionate Agenda* (Minneapolis: University of Minnesota Press, 2002), ix; Matthew Dallek, "The Conservative 1960s," The Atlantic Online (book review of Mary Brennan, *Turning Right in the Sixties: The Conservative Capture of the GOP* (Chapel Hill: University of North Carolina Press, 1995)). U.S. Senator Paul Wellstone, who died in a plane

crash near Eveleth, Minnesota, on the eve of the 2002 election, left us with many inspiring words. Here's a few of my favorites: "The future belongs to those who are passionate and work hard." "Politics is not about big money or power games, it's about the improvement of people's lives." "When we all do better, we all do better." For a well-written biography of Senator Wellstone, see Bill Lofy, *Paul Wellstone: The Life of a Passionate Progressive* (Ann Arbor: University of Michigan Press, 2005).

14. Betty Edwards, *Drawing on the Artist Within: An Inspirational and Practical Guide to Increasing Your Creative Powers* (New York: Simon & Schuster, 1986), 3, 38, 41, 46-47; Ian Jackman, ed., *The Writer's Mentor: Secrets of Success from the World's Greatest Writers* (New York: Random House Reference, 2004), 13; http://www.savident.com/CurrentProductions/thehobbit.htm (last visited July 18, 2005).

15. Linda Trichter Metcalf & Tobin Simon, *Writing the Mind Alive: The Proprioceptive Method for Finding Your Authentic Voice* (New York: Ballantine Books, 2002), 69-70, 187.

16. Christina Davis & Christopher Edgar, eds., *Illuminations: Great Writers on Writing* (New York: T&W Books, 2003), 91, 116; http://www.nobel.se/literature/laureates/1996/szymborska-bio.html (last visited June 26, 2004).

17. Will Blythe, ed., *Why I Write: Thoughts on the Craft of Fiction* (Boston: Little, Brown & Co., 1998), 48-49, 58.

18. Diane Ackerman, *A Natural History of the Senses* (New York: Vintage Books, 1990), 287.

19. John D. Bessler, *Death in the Dark: Midnight Executions in America* (Boston: Northeastern University Press, 1997). *Death in the Dark* is now out of print. I recently got a letter from the publisher inquiring if I wanted to buy the remaining stock of the books at the bargain-basement price of fifty cents apiece. The letter also informed me (in no uncertain terms) that any books not purchased in that manner would be "recycled." Ouch! Needless to say, I bought some copies to preserve at least a few more copies of my first book, though the shipping charges—as you might have guessed—nearly eclipsed the purchase price. But alas, all is not lost. The book got reviewed in several publications, including *Publishers Weekly* and *The Nation*, and the book made a scholarly contribution and a public impact on America's death penalty debate, however modest. According to my last royalty statement from the publisher, in the ten years since it was first published, *Death in the Dark* sold 1,373 hardcopies and 1,104 paperbacks. Since libraries bought many of those books, the book's life will continue well past the out-of-print notice I received.

20. Margaret Atwood, *Negotiating with the Dead: A Writer on Writing* (New York: Anchor Books, 2002), 117; Catherine Dee, ed., *The Girls' Book of Wisdom* (New York: Little Brown & Co., 1999), 86.

21. Ralph Keyes, *The Courage to Write: How Writers Transcend Fear* (New York: Henry Holt & Co., 1995), 99; Patricia Hampl, *I Could Tell You Stories: Sojourns in the Land of Memory* (New York: W.W. Norton & Co., 1999), 27-28; Robert I. Fitzhenry, ed., *The Harper Book of Quotations* (New York: HarperCollins, 1993), 501.

22. Edwards, *Drawing on the Artist Within*, 152; *The 9/11 Commission Report: Final Report of the National Commission on Terrorist Attacks upon the United States* (New York: W.W. Norton & Co., 2004).

23. Fitzhenry, *The Harper Book of Quotations*, 385.

24. E. L. Doctorow, *Reporting the Universe* (Cambridge: Harvard University Press, 2003), 1; Virginia Woolf, *A Room of One's Own* (New York: Harcourt Brace & Co., 1989), 77.

25. http://www.fedex.com/us/about/overview/?link=4 (last visited Mar. 28, 2004); http://www.ralphkeyes.com/pages/books/innovation/press.htm (last visited Mar. 28, 2004).

CHAPTER SEVEN Rest and Relaxation

1. *The Fairview Guide to Positive Quotations* (Minneapolis: Fairview Press, 1996), 504.

2. Stuart Spencer, *The Playwright's Guidebook: An Insightful Primer on the Art of Dramatic Writing* (New York: Faber & Faber, 2002), 45.

3. John D. Bessler, *Legacy of Violence: Lynch Mobs and Executions in Minnesota* (Minneapolis: University of Minnesota Press, 2003); Elizabeth Knowles, ed., *The Oxford Dictionary of Twentieth Century Quotations* (Oxford: Oxford University Press, 1998), 195.

4. Richard Ford, "Goofing Off While the Muse Recharges," in *Writers on Writing: Collected Essays from The New York Times* (New York: Times Books, 2001), 67. Proofreading endnotes for proper citation form and typographical errors might be described as the opposite of goofing off.

5. Robert Pinsky & Maggie Dietz, eds., *Americans' Favorite Poems: The Favorite Poem Project Anthology* (New York: W.W. Norton & Co., 2000), 92-93; Christopher R. Miller, "Books in Brief," *N.Y. Times Book Review* (Mar. 28, 2004): 18 (reviewing Matthew Spencer, ed., *Elected Friends: Robert Frost and Edward Thomas to One Another* (New York: Handsel Books, 2004)).

6. Alice W. Flaherty, *The Midnight Disease: The Drive to Write, Writer's Block, and the Creative Brain* (New York: Houghton Mifflin Co., 2004), 2, 24-25, 46; Cathleen Rountree, *The Writer's Mentor: A Guide to Putting Passion on Paper* (Berkeley, Cal.: Conari Press, 2002), 123.

7. Flaherty, *The Midnight Disease*, 153.

8. Steven R. Quartz and Terrence J. Sejnowski, *Liars, Lovers, and Heroes: What the New Brain Science Reveals About How We Become Who We Are* (New York: HarperCollins, 2003), 248-50. I myself like to bicycle or play tennis. Speaking of which, if you're ever looking to read an eye-opening, heavily footnoted article on the world of *professional* tennis (which is *not* like the tennis I play), I know of a witty one for you to read. *See* David Foster Wallace, "The String Theory," *Esquire* (July 1996). David Foster Wallace, the author of books such as *Infinite Jest* and *Consider the Lobster*, is well-known for his extensive use of notes.

9. David Snowdon, *Aging with Grace: What the Nun Study Teaches Us About Leading Longer, Healthier, and More Meaningful Lives* (New York: Bantam Books, 2002), 3, 33, 38, 61, 79, 148. Some of the nuns who participated in this study lived in Mankato, Minnesota, on Good Counsel Hill—the same place where I attended high school. Ibid., 18-25. My alma mater, Loyola High School, is still located in the same place.

10. Ibid., 65, 84-85, 107, 112-14, 117, 187-88, 193-94.

11. William C. Dement, *The Promise of Sleep* (New York: Dell Publishing, 1999), 314; Stephanie Thurrott, "The Gift of Sleep," *Creative Living* (Autumn 2004): 8, 11; Sora Song, "Sleeping Your Way to the Top," *TIME* (Jan. 16, 2006): 83. If you ask me, one can never get too much sleep. I myself like to get seven to eight hours a night. The unstructured, otherworldly quality of sleep is not only rejuvenating, it is the perfect counterbalance to the intense, focused concentration required when writing and revising.

12. J. Allan Hobson, *Dreaming: An Introduction to the Science of Sleep* (Oxford: Oxford University Press, 2002), 11, 40, 42, 107-9; Quartz and Sejnowski, *Liars, Lovers, and Heroes*, 39, 287-88.

13. Hobson, *Dreaming*, 53-54, 78.

14. Leonard Roy Frank, ed., *Quotationary* (New York: Random House, 2001), 459.

15. Jack Salzman & Pamela Wilkinson, eds., *Major Characters in American Fiction* (New York: Henry Holt & Co., 1994), 880; Leslie Ann Gibson, comp., *The Women's Book of Positive Quotations* (Minneapolis: Fairview Press, 2002), 19, 170.

CHAPTER EIGHT   A Bookshelf of Friends

1. Sven Birkerts, *The Gutenberg Elegies: The Fate of Reading in an Electronic Age* (New York: Ballantine Books, 1994), 80 (emphasis in original).

2. Maxine Rose Schur, ed., *The Reading Woman: A Journal* (San Francisco: Pomegranate Artbooks, 1991) (not paginated); Bill Bradfield, ed., *Books and Reading: A Book of Quotations* (Mineola, N.Y.: Dover Publications, 2002), 36.

3. National Endowment for the Arts, "Reading at Risk: A Survey of Literary Reading in America" (Research Division Report #46), vii, ix, x, 3, 26, 30;

http://www.naa.org/marketscope/databank/tdnpr1299.htm (last visited Sept. 16, 2004); http://www.naa.org/artpage.cfm?AID=1614&SID=75 (last visited Sept. 16, 2004).

4. Margaret Miner & Hugh Rawson, eds., *The New International Dictionary of Quotations* (New York: Signet, 3rd ed. 2000), 56; "Reading at Risk," vii.

5. Leonard Roy Frank, ed., *Quotationary* (New York: Random House, 2001), 71.

6. W. Kenneth Hamblin, *The Earth's Dynamic Systems* (Minneapolis: Burgess Publishing, 4th ed. 1985); John F. Kennedy, *Profiles in Courage* (New York: Harper & Row, 1964); Scott Turow, *One L: The Turbulent True Story of a First Year at Harvard Law School* (New York: Farrar Straus & Giroux, 1977). Having read Scott Turow's book before I started law school nearly 20 years ago, I'm reminded everyday (if not by my daughter, then by something else) that I'm growing older. One of my former law students at the University of Minnesota Law School actually ended up working with Scott Turow as a lawyer in Chicago. It's a small world after all—and the linkages one discovers between people and events (the kind of linkages one discovers while writing) seem to become more apparent all the time as life goes on.

7. Anne Lamott, *Bird by Bird: Some Instructions on Writing and Life* (New York: Anchor Books, 1995), 15, 233; J. Peder Zane, ed., *Remarkable Reads: 34 Writers and Their Adventures in Reading* (New York: W.W. Norton & Co., 2004), 7.

8. Michael C. Corballis, *From Hand to Mouth: The Origins of Language* (Princeton, N.J.: Princeton University Press, 2002), 101, 151; Nicholas Orme, *Medieval Children* (New Haven: Yale University Press, 2001), 130, 238; Steven Pinker, *The Language Instinct: How the Mind Creates Language* (New York: HarperCollins, 1994), 268-73.

9. Mortimer J. Adler & Charles Van Doren, *How to Read a Book: The Classic Guide to Intelligent Reading* (New York: Simon & Schuster, 1972), 40; Pinker, *The Language Instinct*, 186; *The American Heritage Dictionary of the English Language* (Boston: Houghton Mifflin Co., 3rd ed. 1992), 575.

10. C. S. Lewis, *Surprised by Joy: The Shape of My Early Life* (San Diego: Harvest Books, 1955), 10.

11. *Bartlett's Familiar Quotations: A Collection of Passages, Phrases, and Proverbs Traced to Their Sources in Ancient and Modern Literature* (Boston: Little, Brown & Co., 16th ed. 1992), 344; Bradfield, *Books and Reading*, 49, 62; Robert I. Fitzhenry, ed., *The Harper Book of Quotations* (New York: HarperCollins, 1993), 59; Rob Kaplan & Harold Rabinowitz, eds., *Speaking of Books: The Best Things Ever Said About Books and Book Collecting* (New York: Crown Publishers, 2001), 181.

12. Nicholas J. Karolides, Margaret Bald & Dawn B. Sova, *100 Banned Books: Censorship Histories of World Literature* (New York: Checkmark Books, 1999), 274-75; Diane Ravitch, *The Language Police: How Pressure Groups Restrict What Students Learn*

(New York: Vintage Books, 2004), 74-75, 80; *The Literary Almanac: The Best of the Printed Word 1900 to the Present* (Kansas City, Mo.: Andrews McMeel Publishing, 1997), 270-72.

13. Karolides, Bald & Sova, *100 Banned Books*, xi-xii, 169, 171, 249-56; http://www.kirjasto.sci.fi/sara.htm (last visited Sept. 7, 2004).

14. Karolides, Bald & Sova, *100 Banned Books*, 19-21; Richard Lederer, *The Miracle of Language* (New York: Pocket Books, 1991), 5-6.

15. William DeGregorio, *The Complete Book of U.S. Presidents* (New York: Random House, 4th ed. 1993), 89; Louise Erdrich, *Books and Islands in Ojibwe Country* (Washington, D.C.: National Geographic Society, 2003), 55, 141; Frank, *Quotationary*, 432; Lamott, *Bird by Bird*, 237; David McCullough, "Climbing into Another Head," in Marie Arana, ed., *The Writing Life: Writers on How They Think and Work* (New York: Public Affairs, 2003), 167; Miner & Rawson, *The New International Dictionary of Quotations*, 37; Fitzhenry, *The Harper Book of Quotations*, 63.

16. Frank, *Quotationary*, 68; Adler & Van Doren, *How to Read a Book*, 137; Kaplan & Rabinowitz, *Speaking of Books*, 166.

17. George Grant & Karen Grant, *Shelf Life: How Books Have Changed the Destinies and Desires of Men and Nations* (Nashville, Tenn.: Cumberland House, 1999), 171-73; Brian Lamb, *Booknotes: America's Finest Authors on Reading, Writing, and the Power of Ideas* (New York: Times Books, 1997), xvi, 131; R. W. B. Lewis, "Writers at the Century's Turn," in *The Writing Life: A Collection of Essays and Interviews* (New York: Random House, 1995), 41; Michael Olmert, *The Smithsonian Book of Books* (Washington, D.C.: Smithsonian Books, 1992), 211, 280; Malcolm Jones, "Waiting for the Movie," *Newsweek* (July 19, 2004): 58; http://www.loc.gov/about/ (last visited Aug. 28, 2004); http://www.bookwire.com/bookwire/decadebookproduction.html (last visited Sept. 16, 2004); http://www.loc.gov/loc/legacy/loc.html (last visited Jan. 5, 2005).

18. William Safire & Leonard Safir, eds., *Words of Wisdom: More Good Advice* (New York: Simon & Schuster, 1989), 46; Fitzhenry, *The Harper Book of Quotations*, 137.

19. Susan Sontag, "Directions: Write, Read, Rewrite. Repeat Steps 2 and 3 as Needed," in *Writers on Writing: Collected Essays from The New York Times* (New York: Times Books, 2001), 223-24, 226; Anne Fadiman, ed., *The Best American Essays* (Boston: Houghton Mifflin Co., 2003), 332.

20. Adam Gopnik, *Paris to the Moon* (New York: Random House, 2000); Sarah Turnbull, *Almost French: Love and a New Life in Paris* (New York: Gotham Books, 2002). If you can't make it to Paris, there's an excellent replica (1/3 scale) of the Eiffel Tower at Paramount's Kings Island, a great amusement park near Cincinnati, Ohio. I know that because I used to go there as a kid with my family.

21. Grant & Grant, *Shelf Life*, 24.

22. Bradfield, *Books and Reading*, 41.

23. Cathleen Rountree, *The Writer's Mentor: A Guide to Putting Passion on Paper* (Berkeley, Cal.: Conari Press, 2002), 28-29.

24. Corballis, *From Hand to Mouth*, 200; Kaplan & Rabinowitz, *Speaking of Books*, 111. In its 1991 National Literacy Act, Congress defined literacy as "an individual's ability to read, write, and speak in English, and compute and solve problems at levels of proficiency necessary to function on the job and in society, to achieve one's goals, and develop one's knowledge and potential." In 1988, Congress directed the Department of Education to carry out an assessment of literacy skills, resulting in the National Adult Literacy Survey of approximately 26,000 individuals. That survey found that a total of 21 to 23 percent of Americans aged 16 or older—or 40 to 44 million people—operated at Level 1, the lowest literacy level. People in that group could usually read a little but not well enough to fill out an application, read a food label, or read a simple story to a child. Another 25 to 28 percent of the adult population scored in Level 2, the next lowest level, with Level 5 representing the highest possible score. According to the Literacy Volunteers of America, "Literacy experts believe that adults with skills at Levels 1 and 2 lack a sufficient foundation of basic skills to function successfully in our society." The statistics confirm that conclusion. Forty-three percent of adults at Level 1 were living in poverty; the likelihood of being on welfare goes up as literacy levels go down; and seven in ten prisoners performed in the lowest two literacy levels. http://www.literacyvolunteers.org/about/faqs/facts.html (last visited Sept. 18, 2004); http://www.nifl.gov/reders/!intro.htm (last visited Sept. 18, 2004).

25. Adler & Van Doren, *How to Read a Book*, 5-7, 16-20, 25-26 (emphasis in original).

26. Ibid., 32-33, 35; Bradfield, *Books and Reading*, 23. Benjamin Franklin is not the only founding father who liked to jot things down as he read. A recent Boston Public Library exhibition of some 3,700 volumes owned by John Adams, the second U.S. president, shows that Adams often made marginal notes in the things he read, beginning as early as age 20 in a 1755 pamphlet called "A Lecture on Earthquakes." Responding to the writing of John Winthrop, the pamphlet's author, Adams expressed the view that earthquakes were not made worse by lightning rods. When Adams read Mary Wollstonecraft's 1794 book, *Historical and Moral View of the Origin and Progress of the French Revolution*, Adams used marginalia to critique Wollstonecraft's view that a simpler, less fractionalized political system would better avoid "follies." Adams believed strongly in the concept of checks and balances, and he wrote at length in the margins to express that view. "A woman," Adams wrote, "would be more simple if she had but one eye or one breast; yet nature chose she should have two as more

convenient as well as ornamental." "A man," Adams continued, "would be more simple with but one ear, one arm, one leg." "Shall a legislature have but one chamber
then, merely because it is more simple?" Adams queried. "The word 'simplicity,'"
Adams emphasized, has "produced more horrors than monarchy did in a century." *See*
Richard Brookhiser, "John Adams Talks to His Books," *N. Y. Times Book Review* (Sept.
3, 2006): 23.

27. Adler & Van Doren, *How to Read a Book*, 5 (emphasis in original).

28. Corballis, *From Hand to Mouth*, 13; Zane, *Remarkable Reads*, 53.

29. *Great Quotes from Great Teachers* (Glendale Heights, Ill.: Great Quotations Pub.
Co., 2003), 35; National Endowment for the Arts, "Reading at Risk," xii, 1, 3, 5-6.

CHAPTER NINE The Revision Process

1. Brian Lamb, *Booknotes: America's Finest Authors on Reading, Writing, and the Power
of Ideas* (New York: Times Books, 1997), 18; Robert I. Fitzhenry, ed., *The Harper Book
of Quotations* (New York: HarperCollins, 1993), 500; Donald M. Murray, *The Craft of
Revision* (Fort Worth, Tex.: Harcourt Brace & Co., 3rd ed. 1998), 229; William Zinsser,
On Writing Well: The Classic Guide to Writing Nonfiction (New York: HarperCollins,
2001), 136-37.

2. Ann Charters, ed., *The Story and Its Writer: An Introduction to Short Fiction*
(Boston: Bedford Books of St. Martin's Press, 4th ed. 1995), 1528-29.

3. Henry Beston, *The Outermost House: A Year of Life on the Great Beach of Cape Cod*
(New York: Henry Holt & Co., 1992), xix; Peter Elbow, *Writing with Power: Techniques
for Mastering the Writing Process* (Oxford: Oxford University Press, 1998), 134.

4. http://en.thinkexist.com/keyword/revision/ (last visited Oct. 3, 2004).

5. Elbow, *Writing with Power*, 135.

6. Sven Birkerts, *The Gutenberg Elegies: The Fate of Reading in an Electronic Age* (New
York: Ballantine Books, 1994), 70-71; George Grant & Karen Grant, *Shelf Life: How
Books Have Changed the Destinies and Desires of Men and Nations* (Nashville, Tenn.:
Cumberland House, 1999), 60; Nancy M. Malone, *Walking a Literary Labyrinth: A
Spirituality of Reading* (New York: Riverhead Books, 2003), 17-19; William Safire &
Leonard Safir, eds., *Words of Wisdom: More Good Advice* (New York: Simon & Schuster,
1989), 401; Stuart Spencer, *The Playwright's Guidebook: An Insightful Primer on the Art
of Dramatic Writing* (New York: Faber & Faber, 2002), 225.

7. *Bartlett's Familiar Quotations: A Collection of Passages, Phrases, and Proverbs Traced to
Their Sources in Ancient and Modern Literature* (Boston: Little, Brown & Co., 16th ed.
1992), 195, 270; William Strunk Jr. & E. B. White, *The Elements of Style* (New York:
MacMillan Pub. Co., 3rd ed. 1979), xi, 23.

8. Bill Bryson, *The Mother Tongue: English & How It Got that Way* (New York:

William Morrow & Co., 1990), 69; Robert W. Harris, *When Good People Write Bad Sentences: 12 Steps to Better Writing Habits* (New York: St. Martin's Press, 2004), 54; Murray, *The Craft of Revision*, 66; Gwendolyn Bounds, "Get Me Rewrite! Personal Ads Are Big; Big on Clichés, Too," *Wall Street Journal* (Aug. 1, 2004): A7. The notion of people hiring professional copyeditors to write or spruce up personal ads struck me as particularly funny.

9. Harris, *When Good People Write Bad Sentences*, 71-72, 80-81; Jan Venolia, *Write Right! A Desktop Digest of Punctuation, Grammar, and Style* (Berkeley, Cal.: Ten Speed Press, 4th ed. 2001), 159; Stephen Wilbers, *Keys to Great Writing* (Cincinnati: Writer's Digest Books, 2000), 16-18.

10. Steven Johnson, *Mind Wide Open: Your Brain and the Neuroscience of Everyday Life* (New York: Scribner, 2004), 163-64; V. S. Ramachandran, *A Brief Tour of Human Consciousness: From Impostor Poodles to Purple Numbers* (New York: Pi Press, 2004), 13, 85.

11. Johnson, *Mind Wide Open*, 169-71, 173-79, 181, 210.

12. Not every writing teacher is enamored of the pedagogy frequently used in writing courses and workshops in which students critique other students' work. *See* Carol Bly, *Beyond the Writers' Workshop: New Ways to Write Creative Nonfiction* (New York: Anchor Books, 2001), 37. Bly argues with some force that allowing writing to be "workshopped" before the writer has had a chance to wrestle fully—and alone— with the "original inspiration" may be counterproductive. Ibid., 39-40. As Bly writes: "The skills of deepening oneself (in solitude), never mind showing others how to deepen themselves, are very different from the skills of orchestrating group critiquing." Ibid., 37. Although I believe that getting comments from others can be very helpful to a writer, I also believe that the writer should try to fully develop ideas— and take a piece of writing as far as he or she can—before eliciting comments from others. It may also be damaging to the self-esteem of children to allow writing to be critiqued by classmates who may be insensitive to a young writer's feelings.

13. Diane Osen, ed., *The Book that Changed My Life: Interviews with National Book Award Winners and Finalists* (New York: Modern Library, 2002), 152; *The Fairview Guide to Positive Quotations* (Minneapolis: Fairview Press, 1996), 195; *The Writing Life: A Collection of Essays and Interviews* (New York: Random House, 1995), 194.

14. *The Writing Life: Writers on How They Think and Work* (New York: Public Affairs, 2003), 185; Murray, *The Craft of Revision*, 140.

15. Joyce Carol Oates, *The Faith of a Writer: Life, Craft, Art* (New York: HarperCollins, 2003), 36.

16. John D. Bessler, *Death in the Dark: Midnight Executions in America* (Boston: Northeastern University Press, 1997); John D. Bessler, *Kiss of Death: America's Love Affair with the Death Penalty* (Boston: Northeastern University Press, 2003); John D.

Bessler, *Legacy of Violence: Lynch Mobs and Executions in Minnesota* (Minneapolis: University of Minnesota Press, 2003).

17. Murray, *The Craft of Revision*, 16, 76.

18. *Bartlett's Familiar Quotations*, 741; Murray, *The Craft of Revision*, 47.

19. Lewis D. Eigen & Jonathan P. Siegel, *Dictionary of Political Quotations* (London: Robert Hall, 1993), 472; Laura Ward, ed., *Foolish Words: The Most Stupid Words Ever Spoken* (London: PRC Publishing, 2003), 89, 108; http://www.siena.edu/sri/results/2002/02AugPresidentsSurvey.htm (last visited Oct. 3, 2004). Obviously, many factors go into assessing the performance of U.S. presidents. The selected quotes of Kennedy, Coolidge, and Hoover are just examples that I pulled to make a point.

20. Osen, *The Book that Changed My Life*, 32-33, 35-36.

21. Zinsser, *On Writing Well*, 290-91.

22. Janet Burroway, *Writing Fiction: A Guide to Narrative Craft* (New York: HarperCollins, 4th ed., 1996), 64-65; Wilbers, *Keys to Great Writing*, 55; Zinsser, *On Writing Well*, 68.

23. Wilbers, *Keys to Great Writing*, 56-57; http://web.princeton.edu/sites/writing/writing_center/Handouts/passivevoice.pdf (last visited Oct. 4, 2004).

24. Anne Lamott, *Bird by Bird: Some Instructions on Writing and Life* (New York: Anchor Books, 1995), 93; Leonard Roy Frank, ed., *Quotationary* (New York: Random House, 2001), 606; Cathleen Rountree, *The Writer's Mentor: A Guide to Putting Passion on Paper* (Berkeley, Cal.: Conari Press, 2002), 4; http://education.qld.gov.au/publication/style/writing/publication.html (last visited July 2, 2004).

25. Bill Bryson, *Bryson's Dictionary of Troublesome Words: A Writer's Guide to Getting It Right* (New York: Broadway Books, 2002), 228; *compare* "Q&A with John Bessler: A lawyer and author of a history of the death penalty in Minnesota argues that a problem of violence can be solved by violent means," *St. Paul Pioneer Press* (Mar. 7, 2004): 5C (early edition of Sunday paper) *with* "Q&A with John Bessler: A lawyer and author of a history of the death penalty in Minnesota argues that a problem of violence cannot be solved by violent means," *St. Paul Pioneer Press* (Mar. 7, 2004): 5C (Sunday morning edition).

CHAPTER TEN Storytelling

1. Charles Baxter, *Burning Down the House: Essays on Fiction* (St. Paul, Minn.: Graywolf Press, 1997), xii.

2. Cathleen Rountree, *The Writer's Mentor: A Guide to Putting Passion on Paper* (Berkeley, Cal.: Conari Press, 2002), 3; *The Writing Life: A Collection of Essays and Interviews* (New York: Random House, 1995), 53.

3. Ann Charters, ed., *The Story and Its Writer: An Introduction to Short Fiction*

(Boston: Bedford Books of St. Martin's Press, 4th ed., 1995), 243, 270, 733, 1048.

4. "A String of Successful Failures: An Interview with Ann Bancroft," *Speakeasy* (Mar./Apr. 2004): 33. A good story can be found almost anywhere you look, including in the text (or history) of a note. Footnote four in *United States v. Carolene Products Co.*, for example, is a famous footnote in which Justice Harlan Fiske Stone announced that the U.S. Supreme Court would apply only a minimum level of scrutiny when assessing the constitutionality of economic legislation but would require more careful, stringent review of laws affecting individual rights and liberties. *See* United States v. Carolene Prods. Co., 304 U.S. 144, 152 n.4 (1938). That footnote contributed to the development of the "strict scrutiny" test for legislation affecting minorities. Of course, for every famous note, there are scores of not-so-famous, overlooked ones. To read what one commentator calls "a sarcastic and pun-filled look at the excessive use of footnotes" in legal writing, look up Aside, "Don't Cry Over Filled Milk: The Neglected Footnote Three to *Carolene Products*," 136 *University of Pennsylvania Law Review* 1553 (1988) (the commentator, noting that the *Carolene Products* case dealt with milk products, writes that this law review article examines "dairy jurisprudence as a part of bovine law"). *See* Thomas E. Baker, "A Compendium of Clever and Amusing Law Review Writings: An Idiosyncratic Bibliography of Miscellany with in Kind Annotations Intended as a Humorous Diversion for the Gentle Reader," 51 *Drake Law Review* 105, 112 (2002).

5. *Bartlett's Familiar Quotations: A Collection of Passages, Phrases, and Proverbs Traced to Their Sources in Ancient and Modern Literature* (Boston: Little, Brown & Co., 16th ed. 1992), 646.

6. Carol L. Birch & Melissa A. Heckler, *Who Says? Essays on Pivotal Issues in Contemporary Storytelling* (Little Rock, Ark.: August House Publishers, Inc., 1996), 10–11; Rountree, *The Writer's Mentor*, 104; Stuart Spencer, *The Playwright's Guide: An Insightful Primer on the Art of Dramatic Writing* (New York: Faber & Faber, 2002), 58–59.

7. Drew Hansen, *The Dream: Martin Luther King, Jr. and the Speech that Inspired a Nation* (New York: HarperCollins, 2003), 150.

8. Charters, *The Story and Its Writer*, 1381, 1383–84.

9. Margaret Atwood, *Negotiating with the Dead: A Writer on Writing* (New York: Anchor Books, 2002), 48–50, 125.

10. Russell Freedman, "Bringing Them Back Alive: Writing History and Biography for Young Audiences," *Riverbank Review* (Fall 2000): 19–20, 22.

11. Will Blythe, ed., *On Being a Writer* (Cincinnati: Writer's Digest Books, 1989), 25.

12. Spencer, *The Playwright's Guide*, 3–7, 10.

13. Charters, *The Story and Its Writer*, 1385, 1387; Andrew Greeley, "They Leap from Your Brain Then Take Over Your Heart," in *Writers on Writing: More Collected*

*Essays from The New York Times,*Vol. II (New York: Times Books, 2003), 86.

14. Natalie Goldberg, *Writing Down the Bones: Freeing the Writer Within* (Boston: Shambhala, 1986), 68.

15. Les Edgerton, *Finding Your Voice: How to Put Personality in Your Writing* (Cincinnati: Writer's Digest Books, 2003), 6-7, 35, 64, 66, 102.

16. Kingsley Amis, *The King's English: A Guide to Modern Usage* (New York: St. Martin's Griffin, 1997), 11; Ben Yagoda, *The Sound on the Page: Style and Voice in Writing* (New York: HarperCollins, 2004), 38.

17. Patricia Hampl, *I Could Tell You Stories: Sojourns in the Land of Memory* (New York: W.W. Norton & Co., 1999), 34; Spencer, *The Playwright's Guide*, 134.

18. Anne Lamott, *Bird by Bird: Some Instructions on Writing and Life* (New York: Anchor Books, 1995), 237.

CHAPTER ELEVEN Effective Communication

1. Leslie Ann Gibson, comp., *The Women's Book of Positive Quotations* (Minneapolis: Fairview Press, 2002), 204.

2. Ann Charters, ed., *The Story and Its Writer: An Introduction to Short Fiction* (Boston: Bedford Books of St. Martin's Press, 4th ed. 1995), 1491; Robert I. Fitzhenry, ed., *The Harper Book of Quotations* (New York: HarperCollins, 1993), 500; Margaret Miner & Hugh Rawson, eds., *The New International Dictionary of Quotations* (New York: Signet, 3rd ed. 2000), 39, 41, 475.

3. Betty Edwards, *Drawing on the Artist Within: An Inspirational and Practical Guide to Increasing Your Creative Powers* (New York: Simon & Schuster, 1987), 102-3; Cathleen Rountree, *The Writer's Mentor: A Guide to Putting Passion on Paper* (Berkeley, Cal.: Conari Press, 2002), 185.

4. Christina Davis & Christopher Edgar, eds., *Illuminations: Great Writers on Writing* (New York: T&W Books, 2003), 85; Leonard Roy Frank, ed., *Quotationary* (New York: Random House, 2001), 833.

5. Donald M. Murray, *The Craft of Revision* (Fort Worth, Tex.: Harcourt Brace & Co., 3rd ed. 1998), 87-88, 92. The idea of reading a whole book on the craft of revision may strike you as incredibly dull, but you'd be wise to take a look at what Donald Murray has to say on the subject. Remember, one of the keys to effective writing is revision.

6. *Bartlett's Familiar Quotations: A Collection of Passages, Phrases, and Proverbs Traced to Their Sources in Ancient and Modern Literature* (Boston: Little, Brown & Co., 16th ed. 1992), 622; Ralph Keyes, *The Courage to Write: How Writers Transcend Fear* (New York: Henry Holt & Co., 1995), 108; Richard Lederer, *The Miracle of Language* (New York: Pocket Books, 1991), 33-34.

7. Jan Venolia, *Write Right! A Desktop Digest of Punctuation, Grammar, and Style* (Berkeley, Cal.: Ten Speed Press, 4th ed., 2001), 39; Stephen Wilbers, *Keys to Great Writing* (Cincinnati: Writer's Digest Books, 2000), viii.

8. Les Edgerton, *Finding Your Voice: How to Put Personality in Your Writing* (Cincinnati: Writer's Digest Books, 2003), 102-3, 108-9 (emphasis in original).

9. Pat Schneider, *Writing Alone and with Others* (Oxford: Oxford University Press, 2003), 31, 96, 190.

10. Edgerton, *Finding Your Voice*, 102; Richard Rhodes, *How to Write: Advice and Reflections* (New York: HarperCollins, 1995), 46, 192.

11. Edgerton, *Finding Your Voice*, 112, 114; Ian Jackman, ed., *The Writer's Mentor: Secrets of Success from the World's Great Writers* (New York: Random House Reference, 2004), 111.

12. Bonni Goldberg, *Room to Write: Daily Invitations to a Writer's Life* (New York: Jeremy P. Tarcher/Putnam, 1996), 17, 120; Françoise Sagan, *Bonjour Tristesse* (London: Penguin Books, 1958).

13. Lynne Truss, *Eats, Shoots & Leaves: The Zero Tolerance Approach to Punctuation* (New York: Gotham Books, 2003), 20, 71-72, 77, 111; Wilbers, *Keys to Great Writing*, 72-76.

14. Edgerton, *Finding Your Voice*, 130, 134; Jackman, *The Writer's Mentor*, 150.

15. William Strunk Jr. & E. B. White, *The Elements of Style* (New York: MacMillan Pub. Co., 3rd ed. 1979), xi, xiv, 23; Rountree, *The Writer's Mentor*, 178; http://www.kcstar.com/hemingway/ehstarstyle.htm (last visited Apr. 3, 2004).

16. Jackman, *The Writer's Mentor*, 151; Lederer, *The Miracle of Language*, 128; Miner & Rawson, *The New International Dictionary of Quotations*, 41; http://pages.intnet.mu/linx/quote/ (last visited Oct. 7, 2004); http://www.quotegarden.com/bk-km.html (last visited Oct. 7, 2004).

17. Donald Hall & Sven Birkerts, *Writing Well* (New York: Longman, 9th ed. 1998), 89; William Zinsser, *On Writing Well: The Classic Guide to Writing Nonfiction* (New York: HarperCollins, 2001), 69-70. Helpful books on the craft of writing (such as the two cited here) are published every year. The "Writing" or "Reference" section of your local bookstore is an excellent place to find new titles as they come out.

18. *The American Heritage Dictionary of the English Language* (Boston: Houghton Mifflin Co., 3rd ed., 1992), 2008; Diane Ravitch, *The Language Police: How Pressure Groups Restrict What Students Learn* (New York: Vintage Books, 2004), 175.

19. George Orwell, *A Collection of Essays* (New York: Doubleday Anchor Books, 1954), 162-65, 167, 174.

20. Ibid., 169-70.

21. Ibid., 170; Bill Bryson, *The Mother Tongue: English & How It Got that Way* (New

York: William Morrow & Co., 1990), 19; Lederer, *The Miracle of Language*, 156; Robert McCrum, William Cran & Robert MacNeil, *The Story of English* (New York: Penguin Books, 1992), 17.

22. Orwell, *A Collection of Essays*, 163, 171-73.

23. Ibid., 175-76.

24. Ibid., 176.

25. Patricia T. O'Conner, *Woe Is I: The Grammarphobe's Guide to Better English in Plain English* (New York: Riverhead Books, 1996), 187; Steven Pinker, *The Language Instinct: How the Mind Creates Language* (New York: HarperCollins, 1994), 46; Suzy Platt, ed., *Respectfully Quoted: A Dictionary of Quotations Requested from the Congressional Research Service* (Washington, D.C.: Library of Congress, 1989), 302.

26. Charters, *The Story and Its Writer*, 1524.

27. Ben Yagoda, *The Sound on the Page: Style and Voice in Writing* (New York: HarperCollins, 2004), 24.

28. Catherine Dee, ed., *The Girls' Book of Wisdom* (New York: Little Brown & Co., 1999), 125; John B. Kachuba, *How to Write Funny* (Cincinnati: Writer's Digest Books, 2001), 26, 36-37, 154; http://findquotations.com/quote/by/Dave_Barry (last visited May 17, 2006); http://en.wikipedia.org/wiki/Dave_Barry (last visited May 17, 2006).

29. Zinsser, *On Writing Well*, 288; http://www.bartleby.com/63/84/684.html (last visited Oct. 7, 2004).

30. Alice W. Flaherty, *The Midnight Disease: The Drive to Write, Writer's Block, and the Creative Brain* (Boston: Houghton Mifflin Co., 2004), 224, 228-29; Natalie Goldberg, *Writing Down the Bones: Freeing the Writer Within* (Boston: Shambhala, 1986), 54 (emphasis in original); Anne Lamott, *Bird by Bird: Some Instructions on Writing and Life* (New York: Anchor Books, 1995), 77; Susan Goldsmith Wooldridge, *Poemcrazy: Freeing Your Life with Words* (New York: Three Rivers Press, 1996), 32.

31. Frederick Crews, *The Random House Handbook* (New York: Random House, 2nd ed. 1977), 117-18, 437-38, 456.

32. Peter Elbow, *Writing with Power: Techniques for Mastering the Writing Process* (Oxford: Oxford University Press, 1998), 167-68; National Commission on Writing (The College Board), "The Neglected 'R': The Need for a Writing Revolution" (Apr. 2003): 11, 14.

33. William Safire & Leonard Safir, eds., *Words of Wisdom: More Good Advice* (New York: Simon & Schuster, 1989), 213. Odd fact to file away for your next game of *Trivial Pursuit*: William Safire and Leonard Safir are brothers. William Safire added the "e" to the family name because that's the way it's pronounced. Another odd fact: I have five brothers and no sisters. My parents always wanted a girl, but when my mom got pregnant for the last time, she ended up having *identical twin boys*. And a final

morsel (though, in this case, it's certainly not trivial): my brother Andrew—one of the twins—oversaw the design of this handsome book. I will be forever indebted to him for his efforts.

34. O'Conner, *Woe Is I*, 188.

35. Lederer, *The Miracle of Language*, 220; Pinker, *The Language Instinct*, 76-77.

36. Goldberg, *Room to Write*, 82; O'Conner, *Woe Is I*, 168, 170, 174; Zinsser, *On Writing Well*, 237.

37. John D. Bessler, *Kiss of Death: America's Love Affair with the Death Penalty* (Boston: Northeastern University Press, 2003), 90-98; Charles Johnson & Bob Adelman, *King: The Photobiography of Martin Luther King, Jr.* (New York: Viking Studio, 2000), 110; Ronald C. White, Jr., *Lincoln's Greatest Speech: The Second Inaugural* (New York: Simon & Schuster, 2002), 19, 40-42, 48, 162, 164, 184, 199.

38. *Bartlett's Familiar Quotations*, 771; Eudora Welty, *On Writing* (New York: Modern Library, 2002), 70.

CHAPTER TWELVE Parting Advice

1. Donald Hall, *Life Work* (Boston: Beacon Press, 2003), 58. *Life Work* is a well-written book about the importance of work to people's lives, and to writer Donald Hall's life in particular. I really enjoyed this book, so I'm using this note to plug it. It's a slender volume that can be read in a single sitting, so I ask you this: why not read it for yourself?

2. Les Edgerton, *Finding Your Voice: How to Put Personality in Your Writing* (Cincinnati: Writer's Digest Books, 2003), 224.

3. Susan Goldsmith Wooldridge, *Poemcrazy: Freeing Your Life with Words* (New York: Three Rivers Press, 1996), 148; Richard Lederer, *The Miracle of Language* (New York: Pocket Books, 1991), 241.

4. Pat Schneider, *Writing Alone and with Others* (Oxford: Oxford University Press, 2003), 63.

5. David Bayles & Ted Orland, *Art & Fear: Observations on the Perils (and Rewards) of Artmaking* (Santa Cruz, Cal.: Image Continuum Press, 2002), 6.

6. Ian Jackman, ed., *The Writer's Mentor: Secrets of Success from the World's Great Writers* (New York: Random House Reference, 2004), 9.

7. Kurt Vonnegut, Jr., "Despite Tough Guys, Life Is Not the Only School for Real Novelists," in *Writers on Writing: Collected Essays from The New York Times* (New York: Times Books, 2001), 244; http://www.writingcommission.org/pr/pr_4_25_2003 .html (last visited Oct. 7, 2004).

8. Robert I. Fitzhenry, ed., *The Harper Book of Quotations* (New York: HarperCollins, 1993), 159; Bonni Goldberg, *Room to Write: Daily Invitations to a*

Writer's Life (New York: Jeremy P. Tarcher/Putnam, 1996), 91; Mark Robert Waldman, ed., *The Spirit of Writing: Classic and Contemporary Essays Celebrating the Writing Life* (New York: Jeremy P. Tarcher/Putnam, 2001), 2; *Collected Works of Abraham Lincoln*, Vol. 3 (Second Lecture on Discoveries and Inventions, Feb. 11, 1859).

9. Erin Barrett & Jack Mingo, *It Takes a Certain Type To Be a Writer: Facts from the World of Writing and Publishing* (York Beach, Maine: Conari Press, 2003), 50; Cathleen Rountree, *The Writer's Mentor: A Guide to Putting Passion on Paper* (Berkeley, Cal.: Conari Press, 2002), 62; Stuart Spencer, *The Playwright's Guidebook: An Insightful Primer on the Art of Dramatic Writing* (New York: Faber & Faber, 2002), 306.

10. Henriette Anne Klauser, *With Pen in Hand: The Healing Power of Writing* (Cambridge, Mass.: Perseus Publishing, 2003), x-xi, 3, 86.

11. Linda Trichter Metcalf & Tobin Simon, *Writing the Mind Alive: The Proprioceptive Method for Finding Your Authentic Voice* (New York: Balantine Books, 2002), 93-94; Rountree, *The Writer's Mentor*, 7; James Pennebaker, "Writing About Emotional Experience Is a Therapeutic Process," *Psychological Science* 8 (1977): 162-66; Joshua Smyth, et al., "Effects of Writing About Stressful Experiences on Symptom Reduction in Patients with Asthma or Rheumatoid Arthritis: A Randomized Trial," *JAMA* 281 (Apr. 14, 1999): 1304; Walter Kirn, "The Rush of What Is Said," *N.Y. Times Book Review* (Oct. 10, 2004): 6 (reviewing Douglas Brinkley, ed., *Windblown World: The Journals of Jack Kerouac, 1947-1954* (New York: Viking Books, 2004)).

12. Rountree, *The Writer's Mentor*, 7; Waldman, *The Spirit of Writing*, 11, 13.

13. Bert Hölldobler & Edward O. Wilson, *The Ants* (Cambridge, Mass.: Belknap Press of Harvard University Press, 1990); Michael Olmert, *The Smithsonian Book of Books* (Washington, D.C.: Smithsonian Books, 1992), 10, 31, 43, 61, 65; Steven R. Quartz & Terrence J. Sejnowski, *Liars, Lovers, and Heroes: What the New Brain Science Reveals About How We Become Who We Are* (New York: HarperCollins, 2002), 64; Andrew Robinson, *The Story of Writing: Alphabets, Hieroglyphs and Pictograms* (New York: Thames & Hudson, Inc., 1995), 11-12, 16, 50, 53, 71.

14. George Holmes, ed., *The Oxford History of Medieval Europe* (Oxford: Oxford University Press, 1988), v, 319; Kevin Kelly, "Scan This Book!", *N.Y. Times Magazine* (May 14, 2006): 44; "Remains of Oldest University Found," *Star Tribune* (Minneapolis) (May 27, 2004): A11. One of the most famous footnotes in the history of medicine began: "Das Serum gesunder Menschen wirkt nicht nur auf tierische Blutkörperchen agglutinierend, sonders öfters auch auf menschliche von anderen Individuen stammende." This note, authored in 1900 by Karl Landsteiner, led to discovery of A, B, O and AB blood groups and, later, successful blood transfusions in humans. *See* http://www.whonamedit.com/synd.cfm/3362.html (last visited Sept. 15, 2006).

15. Barrett & Mingo, *It Takes a Certain Type To Be a Writer*, 4; John D. Bessler, *Legacy of Violence: Lynch Mobs and Executions in Minnesota* (Minneapolis: University of Minnesota Press, 2003), 220; Will Durant, *The Age of Faith* (New York: Simon & Schuster, 1950); Henry J. Steiner & Philip Alston, *International Human Rights in Context: Law, Politics, Morals* (Oxford: Oxford University Press, 1996), v, 99.

16. *The Essential Writings of Ralph Waldo Emerson* (New York: Modern Library, 2000), 268. Ralph Waldo Emerson and fellow writer (and pencil-maker) Henry David Thoreau, of Walden Pond fame, were neighbors in Concord, Massachusetts—a locale that was also home to writer Louisa May Alcott. Ibid., v-vi; Milton Meltzer & Walter Harding, *A Thoreau Profile* (Lincoln, Mass.: Thoreau Society, 1998), 51-57, 136-39, 299. The tranquil Sleepy Hollow Cemetery in Concord—a place I have visited on more than one occasion—is the burial place of Emerson, Thoreau and Alcott, as well as novelist Nathaniel Hawthorne and Daniel Chester French, the sculptor whose works include the Lincoln Memorial statue in Washington, D.C. The Sleepy Hollow Cemetery in Concord is not to be confused with the cemetery of the same name in Sleepy Hollow, New York, where businessman and philanthropist Andrew Carnegie and writer Washington Irving—the author of "The Legend of Sleepy Hollow"—are buried.

17. *The Fairview Guide to Positive Quotations* (Minneapolis: Fairview Press, 1996), 518; Fitzhenry, *The Harper Book of Quotations*, 13; Suzy Platt, ed., *Respectfully Quoted: A Dictionary of Quotations Requested from the Congressional Research Service* (Washington, D.C.: Library of Congress, 1989), 115; Margaret Miner & Hugh Rawson, eds., *The New International Dictionary of Quotations* (New York: Signet, 3rd ed. 2000), 296.

18. Catherine Dee, ed., *The Girls' Book of Wisdom* (New York: Little Brown & Co., 1999), 191; Leonard Roy Frank, ed., *Quotationary* (New York: Random House, 2001), 721.

19. Herman Melville, "Bartleby, the Scrivener," reprinted in Ann Charters, ed., *The Story and Its Writer: An Introduction to Short Fiction* (Boston: Bedford Books of St. Martin's Press, 4th ed., 1995), 908-34. "Bartleby, the Scrivener" is one of my favorite short stories. I wanted to find a way to work Melville's story into my text; hopefully, you'll find it fits and doesn't seem too out of place.

20. Ibid. It was civil rights leader W. E. B. Du Bois's footnotes that first inspired legendary singer Harry Belafonte—then a young West Indian sailor—to read critically. See Anthony Grafton, *The Footnote: A Curious History* (Cambridge, Mass.: Harvard University Press, 1997), 234-35. As Belafonte tells the story: "I discovered that at the end of some sentences there was a number, and if you looked at the foot of the page the reference was to what it was all about—what source Du Bois gleaned his information from." Ibid. Belafonte recalled how the citations at first baffled him: "So

when I was on leave, going into Chicago, I went to a library with a long list of books. The librarian said, 'That's too many young man. You're going to have to cut it down.' I said, 'I can make it very easy. Just give me everything you got by Ibid.' She said, 'There's no such writer.' I called her a racist. I said, 'Are you trying to keep me in darkness?' And I walked out of there angry." Ibid., 235 n.17. Belafonte went on to release the first album in history to sell over one million copies, and to win an Emmy, a Grammy Award for lifetime achievement, the Martin Luther King Non-Violent Peace Prize, and the first Nelson Mandela Courage Award. He was also named a UNICEF goodwill ambassador in 1987.

21. Platt, *Respectfully Quoted*, 166; *Writers on Writing: Collected Essays from The New York Times* (New York: Times Books, 2001), 104-9.

22. Miner & Rawson, *The New International Dictionary of Quotations*, 446.

23. F. Scott Fitzgerald, "The Crack-Up," *Esquire* (Feb. 1936) (cited in Frank, *Quotationary*, 406). Between 1597 and 1607, Richard White of Basingstoke published an eleven-volume treatise on the history of England. Book I of that history runs from pages 7 to 26, while the book's 38 endnotes occupy pages 27 to 124, filling up almost five times the amount of space within the text. See Grafton, *The Footnote*, 128-29.

24. M. D. Herter Norton, trans., Rainer Maria Rilke, *Letters to a Young Poet* (New York: W.W. Norton & Co., 1993), 18-19. A final interesting tidbit: the poet Rainer Maria Rilke served as the sculptor Auguste Rodin's personal secretary. The two met in 1902 when Rilke arrived at Rodin's Paris studio, and Rilke wrote essays about Rodin's art and work. "Rodin," Rilke wrote, "followed the paths of this life year after year, a humble pilgrim who never stopped thinking of himself as a beginner." See Rainer Maria Rilke, *Auguste Rodin* (Daniel Slager, trans.) (New York: Archipelago Books, 2004), 1, 22, 37. For Rilke, Rodin's genius lay in his enduring passion for his work and his attention to detail, his observational powers, his craft. "Removed from the pretentious and capricious rhetoric," Rilke wrote, "art returns to its humble, dignified place in everyday life, to craft." Ibid., 70, 73. By using craft and through remarkable patience, Rodin created artful and memorable sculptures, including the famous bronze known as *The Thinker* which portrays a man—as Rilke describes him—"thinking with his whole body." Ibid., 71, 86. That is exactly what good writing requires: keen observation, hard work, patience, thinking and craft. With writing, all things are possible, so start where you are (and with whatever blank screen or pieces of paper you have) and *write*, letting your imagination, creativity and talent run wild. Use your head and your hands, as Rodin did, to mold, shape and craft; never stop expanding your mind, your worldview, and your skills; and scrawl, type and revise to your heart's content and for the rest of your life. You will learn and grow as a person. And you will make a difference!

In the life of the human spirit, words are action, much more so than many of us realize who live in countries where freedom of expression is taken for granted. –Jimmy Carter • Great writers are great readers. Writers spend endless hours studying the books of predecessors and contemporaries to learn what worked and what didn't. –Bruce Fellman • Good writers are good not only because of their facility with language but also because of their approach. Good writers position themselves in a way that increases their odds of success. –Stephen Wilbers • A good reader is rarer than a good writer. –Jorge Luis Borges • We read to train the mind, to fill the mind, to rest the mind, to recreate the mind, or to escape the mind. –Holbrook Jackson • The only impeccable writers are those that never wrote. –William Hazlitt • Great writers are not those who tell us we shouldn't play with fire, but those who make our fingers burn. –Stephen Vizinczey • You can never correct your work well until after you have forgotten it. –Voltaire • If becoming a better writer were the only benefit of writing practice, it would be enough. –Judy Reeves • Knowledge is acquired when we succeed in fitting a new experience into the system of concepts based upon our old experiences. –Aldous Huxley • If language is intimately related to being human, then when we study language we are, to a remarkable degree, studying human nature. –Charlton Laird • Talent is like a faucet; while it is open, one must write. –Jean Anouilh • To produce a mighty work, you must choose a mighty theme. –Herman Melville • Anyone who shrinks from ideas ends by having nothing but sensations. –Johann Wolfgang von Goethe • Writers do not merely reflect and interpret life, they inform and shape life. –E. B. White • The best thing about writing is not the actual labor of putting word against word, brick upon brick, but the preliminaries, the spade work, which is done in silence, under any circumstances, in dream as well as in the waking state. In short, the period of gestation. –Henry Miller • We are thinking beings, and we cannot exclude the intellect from participating in any of our functions. –William James • Thought is the strongest thing we have. –Albert Schweitzer • The human brain has a mind of its own. –Joseph Heller • Imagery, delivery, vocabulary spring from the body and the past of the writer and gradually become the very reflexes of his art. Thus under the name of style a self-sufficient language is evolved which has its roots only in the depths of the author's personal and secret mythology. –Roland Barthes • I imitated every style in the hope of finding the clue to the gnawing secret of how to write. –Henry Miller • I write a little each day without hope and without despair. –Isak Dinesen

BIBLIOGRAPHY

Imitation, if it is not forgery, is a fine thing. It stems from a generous impulse, and a realistic sense of what can and cannot be done. –James Fenton • People say that life is the thing, but I prefer reading. –Logan Pearsall Smith • Writing is about growing. –Tayari Jones • Reading is the avenue to writing, and after a while, the sheer bulk of influences begins to eliminate the question of influence. –Siri Hustvedt • We don't write what we know. We write what we wonder about. –Richard Peck • Moving around is good for creativity: the next line of dialogue that you desperately need may well be waiting in the back of the refrigerator or half a mile along your favorite walk. –Will Shetterly • No two people read the same book. –Edmund Wilson • Method of investigation: as soon as we have thought something, try to see in what way the contrary is true. –Simone Weil • Truth never penetrates an unwilling mind. –Jorge Luis Borges • What does the writer want out of life? What does he want to become? These are the things he should write about. The question is who do I wish to become? –Colin Wilson • Most writing problems require effort rather than inspiration (a backbone rather than a wishbone). –Barbara Tomlinson • Sometimes what happens is that you poke your pick into a piece of respectable earth and silver shows up in an iron-ore vein and God knows where you're heading. You follow it and you have to revise everything in light of the silver. –John Gardner • Writing and mining are exhausting, backbreaking work with a recalcitrant substance; the substance must be transformed in order to yield valuable, even invaluable results. –Barbara Tomlinson • Write the truest sentence that you know. –Ernest Hemingway • Writing is not unlike the schoolroom period called "show and tell." The writer should not only tell a story; he should try to make the reader *see* what he is writing about. –William Zinsser • The mastery of any art is the work of a lifetime. –Ezra Pound • In quickness is truth. The faster you blurt, the more swiftly you write, the more honest you are. –Ray Bradbury • I learned to write by listening to people talk. I still feel that the best of my writing comes from having heard rather than having read. –Gayl Jones • If I had to give young writers advice, I would say don't listen to writers talking about writing or themselves. –Lillian Hellman • Writing is like a contact sport, like football. Why do kids play football? They can get hurt on any play, can't they? Yet they can't wait until Saturday comes around. Writing is like that. You can get hurt, but you enjoy it. –Irwin Shaw • The conscious mind is going to suggest the obvious, the cliché, because these things offer the security of having succeeded in the past. Only the mind that has been taken off itself and put on a task is allowed true creativity. –David Mamet • There are two ways of spreading light: to be the candle or the mirror that reflects it. –Edith Wharton • No plagiarist can excuse the wrong by showing how much of his work he did not pirate. –Learned Hand • What's writing? A way of escape, like traveling to a war, or to see the Mau Mau. Escaping what? Boredom. Death. –Graham Greene • The title to a work of writing is like a house's front porch. It should invite you to come on in. –Angela Giles Klocke • Anxious, inexperienced writers obey the rules; rebellious, unschooled writers break the rules; an artist masters the form. –Robert McKee

*Perhaps a few bibliographers are entirely captivated
by the charm of collecting titles for the sake of collecting,
but very few consider this their chief motive.*

–Georg Schneider, THEORY AND HISTORY OF BIBLIOGRAPHY

*What information consumes is rather obvious; it
consumes the attention of its recipients. Hence, a wealth
of information creates a poverty of attention and a need to
allocate that attention efficiently among the overabundance
of information sources that might consume it.*

–Herbert Simon, economist

*English literature is a kind of training in social ethics.
English trains you to handle a body of information
in a way that is conducive to action.*

–Marilyn Butler, British educator

*From the beginning the purpose of bibliography
has been to create a meaningful order among
the records of human experience.*

–Martha Hackman, THE PRACTICAL BIBLIOGRAPHER

Bibliography

Ackerman, Diane. *A Natural History of the Senses*. New York: Vintage Books, 1990.

Adler, Mortimer & Charles Van Doren. *How to Read a Book: The Classic Guide to Intelligent Reading*. New York: Simon & Schuster, 1972.

Alred, Gerald J., Walter E. Oliu & Charles T. Brusaw. *The Handbook of Technical Writing*. New York: St. Martin's Press, 7th ed. 2003.

Alvarez, Al. *The Writer's Voice*. London: Bloomsbury Publishing, 2005.

Amis, Kingsley. *The King's English: A Guide to Modern Usage*. New York: St. Martin's Griffin, 1997.

Arana, Marie, ed. *The Writing Life: Writers on How They Think and Work*. New York: Public Affairs, 2003.

Aronie, Nancy Slonim. *Writing from the Heart: Tapping the Power of Your Inner Voice*. New York: Hyperion, 1998.

Atwood, Margaret. *Negotiating with the Dead: A Writer on Writing*. New York: Anchor Books, 2003.

Axelrod, Rise B. & Charles Raymond Cooper. *Reading Critically, Writing Well: A Reader and Guide*. New York: Bedford/St. Martin's Press, 6th ed. 2002.

Barrett, Erin & Jack Mingo. *It Takes a Certain Type to Be a Writer: Facts from the World of Writing and Publishing.* York Beach, Maine: Conari Press, 2003.

Baugh, L. Sue. *Essentials of English Grammar: A Practical Guide to the Mastery of English.* Lincolnwood, Ill.: Passport Books, 2nd ed. 1993.

Baxter, Charles. *Burning Down the House: Essays on Fiction.* St. Paul: Graywolf Press, 1997.

Bell, Arthur. *Writing Effective Letters, Memos, & E-mail.* Hauppauge, N.Y.: Barron's, 3rd ed. 2004.

Berman, Robert. *Fade In: The Screenwriting Process: A Concise Method for Developing a Story Concept into a Finished Screenplay.* Studio City, Cal.: Michael Wiese Productions, 1988.

Blake, Gary & Robert W. Bly. *Elements of Business Writing: A Guide to Writing Clear, Concise Letters, Memos, Reports, Proposals, and Other Business Documents.* Upper Saddle River, N.J.: Pearson Education, 1992.

Bly, Carol. *Beyond the Writers' Workshop: New Ways to Write Creative Nonfiction.* New York: Anchor Books, 2001.

Blythe, Will, ed. *Why I Write: Thoughts on the Craft of Fiction.* Boston: Back Bay Books, 1998.

Boisseau, Michelle & Robert Wallace. *Writing Poems.* New York: Pearson Longman, 2004.

Bolker, Joan, ed. *The Writer's Home Companion: An Anthology of the World's Best Writing Advice, from Keats to Kunitz.* New York: Henry Holt & Co., 1997.

Booth, Wayne C., Joseph M. Williams & Gregory G. Colomb. *The Craft of Research.* Chicago: University of Chicago Press, 2nd ed. 2003.

Bradbury, Ray. *Zen in the Art of Writing: Releasing the Creative Genius Within You.* New York: Bantam Books, 1992.

Bradfield, Bill, ed. *Books and Reading: A Book of Quotations.* Mineola, N.Y.: Dover Publications, 2002.

Bragg, Melvyn. *The Adventure of English: The Biography of a Language.* New York: Arcade Publishing, 2003.

Brande, Dorothea. *Becoming a Writer.* New York: Tarcher, 1981.

Brennan, Thomas, ed. *Writings on Writing: A Compendium of 1209 Quotations from Authors on Their Craft.* Jefferson, N.C.: McFarland & Company, 1994.

Brodie, Deborah, ed. *Writing Changes Everything: The 627 Best Things Anyone Ever Said About Writing.* New York: St. Martin's Press, 1997.

Bryson, Bill. *Bryson's Dictionary of Troublesome Words: A Writer's Guide to Getting It Right.* New York: Broadway Books, 2002.

_____. *The Mother Tongue: English & How It Got that Way.* New York: William Morrow & Co., 1990.

Burroway, Janet. *Writing Fiction: A Guide to Narrative Craft.* New York: HarperCollins, 4th ed. 1996.

Cameron, Julia. *The Artist's Way: A Spiritual Path to Higher Creativity.* New York: Jeremy P. Tarcher/Putnam, 2002.

_____. *The Right to Write: An Invitation and Initiation into the Writing Life.* New York: Jeremy P. Tarcher/Putnam, 1999.

Casewit, Curtis W. *Freelance Writing: Advice from the Pros.* New York: Collier Books, 1985.

Cerwinske, Laura. *Writing as a Healing Art: The Transforming Power of Self Expression.* New York: Perigee Books, 1999.

Charlton, James, ed. *The Writer's Quotation Book: A Literary Companion.* Wainscott, N.Y.: Pushcart Press, 1985.

Charters, Ann, ed. *The Story and Its Writer: An Introduction to Short Fiction.* Boston: Bedford Books of St. Martin's Press, 4th ed. 1995.

The Chicago Manual of Style: The Essential Guide for Writers, Editors, and Publishers. Chicago: University of Chicago Press, 15th ed. 2003.

Clark, Roy Peter. *Writing Tools: 50 Essential Strategies for Every Writer.* New York: Little, Brown & Co., 2006.

Cohen, Rachel. *A Chance Meeting: Intertwined Lives of American Writers and Artists, 1854-1967.* New York: Random House, 2004.

Corballis, Michael. *From Hand to Mouth: The Origins of Language*. Princeton, N.J.: Princeton University Press, 2002.

Crystal, David & Hilary Crystal, eds. *Words on Words: Quotations About Language and Languages*. Chicago: University of Chicago Press, 2000.

Daigh, Ralph. *Maybe You Should Write a Book*. Englewood Cliffs, N.J.: Prentice-Hall, 1977.

Davis, Christina & Christopher Edgar, eds. *Illuminations: Great Writers on Writing*. New York: T&W Books, 2003.

Dawidziak, Mark, ed. *Mark My Words: Mark Twain on Writing*. New York: St. Martin's Press, 1996.

Dillard, Annie. *The Writing Life*. New York: HarperCollins, 1990.

Doctorow, E. L. *Jack London, Hemingway, and the Constitution: Selected Essays, 1977-1992*. New York: HarperCollins, 1994.

Dumaine, Deborah. *Write to the Top: Writing for Corporate Success*. New York: Random House, 2004.

Edgarian, Carol & Tom Jenks, eds. *The Writer's Life: Intimate Thoughts on Work, Love, Inspiration, and Fame from the Diaries of the World's Great Writers*. New York: Vintage Books, 1997.

Edgerton, Les. *Finding Your Voice: How to Put Personality in Your Writing*. Cincinnati: Writer's Digest Books, 2003.

Edwards, Betty. *Drawing on the Right Side of the Brain: A Course in Enhancing Creativity and Artistic Confidence*. New York: Jeremy P. Tarcher/Perigee Books, 1989.

Eiben, Therese & Mary Gannon, eds. *The Practical Writer: From Inspiration to Publication*. New York: Penguin Books, 2004.

Elbow, Peter. *Writing with Power: Techniques for Mastering the Writing Process*. Oxford: Oxford University Press, 2nd ed. 1998.

Fisher, Jim, ed. *The Writer's Quotebook: 500 Authors on Creativity, Craft, and the Writing Life*. New Brunswick, N.J.: Rutgers University Press, 2006.

Fishman, Roland, comp. *Creative Wisdom for Writers*. St. Leonards, Australia: Allen & Unwin, 2000.

Flaherty, Alice. *The Midnight Disease: The Drive to Write, Writer's Block, and the Creative Brain.* Boston: Houghton Mifflin Co., 2004.

Flynn, Nancy & Tom Flynn. *Writing Effective E-mail: Improving Your Electronic Communication.* Menlo Park, Cal.: Crisp Learning, 2003.

Forche, Carolyn & Philip Gerard, eds. *Writing Creative Nonfiction: Instruction and Insights from Teachers of the Associated Writing Programs.* Cincinnati: F&W Publications, 2001.

Frank, Steven. *The Pen Commandments: A Guide for the Beginning Writer.* New York: Anchor Books, 2003.

Gardner, John. *The Art of Fiction: Notes on Craft for Young Writers.* New York: Vintage Books, 1991.

_____. *On Becoming a Novelist.* New York: W.W. Norton & Co., 1999.

Ghiselin, Brewster, ed. *The Creative Process: Reflections on Invention in the Arts and Sciences.* Berkeley, Cal.: University of California Press, 1985.

Gibaldi, Joseph. *MLA Handbook for Writers of Research Papers.* New York: Modern Language Association of America, 6th ed. 2003.

Gilchrist, Ellen. *The Writing Life.* Jackson: University Press of Mississippi, 2005.

Goldberg, Bonni. *Room to Write: Daily Invitations to a Writer's Life.* New York: Jeremy P. Tarcher/Putnam, 1996.

Goldberg, Natalie. *Thunder and Lightning: Cracking Open the Writer's Craft.* New York: Bantam Books, 2000.

_____. *Writing Down the Bones: Freeing the Writer Within.* Boston: Shambhala Publications, 1986.

Goldsberry, Steven. *The Writer's Book of Wisdom: 101 Rules for Mastering Your Craft.* Cincinnati: Writer's Digest Books, 2004.

Golub, Marcia. *I'd Rather Be Writing.* Cincinnati: Writer's Digest Books, 1999.

Gordimer, Nadine. *Writing and Being.* Cambridge, Mass.: Harvard University Press, 1995.

Gordon, William. *The Quotable Writer: Words of Wisdom from Mark Twain, Aristotle, Oscar Wilde, Robert Frost, Erica Jong, and More.* New York: McGraw-Hill, 2000.

Gray, Dorothy Randall. *Soul Between the Lines: Freeing Your Creative Spirit Through Writing*. New York: Avon Books, 1998.

Hairston, Maxine, John Ruszkiewicz & Christy Friend. *The Scott, Foresman Handbook for Writers*. New York: Longman, 6th ed. 2002.

Hall, Donald & Sven Birkerts. *Writing Well*. New York: Longman, 9th ed. 1998.

Hampl, Patricia. *I Could Tell You Stories: Sojourns in the Land of Memory*. New York: W.W. Norton & Co., 1999.

Harris, Robert. *When Good People Write Bad Sentences: 12 Steps to Better Writing Habits*. New York: St. Martin's Griffin, 2003.

Hayakawa, S.I. & Alan R. Hayakawa. *Language in Thought and Action*. San Diego, Cal.: Harcourt, 5th ed. 1990.

Helitzer, Melvin. *Comedy Writing Secrets*. Cincinnati: F&W Publications, 1992.

Hersey, John, ed. *The Writer's Craft*. New York: Knopf, 1974.

Hills, Rust. *Writing in General and the Short Story in Particular*. New York: Bantam Books, 1980.

Hopper, Vincent F., Benjamin W. Griffith, Ronald C. Foote & Cedric Gale. *Essentials of English: A Practical Handbook Covering All the Rules of English Grammar and Writing Style*. Hauppauge, N.Y.: Barron's Educational Series, 5th ed. 2000.

Jackman, Ian, ed. *The Writer's Mentor: Secrets of Success from the World's Great Writers*. New York: Random House Reference, 2004.

Jacobs, Ben & Helena Hjalmarsson, eds. *The Quotable Book Lover*. New York: Lyons Press, 1999.

Johnson, Steven. *Mind Wide Open: Your Brain and the Neuroscience of Everyday Life*. New York: Scribner, 2004.

Kachuba, John, ed. *How to Write Funny: Add Humor to Every Kind of Writing*. Cincinnati: Writer's Digest Books, 2001.

Kane, Thomas. *The New Oxford Guide to Writing*. Oxford: Oxford University Press, 1988.

Kaplan, Rob & Harold Rabinowitz, eds. *Speaking of Books: The Best Things Ever Said About Books and Book Collecting*. New York: Crown Publishers, 2001.

Kaye, Sanford. *Writing as a Lifelong Skill.* Belmont, Cal.: Wadsworth Pub., 1994.

Kemp, Peter, ed. *The Oxford Dictionary of Literary Quotations.* Oxford: Oxford University Press, 2nd ed. 2003.

Keyes, Ralph. *The Courage to Write: How Writers Transcend Fear.* New York: Owl Books, 1996.

_____. *The Writer's Book of Hope: Getting from Frustration to Publication.* New York: Henry Holt, 2003.

King, Stephen. *On Writing: A Memoir of the Craft.* New York: Scribner, 2000.

Klauser, Henriette Anne. *With Pen in Hand: The Healing Power of Writing.* Cambridge, Mass.: Perseus Publishing, 2003.

Kooser, Ted. *The Poetry Home Repair Manual: Practical Advice for Beginning Poets.* Lincoln, Neb.: University of Nebraska Press, 2005.

Kooser, Ted & Steve Cox. *Writing Brave & Free: Encouraging Words for People Who Want to Start Writing.* Lincoln: University of Nebraska Press, 2006.

Krementz, Jill. *The Writer's Desk.* New York: Random House, 1996.

Lamb, Brian, ed. *Booknotes: America's Finest Authors on Reading, Writing, and the Power of Ideas.* New York: Times Books, 1997.

Lamott, Anne. *Bird by Bird: Some Instructions on Writing and Life.* New York: Anchor Books, 1995.

Lawrence, Mary. *Writing as a Thinking Process.* Ann Arbor: University of Michigan Press, 1996.

Lederer, Richard. *The Miracle of Language.* New York: Pocket Books, 1991.

Lerner, Betsy. *The Forest for the Trees: An Editor's Advice to Writers.* New York: Riverhead Books, 2001.

Lesser, Wendy, ed. *The Genius of Language: Fifteen Writers Reflect on Their Mother Tongues.* New York: Pantheon Books, 2004.

Lingeman, Richard. *Double Lives: American Writers' Friendships.* New York: Random House, 2006.

The Literary Almanac: The Best of the Printed Word, 1900 to the Present. Kansas City, Mo.: High Tide Press, 1997.

Lopate, Phillip. *The Art of the Personal Essay: An Anthology from the Classical Era to the Present.* New York: Anchor Books, 1995.

Lyon, Elizabeth. *A Writer's Guide to Nonfiction.* New York: Perigee Books, 2003.

Mailer, Norman. *The Spooky Art: Thoughts on Writing.* New York: Random House, 2004.

Maisel, Eric. *Write Mind: 299 Things Writers Should Never Say to Themselves (and What They Should Say Instead).* New York: Jeremy P. Tarcher/Putnam, 2002.

Mann, Thomas. *The Oxford Guide to Library Research.* Oxford: Oxford University Press, 1998.

McClanahan, Rebecca. *Word Painting: A Guide to Writing More Descriptively.* Cincinnati: F&W Publications, 2000.

McKee, Robert. *Story: Style, Structure, Substance, and the Principles of Screenwriting.* New York: HarperCollins, 1997.

Metcalf, Linda Trichter & Tobin Simon. *Writing the Mind Alive: The Proprioceptive Method for Finding Your Authentic Voice.* New York: Ballantine Books, 2002.

Moore, Thomas H., ed. *Henry Miller on Writing.* New York: New Directions, 1964.

Murray, Donald. *The Craft of Revision.* Fort Worth, Tex.: Harcourt Brace & Co., 3rd ed. 1998.

Noonan, Peggy. *On Speaking Well: How to Give a Speech with Style, Substance, and Clarity.* New York: ReganBooks, 1999.

Oates, Joyce Carol. *The Faith of a Writer: Life, Craft, Art.* New York: HarperCollins, 2003.

O'Conner, Patricia. *Woe Is I: The Grammarphobe's Guide to Better English in Plain English.* New York: Riverhead Books, 1996.

_____. *Words Fail Me: What Everyone Who Writes Should Know About Writing.* San Diego, Cal.: Harcourt, 1999.

Oliver, Mary. *A Poetry Handbook.* San Diego, Cal.: Harcourt Brace & Co., 1994.

Orwell, George. *Why I Write*. New York: Penguin Books, 2005.

Osen, Diane, ed. *The Book that Changed My Life: Interviews with National Book Award Winners and Finalists*. New York: Modern Library, 2002.

Pack, Robert & Jay Parini, eds. *Writers on Writing: A Bread Loaf Anthology*. Hanover, N.H.: University Press of New England, 1991.

Palumbo, Dennis. *Writing from the Inside Out: Transforming Your Psychological Blocks to Release the Writer Within*. New York: John Wiley & Sons, Inc., 2000.

Paterson, Katherine. *The Invisible Child: On Reading and Writing Books for Children*. New York: Dutton Children's Books, 2001.

Phillips, Larry W., ed. *F. Scott Fitzgerald on Writing*. New York: Charles Scribner's Sons, 1985.

Pinker, Steven. *The Language Instinct: How the Mind Creates Language*. New York: HarperCollins, 1994.

Pipher, Mary. *Writing to Change the World*. New York: Riverhead Books, 2006.

Plimpton, George, ed. *The Paris Review Interviews: Women Writers at Work*. New York: Modern Library, 1998.

_____, ed. *The Writer's Chapbook: A Compendium of Fact, Opinion, Wit, and Advice from the 20th Century's Preeminent Writers*. New York: Penguin Books, 1989.

_____, ed. *Writers at Work: The Paris Review Interviews*. New York: Penguin Books, 1988.

Rasmussen, Kirk. *A Writer's Guide to Research and Documentation*. Upper Saddle River, N.J.: Prentice Hall, 5th ed. 2003.

Rawlins, Jack. *The Writer's Way*. Boston: Houghton Mifflin Co., 5th ed. 2002.

Reeves, Judy. *A Writer's Book of Days: A Spirited Companion and Lively Muse for the Writing Life*. Novato, Cal.: New World Library, 1999.

Rhodes, Richard. *How to Write: Advice and Reflections*. New York: HarperCollins, 1995.

Rico, Gabriele, *Writing the Natural Way: Using Right-Brain Techniques to Release Your Expressive Powers*. New York: Jeremy P. Tarcher/Putnam, 2000.

Rilke, Rainer Maria. *Letters to a Young Poet* (M.D. Herton Norton, trans.). New York: W.W. Norton & Co., 1993.

Robinson, Andrew. *The Story of Writing: Alphabets, Hieroglyphs & Pictograms*. London: Thames & Hudson, 1995.

Roman, Kenneth & Joel Raphaelson. *Writing that Works: How to Communicate Effectively in Business*. New York: HarperCollins, 3rd ed. 2000.

Ross-Larson, Bruce. *Edit Yourself: A Manual for Everyone Who Works with Words*. New York: W.W. Norton & Co., 1985.

Rountree, Cathleen. *The Writer's Mentor: A Guide to Putting Passion on Paper*. Berkeley, Cal.: Conari Press, 2002.

Sacks, David. *Language Visible: Unraveling the Mystery of the Alphabet from A to Z*. New York: Broadway Books, 2003.

Safire, William & Leonard Safir, eds. *Good Advice on Writing: Great Quotations from Writers Past and Present on How to Write Well*. New York: Simon & Schuster, 1992.

Sanders, Scott Russell. *Writing from the Center*. Bloomington: Indiana University Press, 1997.

Schneider, Pat. *Writing Alone and with Others*. Oxford: Oxford University Press, 2003.

Sebranek, Patrick, Verne Meyer & Dave Kemper. *Writers Inc: A Student Handbook for Writing & Learning*. Boston: Houghton Mifflin Co.,1996.

See, Carolyn. *Making a Literary Life: Advice for Writers and Other Dreamers*. New York: Ballantine Books, 2002.

Shaughnessy, Susan. *Walking on Alligators: A Book of Meditations for Writers*. New York: HarperCollins, 1993.

Shertzer, Margaret. *The Elements of Grammar*. New York: Collier Books, 1986.

Siegal, Allan M. & William G. Connolly. *The New York Times Manual for Style and Usage: The Official Style Guide Used by the Writers and Editors of the World's Most Authoritative Newspaper*. New York: Crown Publishing Group, 2002.

Spencer, Stuart. *The Playwright's Guidebook: An Insightful Primer on the Art of Dramatic Writing*. New York: Faber & Faber, 2002.

Springer, Sally & Georg Deutsch. *Left Brain, Right Brain*. New York: W. H. Freeman & Co., 3rd ed. 1989.

Stephens, Meic, comp. *Collins Dictionary of Literary Quotations*. Glasgow: HarperCollins, 1990.

Strickland, Bill, ed. *On Being a Writer*. Cincinnati: Writer's Digest Books, 1989.

Strunk, William & E. B. White. *The Elements of Style*. Upper Saddle River, N.J.: Pearson Education, 4th ed. 1999.

Thornley, Wilson. *Short Story Writing: The Student's Step-by-Step Guide to Writing the Effective Short Story*. New York: Bantam Books, 1976.

Tomlinson, Barbara. *Authors on Writing: Metaphors and Intellectual Labor*. New York: Palgrave MacMillan, 2005.

Trimble, John. *Writing with Style: Conversations on the Art of Writing*. Englewood Cliffs, N.J.: Prentice Hall, 2nd ed. 1999.

Truss, Lynne. *Eats, Shoots & Leaves: The Zero Tolerance Approach to Punctuation*. New York: Gotham Books, 2003.

Turabian, Kate. *A Manual for Writers of Term Papers, Theses, and Dissertations*. Chicago: University of Chicago Press, 6th ed. 1996.

Ueland, Brenda. *If You Want to Write: A Book About Art, Independence and Spirit*. St. Paul: Graywolf Press, 1987.

Underwood, Lamar, ed. *The Quotable Writer*. Guilford, Conn.: Lyons Press, 2004.

Vida, Vendela, ed. *The Believer Book of Writers Talking to Writers*. San Francisco: Believer Books, 2005.

Waldman, Mark Robert, ed. *The Spirit of Writing: Classic and Contemporary Essays Celebrating the Writing Life*. New York: Jeremy P. Tarcher/Putnam, 2001.

Walsh, Bill. *Lapsing into a Comma: A Curmudgeon's Guide to the Many Things that Can Go Wrong in Print – and How to Avoid Them*. New York: McGraw-Hill, 2000.

Welty, Eudora. *On Writing*. New York: Modern Library, 2002.

Wilbers, Stephen. *Keys to Great Writing*. Cincinnati: Writer's Digest Books, 2000.

Winokur, Jon, ed. *Advice to Writers: A Compendium of Quotes, Anecdotes, and Writerly Wisdom from a Dazzling Array of Literary Lights*. New York: Vintage Books, 2000.

Wooldridge, Susan Goldsmith. *Poemcrazy: Freeing Your Life with Words*. New York: Three Rivers Press, 1997.

Woolf, Virginia. *A Room of One's Own*. San Diego, Cal.: Harcourt Brace & Co., 1989.

Writers on Writing: Collected Essays from The New York Times. New York: Times Books, 2001.

Writers on Writing: More Collected Essays from The New York Times. New York: Times Books, 2003.

The Writing Life: A Collection of Essays and Interviews. New York: Random House, 1995.

Yagoda, Ben. *The Sound on the Page: Style and Voice in Writing*. New York: HarperCollins, 2004.

Yolen, Jane. *Take Joy: A Writer's Guide to Loving the Craft*. Cincinnati: Writer's Digest Books, 2006.

Zane, J. Peder, ed. *Remarkable Reads: 34 Writers and Their Adventures in Reading*. New York: W.W. Norton & Co., 2004.

Zimmermann, Susan. *Writing to Heal the Soul: Transforming Grief and Loss Through Writing*. New York: Three Rivers Press, 2002.

Zinsser, William. *On Writing Well: The Classic Guide to Writing Nonfiction*. New York: HarperCollins, 2001.

_____. *Writing About Your Life: A Journey into the Past*. New York: Marlowe, 2004.

_____. *Writing to Learn: How to Write and Think Clearly About Any Subject at All*. New York: Harper & Row, 1989.

Good writing connects people to one another, to other living creatures, to stories and ideas, and to action. It allows readers to see the world from a new perspective. –Mary Pipher • If a writer could truly capture the life of any person for just one day, that writer would be the best writer who ever lived. –Leo Tolstoy • The poet's goal is to light up the sky. –Ted Kooser • Never think of revising as fixing something that is wrong. That starts you off in a negative frame of mind. Rather think of it as an opportunity to improve something you already love. –Marion Dane Bauer • A true piece of writing is a dangerous thing. It can change your life. –Tobias Wolff • Feelings of inadequacy are the black lung disease of writing. –Charles Baxter • A jackass can kick a barn down, but it takes a carpenter to build one. –Sam Rayburn • Voice is like a snowflake—complicated, beautiful, and individual. It is essence of self, distilled and offered in service to the world. –Mary Pipher • Just trust yourself, then you will know how to live. –Johann Wolfgang von Goethe • To work in silence and with all one's heart, that is the writer's lot; he is the only artist who must be solitary, and yet needs the widest outlook on the world. –Sarah Orne Jewett • It's hell writing, but it's hell not writing. The only tolerable state is just having written. –Robert Hass • Why not just tell the truth? –Raymond Carver • The Promised Land always lies on the other side of a wilderness. –Havelock Ellis • The secret of having good ideas is to have a lot of ideas, then throw away the bad ones. –Linus Pauling • Well begun is half done. –Aristotle • Writers work in the solitude of a lighthouse keeper, but the light they keep illuminates the way for distant lives. –Richard Lingeman • Rome was not built in one day. –John Heywood • He listens well who takes notes. –Dante Alighieri • Words are the physicians of a mind diseased. –Aeschylus • As no man is born an artist, so no man is born an angler. –Izaak Walton • In dreams begins responsibility. –William Butler Yeats • All great art is the work of the whole living creature, body and soul, and chiefly of the soul. –John Ruskin • It is not enough to have a good mind. The main thing is to use it well. –René Descartes • Daily life is always extraordinary when rendered precisely. –Bonnie Friedman • If a writer stops observing he is finished. Experience is communicated by small details intimately observed. –Ernest Hemingway • No thing great is created suddenly, any more than a bunch of grapes or a fig. If you tell me that you desire a fig, I answer you that there must be time. Let it first blossom, then bear fruit, then ripen. –Epictetus • Education is not preparation for life; education is life itself. –John Dewey • It is better to know some of the questions than all of the answers. –James Thurber

ABOUT THE AUTHOR

Curiosity is one of the permanent and certain characteristics of a vigorous mind. –Samuel Johnson • What is life? It is the flash of a firefly in the night. It is the breath of a buffalo in the wintertime. It is the little shadow which runs across the grass and loses itself in the sunset. –Crowfoot • Writing a book is a long, exhausting struggle, like a long bout of some painful illness. One would never undertake such a thing if one were not driven by some demon whom one can neither resist nor understand. –George Orwell • Color theory for life: Those who spend their lives only chasing green end up blue. –Tim Hale • Writers love quotations. They love quoting someone else's work almost as much as they enjoy quoting their own. –James Charlton • I don't want to be a doctor, and live by men's diseases; nor a minister to live by their sins; nor a lawyer to live by their quarrels. So I don't see there's anything left for me but to be an author. –Nathaniel Hawthorne • A writer should never be brief at the expense of being clear. –Arthur Schopenhauer • The best thing that governments can do for authors in wartime is to leave them alone. –John Strachey • The good writer seems to be writing about himself, but has his eye always on that thread of the Universe which runs through himself and all things. –Ralph Waldo Emerson • Proofs don't shock me any longer, yet there's still a strange moment with every book when I move from the position of writer to the position of reader, and I suddenly see my words with the eyes of the cold public. It gives me a terrible sense of exposure, as if I'd gotten sunburned. –Eudora Welty • A writer can do nothing for men more necessary, satisfying, than just simply to reveal to them the infinite possibilities of their own souls. –Walt Whitman • A person who publishes a book wilfully appears before the public with his pants down. –Edna St. Vincent Millay • Being a trial lawyer has improved my writing. A trial is basically a problem in narration. Every witness has his or her story to tell. A trial lawyer's function is to help shape that story so it gets across to the audience. –Scott Turow • I want to escape the unrest, to shut out the voices around me and within me, and so I write. –Franz Kafka • An essayist is a lucky person who has found a way to discourse without being interrupted. –Charles Poore • They're fancy talkers about themselves, writers. If I had to give young writers advice, I would say don't listen to writers talking about writing or themselves. –Lillian Hellman • Authors are like cattle going to a fair: those of the same field can never move on without butting one another. –Walter Savage Landor • When I'm near the end of a book, I need to sleep in the same room with it. –Joan Didion • The moment when the finished book or, better yet, a tightly packed carton of finished books arrives on my doorstep is the moment of truth, of culmination; its bliss lasts as much as five minutes, until the first typographical error or production flaw is noticed. –John Updike • The profession of book writing makes horse racing seem like a solid, stable business. –John Steinbeck • Each book is, in a sense, an argument with myself, and I would write it, whether it is ever published or not. –Patricia Highsmith • Writing is a craft you can learn. –Roy Peter Clark • An author ought to write for the youth of his own generation, the critics of the next, and the schoolmasters of ever afterward. –F. Scott Fitzgerald

Writing is like breathing. I believe that.
I believe we all come into life as writers.
We are born with the gift of language and it comes to us
within months as we begin to name our world.

–Julia Cameron, author of THE ARTIST'S WAY

The beginning writer writes his first draft, reads it, and says,
"This is awful. I'm screwed." The experienced writer writes his
first draft, reads it, and says, "This is awful. I'm on my way!"

–Jerry Cleaver, writer

Writing is thinking. It is more than living, for it is being conscious of living.

–Anne Morrow Lindbergh, LOCKED ROOMS AND OPEN DOORS

I write basically because it's so much fun.

–James Thurber, satirst

ABOUT THE AUTHOR

JOHN D. BESSLER, a two-time Minnesota Book Award finalist, is an attorney, writer and adjunct professor at the University of Minnesota Law School. He graduated from the University of Minnesota with a degree in political science, obtained his law degree from the Indiana University School of Law in Bloomington, and has studied international human rights law at Oxford University. He also has an M.F.A. degree from Hamline University, and is the author of *Death in the Dark: Midnight Executions in America*, *Kiss of Death: America's Love Affair with the Death Penalty*, and *Legacy of Violence: Lynch Mobs and Executions in Minnesota*. He lives in Minneapolis with his wife, Amy, and their daughter, Abigail.

I don't think anything I've written has been done in under six or eight drafts. –E. L. Doctorow • Style isn't something added on; it's intrinsic to the perceptions and the way you see life. –Martin Amis • The idea of "inspiration," as it is commonly understood, does a great deal of damage to writers. For one thing, it devalues *craft*, which I think is the most important part of writing. –Dennis Palumbo • A writing career can begin at any point in one's life, even without prior writing experience, and any set of circumstances may give rise to it. It's never too late to start. –Ian Jackman • When I began to write I did so as though it were the most natural thing in the world. I took to it as a duck takes to water. –W. Somerset Maugham • A writer's life is hard. Everybody says so, and everybody is right. –Stephen Koch • The only way to get better as a writer is to write. –C. J. Hribal • Writing should be a snap. We've been telling stories all our lives; we know all of these words; we've got a pen and some paper and a million ideas. –John Dufresne • When I was in college, I revised nothing. I wrote out my papers in longhand, typed them up and turned them in. It would never have crossed my mind that what I had produced was only a first draft and that I had more work to do; the idea was to get to the end, and once you had got to the end you were finished. –Nora Ephron • Many people become writers because of their love of reading. –William Maxwell • Good habits are as easy to form as bad ones. –Tim McCarver • I write because I was meant to write, I was called to write, I was told to write. I write because that's who I am. –Elizabeth George • Writing, at least for me, is a delightfully mysterious business. I poke around and wait for something to explode in my head. –Eleanor Clark • The act of writing is one of the most intensely creative acts we can engage in. –Gabriele Rico • I think that most writers suffer from writer's block because they're trying too hard to make it perfect out of the gate when in fact, they should be writing it for themselves, as if no one is ever going to read it at all. –Terry McMillan • An untitled manuscript is an unfinished piece of work. –Lesley Grant-Adamson • Writing is physical for me. I always have the sense that the words are coming out of my body, not just my mind. –Paul Auster • I find that when I'm writing there's a back and forth process—I'll write, then I'll write some, then what I've written influences the next train of thought, and so on. –ZZ Packer • Concerning *The Jungle* I wrote that "I aimed at the public's heart, and by accident I hit it in the stomach." I helped to clean up the yards and improve the country's meat supply. Now the workers have strong unions and, I hope, are able to look out for themselves. –Upton Sinclair

Writing is life. –Terry Brooks • Mere literary talent is common; what is rare is endurance, the continuing desire to work hard at writing. –Donald Hall • I love writing. I love the swirl and swing of words as they tangle with human emotions. –James Michener • For better or worse, it is a delicious thing to write, to be no longer yourself but to move in an entire universe of your own creating. –Gustave Flaubert • It is dangerous to leave written that which is badly written. –William Carlos Williams • What I had to face, the very bitter lesson that everyone who wants to write has got to learn, was that a thing may in itself be the finest piece of writing one has ever done, and yet have absolutely no place in the manuscript one hopes to publish. –Thomas Wolfe • It is necessary to write, if the days are not to slip emptily by. How else, indeed, to clap the net over the butterfly of the moment? –Vita Sackville-West • Writing is so hard. It's the only time in your life when you have to think. –Elizabeth Hardwick • There are three reasons for becoming a writer. The first is that you need the money; the second, that you have something to say that you think the world should know; and the third is that you can't think what to do with the long winter evenings. –Quentin Crisp • What obsesses a writer starting out on a lifetime's work is the panic-stricken search for a voice of his own. –John Mortimer • Writing is the continuation of politics by other means. –Philippe Sollers • I think the end is implicit in the beginning. It must be. If that isn't there in the beginning, you don't know what you're working toward. You should have a sense of a story's shape and form and its destination, all of which is like a flower inside a seed. –Eudora Welty • I didn't know a thing about writing. I was scared shitless. –Henry Miller • Voice is the quality in writing, more than any other, that makes the reader read on, that makes the reader interested in what is being said and makes the reader trust the person who is saying it. –Donald Murray • Only a life lived for others is the life worthwhile. –Albert Einstein • Give yourself permission to fail. –Janet Burroway • I don't think of myself as a naturally gifted writer when it comes to using language. –Joseph Heller • A bad beginning makes a bad ending. –Euripides • It's like improvising in jazz. You don't ask a jazz musician, "But what are you going to play?" He'll laugh at you. He has a theme, a series of chords he has to respect, and then he takes up his trumpet or his saxophone and he begins. –Julio Cortázar • Never let the fear of striking out get in your way. –Babe Ruth • Education is the movement from darkness to light. –Allan Bloom • The writer must criticize his own work as a reader. Every day I pick up the story or whatever it is I've been working on and read it through. If I enjoy it as a reader then I know I'm getting along all right. –William Styron • Writers aren't born knowing the craft; writers are born with an urge to write, a curiosity, an imagination, and, perhaps, a love of the language. The way to learn the craft is through practice, and your notebook is the place of your apprenticeship. –Judy Reeves • To become a writer was not easy for me. –Henry Miller • Those rituals of getting ready to write produce a kind of trance. –John Barth • If thou art a writer, write as if thy time were short, for it is indeed short at the longest. –Henry David Thoreau • To write is to be self-conscious. –Carol Shields

It is easier to achieve an ambition than to give it up. —Herbert Bluen • To speak with clarity, brevity and wit is like holding a lightning rod. We are drawn to people who know things and are able to express them. —James Salter • We do not invent language; we inherit it. Language has its own genius that re-creates itself through our use of it. We are the means by which it grows and keeps itself alive. —Robert Pack • One test of whether you really understand something is whether you can put it into words in such a way as to teach it to someone else. —Peter Steinhart • Expression surely stands as the final objective of art. —Edward Hill • We have to be proud, not ashamed, about our changes of heart. Changes of heart are the huge glad beasts in the forest of the writing process. —Carol Bly • Verbs are the combustible material of the language; they create the action, they move the writing. Verbs contain the energy of sentences. —Judy Reeves • I only have twenty-six letters of the alphabet; I don't have color or music. I must use my craft to make the reader see the colors and hear the sounds. —Toni Morrison • You develop a style from writing a lot. —Kurt Vonnegut • You do not create a style. You work, and develop yourself; your style is an emanation from your own being. —Katherine Anne Porter • When I give I give myself. —Walt Whitman • Human rights are universal and indivisible. Human freedom is also indivisible: if it is denied to anyone in the world, it is therefore denied, indirectly, to all people. This is why we cannot remain silent in the face of evil or violence; silence merely encourages them. —Václav Havel • Originality is unexplored territory. You get there by carrying a canoe—you can't take a taxi. —Alan Alda • If I knew what was going to happen next, I wouldn't be able to write. I wouldn't be interested in writing. —Walker Percy • One role of the writer today is to sound the alarm. —E. B. White • Writing became such a process of discovery that I couldn't wait to get to work in the morning: I wanted to find out what I was going to say. —Sharon O'Brien • Life is a great big canvas; throw all the paint on it you can. —Danny Kaye • Great writing can be conjured by great injustice. —Lance Morrow • Most of the work is done in the unconscious. —Peter Weir • There is no subject so old that something new cannot be said about it. —Fyodor Dostoevsky • If all my possessions were to be taken from me with one exception, I would choose to keep the power of communication for by it I would regain all the others. —Daniel Webster • Mental life is the result of the brain's serendipitous sidesteps, its knack for discovering new uses for old structures, in turn making leaps to develop new ways of seeing. —William Calvin • It is harder to see than it is to express. —Robert Henri

Drawing is a way to know things, and the more one knows about the world around one, the more one feels at home in it. —Peter Steinhart • One eye sees, the other feels. —Paul Klee • When I'm really writing, I'm listening. —Madeleine L'Engle • All inquiries carry with them some element of risk. —Carl Sagan • If you're going to be a writer, you first of all have to develop unusual powers of observation. —Nadine Gordimer • Painters have often taught writers how to see. And once you've had that experience, you see differently. —James Baldwin • It is simply this: a writer has to take all the risks of putting down what he sees. —John Barth • You never really understand a person until you consider things from his point of view. —Harper Lee • We write because we discover that we have something we alone can say. —Mary Pipher • The habit of compulsive, premature editing doesn't just make writing hard. It also makes writing dead. —Peter Elbow • Organizing is what you do before you do something, so that when you do it, it's not all mixed up. —A. A. Milne • Writers are a fascinating breed, because there are so many kinds of them, they are made by so many circumstances, conditions, and mysteries, and there are so many ways for writing to be done. —William Saroyan • I always do the first line well, but I have trouble doing the others. —Molière • A word is not the same with one writer as with another. One tears it from his guts. The other pulls it out of his overcoat pocket. —Charles Péguy • Write often enough that you miss it if you don't do it. To have a real writing life, you must be writing at least this often. —David Huddle • Creative work is like a faucet: nothing comes unless you turn it on, and the more you turn it on, the more comes. —Brenda Ueland • If you have difficulty writing, do not conclude that there is something wrong with you. —Ayn Rand • Only writers in movies wait for inspiration. Real writers work on schedules, different ones for different writers, but always structured. Ask any writer you know. —Ed McBain • Orville Wright didn't have a pilot's license. —Richard Tait • A lot of young writers wait for inspiration. The inspiration only hits you at the desk. —Robert Anderson • There are stages in bread-making quite similar to the stages of writing. You begin with something shapeless, which sticks to your fingers, a kind of paste. Gradually that paste becomes more and more firm. Then there comes a point when it turns rubbery. Finally, you sense that the yeast has begun to do its work: the dough is alive. —Marguerite Yourcenar • The idea is to get the pencil moving quickly. —Bernard Malamud • You do your best work when you're not conscious of yourself. —Peter Matthiessen • The early stages of any creative product are not accompanied by certainty. Passion maybe, compulsion maybe, momentary visions of enticing clarity maybe, but certainty—that we have come to the right forest and are following the right track—rarely. —Stephen Nachmanovitch • Composing in language is done by feel, rather than by rule. —William Stafford • Anyone can become a writer. The trick is staying a writer. —Harlan Ellison • The typewriter separated me from a deeper intimacy with poetry, and my hand brought me closer to that intimacy again. —Pablo Neruda • The only way to get anything out of a writer's brains is to leave him or her alone until he or she is damn well ready to write it down. —Kurt Vonnegut

I use a notebook, and I write in bed. Ninety-five percent of everything I've written has been done in bed. –Paul Bowles • When you show up at the page and put in the time day after day, you learn to trust your pen and the voice that emerges as your own. –Judy Reeves • While I am working I am not conscious of what I am putting on the canvas. –Pablo Picasso • I shall live badly if I do not write. –Françoise Sagan • What I do for a *life* is write, and that's the part that's hard to explain. –Rebecca McClanahan • A sight, an emotion, creates this wave in the mind, long before it makes words to fit it; and in writing (such is my present belief) one has to recapture this, and set this working (which has nothing apparently to do with words), and then, as it breaks and tumbles in the mind, it makes words to fit it. –Virginia Woolf • I am writing in the garden. To write as one should of a garden one must write not outside it or merely somewhere near it, but in the garden. –Frances Hodgson Burnett • Language—whatever language, English, Swahili, Japanese—is the requisite for the human condition. –James Salter • Punctuation is a matter of care. Care for words, yes, but also, and more important, for what the words imply. A comma can let us hear a voice break, or a heart. Punctuation, in fact, is a labor of love. –Pico Iyer • The secret of all good writing is sound judgment. –Horace • It is well to remember that grammar is common speech formulated. –W. Somerset Maugham • The most important thing about writing is, simply, doing it, and, like practicing a musical instrument, the more you do it, the more familiar you become with the process, the easier it becomes. –Patricia Cumming • In reading and writing, you cannot lay down rules until you have learnt to obey them. Much more so in life. –Marcus Aurelius • Even when we write, we usually speak first, either overtly or covertly. What goes down on paper is then a kind of self-dictation. –B. F. Skinner • Words are, of course, the most powerful drug used by mankind. –Rudyard Kipling • Writing is hard labor, shot through with intervals of joy. –Scott Russell Sanders • I don't think a writer's block is anything more than a loss of confidence. It certainly isn't a loss of talent. –William Maxwell • I heard an angel speak last night / And he said, "write!" –Elizabeth Barrett Browning • The mere habit of writing, of constantly keeping at it, of never giving up, ultimately teaches you how to write. –Gabriel Fielding • Writing, like life (and baseball, for that matter, or marriage, or politics), is totally unpredictable. Every time you start a new writing project, you're sailing off into uncharted waters. –Dennis Palumbro • English usage is sometimes more than mere taste, judgment and education—sometimes it's sheer luck, like getting across the street. –E. B. White

The purpose of paragraphing is to give the reader a rest. –H. W. Fowler • If a writer stops observing he is finished. –Ernest Hemingway • Syntax is the plot of the sentence, a systematic ordering of person and event, of who does what to whom and when and to what end. –Aaron Shurin • We may be bored by the phrase "the writing process," but it is a wonderful process. –Carol Bly • Take care that you never spell a word wrong. Always before you write a word, consider how it is spelled, and, if you do not remember, turn to a dictionary. –Thomas Jefferson • The sound of a word is at least as important as the meaning. –Jack Prelutsky • Words are chameleons, which reflect the color of their environment. –Learned Hand • A child on a farm sees a plane fly overhead and dreams of a faraway place. A traveler on the plane sees the farmhouse and dreams of home. –Carl Burns • It's important to try to write when you are in the wrong mood or the weather is wrong. Even if you don't succeed you'll be developing a muscle that may do it later on. –John Ashbery • An idea just sort of zooms in like a bird out of the sky. –Patricia Highsmith • If you have an important point to make, don't try to be subtle or clever. Use a pile-driver. Hit the point once. Then come back and hit it again. Then hit it a third time—a tremendous whack. –Winston Churchill • Music has often created the wellspring out of which my imaginative efforts have sprung. –William Styron • When you're writing, you're trying to find out something which you don't know. –James Baldwin • Writing begins in thought. –Carolyn See • Knowledge is power. –Francis Bacon • Never express yourself more clearly than you can think. –Niels Bohr • I think with my right hand. –Edmund Wilson • What I tend to do is not so much pick at a thing but sit down and rewrite it. After making notes on one draft I'd sit down and rewrite it again from the beginning. I've found that's much better than patching and amputating things. One has to rethink the thing completely. –Christopher Isherwood • To rewrite ten times is not unusual. –Saul Bellow • I never quite know when I'm not writing. –James Thurber • I would suppose that many of us have experienced more than one crisis of faith—in our talents, in our lives—and yet because we are still at work, still writing, I would also suppose that we have at some point undergone a renewal of that faith. –Tim O'Brien • The written word may be a weak second best to lived experience, but it's still pretty powerful—our only path to meaning and inner order. –Francine du Plessix Gray • All writing is dreaming. –Jorge Luis Borges • I find that what I write when I force myself is generally just as good as what I write when I'm feeling inspired. –Tom Wolfe • I've been working, working, working, and you know, sometimes you look back at your work and you see that it just isn't any good. –Truman Capote • The verb is the business end of a sentence, the sentence's reason for being. That's where the action is. Without a verb, even if it's only suggested, there's nothing going on, just a lot of nouns standing around with their hands in their pockets. –Patricia T. O'Conner • The pen is the tool of the intuitive. –Judy Reeves • Books were my pass to personal freedom. I learned to read at age three, and soon discovered there was a whole world to conquer that went beyond our farm in Mississippi. –Oprah Winfrey

For me, design is like choosing what I'm going to wear for the day—only much more complicated and not really the same at all. –Robynne Raye • The best designers can make music on any instrument. –Anne Traver • To live a creative life, we must lose our fear of being wrong. –Joseph Chilton Pearce • Always design a thing by considering it in its next larger context—a chair in a room, a room in a house, a house in an environment, an environment in a city plan. –Eliel Saarinen • Good design is a form of respect—on the part of the producer for the person who will eventually spend hard-earned cash on the product, uses the product, own the product. –David Brown • Creativity: Take the obvious, add a cupful of brains, a generous pinch of imagination, a bucketful of courage and daring, stir well and bring to a boil. –Bernard M. Baruch • Always think of drawing, getting the forms realized, emphasizing the design. –John Sloan • Naps are completely underestimated and are an essential part of the creative process. –Laura Zeck • No one ever discovered anything new by coloring inside the lines. –Thomas Vasquez • Design is directed toward human beings. To design is to solve human problems by identifying them and executing the best solution. –Ivan Chermayeff • On the smallest level, creativity can alter moods. On the grandest level, it can change lives. –Steffanie Lorig • Creativity is allowing yourself to make mistakes. Art is knowing which ones to keep. –Scott Adams • The object of art is to give life shape. –Jean Anouilh • What perplexes me most these days is that after hundreds of posters, logos, brochures, and digital bits and pieces, I still start every project gripped by the fingers of fear and failure. –Andrew Lewis • Inspiration is for amateurs; the rest of us just get to work. –Chuck Close • Art is the most intense mode of individualism that the world has known. –Oscar Wilde • Graphic design is the spit and polish but not the shoe. –Ellen Lupton • Design can be an elusive mistress. Be good to her, don't rush things, and she'll probably reward you every time. Tread lightly, however, as she will ridicule you in front of your friends and peers if you cross her. –Justin Hampton • Design is a response to social change. –George Nelson • You can never do too much drawing. –Jacopo Robusti • The noun of self becomes a verb. This flashpoint of creation in the present moment is where work and play merge. –Stephen Nachmanovitch • Forcing yourself to design is like exercising: the more you do, the stronger you become. –Michael Cina • The creation of a thousand forests is in one acorn. –Ralph Waldo Emerson • Bad design is smoke, while good design is a mirror. –Juan-Carlos Fernández • The way something looks is the last thing we figure out. –Alexander Isley

A B O U T   T H E   D E S I G N E R S

The creation of something new is not accomplished by the intellect but by the play instinct acting from inner necessity. The creative mind plays with the objects it loves. –Carl Jung • Graphic art is my secret garden, the place where I can get lost but also find territories I didn't even know existed. –Kari Piippo • Design is at base a practical activity, the making of artifacts. –Quenten Newark • A well-defined problem is half solved. –Michael Osborne • Creativity is a continual surprise. –Ray Bradbury • A life in design is a difficult one—a life living in a state of heightened emotional awareness, throwing your entire soul into your very best work, which may be dismissed in an instant for the most trivial and petty of reasons. I can't think of anything else I would rather do more. –Robert Louey • Design can be art. Design can be aesthetics. Design is so simple, that's why it is so complicated. –Paul Rand • Creativity is inventing, experimenting, growing, taking risks, breaking rules, making mistakes, and having fun. –Mary Lou Cook • Anyone who says you can't see a thought simply doesn't know art. –Wynetka Ann Reynolds • Simplicity is not the goal. It is the by-product of a good idea and modest expectations. –Paul Rand • Design is like life: It is an ongoing process of development and discovery. –Thomas Vasquez • Creativity is essentially a lonely art. An even lonelier struggle. To some a blessing. To others a curse. It is in reality the ability to reach inside yourself and drag forth from your very soul an idea. –Lou Dorfsman • If you don't risk it, no biscuit. –Sean Adams • It is only by drawing often, drawing everything, drawing incessantly, that one fine day you discover to your surprise that you have rendered something in its true character. –Camille Pissarro • Creation begins with vision. –Henri Matisse • There are painters who transform the sun to a yellow spot, but there are others who with the help of their art and their intelligence, transform a yellow spot into the sun. –Pablo Picasso • Yes, as a way of determining and influencing people's actions, design is a political act. –Rudy VanderLans • Realize the value of putting down your first impression quickly. –Charles Hawthorne • Passion is in all great searches and is necessary to all creative endeavors. –W. Eugene Smith • If you are seeking creative ideas, go out walking. –Raymond Inman • Do whatever you do intensely. –Robert Henri • Everything you need to know is already in your head. You just have to find it. –Garth Walker • A creative solution always lies at the fingertips holding the drawing pencil. –Raphael Henry • An idea is salvation by imagination. –Frank Lloyd Wright • Design is easy. All you do is stare at the screen until drops of blood form on your forehead. –Marty Neumeier • When inspiration doesn't come, I go halfway to meet it. –Sigmund Freud • Go on working, freely and furiously, and you will make progress. –Paul Gauguin • Technique does not exist in itself, it is only the substance of the creative machinery. –Ansel Adams • Instantly paint what you see. –Édouard Manet • Creativity is a type of learning process where the teacher and pupil are located in the same individual. –Arthur Koestler • Painting is easy when you don't know how, but very difficult when you do. –Edgar Degas • The difference between regulated architects and unregulated designers is, unlike buildings, letterheads don't fall down and kill people. –Brian Webb

Being a famous designer is like being a famous dentist.

–Noreen Morioka, Principal, AdamsMorioka

A camel is a horse designed by committee.

–Sir Alec Issigonis, automobile designer

The kind of effort that goes into graphic expression is essentially lonely and intensive and produces, at its best, a simple logical design. It is sometimes frustrating to find that hardly anyone knows that it is a very complicated job to produce something simple.

–William Golden, NINE PIONEERS IN AMERICAN GRAPHIC DESIGN

Design is not just what it looks like and feels like. Design is how it works.

–Steve Jobs, Apple Computer CEO

ABOUT THE BOOK DESIGNERS

ANDREW BESSLER, according to the Minnesota Department of Motor Vehicles, measures five-feet, nine-inches tall, weighs 130 pounds and has hazel eyes. Additionally, he is a partner of Play, a graphic design firm in the warehouse district in Minneapolis. He is belonephobic, a graduate of the University of Minnesota and lives in St. Paul with his wife Hongji, who is an acupuncturist.

VICTORIA HAKALA, who lives and works in Afton, Minnesota, helped with page layout and typesetting for the book. She and her husband own Hakala Communications Inc., a firm that specializes in the research, writing, design, and production of business and institutional histories.

Typography is the particle physics of design. –Rian Hughes • A good concept is the fruit of an analytical, as well as intuitive, process. –Fang Chen • "No, Watson, this was not done by accident, but by design." –Sherlock Holmes • Every school boy and school girl who has arrived at the age of reflection ought to know something about the history of the art of printing. –Horace Mann • Echo replies to echo, everything reverberates. –Georges Braque • The very greatest is the alphabet, for in it lies the deepest wisdom; yet only he can fathom it, who truly knows how to put it together. –Emmanuel Geibel • Art is a passion or it is nothing. –Roger Fry • Form follows feeling. –David Turner • You know you've achieved perfection in design, not when you have nothing more to add, but when you have nothing more to take away. –Antoine de Saint-Exupéry • There are only two types of graphic design: good and bad. –Ken Cato • A personal style is like a handwriting—it happens as the byproduct of our way of seeing things, enriched by the experiences of everything around us. –Massimo Vignelli • Content comes first…yet excellent design can catch people's eyes and impress the contents on their memory. –Hideki Nakajima • One must always be careful not to let one's work be covered with moss. –Marc Chagall • When Einstein realized, "Dear me, this universe with its wonders all adds up to $E=mc^2$?," he did not stop to think whether this concept would sell better set in Futura or Antikva. –Kari Piippo • Creative work is play. It is free speculation using materials of one's chosen form. –Stephen Nachmanovitch • Design is the art of situations. –Ellen Lupton • What you see is what you see. –Frank Stella • Design is not for philosophy—it's for life. –Issey Miyake • Don't break the rules just to be breaking the rules, but on the other hand, don't let them get in the way either. –Rick Tharp • The canvas upon which the artist paints is the spectator's mind. –Kakuzo Okakura • It isn't a question of enhancement through design. Whether an editor realizes it or not, design is part of what he does every time he prints the paper. –Louis Silverstein • You have to be interested in culture to design for it. –Lorraine Wild • I will do anything to support individual means of expression and if this means there are a million typefaces, I'll support that, because I think people should be allowed to make their own. The ability to design typefaces on the Macintosh is a true revolution. –Neville Brody • Be true to your work, and your work will be true to you. –Charles Pratt • Work lovingly done is the secret of all order and all happiness. –Auguste Rodin • Creativity can solve almost any problem. The creative act, the defeat of habit by originality, overcomes everything. –George Lois

ABOUT THE TYPE

When I am working on a problem, I never think about beauty. I only think about how to solve the problem. But when I have finished, if the solution is not beautiful, I know it is wrong. –Richard Buckminster Fuller • The pursuit of beauty is honorable. –Estee Lauder • I begin with an idea and then it becomes something else. –Pablo Picasso • What I'm trying to produce is the visual equivalent of the chord change that makes the hairs on the back of your neck stand up. –Rian Hughes • My aim is a continuous, sustained, uncontrived image motivated by nothing but passion. –Rico Lebrun • In most people's vocabularies, design means veneer. It's interior decorating. It's the fabric of the curtains or the sofa. But to me, nothing could be further from the meaning of design. Design is the fundamental soul of a human-made creation that ends up expressing itself in successive outer layers of the product or service. –Steve Jobs • Design brings content into focus; design makes function visible. –Jennifer Morla • I find going to bed and pulling my imagination over my head often means waking up with a solution to a design problem. That state of limbo, the time between sleeping and waking, seems to allow ideas to somehow outflank the sentinels of common sense. –Alan Fletcher • A hunch is creativity trying to tell you something. –Frank Capra • What is design? A plan for arranging elements in such a way as to best accomplish a particular purpose. –Charles Eames • You should demand of the writer that he really present what he writes; his ideas reach you through the eye and not through the ear. Therefore typographical form should do by means of optics what the voice and gesture of the writer does to convey his ideas. –El Lissitzky • How do I work? I grope. –Albert Einstein • Less is only more where more is no good. –Frank Lloyd Wright • Typography bears much resemblance to cinema, just as the reading of print puts the reader in the role of movie projector. The reader moves the series of imprinted letters before him with a speed consistent with apprehending the motions of the author's mind. –László Moholoy-Nagy • Begin with the end in mind. –Lana Rigsby • Creativity represents a miraculous coming together of the uninhibited energy of the child with its apparent opposite and enemy, the sense of order imposed on the disciplined adult intelligence. –Norman Podhoretz • Matthew Carter's Bell Centennial font was designed for maximum legibility at a minimum size. It is used in the U.S. phone books. Bell Centennial has saved millions of trees. –Ellen Lupton • How can there be too many typefaces in the world? Are there too many songs, too many books, too many places to go? –Rian Hughes • I generally think that the idea is the starting point of graphic design. The second step is to find the appropriate style to make this idea work the best. –Christoph Niemann • Creativity is a drug I cannot live without. –Cecil B. DeMille • Far from being merely decorative, the artist's awareness is one of the few guardians of the inherent sanity and equilibrium of the human spirit that we have. –Robert Motherwell • Design without thinking is like a story with no plot. –Pat Hansen • The mind is but a barren soil—a soil which is soon exhausted, and will produce no crop, or only one, unless it be continually fertilized and enriched with foreign matter. –Sir Joshua Reynolds • Play! –Peter Vattanatham

Every graphic designer has at least one favorite typeface that he or she uses ad nauseam. If I were not the art director of The New York Times Book Review *(and thus restricted to Franklin Gothic, Imperial and Bookman), mine would be Bembo.*

–Steven Heller, author of *LETTERFORMS: BAWDY, BAD AND BEAUTIFUL*

Typography is what language looks like.

–Ellen Lupton, Director, MFA program, Maryland Institute College of Art

The more uninteresting a letter, the more useful it is to the typographer.

–Piet Zwart, Dutch typographer

When in Rome, use Times Roman.

–Marty Neumeier, Neutron LLC

ABOUT THE TYPE

This book was set in Bembo, an Italian Renaissance letterform originating with "De Aetna," a book by Pietro Bembo about his visit to Mount Etna. A poet, historian and cardinal, Pietro Bembo was born in Venice, was appointed secretary to Pope Leo X, and died in Rome in 1547. "De Aetna" was published in 1495 by Aldus Manutius, a Venetian printer, and the original typeface was cut by master craftsman Francesco Griffo, a goldsmith-turned-punchcutter. The typeface became popular in Italy, was soon duplicated by the French type founder Claude Garamond, and the influence of the design eventually spread throughout Europe. The typeface was revived in the 1920s by Stanley Morison of England's Monotype Corporation and christened Bembo. The stylish, easily readable Bembo font was brought to the United States in the 1930s by the Lanston Monotype Machine Company of Philadelphia. The italic form of Bembo is based on the handwriting of Giovanni Tagliente, a Renaissance scribe.

The book's headings are in Chalet Paris, a typeface released in 2000 by House Industries. The Chalet collection of fonts, the company's website notes, "is the preeminent contribution of René Albert Chalet, one of the most underappreciated yet arguably greatest typeface designers in history." Born in Interlaken, Switzerland in 1923, Chalet served as a printer's apprentice, developed a keen interest in opera and marionettes, then began designing costumes for Marionette du Theatre du Luxembourg in Paris. This work led to his launch of Atelier Chalet, a fashion enterprise that renewed Chalet's long-time passion for typography as he developed his firm's fledgling identity. In 1944, Chalet had proposed a typeface to Deberny & Peignot of Paris, a font the company rejected out of fear of being labeled "cultural Bolshevists" by the occupying Nazi regime. Alas, René Albert Chalet is a fictional creation—a House Industries hoax conjured up to expose people's lack of knowledge of the history of type design!

The small icons or "dingbats" that are found on select pages in this book are in Poppi, which was created by German typeface designer Martin Friedl and released by Emigre in 2003. Friedl studied at the State Academy of Fine Arts in Stuttgart, co-founded a design firm, and is very much a real person.

The most valuable of talents is never using two words when one will do. –Thomas Jefferson • Occasionally you can hit it right the first time. More often, you don't. –John Dos Passos • I love metaphor. It provides two loaves where there seems to be one. Sometimes it throws in a load of fish. –Bernard Malamud • Contrary to general belief, writing isn't something that only "writers" do; writing is a basic skill for getting through life. –William Zinsser • No, I don't think that style is consciously arrived at. Any more than one arrives at the color of one's eyes. After all, your style *is* you. –Truman Capote • Most thinkers write badly, because they communicate not only their thoughts, but also the thinking of them. –Friedrich Nietzsche • Great ideas need landing gear as well as wings. –C. D. Jackson • An idea can turn to dust or magic, depending on the talent that rubs against it. –William Bernbach • To live in the realm of ideas means treating the impossible as though it were possible. –Johann Wolfgang von Goethe • It is obvious that invention or discovery, be it in mathematics or anywhere else, takes place by combining ideas. –Jacques Hadamard • The writer must soak up the subject completely, as a plant soaks up water, until the ideas are ready to sprout. –Marguerite Yourcenar • I keep a small sheath of 3 x 5 cards in my billfold. If I think of a good sentence, I'll write it down. –Joseph Heller • Three hours of writing require twenty hours of preparation. –John Steinbeck • Change is the law of life. –John F. Kennedy • Developing a language of one's own, with its distinct colors and nuances, with maps and charts and images that voice the self, takes a long time. It is the writer's lifelong work. –Burghild Nina Holzer • The title comes afterwards, usually with considerable difficulty. –Heinrich Böll • I want always to write as if my brain has just woken up, because I want it to be exciting to me. The thing that keeps me writing is that it will be new. –Jamaica Kincaid • For me, writing is like breathing. I'm always writing something. –Haruki Murakami • I think that to be a good writer, you have to put yourself on the line, you have to think deeply about what is meaningful to you and you have to make a good-faith effort to speak from the integrity of your own deep experience. –Marilynne Robinson • Writing is the consequence of the desire to tell. –James Salter • I've seen, time and time again, the way that the process of trying to say something that matters dignifies and improves a person. –George Saunders • I feel that writing does good, that it has a purpose in the world. –Joan Silber • Everything we learn to write is a stepping stone for the next level of conversation we are capable of having with ourselves. –Christina Baldwin • As I write I create myself again and again. –Joy Harjo

For constructing any work of art you need some principle of repetition or recurrence; that's what gives you rhythm in music and pattern in painting. –Northrop Frye • Most writers ignore the very thing that would get them results, and that's craft. And how do you get craft? In the trenches. You've got to do it. You got to get in there, you got to write. I say write and then write and write and write some more and go write some more. –August Wilson • Writing is a process of learning and discovery. –Donald Murray • That's why I go on, I suppose. To see what the next sentences I write will be. –Gore Vidal • Writing itself is one of the great, free human activities. There is scope for individuality, and elation, and discovery. –William Stafford • The more I wrote the more I became a human being. –Henry Miller • When you write on a daily basis, your self-confidence increases. You learn what you want to write about and what matters to you as a writer. –Judy Reeves • I can tell you some things by hindsight or from what people have told me. But basically, when I'm writing a story it's like riding a rather wild horse, letting it go where it wants to go. –Madeleine L'Engle • The pencil is an extension of your mind. It turns your thoughts into reality. –D. Daryl Adams • The writing style which is most natural for you is bound to echo speech you heard when a child. –Kurt Vonnegut • History will be kind to me for I intend to write it. –Winston Churchill • For a long time now I have tried simply to write the best I can. Sometimes I have good luck and write better than I can. –Ernest Hemingway • Short sentences are emphatic. Don't underestimate their power. –Stephen Wilbers • Style is not something applied. It is something that permeates. –Wallace Stevens • Wit surprises, humor illuminates. –Eli Schleifer • If you want to say something radical, you should dress conservative. –Steve Biko • To me style is just the outside of content, and content the inside of style, like the outside and the inside of the human body—both go together, they can't be separated. –Jean-Luc Godard • Good writing is supposed to evoke sensation in the reader—not the fact that it is raining, but the feeling of being rained upon. –E. L. Doctorow • We're only really thinking when we can't think out fully what we are thinking about! –Johann Wolfgang von Goethe • The printworks is the artillery of thought. –Antoine de Rivarol • I used to work in bursts of intuition. Now I find the very process of working step by step feeds my imagination. –Anne Truitt • Writing is conscience, scruple and the farming of our ancestors. –Edward Dahlberg • We are truer to ourselves when we write than when we talk, because we write alone. –Comtesse Diane • A writer has to master his craft and learn the rules before he tries to break them. It's much more than just feeling that you have something to say. You have to learn how to say it. –Arthur Kopit • The shameless delight that comes from seeing your name in print is incomparable. –Carolyn See • I write in order to replicate the information, the medicine, the balm we used to find in music. –Toni Morrison • Style is the perfection of the point of view. –Richard Eberhart • The ability to simplify means to eliminate the unnecessary so that the necessary may speak. –Hans Hofmann • Writers need to physically hear the rhythm of their lips forming words—the touching of two lips, of lips to tongue, each to each. –Doug Rice

Writing is hard work. Only those more bothered by shirking it than doing it can ever succeed at it. –George V. Higgins • A writing gift doesn't have to manifest itself in childhood or adolescence in order to exist. For some people it may well be the blessing of their later years. –Deena Metzger • But you can't teach writing, people tell me. And I say, "Who the hell are you, God's dean of admissions?" –Anne Lamott • I write a lot— every day, seven days a week—and I throw a lot away. Sometimes I think I write to throw away. It's a process of distillation. –Donald Barthelme • There's a suspense in the process of writing which I've learned to be both charmed and faintly, decently—terrified by. –John Barth • Writing is a craft, as well as an art, and that craft takes time to develop. –Dennis Palumbro • I write a lot because I'm a writer. –Gore Vidal • A writer must reflect and interpret his society, his world; he must also provide inspiration and guidance and challenge. –E. B. White • The bitterest tears shed over graves are for words left unsaid and deeds left undone. –Harriet Beecher Stowe • If you're a singer you lose your voice. A baseball player loses his arm. A writer gets more knowledge, and if he's good, the older he gets, the better he writes. –Mickey Spillane • The writer is not so different from the farmer toiling in his fields or any other laborer. –Linda Pastan • There is no failure except in no longer trying. –Elbert Hubbard • I can't imagine *not* writing. –William Goyen • Writing is as much discipline as it is desire. Don't wait until you're inspired, because if you do, you'll never finish anything. –Christopher A. Bohjalian • I do enjoy writing, yes. A great deal. And I feel somewhat at a loss, aimless and foolishly senti-mental, and disconnected, when I've finished one work and haven't yet become absorbed in another. –Marianne Moore • So if I were talking to a young writer, I would recommend the cultivation of extreme indifference to both praise and blame because praise will lead you to vanity, and blame will lead you to self-pity, and both are bad for writers. –John Berryman • Printing links the present with forever. It carries personal identity into realms unknown. –Neil Postman • In the end, the best thing a writer can do for his society is to write as well as he can. –Gabriel García Márquez • A professional is someone who can do his best work when he doesn't feel like it. –Alistair Cooke • For a writer, nothing is lost. Research once done can be used again and again, a kind of marvel of recycling. –Jane Yolen • Beginning writers must appreciate the prerequisites if they hope to become writers. You pay your dues—which takes years. –Alex Haley • I do a lot of revising. –John Dos Passos • Revision is one of the true pleasures of writing. –Bernard Malamud

Writing and publishing is nothing more than an act of living. When we think and care and share our thoughts and our feelings, we are participating in the remaking of the world, nothing less. –Donald Murray • Great is the art of beginning, but greater is the art of ending. –Henry Wadsworth Longfellow • If it sounds like writ-ing, I rewrite it. –Elmore Leonard • Let me tell you the secret that has led me to my goal. My strength lies solely in my tenacity. –Louis Pasteur • Vitality shows not only in the ability to persist but in the ability to start over. –F. Scott Fitzgerald • Revisiting your work isn't just an afterthought, something to do if you have the time. If you haven't revised, you're not finished. –Patricia T. O'Conner • I write very quickly; I rewrite very slowly. –John Irving • Elbow-grease is the best polish. –English proverb • When something can be read with-out effort, great effort has gone into its writing. –Enrique Jardiel Poncela • Books are the windows through which the soul looks out. A home without books is like a room without windows. –Henry Ward Beecher • Writers mainly fall into two groups; either they are forest clearers or explorers. Some like to tidy the world and reduce it to a clear and understandable diagram. Others prefer to wander in the wilderness, rejoicing in it for its own sake. I like the wilderness. –Brian W. Aldiss • There are no rules governing the unglamorous work of rewriting, other than the fact that it is necessary and everyone does it. Rewriting is the literary equivalent of sausage-making. –Ian Jackman • The secret is not to try to be perfect. If you try to be perfect, you procras-tinate, you go over and over what you wrote, you make no forward motion. Trying to be perfect doesn't pro-duce masterpieces, only agony and slow writing. –Stephen J. Cannell • When you write, you align yourself with others who are engaged in the same strange, exhilarating pursuit. Although you may sometimes feel alone as you sit at your desk trying to release the next phrase from your pen, you aren't alone. At the same instant, hun-dreds of thousands of writers are sitting at their desks or kitchen tables, speaking into tape recorders, or pacing the floor searching for a word (perhaps the word you're searching for). –Rebecca McClanahan • We write because language is the way we keep a hold on life. –bell hooks • Still, the act of writing is either something the writer dreads or actually likes, and I actually like it. Even rewriting's fun. You're getting somewhere, whether it seems to move or not. –James Thurber • Writing is a kind of free fall that you then go back and edit and shape. –Allan Gurganus • In a very real sense, the writer writes in order to teach himself, to understand him-self, to satisfy himself. The first idea is vague, but I know that it is the generating force—later everything can change. –Alain Robbe-Grillet • The unconscious creates, the ego edits. –Stanley Kunitz • All good writing is built one good line at a time. –Kate Braverman • As a writer of a draft you must keep going and not get hung up on small problems. As a reviser you change hats, becoming a demanding reader who expects perfection. –Thomas Kane • I write slowly because I write badly. I have to rewrite everything many, many times just to achieve mediocrity. –William H. Gass • I do a lot of rewriting. It's very painful. You know it's finished when you can't do anything more to it, though it's never exactly the way you want it. –James Baldwin

A poet is, before anything else, a person who is passionately in love with language. –W. H. Auden • The more you leave out, the more you highlight what you leave in. –Henry Green • For a writer, going back home means back to the pen, pencil, and typewriter—and the blank, implacable sheet of white paper. –Paul Scott • The act of writing is a kind of guerrilla warfare; there is no vacation, no leave, no relief. In actuality there is very little chance of victory. –Walter Mosley • If a writer writes truthfully out of individual experience then what is written inevitably speaks for other people. –Doris Lessing • To get the right word in the right place is a rare achievement. –Mark Twain • As a writer you begin with infinite freedom, and then you must immediately start hemming yourself in. You have to choose a genre, you have to choose a voice that precludes using other voices. You have to choose a time that precludes other times. –Tobias Wolff • Effectiveness of assertion is the alpha and omega of style. –George Bernard Shaw • The great thing about revision is that it's your opportunity to fake being brilliant. –Will Shetterly • I never spent less than two years on the text of one of my picture books, even though each of them is approximately 380 words long. –Maurice Sendak • If you put a poem aside, when you look at it again it tends to rewrite itself. –Stephen Spender • Your only obligation in any lifetime is to be true to yourself. –Richard Bach • I notice that you use plain, simple language, short words and brief sentences. That is the way to write English—it is the modern way and the best way. Stick to it; don't let fluff and flowers and verbosity creep in. –Mark Twain • All writers are discontented with their work as it's being made. That's because they are always aware of a potential, and believe they're not reaching it. –William Saroyan • The first step in all writing is observation. –Mary Pipher • When the writing is really working, I think there is something like dreaming going on. I don't know how to draw the line between the conscious management of what you're doing and this state. It usually takes place in the earlier stages, in the drafting process. I would say that it's related to day-dreaming. –John Hersey • A writer's life stands in relation to his work as a house does to a garden, related but distinct. –Mavis Gallant • Reading is writing's nourishment. –David Huddle • We do not write in order to be understood; we write in order to understand. –C. Day Lewis • Genius is one percent inspiration and ninety-nine percent perspiration. –Thomas Edison • Thought itself needs words. It runs on them like a long wire. And if it loses the habit of words, little by little it becomes shapeless, somber. –Ugo Betti • No man can write who is not first a humanitarian. –William Faulkner

A commitment to writing, in the end, means that you accept, with as much grace as you can muster on any given day, its myriad demands and delights, failures, and triumphs. –Dennis Palumbro • Only the educated are free. –Epictetus • Using language like clothes or the skin on your body, with its sleeves, its patches, its transpirations, and its blood and sweat stains, that's what shows a writer's mettle. This is style. –Pablo Neruda • A written language brings precision, forces ideas into steady shapes, secures against loss. Once the words are on the page they are there to be challenged and embellished by those who come across them later. –Melvyn Bragg • Ideas are like rabbits. You get a couple of them, and pretty soon you have a dozen. –John Steinbeck • I have never developed an orderly approach to the business of studying out something to write. It's like a nail sticking out of the wall: you walk past it for six months without seeing it, and all of the sudden it tears your shirt as you go by. –John Graves • The more you know about a wide range of subjects, the more material you have to make connections with. The more material you have to work with, the more likely you are to produce fresh, unexpected connections, the kind of connections that make good metaphors. –Carol Bly • Often when one works at a hard question, nothing good is accomplished at the first attack. Then one takes a rest, longer or shorter, and sits down anew to the work. During the first half-hour, as before, nothing is found, and then all of a sudden the decisive idea presents itself to the mind. –Henri Poincaré • Life is to be lived. –Katharine Hepburn • I have spent so long erecting partitions around the part of me that writes—learning how to close the door on it when ordinary life intervenes, how to close the door on ordinary life when it's time to start writing again—that I'm not sure I could fit the two parts of me back together now. –Anne Tyler • The act of reading a text is like playing music and listening to it at the same time. –Margaret Atwood • A truly good book teaches me better than to read it. I must soon lay it down, and commence living on its hint. What I begin by reading, I must finish by acting. –Henry David Thoreau • The first help I ever had in writing in my life was from my father who read an utterly imitative Sherlock Holmes story of mine and pretended to like it. –F. Scott Fitzgerald • The alphabet was a great invention, which enabled men to store and to learn with little effort what others had learned the hard way—that is, to learn from books rather than from direct, possibly painful, contact with the real world. –B. F. Skinner • The greatest gift is the passion for reading. It is cheap, it consoles, it distracts, it excites, it gives you knowledge of the world and experience of a wide kind. It is a moral illumination. –Elizabeth Hardwick • Stories teach us how to be human. –Scott Russell Sanders • If you tell me, it's an essay. If you show me, it's a story. –Barbara Greene • What I like to do is to treat words as a craftsman does his wood or stone or what-have-you, to hew, carve, mould, coil, polish, and plane them into patterns, sequences, sculptures, fugues of sound expressing some lyrical impulse, some spiritual doubt or conviction, some dimly realized truth I must try to reach and realize. –Dylan Thomas • Words form the thread on which we string our experiences. –Aldous Huxley • No great thing is created suddenly. –Epictetus

Writing is what I do. I have to do it. –James Michener • A writer has no choice but to be a writer
the goal in mind, but many beautiful scenes are to be observed from each new vantage poi
for the journey. –Harold V. Melchert • The best thing about the future is that it comes only one c
for 15 minutes a day over a course of ten years, you're gonna get muscles. If you write for an
flowers in spring say, "not yet"? –Norman Douglas • I would hurl words into this darkness and w
create a sense of hunger for life that gnaws in us all. –Richard Wright • When you sit down to w
in the matter of writing. –Charlotte Brontë • I write in order to attain that feeling of tension relie
the readers better to enjoy life, or better to endure it. –Samuel Johnson • It is better to light a
themselves. They will arrange themselves as sand strewn upon stretched parchment does—a
life. It is the best gift you can give yourself. –John Truby • Your mind is like any other muscle—i
parents and your street and friends, you'll probably say something beautiful. –Grace Paley • L
keep it accurate, keep it clear. –Ezra Pound • One writes to make a home for oneself, on pape
leads to achievement. Nothing can be done without hope and confidence. –Helen Keller • Th
throwing good stuff into the wastebasket. –Ernest Hemingway • An essential element for goo
writing by reading the work of other writers. –David Huddle • Go confidently in the direction of yo
is the common property of society, and writers are the guardians of language. –Octavio Paz •
let him be first clear in his thoughts; and if any man would write in a noble style, let him first po
that there is just one contribution which every one of us can make: we can give into the comr
dog's life, but the only life worth living. –Gustave Flaubert • Success is dependent on effort. –S
vanish into air. –John Quincy Adams • You always find things you didn't know you were going
stop you from writing. You will write whether it is convenient or inconvenient, whether you are ri
your jobs is to bring news of the world to the world. –Grace Paley • Each time I write, each tim
what words will appear on the page. I follow language, I follow the sound of the words, and I a
the storm terrible, but they have never found these dangers sufficient reason for remaining as
all serious daring starts from within. –Eudora Welty • This ink lasts longer than I do. –Mark Dot
new ones are elaborated. –Thomas Jefferson • That's all we have, finally, the words, and they h
to say. –Raymond Carver • It is never too late to be what you might have been. –George Elio
broader and fuller life. –W. E. B. Du Bois • Everybody can be great, because everybody can ser
in every line. –Joseph Conrad • We all write poems; it is simply that poets are the·ones who wr
to live. You end by writing so as not to die. –Carlos Fuentes • Far and away the best prize that I
I live. –Bernard Malamud • If you can't make a mistake, you can't make anything. –Marva Colli
writing well. It's a skill that just about anyone can learn, more craft than art. –Patricia T. O'Conne
more beautiful life becomes. –Frank Lloyd Wright • The essential human act at the heart of writi
to say. –Anaïs Nin • To become an artist, just as to become a writer or a scientist or a busines
but we make a life by what we give. –Winston Churchill • I write for the same reason I breathe
writer is an amateur who didn't quit. –Richard Bach • Imagination is the highest kite one can f
good writer, you not only have to write a great deal, but you have to care. –Anne Lamott • To sp
own way, to try one's best, to make the thing live. –Vincent van Gogh • Only those that risk goi
adventure is a metaphysical one: it is a way of approaching life indirectly, of acquiring a total i
bad day. –Norman Mailer • In every writer there is a certain amount of scavenger. –William Fa
to forget publishers and just roll a sheet of copy paper into your machine and get lost in you